CONTEMPORARY READINGS

IN

PSYCHOPATHOLOGY

CONTEMPORARY READINGS IN PSYCHOPATHOLOGY

EDITED BY

John M. Neale
Gerald C. Davison
Kenneth P. Price

State University of
New York at Stony Brook

JOHN WILEY & SONS, INC.
NEW YORK • LONDON • SYDNEY • TORONTO

To Gail,
Aaron and Celia,
Hillel and Miriam

Library of Congress Cataloging in Publication Data

Neale, John M   1943–   comp.
  Contemporary readings in psychopathology.

    1.   Psychology, Pathological—Addresses, essays,
lectures.   I.   Davison, Gerald C., joint comp.
II.   Price, Kenneth P., 1947–   joint comp.
III. Title.   [DNLM: 1. Psychopathology—Collected
works.   WM100 N346c 1974]
RC458.N38   157'.08   73-22140
ISBN 0–471–63082–9
ISBN 0–471–63083–7 ((pbk.)

Printed in the United States of America

10 9 8 7 6 5 4 3 2 1

PREFACE

This book differs from the usual book of readings in abnormal psychology. Half the articles have appeared since 1970 and three quarters of them since 1966. Thus the book largely reflects current views on psychopathology. Another significant departure from most collections is our decision not to reprint merely a collection of "classic" articles. We have also deliberately avoided choosing sections that solely represent a diversity of views of psychopathology. Books of this nature already exist, and none of them strikes a balance that is satisfactory to everyone. Instead, we have selected articles from both professional and popular journals that represent significant views on psychopathology and that are likely to be of intrinsic interest to the undergraduate.

The book begins by discussing the nature of psychopathology. On one hand, it is disappointing to realize that mental health workers cannot even agree on a definition of what they are studying, but on the other hand, considering the complex nature of human beings, it is not incomprehensible that answers to all our questions have not yet been found. One reason for continuing disagreements among psychopathologists is the absence of a commonly held *paradigm* for conceptualizing mental disorders. Professionals have theorized and argued from their own particular models, and this has often impeded communication among proponents of differing viewpoints who speak in different languages and accept only evidence compatible with their own paradigm. Clashes are perhaps inevitable with one psychologist jealously guarding his medical approach, a second one his intrapsychic approach, and a third his social-learning approach. Perhaps more than any field of study, psychopathology demands a broad approach that takes cognizance of all pieces of information about man, gleaned from a wide range of sources. In Section 1 there are several readings illustrating different viewpoints of psychopathology, another is critical of psychiatric diagnosis, and two discuss the relationship between mental health workers and our legal system.

Sections 2 and 4 deal with some of the traditional problems in abnormal psychology: neurosis, psychosomatic disorders, depression, and psychosis. In Section 2 is a selection radically reinterpreting a classic psychoanalytic case study of a phobia, another utilizing experimental methods to investigate asthma, and two readings dealing with depression—one suggesting a new view of depression, and a second that is particularly relevant to college students. Section 4 includes outstanding research and review readings concerning one of man's most mystifying disorders: schizophrenia.

Section 3 deals with behaviors that are defined as abnormal because of social mores: psychopathy, alcoholism, drug use, and female homosexuality. It is interesting to note that some of these behaviors are no longer being viewed as necessarily socially inappropriate, and in future texts of abnormal psychology they may, in fact, disappear.

Section 5 describes various psychotherapies. In the past few years psychotherapy has moved from reliance on individual therapy to a dependence on group therapy, the use of paraprofessionals, and the creation of therapeutic environments.

Several people provided valuable assistance in preparing this book. Crysta Casey diligently tracked down many of the readings, Betty Hammer and Patricia Carl rendered typing assistance and Stan Redfern of Wiley ably guided the book through the production process. Our greatest debt, however, is to the authors whose creative endeavors made this collection possible.

John M. Neale
Gerald C. Davison
Kenneth P. Price

CONTENTS

CONTEMPORARY READINGS

IN

PSYCHOPATHOLOGY

SECTION 1
MODELS OF MADNESS

One of the liveliest and most controversial issues in current psychopathology concerns the usefulness of the concepts of mental illness and psychiatric diagnosis and classification. The idea of "mental illness" came into widespread use during the nineteenth century by reformers who hoped to humanize the treatment of that era's "insane" by attributing the cause of their bizarre behavior to an illness instead of to evil spirits or willful malingering. By being classified as ill, the insane became entitled to the same care and solicitude generally accorded to persons suffering from a recognized physical illness.

In another attempt to modernize treatment, nineteenth century psychopathologists began to develop a taxonomy of mental illnesses, believing that a classification scheme would contribute to the scientific understanding of mental disorders and aid in the development of appropriate therapies, as was the case with physical illness. This endeavor culminated in the work of Emil Kraepelin, whose taxonomy of mental disorders *(Lehrbuch der Psychiatrie, 1896)* has survived in modified form down to the present time *(Diagnostic and Statistical Manual II,* published by the American Psychiatric Association, 1968).

Although the concept of mental illness may have succeeded in bringing psychiatry out of the dark ages, many workers in the field now believe that it has little utility, and worse, that it actually impedes the scientific investigation of abnormal behavior. Their principal argument is that mental illness is a circular concept that lacks explanatory value. We allege that someone is "mentally ill" because he exhibits bizarre behavior, and then we "explain" his strange actions as being the result of mental illness. They suggest that unusual behavior is the result of complex interactions between the organism and his social learning history instead of the result of "mental illness."

The current system of psychiatric classification has itself also come under attack. Naturally, if mental illness does not exist, there can be no taxonomy of mental illnesses. However, psychiatric diagnosis could nevertheless be valuable if it accurately described different syndromes of deviant behavior

1

and therefore could provide valuable information on an etiology, course, or treatment. Diagnosticians argue that, at the very least, it does enable the mental health worker to treat specific disorders with appropriate drugs. However, critics feel that subcategories of the major classifications cannot be reliably identified and that prescribing drugs merely on the basis of psychiatric label, instead of on the basis of specific behaviors, constitutes a major error.

Selection 1 is a classic article by Thomas Szasz, perhaps the first to attack "mental illness" as a myth. Szasz does not deny the reality of deviant behavior and personal suffering, but he asserts that deviant behavior is defined in terms of psychosocial, ethical, and legal concepts and therefore ought not to be regarded as a medical problem. He further claims that "mental illness" is used as an explanation for what he considers "problems in living." As such it not only explains nothing but serves to deprive individuals of the responsibility of dealing with their problems.

In addition to eliciting strong support for the position it represented, Szasz's controversial stand also provoked widespread criticism. Ausubel's opinion (Selection 2) illustrates one kind of negative response to Szasz's viewpoint. Ausubel argues that the concept of mental disease has contributed to the humanizing of treatment for behavioral aberrations, that judgments of mental health are no more subjective than judgments of physical well-being, and that "problems in living" cannot account for "gross deviation from a designated range of desirable behavioral variability." He also argues that Szasz is mistaken in identifying the mental illness concept with the idea that a physiological disease produces abnormal behavior. While many of Ausubel's arguments respond to issues raised by Szasz, it can be readily seen that Ausubel holds a number of unstated assumptions that differ from the basic assumptions underlying Szasz's approach. This clash of models makes it difficult for the two to communicate, and they often argue "past" each other.

Ward et al deal with the problem of the reliability of psychiatric diagnosis in Selection 3. In an earlier study, Beck, Ward, Mendelson, Mock, and Erbaugh (1962) examined the degree of agreement between psychiatrists diagnosing psychiatric outpatients and found 70 percent agreement on broad categories (neurosis, psychosis, and personality disorder) but only 56 percent agreement on narrower judgments (neurotic-depressive reaction and schizophrenic reaction). They report their subsequent attempt to assess the reasons for diagnostic disagreement. They found that one third of the disagreements could be attributed to inconsistencies by one of the psychiatrists and two-thirds to inadequacies in the diagnostic system. These disappointing findings led the authors to abandon the use of the traditional psychiatric classification in their study of depression and to substitute for it an alternative psychometric inventory.

Such dissatisfaction with traditional concepts of mental illness and psychiatric diagnosis led Rosenhan (Selection 4) to undertake an unusual study. He had several psychologists, graduate students, and physicians approach a number of mental hospitals with the complaint that they heard voices saying "thud." All but one were diagnosed as schizophrenic and admitted to the hospital, where they then acted "sane" in every respect. The pseudopatients were kept in the hospital from one week to nearly two months and then released with the diagnosis of schizophrenia in remission. The readiness of the hospital staffs to hospitalize for up to two months individuals who were exhibiting no bizarre behaviors—if not an indictment of the diagnostic enterprise—at the very least highlights the apparent tendency on the part of mental health professionals to see illness even in ordinary behavior providing that the person they are observing is labeled a mental patient.

Additional support for the belief that sociocultural norms influence the perception of normality and deviance is provided by Broverman et al. (Selection 5). They administered a questionnaire to a group of clinicians and found that their judgments of the ideal healthy adult matched their judgments of the ideal healthy male, while the characteristics of the male were opposite to those attributed to the ideal healthy female. The authors suggest that attitudes of clinicians stem from an adjustment notion of mental health: to be mentally healthy means being able to fit in with society's expectations and role demands. Thus, to be considered a normal woman means to fit the typical stereotypes of the passive female. This article raises important issues about the role of a clinician. Is he an agent of the state whose goal is to help people conform to societal demands with a smile, or does he owe allegiance to the client and should he therefore work to make the client less concerned about what other people think of him? Is the clinician always doing his client a favor by encouraging unconventional behavior and forcing the client to suffer considerable anguish while waiting for society to catch up to his and his therapist's values?

The last two readings (Selections 6 and 7) deal with the relationship between psychiatrists/psychologists and legal definitions of mental health. There is a growing feeling that mental health specialists should not be involved in determining legal responsibility for a criminal act. According to this view, the courts should determine guilt or innocence and then heed the recommendations of mental health professionals regarding possibilities for treatment and rehabilitation when it comes to sentencing. Such disillusionment with the psychiatrist as an expert witness has stemmed from the rebellion against the concept of "mental illness" as a cause of behavior, from dissatisfaction with with the diagnostic system, and from other, ethical considerations. Leifer argues that the expert witness usurps the function of the jury. Jeffery presents transcripts of courtroom proceedings that question the usefulness of psychological testing. While the prosecutor in Jeffery's reading often makes his points through ridicule, psychologists themselves have often recognized the limitations of traditional assessment methods (cf. Mischel, 1968)

SUGGESTED READINGS

Beck, A. T., Ward, C. H., Mendelson, M., Mock, J. E., & Erbaugh, J. K. Reliability of psychiatric diagnoses: 2. A study of consistency of clinical judgments and ratings. *American Journal of Psychiatry,* 1962, *119,* 351–357.

Klein, D. F. & Davis, J. M. *Diagnosis and drug treatment of psychiatric disorders.* Baltimore, Md.: Williams & Wilkins, 1969.

Kuhn, T. S. *The structure of scientific revolutions.* Chicago: Chicago University Press, 1962.

Mischel, W. *Personality and assessment. New* York: Wiley, 1968

Price, R. H. *Abnormal behavior: Perspectives in conflict.* New York: Holt, Rinehart & Winston, 1972.

Reiss, S. A critique of T. S. Szasz's "Myth of mental illness." *American Journal of Psychiatry,* 1972, *128,* 1081–1085.

Science, 1973, *180* (4084), 356–369 (letters to the editor reacting to Rosenhan).

Stuart, R. B. *Trick or treatment: How and when psychotherapy fails.* Champaign, Ill: Research Press, 1970.

Zilboorg, G. *A history of medical psychology.* New York: Norton, 1941.

1. The Myth of Mental Illness
THOMAS S. SZASZ

My aim in this essay is to raise the question "Is there such a thing as mental illness?" and to argue that there is not. Since the notion of mental illness is extremely widely used nowadays, inquiry into the ways in which this term is employed would seem to be especially indicated. Mental illness, of course, is not literally a "thing"—or physical object— and hence it can "exist" only in the same sort of way in which other theoretical concepts exist. Yet, familiar theories are in the habit of posing, sooner or later—at least to those who come to believe in them—as "objective truths" (or "facts"). During certain historical periods, explanatory conceptions such as deities, witches, and microorganisms appeared not only as theories but as self-evident *causes* of a vast number of events. I submit that today mental illness is widely regarded in a somewhat similar fashion, that is, as the cause of innumerable diverse happenings. As an antidote to the complacent use of the notion of mental illness—whether as a self-evident phenomenon, theory, or cause—let us ask this question: What is meant when it is asserted that someone is mentally ill?

In what follows I shall describe briefly the main uses to which the concept of mental illness has been put. I shall argue that this notion has outlived whatever usefulness it might have had and that it now functions merely as a convenient myth.

MENTAL ILLNESS AS A SIGN OF BRAIN DISEASE

The notion of mental illness derives its main support from such phenomena as syphilis of the brain or delirious conditions—intoxications, for instance—in which persons are known to manifest various peculiarities or disorders of thinking and behavior. Correctly speaking, however, these are diseases of the brain, not of the mind. According to one school of thought, *all* so-called mental illness is of this type. The assumption is made that some neurological defect, perhaps a very subtle one, will ultimately be found for all the disorders of thinking and behavior. Many contemporary psychiatrists, physicians, and other scientists hold this view. This position implies that people *cannot* have troubles—expressed in what are *now called* "mental illnesses"—because of differences in personal needs, opinions, social aspirations, values, and so on. *All problems in living* are attributed to physiochemical processes which in due

T. S. Szasz, "The myth of mental illness," *American Psychologist*, 1960, *15*, 113–118. Copyright 1960 by the American Psychological Association, and reproduced by permission.

time will be discovered in medical research.

"Mental illnesses" are thus regarded as basically no different than all other diseases (that is, of the body). The only difference, in this view, between mental and bodily diseases is that the former, affecting the brain, manifest themselves by means of mental symptoms; whereas the latter, affecting other organ systems (for example, the skin, liver, etc.), manifest themselves by means of symptoms referable to those parts of the body. This view rests on and expresses what are, in my opinion, two fundamental errors.

In the first place, what central nervous system symptoms would correspond to a skin eruption or a fracture? It would *not* be some emotion or complex bit of behavior. Rather, it would be blindness or a paralysis of some part of the body. The crux of the matter is that a disease of the brain, analogous to a disease of the skin or bone, is a neurological defect, and not a problem in living. For example, a *defect* in a person's visual field may be satisfactorily explained by correlating it with certain definite lesions in the nervous system. On the other hand, a person's *belief*—whether this be a belief in Christianity, in Communism, or in the idea that his internal organs are "rotting" and that his body is, in fact, already "dead"—cannot be explained by a defect or disease of the nervous system. Explanations of this sort of occurrence—assuming that one is interested in the belief itself and does not regard it simply as a "symptom" or expression of something else that is *more interesting*—must be sought along different lines.

The second error in regarding complex psychosocial behavior, consisting of communications about ourselves and the world about us, as mere symptoms of neurological functioning is *epistemological.* In other words, it is an error pertaining not to any mistakes in observation or reasoning, as such, but rather to the way in which we organize and express our knowledge. In the present case, the error lies in making a symmetrical dualism between mental and physical (or bodily) symptoms, a dualism which is merely a habit of speech and to which no known observations can be found to correspond. Let us see if this is so. In medical practice, when we speak of physical disturbances, we mean either signs (for example, a fever) or symptoms (for example, pain). We speak of mental symptoms on the other hand, when we refer to a patient's *communications about himself, others, and the world about him.* He might state that he is Napoleon or that he is being persecuted by the Communists. These would be considered mental symptoms *only* if the observer believed that the patient was *not* Napoleon or that he was *not* being persecuted by the Communists. This makes it apparent that the statement that "*X* is a mental symptom" involves rendering a judgment. The judgment entails, moreover, a covert comparison or matching of the patient's ideas, concepts, or beliefs with those of the observer and the society in which they live. The notion of mental symptom is therefore inextricably tied to the *social* (including *ethical) context* in which it is made in much the same way as the notion of bodily symptom is tied to an *anatomical* and *genetic context (Szasz,* 1957a, 1957b).

To sum up what has been said thus far: I have tried to show that for those who regard mental symptoms as signs of brain disease, the concept of mental illness is unnecessary and misleading. For what they mean is that people so labeled suffer from diseases of the brain; and, if that is what they mean, it would seem better for the sake of clarity to say that and not something else.

MENTAL ILLNESS AS A NAME FOR PROBLEMS IN LIVING

The term "mental illness" is widely used to describe something which is very different than a disease of the brain. Many people today take it for granted that living is an arduous process. Its hardship for modern man, moreover, derives not so much from a struggle for biological survival as from the stresses and strains inherent in the social intercourse of complex human personalities. In this context, the notion

THE MYTH OF MENTAL ILLNESS

of mental illness is used to identify or describe some feature of an individual's so-called personality. Mental illness—as a deformity of the personality, so to speak—is then regarded as the *cause* of the human disharmony. It is implicit in this view that social intercourse between people is regarded as something *inherently harmonious,* its disturbance being due solely to the presence of "mental illness" in many people. This is obviously fallacious reasoning, for it makes the abstraction "mental illness" into a *cause*, even though this abstraction was created in the first place to serve only as a shorthand expression for certain types of human behavior. It now becomes necessary to ask: "What kinds of behavior are regarded as indicative of mental illness, and by whom?"

The concept of illness, whether bodily or mental, implies *deviation from some clearly defined norm.* In the case of physical illness, the norm is the structural and functional integrity of the human body. Thus, although the desirability of physical health, as such, is an ethical value, what health *is* can be stated in anatomical and physiological terms. What is the norm deviation from which is regarded as mental illness? This question cannot be easily answered. But whatever this norm might be, we can be certain of only one thing: namely, that it is a norm that must be stated in terms of *psychosocial, ethical,* and *legal* concepts. For example, notions such as "excessive repression" or "acting out of an unconscious impulse" illustrate the use of psychological concepts for judging (so-called) mental health and illness. The idea that chronic hostility, vengefulness, or divorce are indicative of mental illness would be illustrations of the use of ethical norms (that is, the desirability of love, kindness, and a stable marriage relationship). Finally, the widespread psychiatric opinion that only a mentally ill person would commit homicide illustrates the use of a legal concept as a norm of mental health. The norm from which deviation is measured whenever one speaks of a mental illness is a *psychosocial and ethical one.* Yet, the remedy is sought in terms of *medical* measures which—it is hoped and assumed—are free from wide differences of ethical value. The definition of the disorder and the terms in which its remedy are sought are therefore at serious odds with one another. The practical significance of this covert conflict between the alleged nature of the defect and the remedy can hardly be exaggerated.

Having identified the norms used to measure deviations in cases of mental illness, we will now turn to the question: "Who defines the norms and hence the deviation?" Two basic answers may be offered: *(a)* It may be the person himself (that is, the patient) who decides that he deviates from a norm. For example, an artist may believe that he suffers from a work inhibition; and he may implement this conclusion by seeking help *for* himself from a psychotherapist. *(b)* It may be someone other than the patient who decides that the latter is deviant (for example, relatives, physicians, legal authorities, society generally, etc.). In such a case a psychiatrist may be hired by others to do something *to* the patient in order to correct the deviation.

These considerations underscore the importance of asking the question "Whose agent is the psychiatrist?" and of giving a candid answer to it (Szasz, 1956, 1958). The psychiatrist (psychologist or nonmedical psychotherapist), it now develops, may be the agent of the patient, of the relatives, of the school, of the military services, of a business organization, of a court of law, and so forth. In speaking of the psychiatrist as the agent of these persons or organizations, it is not implied that his values concerning norms, or his ideas and aims concerning the proper nature of remedial action, need to coincide exactly with those of his employer. For example, a patient in individual psychotherapy may believe that his salvation lies in a new marriage; his psychotherapist need not share this hypothesis. As the patient's agent, however, he must abstain from bringing social or legal force to bear on the patient which would prevent him from putting his beliefs into action. If his *contract* is with the patient, the psychiatrist (psychotherapist) may disagree with him or stop his treatment; but he cannot engage others to obstruct the patient's aspirations. Similarly, if a psychiatrist is engaged by a court to determine the sanity of a criminal, he need not fully share the legal authorities' values and intentions in regard to the criminal and the means available for dealing with him. But the psychiatrist is expressly barred from stating, for example, that it is not the criminal who is "insane" but the men who wrote the law on the basis of which the very actions that are being judged are regarded as "criminal." Such an opinion could be voiced, of course, but not in a courtroom, and not by a psychiatrist who makes it his practice to assist the court in performing its daily work.

To recapitulate: In actual contemporary social usage, the finding of a mental illness is made by establishing a deviance in behavior from certain psychosocial, ethical, or legal norms. The judgment may be made, as in medicine, by the patient, the physician (psychiatrist), or others. Remedial action, finally, tends to be sought in a therapeutic—or covertly medical—framework, thus creating a situation in which *psychosocial, ethical,* and/or *legal deviations* are claimed to be correctible by (so-called) *medical action.* Since medical action is designed to correct only medical deviations, it seems logically absurd to expect that it will help solve problems whose very existence had been defined and established on nonmedical grounds. I think that these considerations may be fruitfully applied to the present use of tranquilizers and, more generally, to what might be expected of drugs of whatever type in regard to the amelioration or solution of problems in human living.

THE ROLE OF ETHICS IN PSYCHIATRY

Anything that people *do*—in contrast to things that *happen* to them (Peters, 1958)—takes palce in a context of value. In this broad sense, no human activity is devoid of ethical implications. When the values underlying certain activities are widely shared, those who participate in their pursuit may lose sight of them altogether. The discipline of medicine, both as a pure science (for example, research) and as a technology (for example, therapy), contains many ethical considerations and judgments. Unfortunately, these are often denied, minimized, or merely kept out of focus; for the ideal of the medical profession as well as of the people whom it serves seems to be having a system of medicine (allegedly) free of ethical value. This sentimental notion is expressed by such things as the doctor's willingness to treat and help patients irrespective of their religious or political beliefs, whether they are rich or poor, etc. While there may be some grounds for this belief—albeit it is a view that is not impressively true even in these regards—the fact remains that ethical considerations encompass a vast range of human affairs. By making the practice of medicine neutral in regard to some specific issues of value need not, and cannot, mean that it can be kept free from all such values. The practice of medicine is intimately tied to ethics; and the first thing that we must do, it seems to me, is to try to make this clear and explicit. I shall let this matter rest here, for it does not concern us specifically in this essay. Lest there be any vagueness, however, about how or where ethics and medicine meet, let me remind the reader of such issues as birth control, abortion, suicide, and euthanasia as only a few of the major areas of current ethicomedical controversy.

Psychiatry, I submit, is very much more intimately tied to problems of ethics than is medicine. I use the word "psychiatry" here to refer to that contemporary discipline which is concerned with *problems in living* (and not with diseases of the brain, which are problems for neurology). Problems in human relations can be analyzed, interpreted, and given meaning only within given social and ethical contexts. Accordingly, it *does* make a difference—arguments to the contrary notwithstanding—what the psychiatrists's socioethical orientations happen to be; for these will influence his ideas on what is wrong with the patient, what deserves comment or interpretation, in what possible directions change might be desirable, and so forth. Even in medicine proper, these factors play a role, as for instance, in the divergent orientations which physicians, depending on their religious affiliations, have toward such things as birth control and therapeutic abortion. Can anyone really believe that a psychotherapist's ideas concerning religious belief, slavery, or other similar issues play no role in his practical work? If they do make a difference, what are we to infer from it? Does it not seem reasonable that we ought to have different psychiatric therapies—each expressly recognized for the ethical positions which they embody—for, say Catholics and Jews, religious persons and agnostics, democrats and communists, white supremacists and Negroes, and so on? Indeed, if we look at how psychiatry is actually practiced today (especially in the United States), we find that people do seek psychiatric help in accordance with the social status and ethical beliefs (Hollingshead & Redlich, 1958). This should not really surprise us more than being told that practicing Catholics rarely frequent birth control clinics.

The foregoing position which holds that contemporary psychotherapists deal with problems in living, rather than with mental illnesses and their cures, stands in opposition to a currently prevalent claim, according to which mental illness is just as "real" and "objective" as bodily illness. This is a confusing claim since it is never known exactly what is meant by such words as "real" and "objective." I suspect, however, that what is intended by the proponents of this view is to create the idea in the popular mind that mental illness is some sort of disease entity, like an infection or a malignancy. If this were true, one could catch or get a "mental illness," one might *have* or *harbor* it, one might transmit it to others and finally one could get *rid* of it. In my opinion, there is not a shred of evidence to support this idea. To the contrary, all the evidence is the other way and supports the view that what people now call mental illnesses are for the most part *communications* expressing unacceptable ideas, often framed, moreover, in an unusual idiom. The scope of this essay allows me to do no more than mention this alternative theoretical approach to this problem (Szasz, 1957c).

This is not the place to consider in detail the similarities and differences between bodily and mental illnesses. It shall suffice for us here to emphasize only one important difference between them: namely that whereas bodily disease refers to public, physicochemical occurrences, the notion of mental illness is used to codify relatively more private, sociopsychological happenings of which the observer (diagnostician) forms a part. In other words, the psychiatrist does not stand *apart* from what he observes, but is, in Harry Stack Sullivan's apt words, a "participant observer." This means that he is *committed* to some picture of what he considers reality—and to what he thinks society considers reality—and he observes and judges the patient's behavior in the light of these considerations. This touches on our earlier observation that the notion of mental symptom itself implies a comparison between observer and observed, psychiatrist and patient. This is so obvious that I may be charged with belaboring trivialities. Let me therefore say once more that my aim in presenting this argument was expressly to criticize and counter a prevailing contemporary tendency to deny the moral aspects of psychiatry (and psychotherapy) and to substitute for them allegedly value-free medical considerations. Psychotherapy for example, is being widely practiced as though it entailed nothing other than restoring the patient from a state of mental sickness to one of mental health. While it is generally accepted that mental illness has something to do with man's social (or interpersonal) relations, it is paradoxically maintained that problems of values (that is, of ethics) do not arise in this process.[1] Yet, in one sense, much of psychotherapy may revolve around nothing other than the elucidation and weighing of goals and values—many of which may be mutually contradictory—and the means whereby they might best be harmonized, realized, or relinquished.

The diversity of human values and methods by means of which they may be realized is so vast, and so many of them remain so unacknowledged, that they cannot fail but lead to conflicts in human relations. Indeed, to say that human relations at all

[1]Freud went so far as to say that: "I consider ethics to be taken for granted. Actually I have never done a mean thing" (Jones, 1957, p. 247). This surely is a strange thing to say for someone who has studied man as a social being as closely as did Freud. I mention it here to show how the notion of "illness" (in the case of psychoanalysis, "psychopathology," or "mental illness") was used by Freud—and by most of his followers—as a means for classifying certain forms of human behavior as falling within the scope of medicine, and hence (by *fiat*) outside that of ethics!

levels—from mother to child, through husband and wife, to nation and nation—are fraught with stress, strain, and disharmony is, once again, making the obvious explicit. Yet, what may be obvious may be also poorly understood. This I think is the case here. For it seems to me that—at least in our scientific theories of behavior—we have failed to *accept* the simple fact that human relations are inherently fraught with difficulties and that to make them even relatively harmonious requires much patience and hard work. I submit that the idea of mental illness is now being put to work to obscure certain difficulties which at present may be inherent—not that they need be unmodifiable—in the social intercourse of persons. If this is true, the concept functions as a disguise; for instead of calling attention to conflicting human needs, aspirations, and values, the notion of mental illness provides an amoral and impersonal "thing" (an "illness") as an explanation for *problems in living* (Szasz, 1959). We may recall in this connection that not so long ago it was devils and witches who were held responsible for men's problems in social living. The belief in mental illness, as something other than man's trouble in getting along with his fellow man, is the proper heir to the belief in demonology and witchcraft. Mental illness exists or is "real" in exactly the same sense in which witches existed or were "real."

CHOICE, RESPONSIBILITY, AND PSYCHIATRY

While I have argued that mental illnesses do not exist, I obviously did not imply that the social and psychological occurrences to which this label is currently being attached also do not exist. Like the personal and social troubles which people had in the Middle Ages, they are real enough. It is the labels we give them that concerns us and, having labelled them, what we do about them. While I cannot go into the ramified implications of this problem here, it is worth noting that a demonologic conception of problems in living gave rise to therapy along theological lines. Today, a belief in mental illness implies—nay, requires—therapy along medical or psychotherapeutic lines.

What is implied in the line of thought set forth here is something quite different. I do not intend to offer a new conception of "psychiatric illness" nor a new form of "therapy." My aim is more modest and yet also more ambitious. It is to suggest that the phenomena now called mental illnesses be looked at afresh and more simply, that they be removed from the category of illnesses, and that they be regarded as the expressions of man's struggle with the problem of *how* he should live. The last mentioned problem is obviously a vast one, its enormity reflecting not only man's inability to cope with his environment, but even more his increasing self-reflectiveness.

By problems in living, then, I refer to that truly explosive chain reaction which began with man's fall from divine grace by partaking of the fruit of the tree of knowledge. Man's awareness of himself and of the world about him seems to be a steadily expanding one, bringing in its wake an ever larger *burden of understanding* (an expression borrowed from Susanne Langer, 1953). *This burden, then, is to be expected and must not be misinterpreted.* Only our *rational* means for lightening it is *more understanding,* and appropriate *action* based on such understanding. The main alternative lies in acting as though the burden were not what in fact we perceive it to be and taking refuge in an outmoded theological view of man. In the latter view, man does not fashion his life and much of his world about him, but merely lives out his fate in a world created by superior beings. This may logically lead to pleading nonresponsibility in the face of seemingly unfathomable problems and difficulties. Yet, if man fails to take increasing responsibilities for his actions, individually as well as collectively, it seems unlikely that some higher power or being would assume this task and carry this burden for him. Moreover, this seems hardly the proper time in human history for obscuring the issue of man's responsibility for his actions by hiding it behind the skirt of an all-explaining conception of mental illness.

CONCLUSIONS

I have tried to show that the notion of mental illness has outlived whatever usefulness it might have had and that it now functions merely as a convenient myth. As such, it is a true heir to religious myths in general, and to the belief in witchcraft in particular; the role of all these belief-systems was to act as *social tranquilizers,* thus encouraging the hope that mastery of certain specific problems may be achieved by means of substitutive (symbolic-magical) operations. The notion of mental illness thus serves mainly to obscure the everyday fact that life for most people is a continuous struggle, not for biological survival, but for a "place in the sun," "peace of mind," or some other human value. For man aware of himself and of the world about him, once the needs for preserving the body (and perhaps the race) are more or less satisfied, the problem arises as to what he should do with himself. Sustained adherence to the myth of mental illness allows people to avoid facing this problem, believing that mental health, conceived as the absence of mental illness, automatically insures the making of right and safe choices in one's conduct of life. But the facts are all the other way. It is the making of good choices in life that others regard, retrospectively, as good mental health!

The myth of mental illness encourages us, moreover, to believe in its logical corollary: that social intercourse would be harmonious, satisfying, and the secure basis of a "good life" were it not for the disrupting influences of mental illness or "psychopathology." The potentiality for universal human happiness, in this form at least, seems to me but another example of the I-wish-it-were-true type of fantasy. I do believe that human happiness or well-being on a hitherto unimaginably large scale, and not just for a select few, is possible. This goal could be achieved, however, only at the cost of many men, and not just a few being willing and able to tackle their personal, social, and ethical conflicts. This means having the courage and integrity to forego waging battles on false fronts, finding solutions for substitute problems—for instance, fighting the battle of stomach acid and chronic fatigue instead of facing up to a marital conflict.

Our adversaries are not demons, witches, fate, or mental illness. We have no enemy whom we can fight, exorcise, or dispel by "cure." What we do have are *problems in living*—whether these be biologic, economic, political, or sociopsychological. In this essay I was concerned only with problems belonging in the last mentioned category, and within this group mainly with those pertaining to moral values. The field to which modern psychiatry addresses itself is vast, and I made no effort to encompass it all. My argument was limited to the proposition that mental illness is a myth, whose function it is to disguise and thus render more palatable the bitter pill of moral conflicts in human relations.

REFERENCES

Hollingshead, A. B., & Redlich, F. C. *Social class and mental illness.* New York: Wiley, 1958.

Jones, E. *The life and work of Sigmund Freud.* Vol. III, New York: Basic Books, 1957.

Langer, S. K. *Philosophy in a new key.* New York: Mentor Books, 1953. 1953.

Peters, R. S. *The concept of motivation.* London: Routledge & Kegan Paul, 1958.

Szasz, T. S. Malingering: "Diagnosis" or social condemnation? *AMA Arch Neurol. Psychiat.,* 1956, 76, 432–443.

Szasz, T. S. *Pain and pleasure: A study of bodily feelings,* New York: Basic Books, 1957. (a)

Szasz, T. S. The problem of psychiatric nosology: A contribution to a situational analysis of psychiatric operations. *Amer. J. Psychiat.,* 1957, *114,* 405–413. (b)

Szasz, T. S. On the theory of psychoanalytic treatment. *Int. J. Psycho-Anal.,* 1957, *38,* 166–182. (c)

Szasz, T. S. Psychiatry, ethics and the criminal law. *Columbia law Rev.,* 1958, *58,* 183–198.

Szasz, T. S. Moral conflict and psychiatry, *Yale Rev.,* 1959, in press.

2. Personality Disorder is Disease
DAVID P. AUSUBEL

In two recent articles in the *American Psychologist,* Szasz (1960) and Mowrer (1960) have argued the case for discarding the concept of mental illness. The essence of Mowrer's position is that since medical science lacks "demonstrated competence . . . in psychiatry," psychology would be wise to "get out" from "under the penumbra of medicine," and to regard the behavior disorders as manifestations of sin rather than of disease (p. 302). Szasz' position, as we shall see shortly, is somewhat more complex than Mowrer's, but agrees with the latter in emphasizing the moral as opposed to the psychopathological basis of abnormal behavior.

For a long time now, clinical psychology has both repudiated the relevance of moral judgment and accountability for assessing behavioral acts and choices, and has chafed under medical (psychiatric) control and authority in diagnosing and treating the personality disorders. One can readily appreciate, therefore, Mowrer's eagerness to sever the historical and professional ties that bind clinical psychology to medicine, even if this means denying that psychological disturbances constitute a form of illness, and even if psychology's close working relationship with psychiatry must be replaced by a new rapprochement with sin and theology, as "the lesser of two evils"

David P. Ausubel. Personality disorder *is* disease. *American Psychologist, 16,* 1961, 69–74. Copyright ©1961 by the American Psychological Association and reproduced by permission.

(pp. 302–303). One can also sympathize with Mowrer's and Szasz' dissatisfaction with prevailing amoral and nonjudgmental trends in clinical psychology and with their entirely commendable efforts to restore moral judgment and accountability to a respectable place among the criteria used in evaluating human behavior, both normal and abnormal.

Opposition to these two trends in the handling of the behavior disorders (i.e., to medical control and to nonjudgmental therapeutic attitudes), however—does not necessarily imply abandonment of the concept of mental illness. There is no inconsistency whatsoever in maintaining, on the one hand that most purposeful human activity has a moral aspect the reality of which psychologists cannot afford to ignore (Ausubel, 1952, p. 462), that man is morally accountable for the majority of his misdeeds (Ausubel, 1952, p. 469), and that psychological rather than medical training and sophistication are basic to competence in the personality disorders (Ausubel, 1956, p. 101), and affirming, on the other hand, that the latter disorders are genuine manifestations of illness. In recent years psychology has been steadily moving away from the formerly fashionable stance of ethical neutrality in the behavioral sciences; and in spite of strident medical claims regarding superior professional qualifications and preclusive legal responsibility for treating psychiatric patients, and notwithstanding the nominally restrictive provisions of medical practice acts, clinical psychologists have been assuming an increasingly more important, independent, and responsible role in treating the mentally ill population of the United States.

It would be instructive at this point to examine the tactics of certain other medically allied professions in freeing themselves from medical control and in acquiring independent, legally recognized professional status. In no instance have they resorted to the devious stratagem of denying that they were treating diseases, in the hope of mollifying medical opposition and legitimizing their own professional activities. They took the position instead that simply because a given condition is defined as a disease, its treatment need not necessarily be turned over to doctors of medicine if other equally competent professional specialists were available. That this position is legally and politically tenable is demonstrated by the fact that an impressively large number of recognized diseases are legally treated today by both medical *and* nonmedical specialists (e.g., diseases of the mouth, face, jaws, teeth, eyes, and feet). And there are few convincing reasons for believing that psychiatrists wield that much more political power than physicians. maxillofacial surgeons, ophthalmologists, and orthopedic surgeons, that they could be successful where these latter specialists have failed, in legally restricting practice in their particular area of competence to holders of the medical degree. Hence, even if psychologists were not currently managing to hold their own vis-a-vis psychiatrists, it would be far less dangerous and much more forthright to press for the necessary ameliorative legislation than to seek cover behind an outmoded and thoroughly discredited conception of the behavior disorders.

THE SZASZ-MOWRER POSITION

Szasz' (1960) contention that the concept of mental illness "now functions merely as a convenient myth" (p. 118) is grounded on four unsubstantiated and logically untenable propositions, which can be fairly summarized as follows:

1. Only symptoms resulting from demonstrable physical lesions qualify as legitimate manifestations of disease. Brain pathology is a type of physical lesion, but its symptoms properly speaking, are neurological rather than psychological in nature. Under no circumstances, therefore, can mental symptoms be considered a form of illness.
2. A basic dichotomy exists between *mental* symptoms, on the one hand, which are subjective in nature, dependent on subjective judgment and personal involvement of the observer, and referable to cultural-ethical norms, and *physical* symptoms on the other hand, which are allegedly objective in nature, ascertainable without personal involvement of the observer, and independent of cultural norms and ethical standards. Only symptoms possessing the latter set of characteristics are genuinely reflective of illness and amenable to medical treatment.

3. Mental symptoms are merely expressions of problems of living and, hence, cannot be regarded as manifestations of a pathological condition. The concept of mental illness is misleading and demonological because it seeks to explain psychological disturbance in particular and human disharmony in general in terms of metaphorical but nonexistent disease entity, instead of attributing them to inherent difficulties in coming to grips with elusive problems of choice and responsibility.
4. Personality disorders, therefore, can be most fruitfully conceptualized as products of moral conflict, confusion, and aberration. Mowrer (1960) extends this latter proposition to include the dictum that psychiatric symptoms are primarily reflective of unacknowledged sin, and that individuals manifesting these symptoms are responsible for and deserve their suffering, both because of their original transgressions and because they re-

fuse to avow and expiate their guilt (pp. 301, 304).

Widespread adoption of the Szasz-Mowrer view of the personality disorders would, in my opinion, turn back the psychiatric clock twenty-five hundred years. The most significant and perhaps the only real advance registered by mankind in evolving a rational and humane method of handling behavioral aberrations has been in substituting a concept of disease for the demonological and retributional doctrines regarding their nature and etiology that flourished until comparatively recent times. Conceptualized as illness, the symptoms of personality disorders can be interpreted in the light of underlying stresses and resistances, both genic and environmental, and can be evaluated in relation to *specifiable* quantitative and qualitative norms of appropriately adaptive behavior, both cross-culturally and within a particular cultural context. It would behoove us, therefore, before we abandon the concept of mental illness and return to the medieval doctrine of unexpiated sin or adopt Szasz' ambiguous criterion of difficulty in ethical choice and responsibility, to subject the foregoing propositions to careful and detailed study.

Mental Symptoms and Brain Pathology

Although I agree with Szasz in rejecting the doctrine that ultimately some neuroanatomic or neurophysiologic defect will be discovered in *all* cases of personality disorder, I disagree with his reasons for not accepting this proposition. Notwithstanding Szasz' straw man presentation of their position, the proponents of the extreme somatic view do not really assert that the *particular nature* of a patient's disordered beliefs can be correlated with "certain definite lesions in the nervous system" (Szasz, 1960, P. 113). They hold rather that normal cognitive and behavioral functioning depends on the anatomic and physiologic integrity of certain key areas of the brain, and that impairment of this substrate integrity, therefore, provides a physical basis for disturbed ideation and behavior, but does not explain, except in a very gross way, the particular kinds of symptoms involved. In fact, they are generally inclined to attribute the

specific character of the patient's symptoms to the nature of his pre-illness personality structure, the substrate integrity of which is impaired by the lesion or metabolic defect in question.

Nevertheless, even though this type of reasoning plausibly accounts for the psychological symptoms found in general paresis, various toxic deleria, and other comparable conditions, it is an extremely improbable explanation of *all* instances of personality disorder. Unlike the tissues of any other organ, brain tissue possesses the unique property of making possible awareness of and adjustment to the world of sensory, social, and symbolic stimulation. Hence by virtue of this unique relationship of the nervous system to the environment, diseases of behavior and personality may reflect abnormalities in personal and social adjustment, quite apart from any structural or metabolic disturbance in the underlying neural substrate. I would conclude, therefore, that although brain pathology is probably not the most important cause of behavior disorder, it is undoubtedly responsible for the incidence of *some* psychological abnormalites *as well as* for various neurological signs and symptoms.

But even if we completely accepted Szasz' view that brain pathology does not account for any symptoms of personality disorder, it would still be unnecessary to accept his assertion that to qualify as a genuine manifestation of disease a given symptom must be caused by a physical lesion. Adoption of such a criterion would be arbitrary and inconsistent both with medical and lay connotations of the term "disease," which in current usage is generally regarded as including any marked deviation, physical, mental, or behavioral, from normally desirable standards of structural and functional integrity.

Mental versus Physical Symptoms

Szasz contends that since the analogy between physical and mental symptoms is patently fallacious, the postulated parallelism between physical and mental disease is logically untenable. This line of reasoning is based on the assumption that the two categories of symptoms can be sharply dichotomized with respect to such basic dimensions as objectivity-subjectivity, the relevance of cultural norms, and the need for personal involvement of the observer. In my opinion, the existence of such a dichotomy cannot be empirically demonstrated in convincing fashion.

Practically all symptoms of bodily disease involve some elements of subjective judgment—both on the part of the patient and of the physician. Pain is perhaps the most important and commonly used criterion of physical illness. Yet, any evaluation of its reported locus, intensity, character, and duration is dependent upon the patient's subjective appraisal of his own sensations and on the physician's assessment of the latter's pain threshold, intelligence, and personality structure. It is also a medical commonplace that the severity of pain in most instances of bodily illness may be mitigated by the administration of a placebo. Furthermore, in taking a meaningful history the physician must not only serve as a participant observer but also as a skilled interpreter of human behavior. It is the rare patient who does not react psychologically to the signs of physical illness; and hence physicians are constantly called upon to decide, for example, to what extent precordial pain and reported tightness in the chest are manifestations of coronary insufficiency, or fear of cardiac disease impending death, or of combinations of both conditions. Even such allegedly objective signs as pulse rate, BMR, blood pressure, and bood cholesterol have their subjective and relativistic aspects. Pulse rate and blood pressure are notoriously susceptible to emotional influences, and BMR and blood cholesterol fluctuate widely from one cultural environment to another (Dreyfuss & Czaczkes, 1959). And anyone who believes that ethical norms have no relevance for physical illness has obviously failed to consider the problems confronting Catholic patients and/or physicians when issues of contraception, abortion, and preferential saving of the mother's as against the fetus' life must be faced in the context of various obstetrical emergencies and medical contraindications to pregnancy.

It should now be clear, therefore, that symptoms not only do not need a physical basis to qualify as manifestations of illness, but also that the evaluation of *all* symptoms, physical as well as mental, is dependent in large measure on subjective judgment, emotional factors, cultural-ethical norms, and personal involvement on the part of the observer. These considerations alone render no longer tenable Szasz' contention (1960, p. 114) that there is an inherent contradiction between using cultural and ethical norms as criteria of mental disease, on the one hand, and of employing medical measures of treatment on the other. But even if the postulated dichotomy between mental and physical symptoms were valid, the use of physical measures in treating subjective and relativistic psychological symptoms would still be warranted. Once we accept the proposition that impairment of the neutral substrate of personality can result in behavior disorder, it is logically consistent to accept the corollary proposition that other kinds of manipulation of the same neutral substrate can conceivably have therapeutic effects, irrespective of whether the underlying cause of the mental symptoms is physical or psychological.

Mental Illness and Problems of Living

"The phenomena now called mental illness," argues Szasz (1960), can be regarded more forthrightly and simply as "expressions of man's struggle with the problem of how he should live" (p. 117). This statement undoubtedly oversimplifies the nature of personality disorders; but even if it were adequately inclusive it would not be inconsistent with the position that these disorders are a manifestation of illness. There is no valid reason why a particular symptom cannot both reflect a problem in living *and* constitute a manifestation of disease. The notion of mental illness, conceived in this way, would not "obscure the everyday fact that life for most people is a continuous struggle . . . for a 'place in the sun,' 'peace of mind,' or some other human value" (p.118) It is quite true, as Szasz points out, that "human relations are inherently fraught with difficulties" (p. 117), and that most people manage to cope with such difficulties without becoming mentally ill. But conceding this fact hardly precludes the possibility that some individuals, either because of the magnitude of the stress involved, or because of genically or environmentally induced susceptibility to ordinary degrees of stress, respond to the problems of living with behavior that is either seriously distorted or sufficiently unadaptive to prevent normal interpersonal relations and vocational functioning. The latter outcome—gross deviation from a designated range of desirable behavioral variability—conforms to the generally understood meaning of mental illness.

The plausibility of subsuming abnormal behavioral reactions to stress under the general rubric of disease is further enhanced by the fact that these reactions include the same three principal categories of symptoms found in physical illness. Depression and catastrophic impairment of self-esteem, for example, are manifestations of personality disorder which are symptomologically comparable to edema in cardiac failure or to heart murmurs in valvular disease. They are indicative of underlying pathology but are neither adaptive nor adjustive. Symptoms such as hypomanic overactivity and compulsive striving toward unrealistically high achievement goals, on the other hand, are both adaptive and adjustive, and constitute a type of compensatory response to the basic feelings of inadequacy, which is not unlike cardiac hypertrophy in hypertensive heart disease or elevated white blood cell count in acute infections. And finally, distortive psychological defenses that have some adjustive value but are generally maladaptive (e.g., phobias, delusions, autistic fantasies) are analogous to the pathological situation found in conditions like pneumonia, in which the excessive outpouring of serum and phagocytes in defensive response to pathogenic bacteria literally causes the patient to drown in his own fluids.

Within the context of this same general proposition, Szasz repudiates the concept of mental illness as demonological in nature, i.e., as the "true heir to religious myths in general and to the belief in witchcraft in particular" (p. 118) because it allegedly employs a reified abstraction ("a deformity of personality") to account in causal terms both for "human disharmony" and for symptoms of behavior disorder (p. 114). But again he appears to be demolishing a straw man. Modern students of personality disorder do not regard mental illness as a cause of human disharmony, but as a comanifestation with it of inherent difficulties in personal adjustment and interpersonal realations; and in so far as I can accurately interpret the literature, psychopathologists do not conceive of mental illness as a cause of particular behavioral symptoms but as a generic term under which these symptoms can be subsumed.

Mental Illness and Moral Responsibility

Szasz' final reason for regarding mental illness as a myth is really a corollary of his previously considered more general proposition that mental symptoms are essentially reflective of problems of living and hence do not legitimately qualify as manifestations of disease. It focuses on difficulties of ethical choice and responsibility as the particular life problems most likely to be productive of personality disorder. Mowrer (1960) further extends this corollary by asserting that neurotic and psychotic individuals are responsible for their suffering (p. 301), and that unacknowledged and unexpiated sin, in turn, is the basic cause of this suffering (p. 304). As previously suggested, however, one can plausibly accept the proposition that psychiatrists and clinical psychologists have erred in trying to divorce behavioral evaluation from ethical considerations, in conducting psychotherapy in an amoral setting, and in confusing the psychological explanation of unethical behavior with absolution from accountability for same, *without* necessarily endorsing the view that personality disorders are basically a reflection of sin, and that victims of these disorders are less ill than responsible for their symptoms (Ausubel, 1952, pp. 392–397, 465–471).

In the first place, it is possible in most instances (although admittedly difficult in some) to distinguish quite unambiguously between mental illness and ordinary cases of immorality. The vast majority of persons who are guilty of moral lapses knowingly violate their own ethical precepts for expediential reasons—despite being volitionally capable at the time, both of choosing the more moral alternative and of exercising the necessary inhibitory control (Ausubel, 1952, pp. 465–471). Such persons, also, usually do not exhibit any signs of behavior disorder. At crucial choice points in facing problems of living they simply choose the opportunistic instead of the moral alternative. They are not mentally ill, but they are clearly accountable for their misconduct. Hence, since personality disorder and immorality are neither coextensive nor mutually exclusive conditions, the concept of mental illness need not necessarily obscure the issue of moral accountability.

Second, guilt may be a contributory factor in behavior disorder, but is by no means the only or principal cause thereof. Feelings of guilt may give rise to anxiety and depression; but in the absence of catastrophic impairment of self-esteem induced by *other* factors, these symptoms tend to be transitory and peripheral in nature (Ausubel, 1952, pp. 362–363). Repression of guilt, is more a consequence than a cause of anxiety. Guilt is repressed in order to avoid the anxiety producing trauma to self-esteem that would otherwise result if it were acknowledged. Repression per se enters the causal picture in anxiety only secondarily—by obviating "the possibility of punishment, confession, expiation, and other guilt reduction mechanisms" (Ausubel, 1952, p. 456). Furthermore, in most types of personality disorder other than anxiety, depression, and various complications of anxiety, such as phobias, obessions, and compulsions, guilt feelings are either not particularly prominent (schizophrenic reactions), or are conspicuously absent (e.g., classical cases of inadequate or aggressive, antisocial psychopathy).

Third, it is just as unreasonable to hold an individual responsible for symptoms of behavior disorder as to deem him accountable for symptoms of physical illness. He is no more culpable for his inability to cope with sociopsychological stress than he would be for his inability to resist the spread of infectious organisms. In those instances where warranted guilt feelings *do* contribute to personality disorder, the patient is accountable for the misdeeds underlying his guilt, but is hardly responsible for the symptoms brought on by the guilt feelings or for unlawful acts committed during his illness. Acknowledgment of guilt may be therapeutically beneficial under these circumstances, but punishment for the original misconduct should obviously be deferred until after recovery.

Lastly, even if it were true that all personality disorder is a reflection of sin and that people are accountable for their behavioral symptoms, it would still be unnecessary to deny that these symptoms are manifestations of disease. Illness is no less real because the victim happens to be culpable for his illness. A glutton with hypertensive heart disease undoubtedly aggravates his condition by overeating, and is culpable in part for the often fatal symptoms of his disease, but what reasonable person would claim that for this reason he is not really ill?

CONCLUSIONS

Four propositions in support of the argument for discarding the concept of mental illness were carefully examined, and the following conclusions were reached:

First, although brain pathology is probably not the major cause of personality disorder, it does account for *some* psychological symptoms by impairing the neural substrate of personality. In any case, however, a symptom need not reflect a physical lesion in order to qualify as a genuine manifestation of disease.

Second, Szasz' postulated dichotomy between mental and physical symptoms is untenable because the assessment of *all* symptoms is dependent to some extent on subjective judgment, emotional factors, cultural-ethical norms, and personal involvement of the observer. Furthermore, the use of medical measures in treating behavior disorders—irrespective of whether the underlying causes are neural or psychological is defensible on the grounds that if inadvertent impairment of the neural substrate of personality can have distortive effects on behavior, directed manipulation of the same substrate may have therapeutic effects.

Third, there is no inherent contradiction in regarding mental symptoms both as expressions of problems in living *and* as manifestations of illness. The latter situation results when individuals are for various reasons unable to cope with such problems, and react with seriously distorted or maladaptive behavior. The three principal categories of behavioral symptoms—manifestations of impaired functioning, adaptive compensation, and defensive overreaction—are also found in bodily disease. The concept of mental illness has never been advanced as a demonological cause of human disharmony, but only as a comanifestation with it of certain inescapable difficulties and hazards in personal and social adjustment. The same concept is also generally accepted as a generic term for all behavioral symptoms rather than as a reified cause of these symptoms.

Fourth, the view that personality disorder is less a manifestation of illness than of sin, i.e., of culpable inadequacy in meeting problems of ethical choice and responsibility, and that victims of behavior disorder are therefore morally accountable for their symptoms, is neither logically nor empirically tenable. In most instances immoral behavior and mental illness are clearly distinguishable conditions. Guilt is only a secondary etiological factor in anxiety and depression, and in other personality disorders is either not prominent or conspicuously absent. The issue of culpability for symptoms is largely irrelevant in handling the behavior disorders, and in any case does not detract from the reality of the illness.

In general, it is both unnecessary and potentially dangerous to discard the concept of mental illness on the grounds that only in this way can clinical psychology escape from the professional domination of medicine. Dentists, podiatrists, optometrists, and osteopaths have managed to acquire an independent professional status without rejecting the concept of the disease. It is equally unnecessary and dangerous to substitute the doctrine of sin for illness in order to counteract prevailing amoral and nonjudgmental trends in psychotherapy. The hypothesis of repressed guilt does not adequately explain most kinds and instances of personality disorder, and the concept of mental illness does not preclude judgments of moral accountability where warranted. Definition of behavior disorder in terms of sin or of difficulties associated with ethical choice and responsibility would substitute theological disputation and philosophical wrangling about values for specifiable quantitative and qualitative criteria of disease.

REFERENCES

Ausubel, D. P. *Ego development and the personality disorders.* New York: Grune & Stratton, 1952.

Ausubel, D. P. Relationships between psychology and psychiatry: The hidden issues. *Amer. Psychologist,* 1956, *11,* 99–105.

Dreyfuss, F., & Czaczkes, J. W. Blood cholesterol and uric acid of healthy medical students under the stress of an examination. *AMA Arch, intern. Med.,* 1959, *103,* 708.

Mowrer, O. H. "Sin." the lesser of two evils. *Amer. Psychologist,* 1960, *15,* 301–304.

Szasz, T. S. The myth of mental illness. *Amer. Psychologist* 1960, *15,* 113–118.

3. The Psychiatric Nomenclature

C. H. WARD, A. T. BECK, M. MENDELSON, J. E. MOCK, & J. K. ERBAUGH

Much current thinking holds psychiatric diagnosis to be "the soft underbelly of psychiatry"[4] and "an indictment of the present state of psychiatry."[7] Diagnosis is said to cause behavioral scientists "marked feelings of inferiority"[6] because of their alleged inability to obtain agreement rates significantly better than chance.[5] To the extent that these opinions are accurate, it is clearly an important question why a nomenclature, which is the distillation of so much experience over so many years,[1] should so fail the test of clinical usefulness. It is equally clear that the problems involved are complex and vexing, not likely amendable to any quick or easy solution.

A previous paper[2] reviewed the literature on concurrence of diagnoses and pointed out that prior studies had methodological limitations which may have spuriously lowered diagnostic agreement. In another article,[3] we reported the results of a more refined procedure which indicated an agreement rate for the various subcategories (schizophrenic reaction, anxiety reaction, neurotic depressive reaction,

etc.) of 56%, a degree of concurrence higher than that generally reported in the literature. This agreement rate was found to be significantly greater than chance; and it was further suggested that the diagnosticians were probably closer to agreement than the simple comparison of preferred diagnoses would indicate, since concurrence increased to 82% when alternate choices of diagnoses were included in determining agreement. Moreover, in 99% of the cases there was not more than 1 scale point difference in 4-point ratings of a single clinical dimension, the degree of depression present regardless of nosological category.

Despite the methodological improvement, it was evident that there remained a substantial problem of diagnostic disagreement. The present article reports the results of an investigation designed to identify the reasons for disagreement on diagnosis when the current revised nomenclature of the American Psychiatric Association[1] is used as a basis for classification.

C. H. Ward, A. T. Beck, M. Mendelson, J. E. Mock & J. K. Erbaugh. The psychiatric nomenclature. *Archives of General Psychiatry*, 1962, 7, 198–205. Reproduced by permission.

Submitted for publication Nov. 21, 1961.

From the Departments of Psychiatry, University of Pennsylvania School of Medicine and Philadeliphia General Hospital.

This investigation was supported by Research Grant M 3358 from the National Institute of Mental Health.

METHOD

Four experienced psychiatrists participated in the diagnostic studies.[3] Before engaging in the formal aspects of the investigation, they had several preliminary meetings during which they discussed the various diagnostic categories, ironed out semantic obscurities, and reached a consensus regarding the specific criteria for each of the nosological entities as outlined in the *Diagnostic and Statistical Manual: Mental Disorders* of the American Psychiatric Association.[1]

The psychiatrists were randomly paired so that each of the patients was seen separately by 2 different diagnosticians. The procedure was to have one psychiatrist interview the patient, and then after a resting period of a few minutes the other psychiatrist would interview the patient. Each psychiatrist independently wrote out his diagnostic conclusions. After the second interview was completed, the pair of psychiatrists met, discussed their diagnoses, and established the reasons for whatever disagreement had arisen.

On the basis of their experience in the joint diagnosis of a preliminary group of more than 75 cases, the 4 diagnosticians prepared a list of the various reasons which, in their opinion, accounted for the differences in the diagnoses. Subsequently, each pair of diagnosticians conferred after their separate interviews with the patients and selected the appropriate reasons from the list. When more than one category appeared to account for the disagreement, they decided on which was the primary or major cause of disagreement. The reasons for disagreement were systematically recorded as seen in 40 consecutive cases in which there were diagnostic disagreements.*

RESULTS

Nine causes for disagreement were identified. These were grouped into 3 categories which, from least to most prominent, are: inconstancy on the part of the patient (5%), inconstancy on the part of the diagnostician (32.5%), and inadequacy of the nosology (62.5%). An outline of these reasons is given below. (Examples and supplementary discussion follow under comments).

Although the numbers involved are not large, they are considered representative of the preliminary group of cases studied when the reasons for disagreement were being conceptualized and also representative of more than 50 cases studied subsequently in experimental diagnostic exercises to be reported in a separate article.

REASONS FOR DIAGNOSTIC DISAGREEMENT

A. Inconstancy on the part of the patient (2 disagreements: 5%).
   1. The patient spontaneously offers different material to each diagnostician (1 disagreement: 2.5%).
   2. The patient changes as a result of the first interview (1 disagreement: 2.5%).

B. Inconstancy on the part of the diagnostician (13 disagreements: 32.5%).
   1. Differences in interviewing technique lead to

*These cases were drawn from the latter portion of the previously mentioned reliability study of 153 cases which were jointly diagnosed and which showed an overall rate of concurrence of 56%.[3]

differences in material elicited (2 disagreements: 5%).

2. Weighing symptoms differently (7 disagreements: 17.5%).
3. Differences in interpretation of the same pathology (2 disagreements: 5%).
4. Other types of variability (2 disagreements: 5%).

C. Inadequacies of the nosology (25 disagreements: 62.5%).

1. Impractically fine distinction required (3 disagreements: 7.5%). (Clinical picture is ambiguous and cannot be classified according to the requirements of the nosology.)
2. Forced choice of predominant major category (12 disagreements: 30.0%). (Present nosology requires a determination of the relative predominance of psychoneurotic disorder and personality disorder when both entities are present.)
3. Unclear criteria (10 disagreements: 25%). (Uncertainty regarding the criteria for a specific diagnosis stemming from insufficient clarification by present nomenclature.)

COMMENT

Our findings are restricted by the limitations of the study. Of these limitations the most prominent is that the diagnostician was confined to material elicited from the patient alone, during an interview of approximately 1 hour. Additional information, had it been available, might have reduced diagnostic disagreement somewhat, especially in areas of "physician inconstancy." It is not considered likely, however, that the conclusions derived from the study would have been substantially altered.

Inconstancy on the part of the patient was considered a minor factor. For the patient to volunteer contradictory material was a rare occurrence (2.5%), and in only 1 case was it considered a determining factor in disagreement. In this case, a young woman was referred for evaluation of a somatic complaint which neither diagnostician could be sure was psychogenic in nature. One of the diagnosticians could therefore make only the diagnosis of "no psychiatric disease." However, to the other examiner, the patient volunteered the history of a previous gastric ulcer with continuing symptomatology, which information she had previously directly denied to the first examiner. The second physician therefore diagnosed psychophysiological gastro-intestinal reaction.

An appreciable change in the clinical picture as a result of the diagnostic interview was considered crucial in a single case (2.5%) in which the effect of the first interview was to make the patient aware of a sizable amount of previously unrealized depression, which then became the center of the patient's presenting complaints in the second interview. The diagnostic difference thus became that of anxiety reaction with depressive features vs. neurotic depressive reaction with anxiety features.

Inconstancy on the part of the diagnostician accounted for nearly a third (32.5%) of diagnostic disagreements. Differences in interviewing technique leading to differences in material elicited was a deciding factor in 2 cases (5%), both involving a question of psychosis. Much has been written about the need for alertness to the existence of hidden delusional systems, of techniques for inquiring into the patient's own ideas as to the mechanisms of his symptoms, and of other approaches for eliciting guarded hallucinatory or delusional phenomena. This comparative experience left us impressed with how easily a seasoned examiner can, at times, be deceived about very active and extensive delusional systems; for example, by more persistent questioning, one examiner elicited a delusional system in reference to physical complaints which the first examiner had diagnosed as conversion. Diagnostic difference: paranoid schizophrenia vs. conversion reaction.

Weighing symptoms differently was a sizable factor, crucial in a fifth of the cases in disagreement (17.5%), especially in cases where the diagnostic choice fell between 2 neuroses. Concerning this difficulty, it was surprising how easy it was to miss the focus and ascribe priority only to the first complaint. Often what was initially advanced as a chief complaint did not develop to be the predominant area of distress, so that we have become convinced of the importance of focusing insistently at the beginning and at the end of the diagnostic interview on what, of all the mentioned difficulties, is *hardest to bear* or is what the patient *would most like help with*. For example, a patient whose chief complaints were of tension and palpitation was considered by the second examiner to be actually more disturbed by symptons of mood impairment, fatigue, self-depreciative thoughts, and loss of interest. When directly asked in the second examination, the patient gave his opinion that the low spirits were more troublesome than the tension. Diagnostic conflict: anxiety reaction with depressive features vs. neurotic depressive reaction with anxiety features.

Difference in interpretation of the same pathology was the determining reason for disagreement in 2 cases (5.0%). For example, 2 observers heard a middle-aged woman complain of recurrent painful thoughts that she had venereal disease or leprosy. She stated that she knew these thoughts were irrational, that she had been reassured by several doctors, but still they persisted. The first diagnostician discredited her statement regarding being aware of the irrationality of her thoughts and considered the symptoms to be somatic delusions, since she had seen several doctors about her condition, and since there was a fixity and conviction which he sensed in her relating it. The second diagnostician credited her awareness of the irrationality of these thoughts, and attributed her having visited several doctors to her anxiety, dependency, and guilt which underlay the obsession. Diagnostic conflict: involutional psychosis vs. neurotic obsessive compulsive reaction.

The occurrence of errors, such as forgetting about major segments of elicited pathology, or making an incorrect inference, was also a critical factor in 2 cases (5%). For example, one observer preferred a diagnosis of schizophrenic reaction, in remission, on very limited grounds (a depressed young girl gave a history of some withdrawal under stress, of excessive fantasy life, and of a frequent feeling that no one was on her side). In discussion afterwards, the diagnostician decided that his diagnosis could not be substantiated and wished to withdraw it. Diagnostic conflict: neurotic depressive reaction in a schizoid personality vs. paranoid schizophrenia in remission. (Had it not been agreed that the diagnostician was in error, other reasons for disagreement would have been considered.)

The largest source of variability was considered to result from the present nosology (62.5%). Because of this predominance and because important problems beyond training the experience are involved, we will devote more discussion to this group and to the current nomenclature as it relates to this group.

Requiring an impractically fine distinction was considered the cause of disagreement in 3 cases (7.5%). Each of these involved a diagnosis of psychophysiological reaction. In 2 cases this diagnosis was in conflict with that of conversion reaction and in the third case with that of anxiety reaction. The nomenclature presently requires a distinction between psychophysiological and conversion reactions on the bases of inferred intrapsychic mechanisms. Often it is not possible to delineate such a mechanism within the ordinary time limits of a diagnostic interview. The diagnostician is forced to guess or speculate at such times. For example, a 26-year-old man, of passive-dependent personality, had experienced, since the age of 17, intermittent attacks of painful gastric cramping usually accompanied by gas and heartburn, for which complaints he was referred for psychiatric evaluation after a negative medical workup. He had also had symptoms of anxiety and depression, both of which seemed clearly less important than the chief complaint. There was no history of hunger pains, of association with diet, or nausea, vomiting, or melena. His first attack occurred while working for an exploitative father, towards whom the patient expressed resentment and estrangement. These attacks had recurred fairly often and with increasing frequency since the patient encountered severe marital difficulties. The mother had, for many years, been subject to "attacks of acute indigestion if she works too hard." One examiner thought the probabilities favored a gastrointestinal psychophysiological reaction with dyspepsia, resulting from the disequilibrium produced by prolonged and intense stimulation of the visceral components of the fight-flight mechanism. The mother's similar difficulty was considered related, if at all, via the mechanism of constitutional predisposition. The second observer considered some part of the reaction to be probably psychophysiological (the gas) but felt the sudden painful cramping, the preponderant symptomatology, to be a conversion reaction based on identification with the mother. The situation of conflict with the father at onset of the reaction was considered confirmatory of this formulation. Both diagnosticians credited the feasibility of the alternate diagnosis and selected it as their second choice for differential diagnosis. Both agreed that a much more thorough investigation of the psychological determinants would be necessary to finally resolve the question of conversion vs. autonomic reaction. Neither disagreed as to the basic criteria for the 2 diagnoses in conflict, and the difference was considered to derive, not from the different weighing of separate clusters of symptomatology, but from differences in selecting the probabilities, on a basis which can only be problematic, of one or the other mechanism involved. The nosology was, therefore, faulted for requiring a distinction that cannot be accurately made without a great deal more time than is available for most diagnostic interviews, at least in a clinical setting. The likelihood that the present differentiation is not clinically practical seems further indicated by the findings that, in our larger series, psychophysiological disorders represent the least agreed-upon broad diagnostic category,* conversion reaction is one of the most frequently disagreed-upon primary diagnoses, and conversion reaction/psychophysiological reaction is the most frequently confused diagnostic pair.

A second type of inadequacy of the nomenclature was that of requiring a choice as to the relative predominance of neurotic symptoms and personality disorder when both entities were present. This was the largest single reason for diagnostic disagreement in the series and was considered crucial in a third (30%) of the cases studied systematically. For example, a 28-year-old married woman, recommended to the clinic by a psychiatrist friend, appeared with the chief complaint: "My relationship to my mother—can I get so I have a happy relationship with her?" She described a great deal of tension, apprehension, and agitation, at times culminating in tantrums and almost all centering around aggressive conflict with a possessive, controlling mother. She was much less aware of the passive-dependent aspects of her problem, or the probable displacement onto the mother of other tensions, especially those generated by the patient's tendency to establish the same relationship with her own 3-year-old daughter. Both examiners saw anxiety and personality-trait disturbance. One examiner rated the personality-trait disturbance as predominant. Diagnostic conflict: anxiety reaction with passive-dependent personality features vs. passive-dependent personality with anxiety features.

Such cases comprise a group which may be increasing in our present culture: those patients who, often with partial insight and often through personal contact with medical psychology or its representatives, come for help with troubled interpersonal relationships combined with neurotic distress. The individual may be somewhat more concerned with such neurotic symptoms as chronic intermittent anxiety and/or depression, or he may somewhat more emphasize his marital difficulties, bad temper, interpersonal problems, or other symptoms of behavioral nature. Regardless of whether the patient

*The phrase ("broad diagnostic category") refers to the 4 major divisions of the present nomenclature: psychotic disorders, psychophysiological disorders, psychoneurotic disorders, and personality disorders.

somewhat emphasizes one element or the other (and they do not always make a clear choice as to their major distress), it is often very difficult to determine whether the neurotic symptomatology or the characterological pathology is more extensive or "basic" in the sense of the present nomenclature.

This is a difficulty which the present APA Diagnostic Manual[1] seems to present with insufficient emphasis if not with distortion. The discussion of qualifying phrases (pp. 12–13), multiple psychiatric diagnoses (p. 46), predisposition (pp. 48–49), and manner of recording (pp. 50–51), combine to favor the impression that such distinctions are relatively rare and relatively easy to make (e.g., acute anxiety in a homosexual, or obsessive-compulsive reaction in compulsive personality); or that the personality disorder can readily be seen as a background, preceding, predisposing factor which does not compete with the neurotic symptomatology for the current diagnostic foreground. In our experience, the converse of both points is often true, especially with combinations of anxiety and/or depression, with passive-aggressive or schizoid personality disorder.

Our basic question here is: Is this decision necessary or helpful? Our experience indicates that weighing choices in a nonquantitative clinical system is a very ready source of disagreement. Such judgments are probably nevertheless necessary in assigning priority among several types of neurotic symptoms occurring together, or in selecting among mixtures of personality disorder features in the same patient. We question, however, the necessity of compounding the chances for disagreement by forcing a weighing choice between the basically different, broader categories of neurosis and personality disorder. The concept that indicates that most often the 2 processes occur together, with the symptoms of the neurosis deriving from decompensation of the personality disorder, is consistent with current theory. One might not, however, have to accept this theory to consider making diagnosis bidimensional at this point, with a predetermined policy as to the order in which the combination is expressed.

A final inadequacy of the nosological system, unclear criteria, was the second most frequent cause of diagnostic disagreement (25%). These were all conflicts involving psychosis, and 8 of the 10 involved the effort to distinguish chronic undifferentiated schizophrenia from nonpsychotic disorders. A disagreement in weighing was also frequently noted as a contributary reason. In fact, it is probable that the whole difficulty hinges around the lack of any clear definition of the critical dividing line between psychosis and other syndromes, especially when the decision rests on quantitative rather than qualitative differences. For example, a 21-year-old single white female (very thin, overly tense, with overly active and somewhat bulging eyes, and communicating a diffuse effect of hostility, yet of distance) was seen whose chief complaints were nervous tension and self-consciousness since she was 3 years old. In recent years, she had been unable to hold down a job, although she had some secretarial training. "Always there's something I can't do, or someone I don't like, so I get to feeling incapable or to hating the boss, and I get depressed and I quit." She had had a long series of jobs, holding the longest for a 9-month period after graduation from high school. She had received various forms of psychiatric treatment over the past 4 years and had seen 12 psychiatrists in all, remaining with only 1 for a period as long as 7 months and leaving all of them with open hostility. She agreed with the previous interpretation of her having been very hostile, was in fact aware of having been so from earliest childhood. Her 2-year-younger sister always was more admired and accepted in the family, and better adjusted than she. It was open knowledge in the family that the patient was supposed to have been a boy; and her parents, especially the somewhat alcoholic father, had told her that she was no good because she was a girl and had approved of her only when she was successfully competitive with boys. The patient finished high school with difficulty, having to leave one school because of her marked discomfort in efforts to make speeches before mixed groups, and also because of much daydreaming, which still continued. She now felt frustrated, bitter, and had long felt that life was not worthwhile. She had never had a serious interpersonal involvement of a positive nature, and to the extent that she let herself react with others, the pattern was that of hostile anticipation, poorly modulated aggression, and suspiciousness. She often wished she were dead and had frequent thoughts of turning on the gas or jumping in front of a car, but at the same time she was aware of an excessively strong fear of death. She was compelled to wash her hands after touching certain articles of furniture; she had phobias of eating with other people. She had many physical symptoms of an anxiety and autonomic tension nature (increased urinary frequency, frequent nuchal headaches, palpitation and tachycardia, acne, and frequent indigestion). She had a sleep pattern which was a mixture of anxiety and depression, was not rarely awakened by nightmares in which she saw herself dead or bad things happening to her family. She had on several occasions had hypnogogic visual images upon awakening from these dreams and had remained anxious and unable to sleep long afterwards. However, she definitely had had no auditory or visual hallucinations in the waking state and had had no clear delusions. There was a peculiar quality to her affect which suggested flatness or a manifestation of depression, though it was hard to distinguish between the two, and neither observer felt that she was making any substantial attempt to be melodramatic or impressive.

Both observers were impressed with the borderline nature of her problem. One was reminded of a previous patient who became "overtly psychotic"; the resemblance was less in specific, recognizable details and more in terms of a vague general feeling of the examiner's. He was also impressed with the chronicity, quantity, and multiplicity of her symptoms. The other examiner volunteered that on another day he might well agree, but as the patient struck him now, after an hour's interview, he felt she had a certain integration and inner consistency; he had seen similar patients who consolidated themselves and improved their adjustment without any clearly psychotic episode. In view of the absence of any clear break with reality, because of the reactive elements in the picture; because the patient was intelligent and did well on routine tests of similarities, differences, and proverb interpreta-

tion; because of the potential damage to the patient of being labeled with a psychotic diagnosis; and because of personal antipathy to the poorly conceived phrase "chronic undifferentiated schizophrenic," he gave the patient the benefit of a very sizable doubt as to where schizoid personality left off and schizophrenia began. Diagnostic conflict: chronic undifferentiated schizophrenic reaction vs. chronic anxiety reaction in a severely schizoid personality.

The Diagnostic Manual insists on quantitative estimates in diagnosing psychosis: page 12, "*Severe* affective disturbance, *profound* autism and withdrawal (*and/or* formation of delusions and hallucinations)"; page 26, "a *strong* tendency to retreat from reality;" and, page 27, "*beyond* that of the schizoid personality." Although the system requires quantitative distinctions, it makes no allowance for any intermediate group except that which is offered by the term "chronic undifferentiated schizophrenic."

In our view this term seems unfortunate. The words "chronic" and "schizophrenic" appear, rightly or wrongly, to associate themselves with the most malignant pathology and prognosis. Our group considered as still insufficiently substantiated the implication that such borderline cases represent a schizophrenic reaction in the usual sense of autistic reordering of the interpretation of experience. The appended synonyms "latent," "incipient," especially "prepsychotic," may better designate the in-between nature of the group but are still weighted by the values associated with the term schizophrenia and do not convey the essence of the diagnostic entity as we construed it to be: a group of problematic borderline cases. Perhaps the term "borderline" itself has enough currency to serve as designation for this group of syndromes[8] characterized by such depth and intensity of distress as to result in a multiplicity of defensive patterns, most of which seem strained to the limit. Patients in the group are often overly insightful or have marked shifts between deep insight and massive denial. They communicate a diffuse hostility; their reality testing is often marginal, and marginal idiosyncrasies of speech are often present. However, there are usually no overt psychotic phenomena, and there is substantial remaining capacity for extramural functioning. The distinction between borderline syndrome (or chronic undifferentiated schizophrenia in the present nosological system) and psychoneurosis or perhaps schizoid personality is largely quantitative, and we are impressed with the notable differences between diagnosticians in making this distinction as well as variations in the same diagnostician over time. It is clear that there is a difference in criteria, but it is difficult to specify the difference other than to say that it is quantitative. We have also been impressed by the degree to which the individual diagnostician's reaction is influenced by his previous chance exposure to somewhat analogous previous cases in this spectrum and also by a difference of criteria in evaluating the history of a previous psychotic episode, some diagnosticians feeling "once psychotic always psychotic" and others quite the contrary.

SUMMARY

A series of psychiatric outpatients was interviewed separately and diagnosed independently by pairs of experienced psychiatrists. In 40 cases in which there was disagreement on the specific diagnosis, a determination was made of the reasons for the disagreement.

One-third of the disagreements were considered to be caused by variability on the part of the diagnostician, with differences in eliciting covert material and identifying the predominant pathology in mixed pictures being the 2 most prominent factors.

Two-thirds of the disagreements were charged to inadequacies of the nosological system itself. The 3 chief difficulties intrinsic in the present nomenclature were identified as: requiring impractically fine distinctions, as in the diagnosis of psychophysiological reaction as opposed to conversion reaction; requiring unnecessary decisions of weighing, as in the forced decision of predominance between neurotic symptoms and personality disorder when both are present; the lack of clear criteria, as in distinguishing certain reactions now labeled schizophrenic, from neuroses or schizoid personalities.

REFERENCES

1. American Psychiatric Association. Diagnostic and statistical manual of mental disorders. Washington, D.C., American Psychiatric Association, 1952.
2. Beck, A. T., Reliability of psychiatric diagnosis: 1. A critique of systematic studies, *Amer. J. Psychiat.,* to be published.
3. Beck, A. T., Ward, C. H., Mendelson, M., Mock, J. E., and Erbaugh, J. K., Reliability of psychiatric diagnosis: 2. A study of consistency of clinical judgments and ratings, *Amer. J. Psychiat.,* to be published.
4. Giffen, M. B., Kenny, J. A., and Kah, T. C., Psychic ingredients of various personality types, *Amer. J. Psychiat, 117*:211-214 (Sept.) 1960.
5. Goldfarb, A., Reliability of diagnostic judgments made by psychologists, *J. Clin. Psychol. 15:*392-396 (Oct.) 1959.

6. Kline, N. S., Comprehensive therapy of depressions, *J. Neuropsychiat.* (Suppl. 1) *2:*15-26 (Feb.) 1961.
7. Pasamanick, B., Dinitz, S., and Lefton, M. Psychiatric orientation and its relation to diagnosis and treatment in a mental hospital, *Amer. J. Psychiat. 116:*127-132 (Aug.) 1959.
8. Schmideberg, M., The borderline patient, in: *American Handbook of Psychiatry,* edited by S. Arieti, New York, Basic Books, Inc., 1959.

4. On Being Sane in Insane Places
D. L. ROSENHAN

If sanity and insanity exist, how shall we know them?

The question is neither capricious nor itself insane. However much we may be personally convinced that we can tell the normal from the abnormal, the evidence is simply not compelling. It is commonplace, for example, to read about murder trials wherein eminent psychiatrists for the defense are contradicted by equally eminent psychiatrists for the prosecution on the matter of the defendant's sanity. More generally, there are a great deal of conflicting data on the reliability, utility, and meaning of such terms as "sanity," "insanity," "mental illness," and "schizophrenia" *(1)*. Finally, as early as 1934, Benedict suggested that normality and abnormality are not universal *(2)*. What is viewed as normal in one culture may be seen as quite aberrant in another. Thus, notions of normality and abnormality may not be quite as accurate as people believe they are.

To raise questions regarding normality and abnormality is in no way to question the fact that some behaviors are deviant or odd. Murder is deviant. So, too, are hallucinations. Nor does raising such questions deny the existence of the personal anguish that is often associated with "mental ill-ness." Anxiety and depression exist. Psychological suffering exists. But normality and abnormality, sanity and insanity, and the diagnoses that flow from them may be less substantive than many believe them to be.

At its heart, the question of whether the sane can be distinguished from the insane (and whether degrees of insanity can be distinguished from each other) is a simple matter: do the salient characteristics that lead to diagnoses reside in the patients themselves or in the environments and contexts in which observers find them? From Bleuler, through Kretchmer, through the formulators of the recently revised *Diagnostic and Statistical Manual* of the American Psychiatric Association, the belief has been strong that patients present symptoms, that those symptoms can be categorized, and, implicitly, that the sane are distinguishable from the insane. More recently, however, this belief has been questioned. Based in part on theoretical and anthropological considerations, but also on philosophical, legal, and therapeutic ones, the view has grown that psychological categorization of mental illness is useless at best and downright harmful, misleading, and pejorative at worst. Psychiatric diagnoses, in this view, are in the minds of the observers and are not valid summaries of characteristics displayed by the observed *(3-5)*.

Gains can be made in deciding which of these is more nearly accurate by getting normal people (that

D. L. Rosenhan, On being sane in insane places, *Science, 179*, 250-258, 19 January 1973. Copyright © 1973 by the American Association for the Advancement of Science. Reproduced by permission.

is, people who do not have, and have never suffered, symptoms of serious psychiatric disorders) admitted to psychiatric hospitals and then determining whether they were discovered to be sane and, if so, how. If the sanity of such pseudo-patients were always detected, there would be prima facie evidence that a sane individual can be distinguished from the insane context in which he is found. Normality (and presumably abnormality) is distinct enough that it can be recognized wherever it occurs, for it is carried within the person. If, on the other hand, the sanity of the pseudopatients were never discovered, serious difficulties would arise for those who support traditional modes of psychiatric diagnosis. Given that the hospital staff was not incompetent, that the pseudopatient had been behaving as sanely as he had been outside of the hospital, and that it had never been previously suggested that he belonged in a psychiatric hospital, such an unlikely outcome would support the view that psychiatric diagnosis betrays little about the patient but much about the environment in which an observer finds him.

This article describes such an experiment. Eight sane people gained secret admission to 12 different hospitals (6). Their diagnostic experiences constitute the data of the first part of this article; the remainder is devoted to a description of their experiences in psychiatric institutions. Too few psychiatrists and psychologists, even those who have worked in such hospitals, know what the experience is like. They rarely talk about it with former patients, perhaps because they distrust information coming from the previously insane. Those who have worked in psychiatric hospitals are likely to have adapted so thoroughly to the settings they they are insensitive to the impact of that experience. And while there have been occasional reports of researchers who submitted themselves to psychiatric hospitalization (7), these researchers have commonly remained in the hospitals for short periods of time, often with the knowledge of the hospital staff. It is difficult to know the extent to which they were treated like patients or like research colleagues. Nevertheless, their reports about the inside of the psychiatric hospital have been valuable. This article extends those efforts.

PSEUDOPATIENTS AND THEIR SETTINGS

The eight pseudopatients were a varied group. One was a psychology graduate student in his 20's. The remaining seven were older and "established." Among them were three psychologists, a pediatrician, a psychiatrist, a painter, and a housewife. Three pseudopatients were women, five were men. All of them employed pseudonyms, lest their alleged diagnoses embarrass them later. Those who were in mental health professions alleged another occupation in order to avoid the special attentions that might be accorded by staff, as a matter of courtesy or caution, to ailing colleagues (8). With the exception of myself (I was the first pseudopatient and my presence was known to the hospital administrator and chief psychologist and, so far as I can tell, to them alone), the presence of pseudopatients and the nature of the research program was not known to the hospital staffs (9).

The settings were similarly varied. In order to generalize the findings, admission into a variety of hospitals was sought. The 12 hospitals in the sample were located in five different states on the East and West coasts. Some were old and shabby, some were quite new. Some were research-oriented, others not. Some had good staff-patient ratios, others were quite understaffed. Only one was a strictly private hospital. All of the others were supported by state or federal funds or, in one instance, by university funds.

After calling the hospital for an appointment, the pseudopatient arrived at the admissions office complaining that he had been hearing voices. Asked what the voices said, he replied that they were often unclear, but as far as he could tell they said "empty," "hollow," and "thud." The voices were unfamiliar and were of the same sex as the pseudopatient. The choice of these symptoms was occasioned by their apparent similarity to existential symptoms. Such symptoms are alleged to arise from painful concerns about the perceived meaninglessness of one's life. It is as if the hallucinating person were saying, "My life is empty and hollow." The choice of these symptoms was also determined by the *absence* of a single report of existential psychoses in the literature.

Beyond alleging the symptoms and falsifying name, vocation, and employment, no further alterations of person, history, or circumstances were made. The significant events of the pseudopatient's life history were presented as they had actually occurred. Relationships with parents and siblings, with spouse and children, with people at work and in school, consistent with the aforementioned exceptions, were described as they were or had been. Frustrations and upsets were described along with joys and satisfactions. These facts are important to remember. If anything, they strongly biased the subsequent results in favor of detecting sanity, since none of their histories or current behaviors were seriously pathological in any way.

Immediately upon admission to the psychiatric ward, the pseudopatient ceased simulating *any* symptoms of abnormality. In some cases, there was a brief period of mild nervousness and anxiety, since none of the pseudopatients really believed that they would be admitted so easily. Indeed, their shared fear was that they would be immediately exposed as frauds and greatly embarrassed. Moreover, many of them had never visited a psychiatric ward; even those who had, nevertheless had some genuine fears about what might happen to them. Their nervousness, then, was quite appropriate to the novelty of the hospital setting, and it abated rapidly.

Apart from that short-lived nervousness, the pseudopatient behaved on the ward as he "normally" behaved. The pseudopatient spoke to patients and staff as he might ordinarily. Because there is uncommonly little to do on a psychiatric ward, he attempted to engage others in conversation. When asked by staff how he was feeling, he indicated that he was fine, that he no longer experienced symptoms. He responded to instructions from attendants, to calls for medication (which was not swallowed), and to dining-hall instructions. Beyond such activities as were available to him on the admissions ward, he spent his time writing down his observations about the ward, its patients, and the staff. Initially these notes were written "secretly," but as it soon became clear that no one much cared, they were subsequently written on standard tablets of paper in such public places as the dayroom. No secret was made of these activities.

The pseudopatient, very much as a true psychiatric patient, entered a hospital with no foreknowledge of when he would be discharged. Each was told that he would have to get out by his own devices, essentially by convincing the staff that he was sane. The psychological stresses associated with hospitalization were considerable, and all but one of the pseudopatients desired to be discharged almost immediately after being admitted. They were, therefore, motivated not only to behave sanely, but to be paragons of cooperation. That their behavior was in no way disruptive is confirmed by nursing reports, which have been obtained on most of the patients. These reports uniformly indicate that the patients were "friendly," "cooperative," and "exhibited no abnormal indications."

THE NORMAL ARE NOT DETECTABLY SANE

Despite their public "show" of sanity, the pseudopatients were never detected. Admitted, except in one case, with a diagnosis of schizophrenia *(10)*, each was discharged with a diagnosis of schizophrenia "in remission." The label "in remission" should in no way be dismissed as a formality, for at no time during any hospitalization had any question been raised about any pseudopatient's simulation. Nor are there any indications in the hospital records that the pseudopatient's status was suspect. Rather, the evidence is strong that, once labeled schizophrenic, the pseudopatient was stuck with that label. If the pseudopatient was to be discharged, he must naturally be "in remission"; but he was not sane, nor, in the institution's view, had he ever been sane.

The uniform failure to recognize sanity cannot be attributed to the quality of the hospitals, for, although there were considerable variations among them, several are considered excellent. Nor can it be alleged that there was simply not enough time to observe the pseudopatients. Length of hospitalization ranged from 7 to 52 days, with an average of 19 days. The pseudopatients were not, in fact, carefully observed, but this failure clearly speaks more to traditions within psychiatric hospitals than to lack of opportunity.

Finally, it cannot be said that the failure to recognize the pseudopatients' sanity was due to the fact that they were not behaving sanely. While there was clearly some tension present in all of them, their daily visitors could detect no serious behavioral consequences—nor, indeed, could other patients. It was quite common for the patients to "detect" the pseudopatients' sanity. During the first three hospitalizations, when accurate counts were kept, 35 of a total of 118 patients on the admissions ward voiced their suspicions, some vigorously. "You're not crazy. You're a journalist, or a professor [referring to the continual note-taking]. You're checking up on the hospital." While most of the patients were reassured by the pseudopatient's insistence that he had been sick before he came in but was fine now, some continued to believe that the pseudopatient was sane throughout his hospitalization *(11)*. The fact that the patients often recognized normality when staff did not raises important questions.

Failure to detect sanity during the course of hospitalization may be due to the fact that physicians operate with a strong bias toward what statisticians call the type 2 error *(5)*. This is to say that physicians are more inclined to call a healthy person sick (a false positive, type 2) than a sick person healthy (a false negative, type 1). The reasons for this are not hard to find: it is clearly more dangerous to misdiagnose illness than health. Better to err on the side of caution, to suspect illness even among the healthy.

But what holds for medicine does not hold equally well for psychiatry. Medical illnesses, while unfortunate, are not commonly pejorative. Psychiatric diagnoses, on the contrary, carry with them personal, legal, and social stigmas *(12)*. It was therefore important to see whether the tendency toward diagnosing the sane insane could be reversed. The following experiment was arranged at a research and teaching hospital whose staff had heard these findings but doubted that such an error could occur in their hospital. The staff was informed that at some time during the following 3 months, one or more pseudopatients would attempt to be admitted into the psychiatric hospital. Each staff member was asked to rate each patient who presented himself at admissions or on the ward according to the likelihood that the patient was a pseudopatient. A 10-point scale was used, with a 1 and 2 reflecting high confidence that the patient was a pseudopatient.

Judgments were obtained on 193 patients who were admitted for psychiatric treatment. All staff who had had sustained contact with or primary responsibility for the patient—attendants, nurses, psychiatrists, physicians, and psychologists—were asked to make judgments. Forty-one patients were alleged, with high confidence, to be pseudopatients by at least one member of the staff. Twenty-three were considered suspect by at least one psychiatrist. Nineteen were suspected by one psychiatrist *and* one other staff member. Actually, no genuine pseudopatient (at least from my group) presented himself during this period.

The experiment is instructive. It indicates that the tendency to designate sane people as insance can be reversed when the stakes (in this case, prestige and diagnostic acumen) are high. But what can be said of the 19 people who were suspected of being "sane" by one psychiatrist and another staff member? Were these people truly "sane," or was it rather the case that in the course of avoiding the type 2 error the staff tended to make more errors of the first sort—calling the crazy "sane"? There is no way of knowing. But one thing is certain: any diagnostic process that lends itself so readily to massive errors of this sort cannot be a very reliable one.

THE STICKINESS OF PSYCHODIAGNOSTIC LABELS

Beyond the tendency to call the healthy sick—a tendency that accounts better for diagnostic behavior on admission than it does for such behavior after a lengthy period of exposure—the data speak to the massive role of labeling in psychiatric assessment. Having once been labeled schizophrenic, there is nothing the pseudopatient can do to overcome the tag. The tag profoundly colors others' perceptions of him and his behavior.

From one viewpoint, these data are hardly surprising, for it has long been known that elements are given meaning by the context in which they occur. Gestalt psychology made this point vigorously, and Asch *(13)* demonstrated that there are "central" personality traits (such as "warm" versus "cold") which are so powerful that they markedly color the meaning of other information in forming an impression of a given personality *(14)*. "Insane," "schizophrenic," "manic-depressive," and "crazy" are probably among the most powerful of such central traits. Once a person is designated abnormal, all of his other behaviors and characteristics are colored by that label. Indeed, that label is so powerful that many of the pseudopatients' normal behaviors were overlooked entirely or profoundly misinterpreted. Some examples may clarify this issue.

Earlier I indicated that there were no changes in the pseudopatient's personal history and current status beyond those of name, employment, and, where necessary, vocation. Otherwise, a veridical description of personal history and circumstances was offered. Those circumstances were not psychotic. How were they made consonant with the diagnosis of psychosis? Or were those diagnoses modified in such a way as to bring them into accord with the circumstances of the pseudopatient's life, as described by him?

As far as I can determine, diagnoses were in no way affected by the relative health of the circumstances of a pseudopatient's life. Rather, the reverse occurred: the perception of his circumstances was shaped entirely by the diagnosis. A clear example of such translation is found in the case of a pseudopatient who had had a close relationship with his mother but was rather remote from his father during his early childhood. During adolescence and beyond, however, his father became a close friend, while his relationship with his mother cooled. His present relationship with his wife was characteristically close and warm. Apart from occasional angry exchanges, friction was minimal. The children had rarely been spanked. Surely there is nothing especially pathological about such a history. Indeed, many readers may see a similar pattern in their own experiences, with no markedly deleterious consequences. Observe, however, how such a history was translated in the psychopathological context, this from the case summary prepared after the patient was discharged.

This white 39-year-old male . . . manifests a long history of considerable ambivalence in close relationships, which begins in early childhood. A warm relationship with his mother cools during his adolescence. A distant relationship to his father is described as becoming very intense. Affective stability is absent. His attempts to control emotionality with his wife and children are punctuated by angry outbursts and, in the case of the children, spankings. And while he says that he has several good friends, one senses considerable ambivalence embedded in those relationships also. . . .

The facts of the case were unintentionally distorted by the staff to achieve consistency with a popular theory of the dynamics of a schizophrenic reaction *(15)*. Nothing of an ambivalent nature had been described in relations with parents, spouse, or friends. To the extent that ambivalence could be inferred, it was probably not greater than is found in all human relationships. It is true the pseudopatient's relationships with his parents changed over time, but in the ordinary context that would hardly be remarkable—indeed, it might very well be expected. Clearly, the meaning ascribed to his verbalizations (that is, ambivalence, affective instability) was determined by the diagnosis: schizophrenia. An entirely different meaning would have been ascribed if it were known that the man was "normal."

All pseudopatients took extensive notes publicly. Under ordinary circumstances, such behavior would have raised questions in the minds of observers, as, in fact, it did among patients. Indeed, it seemed so certain that the notes would elicit suspicion that elaborate precautions were taken to remove them from the ward each day. But the precautions proved needless. The closest any staff member came to questioning these notes occurred when one pseudopatient asked his physician what kind of medication he was receiving and began to write down the response. "You needn't write it," he was told gently. "If you have trouble remembering, just ask me again."

If no questions were asked of the pseudopatients, how was their writing interpreted? Nursing records for three patients indicate that the writing was seen as an aspect of their pathological behavior. "Patient engages in writing behavior" was the daily nursing comment on one of the pseudopatients who was never questioned about his writing. Given that the patient is in the hospital, he must be psychologically disturbed. And given that he is disturbed, continuous writing must be a behavioral manifestation of that disturbance, perhaps a subset of the compulsive behaviors that are sometimes correlated with schizophrenia.

One tacit characteristic of psychiatric diagnosis is that it locates the sources of aberration within the individual and only rarely within the complex of stimuli that surrounds him. Consequently, behaviors that are stimulated by the environment are commonly misattributed to the patient's disorder. For example, one kindly nurse found a pseudopatient pacing the long hospital corridors. "Nervous, Mr. X?" she asked. "No, bored," he said.

The notes kept by pseudopatients are full of patient behaviors that were misinterpreted by well-intentioned staff. Often enough, a patient would go "berserk" because he had, wittingly or unwittingly, been mistreated by, say, an attendant. A nurse coming upon the scene would rarely inquire even cursorily into the environmental stimuli of the patient's behavior. Rather, she assumed that his upset derived from his pathology, not from his present interactions with other staff members. Occasionally, the staff might assume that the patient's family (especially when they had recently visited) or other patients had stimulated the outburst. But never were the staff found to assume that one of themselves or the structure of the hospital had anything to do with a patient's behavior. One psychiatrist pointed to a group of patients who were sitting outside the cafeteria entrance half an hour before lunch time. To a group of young residents he indicated that such behavior was characteristic of the oral-acquisitive nature of the syndrome. It seemed not to occur to him that there were very few things to anticipate in a psychiatric hospital besides eating.

A psychiatric label has a life and an influence of its own. Once the impression has been formed that the patient is schizophrenic, the expectation is that he will continue to be schizophrenic. When a sufficient amount of time has passed, during which the patient has done nothing bizarre, he is considered to be in remission and available for discharge. But the label endures beyond discharge, with the unconfirmed expectation that he will behave as a schizophrenic again. Such labels, conferred by mental health professionals, are as influential on the patient as they are on his relatives and friends, and it should not surprise anyone that the diagnosis acts on all of them as a self-fulfilling prophecy. Eventually, the patient himself accepts the diagnosis, with all of its surplus meanings and expectations, and behaves accordingly *(5)*.

The inferences to be made from these matters are quite simple. Much as Zigler and Phillips have demonstrated that there is enormous overlap in the symptoms presented by patients who have been variously diagnosed *(16)*, so there is enormous overlap in the behaviors of the sane and the insane. The sane are not "sane" all of the time. We lose our tempers "for no good reason." We are occasionally depressed or anxious, again for no good reason. And we may find it difficult to get along with one or another person—again for no reason that we can specify. Similarly, the insane are not always insane. Indeed, it was the impression of the pseudopatients while living with them that they were sane for long periods of time—that the bizarre behaviors upon which their diagnoses were allegedly predicated constituted only a small fraction of their total behavior. If it makes no sense to label ourselves permanently depressed on the basis of an occasional depression, then it takes better evidence than is presently available to label all patients insane or schizophrenic on the basis of bizarre behaviors or cognitions. It seems more useful, as Mischel *(17)* has pointed out, to limit our discussions to *behaviors*, the stimuli that provoke them, and their correlates.

It is not known why powerful impressions of personality traits, such as "crazy" or "insane," arise. Conceivably, when the origins of and stimuli that give rise to a behavior are remote or unknown, or when the behavior strikes us as immutable, trait labels regarding the *behaver* arise. When, on the other hand, the origins and stimuli are known and available, discourse is limited to the behavior itself. Thus, I may hallucinate because I am sleeping, or I may hallucinate because I have ingested a peculiar drug. These are termed sleep-induced hallucinations, or dreams, and drug-induced hallucinations, respectively. But when the stimuli to my hallucinations are unknown, that is called craziness, or schizophrenia—as if that inference were somehow as illuminating as the others.

THE EXPERIENCE OF PSYCHIATRIC HOSPITALIZATION

The term "mental illness" is of recent origin. It was coined by people who were humane in their inclinations and who wanted very much to raise the station of (and the public's sympathies toward) the psychologically disturbed from that of witches and "crazies" to one that was akin to the physically ill. And they were at least partially successful, for the treatment of the mentally ill *has* improved considerably over the years. But while treatment has improved, it is doubtful that people really regard the mentally ill in the same way that they view the physically ill. A broken leg is something one recovers from, but mental illness allegedly endures forever *(18)*. A broken leg does not threaten the observer, but a crazy schizophrenic? There is by now a host of evidence that attitudes toward the mentally ill are characterized by fear, hostility, aloofness, suspicion, and dread *(19)*. The mentally ill are society's lepers.

That such attitudes infect the general population is perhaps not surprising, only upsetting. But that they affect the professionals—attendants, nurses, physicians, psychologists, and social workers—who treat and deal with the mentally ill is more disconcerting, both because such attitudes are self-evidently pernicious and because they are unwitting. Most mental health professionals would insist that they are sympathetic toward the mentally ill, that they are neither avoidant nor hostile. But it is more likely that an exquisite ambivalence characterizes their relations with psychiatric patients, such that their avowed impulses are only part of their entire attitude. Negative attitudes are there too and can easily be detected. Such attitudes should not surprise us. They are the natural offspring of the labels patients wear and the places in which they are found.

Consider the structure of the typical psychiatric hospital. Staff and patients are strictly segregated.

Staff have their own living space, including their dining facilities, bathrooms, and assembly places. The glassed quarters that contain the professional staff, which the pseudopatients came to call "the cage," sit out on every dayroom. The staff emerge primarily for caretaking purposes—to give medication, to conduct a therapy or group meeting, to instruct or reprimand a patient. Otherwise, staff keep to themselves, almost as if the disorder that afflicts their charges is somehow catching.

So much is patient-staff segregation the rule that, for four public hospitals in which an attempt was made to measure the degree to which staff and patients mingle, it was necessary to use "time out of the staff cage" as the operational measure. While it was not the case that all time spent out of the cage was spent mingling with patients (attendants, for example, would occasionally emerge to watch television in the dayroom), it was the only way in which one could gather reliable data on time for measuring.

The average amount of time spent by attendants outside of the cage was 11.3 percent (range, 3 to 52 percent). This figure does not represent only time spent mingling with patients, but also includes time spent on such chores as folding laundry, supervising patients while they shave, directing ward cleanup, and sending patients to off-ward activities. It was the relatively rare attendant who spent time talking with patients or playing games with them. It proved impossible to obtain a "percent mingling time" for nurses, since the amount of time they spent out of the cage was too brief. Rather, we counted instances of emergence from the cage. On the average, daytime nurses emerged from the cage 11.5 times per shift, including instances when they left the ward entirely (range, 4 to 39 times). Late afternoon and night nurses were even less available, emerging on the average 9.4 times per shift (range, 4 to 41 times). Data on early morning nurses, who arrived usually after midnight and departed at 8 a.m., are not available because patients were asleep during most of this period.

Physicians, especially psychiatrists, were even less available. They were rarely seen on the wards. Quite commonly, they would be seen only when they arrived and departed, with the remaining time being spent in their offices or in the cage. On the average, physicians emerged on the ward 6.7 times per day (range, 1 to 17 times). It proved difficult to make an accurate estimate in this regard, since physicians often maintained hours that allowed them to come and go at different times.

The hierarchical organization of the psychiatric hospital has been commented on before [20], but the latent meaning of that kind of organization is worth noting again. Those with the most power have least to do with patients, and those with the least power are most involved with them. Recall, however, that the acquisition of role-appropriate behaviors occurs mainly through the observation of others, with the most powerful having the most influence. Consequently, it is understandable that attendants not only spend more time with patients than do any other members of the staff—that is required by their station in the hierarchy—but also, insofar as they learn from their superiors' behavior, spend as little time with patients as they can. Attendants are seen mainly in the cage, which is where the models, the action, and the power are.

I turn now to a different set of studies, these dealing with staff response to patient-initiated contact. It has long been known that the amount of time a person spends with you can be an index of your significance to him. If he initiates and maintains eye contact, there is reason to believe that he is considering your requests and needs. If he pauses to chat or actually stops and talks, there is added reason to infer that he is individuating you. In four hospitals, the pseudopatient approached the staff member with a request which took the following form' "Pardon me, Mr. [or Dr. or Mrs.] X, could you tell me when I will be eligible for grounds privileges?" (or " . . . when I will be presented at the staff meeting?" or ". . . when I am likely to be discharged?"). While the content of the question varied according to the appropriateness of the target and the pseudopatient's (apparent) current needs the form was always a courteous and relevant request for information. Care was taken never to approach a particular member of the staff more than once a day, lest the staff member become suspicious or irritated. In examining these data, remember

TABLE 1. *Self-initiated Contact by Pseudopatients with Psychiatrists and Nurses and Attendants, Compared to Contact with Other Groups*

Contact	Psychiatric Hospitals		University Campus (Nonmedical)	University Medical Center Physicians		
	(1) Psychiatrists	(2) Nurses and Attendants	(3) Faculty	(4) "Looking for a psychiatrist"	(5) "Looking for an internist"	(6) No Additional Comment
Responses						
Moves on, head averted (%)	71	88	0	0	0	0
Makes eye contact (%)	23	10	0	11	0	0
Pauses and chats (%)	2	2	0	11	0	10
Stops and talks (%)	4	0.5	100	78	100	90
Mean number of questions answered (out of 6)	*	*	6	3.8	4.8	4.5
Respondents (No.)	13	47	14	18	15	10
Attempts (No.)	185	1283	14	18	15	10

*Not applicable.

that the behavior of the pseudopatients was neither bizarre nor disruptive. One could indeed engage in good conversation with them.

The data for these experiments are shown in Table 1, separately for physicians (column 1) and for nurses and attendants (column 2). Minor differences between these four institutions were overwhelmed by the degree to which staff avoided continuing contacts that patients had initiated. By far, their most common response consisted of either a brief response to the question, offered while they were "on the move" and with head averted, or no response at all.

The encounter frequently took the following bizarre form: (pseudopatient) "Pardon me, Dr. X. Could you tell me when I am eligible for grounds privileges?" (physician) "Good morning, Dave. How are you today?" (Moves off without waiting for a response.)

It is instructive to compare these data with data recently obtained at Stanford University. It has been alleged that large and eminent universities are characterized by faculty who are so busy that they have no time for students. For this comparison, a young lady approached individual faculty members who seemed to be walking purposefully to some meeting or teaching engagement and asked them the following six questions.

1. "Pardon me, could you direct me to Encina Hall?" (at the medical school: ". . . to the Clinical Research Center?").
2. "Do you know where Fish Annex is?" (there is no Fish Annex at standord).
3. "Do you teach here?"
4. "How does one apply for admission to the college?" (at the medical school: ". . . to the medical school?").
5. "Is it difficult to get in?"
6. "Is there financial aid?"

Without exception, as can be seen in Table 1 (column 3), all of the questions were answered. No matter how rushed they were, all respondents not only maintained eye contact, but stopped to talk. Indeed, many of the respondents went out of their way to direct or take the questioner to the office she was seeking, to try to locate "Fish Annex," or to discuss with her the possibilities of being admitted to the university.

Similar data, also shown in Table 1 (columns 4, 5, and 6), were obtained in the hospital. Here too, the young lady came prepared with six questions. After the first question, however, she remarked to 18 of her respondents (column 4), "I'm looking for a psychiatrist," and to 15 others (column 5), "I'm looking for an internist." Ten other respondents received no inserted comment (column 6). The general degree of cooperative responses is considerably higher for these university groups than it was for pseudopatients in psychiatric hospitals. Even so, differences are apparent within the medical school setting. Once having indicated that she was looking for a psychiatrist, the degree of cooperation elicited was less than when she sought an internist.

POWERLESSNESS AND DEPERSONALIZATION

Eye contact and verbal contact reflect concern and individuation; their absence, avoidance and depersonalization. The data I have presented do not do justice to the rich daily encounters that grew up around matters of depersonalization and avoidance. I have records of patients who were beaten by staff for the sin of having initiated verbal contact. During my own experience, for example, one patient was beaten in the presence of other patients for having approached an attendant and told him, "I like you." Occasionally, punishment meted out to patients for misdemeanors seemed so excessive that it could not be justified by the most radical interpretations of psychiatric canon. Nevertheless, they appeared to go unquestioned. Tempers were often short. A patient who had not heard a call for medication would be roundly excoriated, and the morning attendants would often wake patients with, "Come on, you m-----f-----s, out of bed!"

Neither anecdotal nor "hard" data can convey the overwhelming sense of powerlessness which invades the individual as he is continually exposed to the depersonalization of the psychiatric hospital. It hardly matters *which* psychiatric hospital—the excellent public ones and the very plush private hospital were better than the rural and shabby ones in this regard, but, again, the features that psychiatric hospitals had in common overwhelmed by far their apparent differences.

Powerlessness was evident everywhere. The patient is deprived of many of his legal rights by dint of his psychiatric commitment *(21)*. He is shorn of credibility by virtue of his psychiatric label. His freedom of movement is restricted. He cannot initiate contact with the staff, but may only respond to such overtures as they make. Personal privacy is minimal. Patient quarters and possessions can be entered and examined by any staff member, for whatever reason. His personal history and anguish is available to any staff member (often including the "grey lady" and "candy striper" volunteer) who chooses to read his folder, regardless of their therapeutic relationship to him. His personal hygiene and waste evacuation are often monitored. The water closets may have no doors.

At times, depersonalization reached such proportions that pseudopatients had the sense that they were invisible, or at least unworthy of account. Upon being admitted, I and other pseudopatients took the initial physical examinations in a semi-public room, where staff members went about their own business as if we were not there.

On the ward, attendants delivered verbal and occasionally serious physical abuse to patients in the presence of other observing patients, some of whom (the pseudopatients) were writing it all down. Abusive behavior, on the other hand, terminated quite abruptly when other staff members were known to be coming. Staff are credible witnesses. Patients are not.

A nurse unbuttoned her uniform to adjust her brassiere in the presence of an entire ward of viewing men. One did not have the sense that she was being seductive. Rather, she didn't notice us. A group of staff persons might point to a patient in the dayroom and discuss him animatedly, as if he were not there.

One illuminating instance of depersonalization and invisibility occurred with regard to medications. All told, the pseudopatients were administered nearly 2100 pills, including Elavil, Stelazine, Compazine, and Thorazine, to name but a few. (That such a variety of medications should have been administered to patients presenting identical symptoms is itself worthy of note.) Only two were swallowed. The rest were either pocketed or deposited in the toilet. The pseudopatients were not alone in this. Although I have no precise record on how many patients rejected their medications, the pseudopatients frequently found the medications of other patients in the toilet before they deposited their own. As long as they were cooperative, their behavior and the pseudopatients' own in this matter, as in other important matters, went unnoticed thoughout.

Reactions to such depersonalization among pseudopatients were intense. Although they had come to the hospital as participant observers and were fully aware that they did not "belong," they nevertheless found themselves caught up in and fighting the process of depersonalization. Some examples: a graduate student in psychology asked his wife to bring his textbooks to the hospital so he could "catch up on his homework"—this despite the elaborate precautions taken to conceal his professional association. The same student, who had trained for quite some time to get into the hospital, and who had looked forward to the experience, "remembered" some drag races that he had wanted to see on the weekend and insisted that he be discharged by that time. Another pseudopatient attempted a romance with a nurse. Subsequently, he informed the staff that he was applying for admission to graduate school in psychology and was very likely to be admitted, since a graduate professor was one of his regular hospital visitors. The same person began to engage in psychotherapy with other patients—all of this as a way of becoming a person in an impersonal environment.

THE SOURCES OF DEPERSONALIZATION

What are the origins of depersonalization? I have already mentioned two. First are attitudes held by all of us toward the mentally ill—including those who treat them—attitudes characterized by fear, distrust, and horrible expectations on the one hand, and benevolent intentions on the other. Our ambivalence leads, in this instance as in others, to avoidance.

Second, and not entirely separate, the hierarchical structure of the psychiatric hospital facilitates depersonalization. Those who are at the top have least to do with patients, and their behavior inspires the rest of the staff. Average daily contact with psychiatrists, psychologists, residents, and physicians combined ranged from 3.9 to 25.1 minutes,

with an overall mean of 6.8 (six pseudopatients over a total of 129 days of hospitalization). Included in this average are time spent in the admissions interview, ward meetings in the presence of a senior staff member, group and individual psychotherapy contacts, case presentation conferences, and discharge meetings. Clearly, patients do not spend much time in interpersonal contact with doctoral staff. And doctoral staff serve as models for nurses and attendants.

There are probably other sources. Psychiatric installations are presently in serious financial straits. Staff shortages are pervasive, staff time at a premium. Something has to give, and that something is patient contact. Yet, while financial stresses are realities, too much can be made of them. I have the impression that the psychological forces that result in depersonalization are much stronger than the fiscal ones and that the addition of more staff would not correspondingly improve patient care in this regard. The incidence of staff meetings and the enormous amount of record-keeping on patients, for example, have not been as substantially reduced as has patient contact. Priorities exist, even during hard times. Patient contact is not a significant priority in the traditional psychiatric hospital, and fiscal pressures do not account for this. Avoidance and depersonalization may.

Heavy reliance upon psychotropic medication tacitly contributes to depersonalization by convincing staff that treatment is indeed being conducted and that further patient contact may not be necessary. Even here, however, caution needs to be exercised in understanding the role of psychotropic drugs. If patients were powerful rather than powerless, if they were viewed as interesting individuals rather than diagnostic entities, if they were socially significant rather than social lepers, if their anguish truly and wholly compelled our sympathies and concerns, would we not *seek* contact with them, despite the availability of medications? Perhaps for the pleasure of it all?

THE CONSEQUENCES OF LABELING AND DEPERSONALIZATION

Whenever the ratio of what is known to what needs to be known approaches zero, we tend to invent "knowledge" and assume that we understand more than we actually do. We seem unable to acknowledge that we simply don't know. The needs for diagnosis and remediation of behavioral and emotional problems are enormous. But rather than acknowledge that we are just embarking on understanding, we continue to label patients "schizophrenic," "manic-depressive," and "insane," as if in those words we had captured the essence of understanding. The facts of the matter are that we have known for a long time that diagnoses are often not useful or reliable, but we have nevertheless continued to use them. We now know that we cannot distinguish insanity from sanity. It is depressing to consider how that information will be used.

Not merely depressing, but frightening. How many people, one wonders, are sane but not recognized as such in our psychiatric institutions? How many have been needlessly stripped of their privileges of citizenship, from the right to vote and drive to that of handling their own accounts? How many have feigned insanity in order to avoid the criminal consequences of their behavior, and, conversely, how many would rather stand trial than live interminably in a psychiatric hospital—but are wrongly thought to be mentally ill? How many have been stigmatized by well-intentioned, but nevertheless erroneous, diagnoses? On the last point, recall again that a "type 2 error" in psychiatric diagnosis does not have the same consequences it does in medical diagnosis. A diagnosis of cancer that has been found to be in error is cause for celebration. But psychiatric diagnoses are rarely found to be in error. The label sticks, a mark of inadequacy forever.

Finally, how many patients might be "sane" outside the psychiatric hospital but seem insane in it— not because craziness resides in them, as it were, but because they are responding to a bizarre setting, one that may be unique to institutions which harbor neither people? Goffman *(4)* calls the process of socialization to such institutions "mortification"— an apt metaphor that includes the processes of depersonalization that have been described here. And while it is impossible to know whether the pseudo-patients' responses to these processes are characteristic of all inmates—they were, after all, not real patients—it is difficult to believe that these processes of socialization to a psychiatric hospital provide useful attitudes or habits of response for living in the "real world."

SUMMARY AND CONCLUSIONS

It is clear that we cannot distinguish the sane from the insane in psychiatric hospitals. The hospital itself imposes a special environment in which the meanings of behavior can easily be misunderstood. The consequences to patients hospitalized in such an environment—the powerlessness, depersonalization, segregation, mortification, and self-labeling—seem undoubtedly counter-therapeutic.

I do not, even now, understand this problem well enough to perceive solutions. But two matters seem to have some promise. The first concerns the proliferation of community mental health facilities, of crisis intervention centers, of the human potential movement, and of behavior therapies that, for all of their own problems, tend to avoid psychiatric labels, to focus on specific problems and behaviors and to retain the individual in a relatively nonpejorative environment. Clearly, to the extent that we refrain from sending the distressed to insane places, our impressions of them are less likely to be distorted. (The risk of distorted perceptions, it seems to me, is always present, since we are much more sensitive to an individual's behaviors and verbalizations than we are to the subtle contextual stimuli that often promote them. At issue here is a matter of magnitude. And, as I have shown, the magnitude of distortion is exceedingly high in the extreme context that is a psychiatric hospital.)

The second matter that might prove promising speaks to the need to increase the sensitivity of mental health workers and researchers to the *Catch 22* position of psychiatric patients. Simply reading materials in this area will be of help to some such workers and researchers. For others, directly experiencing the impact of psychiatric hospitalization will be of enormous use. Clearly, further research into the social psychology of such total institutions will both facilitate treatment and deepen understanding.

I and the other pseudopatients in the psychiatric setting had distinctly negative reactions. We do not pretend to describe the subjective experiences of true patients. Theirs may be different from ours, particularly with the passage of time and the necessary process of adaptation to one's environment. But we can and do speak to the relatively more objective indices of treatment within the hospital. It could be a mistake, and a very unfortunate one, to consider that what happened to us derived from malice or stupidity on the part of the staff. Quite the contrary, our overwhelming impression of them was of people who really cared, who were committed and who were uncommonly intelligent. Where they failed, as they sometimes did painfully, it would be more accurate to attribute those failures to the environment in which they, too, found themselves than to personal callousness. Their perceptions and behavior were controlled by the situation, rather than being motivated by a malicious disposition. In a more benign environment, one that was less attached to global diagnosis, their behaviors and judgments might have been more benign and effective.

REFERENCES AND NOTES

1. P. Ash, *J. Abnorm. Soc. Psychol. 44,* 272 (1949); A. T. Beck, *Amer. J. Psychiat.* 119, 210 (1962); A. T. Boisen, *Psychiatry 2,* 233 (1938); N. Kreitman, *J. Ment. Sci. 107,* 876 (1961); N. Kreitman, P. Sainsbury, J. Morrisey, J. Towers, J. Scrivener, *ibid.,* p. 887; H. O. Schmitt and C. P. Fonda, *J. Abnorm. Soc. Psychol. 52,* 262 (1956); W. Seeman, *J. Nerv. Ment. Dis. 118,* 541 (1953). For an analysis of these artifacts and summaries of the disputes, see J. Zubin, *Annu. Rev. Psychol. 18,* 373

(1967); L. Phillips and J. G. Draguns, *ibid. 22,* 447 (1971).

2. R. Benedict, *J. Gen. Psychol. 10,* 59 (1934).

3. See in this regard H. Becker, *Outsiders: Studies in the Sociology of Deviance* (Free Press, New York, 1963); B. M. Braginsky, D. D. Braginsky, K. Ring. *Methods of Madness: The Mental Hospital as a Last Resort* (Holt, Rinehart & Winston, New York, 1969); G. M. Crocetti and P. V. Lemkau, *Amer. Sociol. Rev. 30,* 577 (1965); E. Goffman, *Behavior in Public Places* (Free Press, New York, 1964); R. D. Laing, *The Divided Self: A Study of Sanity and Madness* (Quadrangle, Chicago, 1960); D. L. Phillips, *Amer. Sociol. Rev. 28,* 963 (1963); T. R. Sarbin, *Psychol. Today 6,* 18 (1972); E. Schur, *Amer. J. Sociol. 75,* 309 (1969); T. Szasz, *Law, Liberty and Psychiatry* (Macmillan, New York, 1963); *The Myth of Mental Illness: Foundations of a Theory of Mental Illness* (Hoeber-Harper, New York, 1963). For a critique of some of these views, see W. R. Gove, *Amer. Sociol. Rev. 35,* 873 (1970).

4. E. Goffman, *Asylums* (Doubleday, Garden City, N.Y., 1961).

5. T. J. Scheff, *Being Mentally Ill: A Sociological Theory* (Aldine, Chicago, 1966).

6. Data from a ninth pseudopatient are not incorporated in this report because, although his sanity went undetected, he falsified aspects of his personal history, including his marital status and parental relationships. His experimental behaviors therefore were not identical to those of the other pseudopatients.

7. A. Barry, *Bellevue Is a State of Mind* (Harcourt Brace Jovanovich, New York, 1971); I. Belknap, *Human Problems of a State Mental Hospital* (McGraw-Hill, New York, 1956); W. Caudill, F. C. Redlich, H. R. Gilmore, E. B. Brody, *Amer. J. Orthopsychiat. 22,* 314 (1952); A. R. Goldman, R. H. Bohr, T. A. Steinberg, *Prof. Psychol. 1,* 427 (1970); unauthored, *Roche Report 1* (No. 13), 8 (1971).

8. Beyond the personal difficulties that the pseudopatient is likely to experience in the hospital, there are legal and social ones that, combined, require considerable attention before entry. For example, once admitted to a psychiatric institution, it is difficult, if not impossible, to be discharged on short notice, state law to the contrary notwithstanding. I was not sensitive to these difficulties at the outset of the project, nor to the personal and situational emergencies that can arise, but later a writ of habeas corpus was prepared for each of the entering pseudopatients and an attorney was kept "on call" during every hospitalization. I am grateful to John Kaplan and Robert Bartels for legal advice and assistance in these matters.

9. However distasteful such concealment is, it was a necessary first step to examining these questions. Without concealment, there would have been no way to know how valid these experiences were; nor was there any way of knowing whether whatever detections occurred were a tribute to the diagnostic acumen of the staff or to the hospital's rumor network. Obviously, since my concerns are general ones that cut across

individual hospitals and staffs, I have respected their anonymity and have eliminated clues that might lead to their identification.

10. Interestingly, of the 12 admissions, 11 were diagnosed as schizophrenic and one, with the identical symptomatology, as manic-depressive psychosis. This diagnosis has a more favorable prognosis, and it was given by the only private hospital in our sample. On the relations between social class and psychiatric diagnosis, see A. deB. Hollingshead and F. C. Redlich, *Social Class and Mental Illness: A Community Study* (Wiley, New York, 1958).

11. It is possible, of course, that patients have quite broad latitudes in diagnosis and therefore are inclined to call many people sane, even those whose behavior is patently aberrant. However, although we have no hard data on this matter, it was our distinct impression that this was not the case. In many instances, patients not only singled us out for attention, but came to imitate our behaviors and styles.

12. J. Cumming and E. Cumming, *Community Ment. Health 1,* 135 (1965); A. Farina and K. Ring, *J. Abnorm. Psychol. 70,* 47 (1965); H. E. Freeman and O. G. Simmons, *The Mental Patient Comes Home* (Wiley, New York, 1963); W. J. Johannsen, *Ment. Hygiene 53,* 218 (1969); A. S. Linsky, *Soc. Psychiat. 5,* 166 (1970).

13. S. E. Asch, *J. Abnorm. Soc. Psychol. 41,* 258 (1946); *Social Psychology* (Prentice-Hall, New York, 1952).

14. See also I. N. Mensh and J. Wishner, *J. Personality 16,* 188 (1947); J. Wishner, *Psychol. Rev. 67,* 96 (1960); J. S. Bruner and R. Tagiuri, in *Handbook of Social Psychology,* G. Lindzey, Ed. (Addison-Wesley, Cambridge, Mass., 1954), vol. 2, pp. 634–654; J. S. Bruner, D. Shapiro, R. Tagiuri, in *Person Perception and Interpersonal Behavior.* R. Tagiuri and L. Petrullo, Eds. (Standford Univ. Press, Stanford, Calif., 1958), pp. 277–288.

15. For an example of a similar self-fulfilling prophecy, in this instance dealing with the "central" trait of intelligence, see R. Rosenthal and L. Jacobson, *Pygmalion in the Classroom* (Holt, Rinehart & Winston, New York, 1968).

16. E. Zigler and L. Phillips, *J. Abnorm. Soc. Psychol. 63,* 69 (1961). See also R. K. Freudenberg and J. P. Robertson, *A.M.A. Arch. Neurol. Psychiatr. 76,* 14 (1956).

17. W. Mischel, *Personality and Assessment* (Wiley, New York, 1968).

18. The most recent and unfortunate instance of this tenet is that of Senator Thomas Eagleton.

19. T. R. Sarbin and J. C. Mancuso, *J. Clin. Consult. Psychol. 35,* 159 (1970); T. R. Sarbin, *ibid. 31,* 447 (1967); J. C. Nunnally, Jr. *Popular Conceptions of Mental Health* (Hold, Rinehart & Winston, New York, 1961).

20. A. H. Stanton and M. S. Schwartz, *The Mental Hospital: A Study of Institutional Participation in Psychiatric Illness and Treatment* (Basic, New York, 1954)..

21. D. B. Wexler and S. E. Scoville, *Ariz. Law Rev. 13,* 1 (1971).
22. I thank W. Mischel, E. Orme, and M. S. Rosenhan for comments on an earlier draft of this manuscript.

5. Sex-Role Stereotypes and Clinical Judgments of Mental Health
INGE K. BROVERMAN, DONALD M. BROVERMAN, FRANK E. CLARKSON, PAUL S. ROSENKRANTZ, & SUSAN R. VOGEL

A sex-role Stereotype Questionnaire consisting of 122 bipolar items was given to actively functioning clinicians with one of three sets of instructions: To describe a healthy, mature, socially competent (a) adult, sex unspecified, (b) a man, or (c) a woman. It was hypothesized that clinical judgments about the characteristics of healthy individuals would differ as a function of sex of person judged, and furthermore, that these differences in clinical judgments would parallel stereotypic sex-role differences. A second hypothesis predicted that behaviors and characteristics judged healthy for an adult, sex unspecified, which are presumed to reflect an ideal standard of health, will resemble behaviors judged healthy for men, but differ from behaviors judged healthy for women. Both hypotheses were confirmed. Possible reasons for and the effects of this double standard of health are discussed.

Evidence of the existence of sex-role stereotypes, that is, highly consensual norms and beliefs about the differing characteristics of men and women, is abundantly present in the literature (Anastasi & Foley, 1949; Fernberger, 1948; Komarovsky, 1950; McKee & Sherriffs, 1957; Seward, 1946; Seward & Larson, 1968; Wylie, 1961; Rosenkrantz, Vogel, Bee, Bro-

Inge K. Broverman, Donald M. Broverman, Frank E. Clarkson, Paul S. Rosenkrantz, & Susan R. Vogel, Sex-role stereotypes and clinical judgment of mental health, *Journal of Consulting and Clinical Psychology, 34,* 1970, 1-7. Copyright © 1970 by the American Psychological Association and reproduced by permission.

verman, & Broverman, 1968). Similarly, the differential valuations of behaviors and characteristics stereotypically ascribed to men and women are well established (Kitay, 1940; Lynn, 1959; McKee & Sherriffs, 1959; Rosenkrantz et al., 1968; White, 1950), that is, stereotypically masculine traits are more often perceived as socially desirable than are attributes which are stereotypically feminine. The literature also indicates that the social desirabilities of behaviors are positively related to the clinical ratings of these same behaviors in terms of "normality-abnormality" (Cowen, 1961), "adjustment" (Wiener, Blumberg, Segman, & Cooper, 1959), and "health-sickness" (Kogan, Quinn, Ax, & Ripley, 1957).

Given the relationships existing between masculine versus feminine characteristics and social desirability, on the one hand, and between mental health and social desirability on the other, it seems reasonable to expect that clinicians will maintain parallel distinctions in their concepts of what, behaviorally, is healthy or pathological when considering men versus women. More specifically, particular behaviors and characteristics may be thought indicative of pathology in members of one sex, but not pathological in members of the opposite sex.

The present paper, then, tests the hypothesis that clinical judgments about the traits characterizing healthy, mature individuals will differ as a function of the sex of the person judged. Furthermore, these differences in clinical judgments are expected to parallel the stereotypic sex-role differences previously reported (Rosenkrantz et al., 1968).

Finally, the present paper hypothesizes that behavioral attributes which are regarded as healthy for an adult, sex unspecified, and thus presumably viewed from an ideal, absolute standpoint, will more often be considered by clinicians as healthy or appropriate for men than for women. This hypothesis derives from the assumption that abstract notions of health will tend to be more influenced by the greater social value of masculine stereotypic characteristics than by the lesser valued femine stereotypic characteristics.

The authors are suggesting, then, that a double standard of health exists wherein ideal concepts of health for a mature adult, sex unspecified, are meant primarily for men, less so for women.

METHOD

Subjects

Seventy-nine clinically-trained psychologists, psychiatrists, or social workers (46 men, 33 women) served as Ss. Of these, 31 men and 18 women had PhD or MD degrees. The Ss were all actively functioning in clinical settings. The ages varied between 23 and 55 years and experience ranged from internship to extensive professional experience.

Instrument

The authors have developed a Stereotype Questionnaire which is described in detail elsewhere (Rosenkrantz et al., 1968). Briefly, the questionnaire consists of 122 bipolar items each of which describes, with an adjective or a short phrase, a particular behavior trait or characteristic such as:

Very aggressive   Not at all aggressive
Doesn't hide emotions at all   Always hides emotions

One pole of each item can be characterized as typically masculine, the other as typically feminine (Rosenkrantz et al., 1968). On 41 items, 70% or better agreement occurred as to which pole characterizes men or women, respectively, in both a sample of college men and in a sample of college women (Rosenkrantz et al., 1968). These items have been classified as "stereotypic."

The questionnaire used in the present study differs slightly from the original questionnaire. Seven original items seemed to reflect adolescent concerns with sex, for example, "very proud of sexual ability . . . not at all concerned with sexual ability." These items were replaced by seven more general items. Since three of the discarded items were stereotypic, the present questionnaire contains only 38 stereotypic items. These items are shown in Table 1.

Finally, in a prior study, judgments have been obtained from samples of Ss as to which pole of each item represents the more socially desirable behavior or trait for an adult individual in general, regardless of sex. On 27 of the 38 stereotypic items, the masculine pole is more socially desirable, (male-valued items), and on the remaining 11 stereotypic items, the feminine pole is the more socially desirable one (female-valued items).

Instructions

The clinicians were given the 122-item questionnaire with one of three sets of instructions, "male," "female," or "adult." Seventeen men and 10 women were given the "male" instructions which stated "think of normal, adult men and then indicate on each item the pole to which a mature, healthy, soc-

ially competent adult man would be closer." The Ss were asked to look at the opposing poles of each item in terms of directions rather than extremes of behavior. Another 14 men and 12 women were given "female" instructions, that is, they were asked to describe a "mature, healthy, socially competent adult woman." Finally, 15 men and 11 women were given "adult" instructions. These Ss were asked to describe a "healthy, mature, socially competent adult person" (sex unspecified). Responses to these "adult" instructions may be considered in-

TABLE 1. *Male–Valued and Female–Valued Stereotypic Items*

Feminine Pole	Masculine Pole
Male-Valued Items	
Not at all aggressive	Very aggressive
Not at all independent	Very independent
Very emotional	Not at all emotional
Does not hide emotions at all	Almost always hides emotions
Very subjective	Very objective
Very easily influenced	Not at all easily influenced
Very submissive	Very dominant
Dislikes math and science very much	Likes math and science very much
Very excitable in a minor crisis	Not at all excitable in a minor crisis
Very passive	Very active
Not at all competitive	Very competitive
Very illogical	Very logical
Very home oriented	Very worldly
Not at all skilled in business	Very skilled in business
Very sneaky	Very direct
Does not know the way of the world	Knows the way of the world
Feelings easily hurt	Feelings not easily hurt
Not at all adventurous	Very adventurous
Has difficulty making decisions	Can make decisions easily
Cries very easily	Never cries
Almost never acts as a leader	Almost always acts as a leader
Not at all self-confident	Very self-confident
Very uncomfortable about being aggressive	Not at all uncomfortable about being aggressive
Not at all ambitious	Very ambitious
Unable to separate feelings from ideas	Easily able to separate feelings from ideas
Very dependent	Not at all dependent
Very conceited about appearance	Never conceited about appearance

TABLE 1. *continued*

Feminine Pole	Masculine Pole
Female-Valued Items	
Very talkative	Not at all talkative
Very tactful	Very blunt
Very gentle	Very rough
Very aware of feelings of others	Not at all aware of feelings of others
Very religious	Not at all religious
Very interested in own appearance	Not at all interested in own appearance
Very neat in habits	Very sloppy in habits
Very quiet	Very loud
Very strong need for security	Very little need for security
Enjoys art and literature very much	Does not enjoy art and literature at all
Easily expresses tender feeling	Does not express tender feelings at all

dicative of "ideal" health patterns, without respect to sex.

Scores

Although Ss responded to all 122 items, only the stereotypic items which reflect highly consensual, clear distinctions between men and women, as perceived by lay people were analyzed. The questionnaires were scored by counting the number of Ss that marked each pole of each stereotypic item, within each set of instructions. Since some Ss occasionally left an item blank, the proportion of Ss marking each pole was computed for each item. Two types of scores were developed: "agreement" scores and "health" scores.

The agreement scores consisted of the proportion of Ss on that pole of each item which was marked by the majority of the Ss. Three agreement scores for each item were computed; namely, a "masculinity agreement score" based on Ss receiving the "male" instructions, a "femininity agreement score," and an "adult agreement score" derived from the Ss receiving the "female" and "adult" instructions, respectively.

The health scores are based on the assumption that the pole which the majority of the clinicians consider to be healthy for an adult, independent of sex, reflects an ideal standard of health. Hence, the proportion of Ss with either male or female instructions who marked that pole of an item which was most often designated as healthy for an adult was taken as a "health" score. Thus, two health scores were computed for each of the stereotypic items: a "masculinity health score" from Ss with "male" instructions, and a "femininity health score" from Ss with "female" instructions.

TABLE 2. *Means and Standard Deviations for Adult, Masculinity, and Femininity Agreement Scores on 38 Stereotypic Items*

Agreement Score	M	SD	Deviation from Chance	
			Z	p
Adult	.866	.116	3.73	< .001
Masculinity	.831	.122	3.15	< .001
Femininity	.763	.164	2.68	< .005

RESULTS

Sex Differences in Subject Responses

The masculinity, femininity, and adult health and agreement scores of the male clinicians were first compared to the comparable scores of the female clinicians via t tests. None of these t tests were significant (the probability levels ranged from .25 to .90). Since the male and female Ss did not differ significantly in any way, all further analyses were performed with the samples of men and women combined.

Agreement Scores

The means and sigmas of the adult, masculinity, and femininity agreement scores across the 38 stereotypic items are shown in Table 2. For each of these three scores, the average proportion of Ss agreeing as to which pole reflects the more healthy behavior or trait is significantly greater than the .50 agreement one would expect by chance. Thus, the average masculinity agreement score is .831 ($z = 3.15$, $p < .001$), the average femininity agreement score is .763 ($z = 2.68$, $p < .005$), and the average adult agreement score is .866 ($z = 3.73$, $p < .001$). These means indicate that on the stereotypic items clinicians strongly agree on the behaviors and attributes which characterize a healthy man, a healthy woman, or a healthy adult independent of sex, respectively.

Relationship between Clinical Judgments of Health and Student Judgments of Social Desirability

Other studies indicate that social desirability is related to clinical judgments of mental health (Cowen, 1961; Kogan et al., 1957; Wiener et al., 1959). The relation between social desirability and clinical judgment was tested in the present data by comparing the previously established socially desirable poles of the stereotypic items (Rosenkrantz et al., 1968) to the poles of those items which the clinicians judged to be the healthier and more mature

for an *adult*. Table 3 shows that the relationship is, as predicted, highly significant ($\chi^2 = 23.64$, $p < .001$). The present data, then, confirm the previously reported relationships that social desirability, as perceived by nonprofessional Ss, is strongly related to professional concepts of mental health.

The four items on which there is disagreement between health and social desirability ratings are: to be emotional; not to hide emotions; to be religious; to have a very strong need for security. The first two items are considered to be healthy for adults by clinicians but not by students; the second two items have the reverse pattern of ratings.

TABLE 3. *Chi-Square Analysis of Social Desirability versus Adult Health Scores on 38 Stereotypic Items*

Item	Pole Elected by Majority of Clinicians for Healthy Adults
Socially desirable pole	34
Socially undesirable pole	4

Note.—$\chi^2 = 23.64$, $p < .001$.

Sex-Role Stereotype and Masculinity versus Femininity Health Scores

On 27 of the 38 stereotypic items, the male pole is perceived as more socially desirable by a sample of college students (male-valued items); while on 11 items, the feminine pole is seen as more socially desirable (female-valued items). A hypothesis of this paper is that the masculinity health scores will tend to be greater than the femininity health scores on the male-valued items, while the femininity health scores will tend to be greater than the masculinity health scores on the female-valued items. In other words, the relationship of the clinicians' judgments of health for men and women are expected to parallel the relationship between stereotypic sex-role behaviors and social desirability. The data support the hypothesis. Thus, on 25 of the 27 male-valued items, the masculinity health score exceeds the femininity health score; while 7 of the 11 female-valued items have higher femininity health scores than masculinity health scores. On four of the female-valued items, the masculinity health score exceeds the femininity health score. The chi-square derived from these data is 10.73 (df = 1, p < .001). This result indicates that clinicians tend to consider socially desirable masculine characteristics more often as healthy for men than for women. On the other hand, only about half of the socially desirable feminine characteristics are considered more often as healthy for women rather than for men.

On the face of it, the finding that clinicians tend to ascribe male-valued stereotypic traits more often to healthy men than to healthy women may seem trite. However, an examination of the content of these items suggests that this trite-seeming phenomenon conceals a powerful, negative assessment of women. For instance, among these items, clinicians are more likely to suggest that healthy women differ from healthy men by being more submissive, less independent, less adventurous, more easily influenced, less aggressive, less competitive, more excitable in minor crises, having their feelings more easily hurt, being more emotional, more conceited about their appearance, less objective, and disliking math and science. This constellation seems a most unusual way of describing any mature, healthy individual.

Mean Differences between Masculinity Health Scores and Femininity Health Scores

The above chi-square analysis reports a significant pattern of differences between masculine and feminine health scores in relationship to the stereotypic items. It is possible, however, that the differences, while in a consistent, predictable direction, actually are trivial in magnitude. A t test, performed between the means of the masculinity and femininity health scores, yielded a t of 2.16 (p < .05), indicating that the mean masculinity health score (.827) differed significantly from the mean femininity health score (.747). Thus, despite massive agreement about the health dimension per se, men and women appear to be located at significantly different points along this well-defined dimension of health.

Concepts of the Healthy Adult versus Concepts of Healthy Men and Healthy Women

Another hypothesis of this paper is that the concepts of health for a sex-unspecified adult, and for a man, will not differ, but that the concepts of health for women will differ significantly from those of the adult.

This hypothesis was tested by performing t tests between the adult agreement scores versus the masculinity and femininity healthy scores. Table 4 indicates, as predicted, that the adult and masculine concepts of health do not differ significantly (t = 1.38, p > .10), whereas, a significant difference does exist between the concepts of health for adults versus females (t = 3.33, p < .01).

These results, then, confirm the hypothesis that a double standard of health exists for men and women, that is, the general standard of health is actually applied only to men, while healthy women are perceived as significantly less healthy by adult standards.

TABLE 4. *Relation of Adult Health Scores to Masculinity Health Scores and to Femininity Health Scores on 38 Stereotypic Items*

Health Score	M	SD
Masculinity	.827	.130
		t = 1.38*
Adult	.866	.115
		t = 3.33*
Femininity	.747	.187

*df = 74, p < .05.
**df = 74, p < .01.

DISCUSSION

The results of the present study indicate that high agreement exists among clinicians as to the attributes characterizing healthy adult men, healthy adult women, and healthy adults, sex unspecified. This agreement, furthermore, holds for both men and women clinicians. The results of this study also support the hypotheses that *(a)* clinicians have different concepts of health for men and women and *(b)* these differences parallel the sex-role stereotypes prevalent in our society.

Although no control for the theoretical orientation of the clinicians was attempted, it is unlikely that a particular theoretical orientation was disproportionately represented in the sample. A counterindication is that the clinicians' concepts of health for a mature adult are strongly related to the concepts of social desirability held by college students. This positive relationship between social desirability and concepts of health replicates findings by a number of other investigators (Cowen, 1961; Kogan et al., 1957; Wiener et al., 1959).

The clinicians' concepts of a healthy, mature man do not differ significantly from their concepts of a healthy adult. However, the clinicians' concepts of a mature healthy woman do differ significantly from their adult health concepts. Clinicians are significantly less likely to attribute traits which characterize healthy adults to a woman than they are likely to attribute these traits to a healthy man.

Speculation about the reasons for and the effects of this double standard of health and its ramifications seems appropriate. In the first place, men and women do differ biologically, and these biological differences appear to be reflected behaviorally, with each sex being more effective in certain behaviors (Broverman, Klaiber, Kobayashi & Vogel, 1968). However, we know of no evidence indicating that these biologically-based behaviors are the basis of the attributes stereotypically attributed to men and to women. Even if biological factors did contribute to the formation of the sex-role stereotypes, enormous overlap undoubtedly exists between the sexes with respect to such traits as logical ability, objectivity, independence, etc., that is, a great many women undoubtedly possess these characteristics to

a greater degree than do many men. In addition, variation in these traits within each sex is certainly great. In view of the within-sex variability, and the overlap between sexes, it seems inappropriate to apply different standards of health to men compared to women on purely biological grounds.

More likely, the double standard of health for men and women stems from the clinicians' acceptance of an "adjustment" notion of health, for example, health consists of a good adjustment to one's environment. In our society, men and women are systematically trained, practically from birth on, to fulfill different social roles. An adjustment notion of health, plus the existence of differential norms of male and female behavior in our society, automatically lead to a double standard of health. Thus, for a woman to be healthy, from an adjustment viewpoint, she must adjust to and accept the behavioral norms for her sex, even though these behaviors are generally less socially desirable and considered to be less healthy for the generalized competent, mature adult.

By way of analogy, one could argue that a black person who conformed to the "pre-civil rights" southern Negro stereotype, that is, a docile, unambitious, childlike, etc., person, was well adjusted to his environment and, therefore, a healthy and mature adult. Our recent history testifies to the bankruptcy of this concept. Alternative definitions of mental health and maturity are implied by concepts of innate drives toward self-actualization, toward mastery of the environment, and toward fulfillment of one's potential (Allport, 1955; Buhler, 1959, Erikson, 1950; Maslow, 1954; Rogers, 1951). Such innate drives, in both blacks and women, are certainly in conflict with becoming adjusted to a social environment with associated restrictive stereotypes. Acceptance of an adjustment notion of health, then, places women in the conflictual position of having to decide whether to exhibit those positive characteristics considered desirable for men and adults, and thus have their "femininity" questioned, that is, be deviant in terms of being a woman; or to behave in the prescribed feminine manner, accept second-class adult status, and possible live a lie to boot.

Another problem with the adjustment notion of health lies in the conflict between the overt laws and ethics existing in our society versus the covert but real customs and mores which significantly shape an individual's behavior. Thus, while American society continually emphasizes equality of opportunity and freedom of choice, social pressures toward conformity to the sex-role stereotypes tend to restrict the actual career choices open to women, and, to a lesser extent, men. A girl who wants to become an engineer or business executive, or a boy who aspires to a career as a ballet dancer or a nurse, will at least encounter raised eyebrows. More likely, considerable obstacles will be put in the path of each by partents, teachers, and counselors.

We are not suggesting that it is the clinicians who pose this dilemma for women. Rather, we see the judgments of our sample of clinicians as merely reflecting the sex-role stereotypes, and the differing valuations of these stereotypes, prevalent in our society. It is the attitudes of our society that create the difficulty. However, the present study does provide evidence that clinicians do accept these sex-role stereotypes, at least implicitly, and, by so doing, help to perpetuate the stereotypes. Therapists should be concerned about whether the influence of the sex-role stereotypes on their professional activities acts to reinforce social and intrapsychic conflict. Clinicians undoubtedly exert an influence on social standards and attitudes beyond that of other groups. This influence arises not only from their effect on many individuals through conventional clinical functioning, but also out of their role as "expert" which leads to consultation to governmental and private agencies of all kinds, as well as guidance of the general public.

It may be worthwhile for clinicians to critically examine their attitudes concerning sex-role stereotypes, as well as their position with respect to an adjustment notion of health. The cause of mental health may be better served if both men and women are encouraged toward maximum realization of individual potential, rather than to an adjustment to existing restrictive sex roles.

REFERENCES

Allport, G. W. *Becoming.* Princeton: Yale University Press, 1955.

Anastast, A., & Foley, J. P., Jr. *Differential psychology,* New York: Macmillan, 1949.

Broverman, D. M., Klaiber, E. L., Kobayashi, Y., & Vogel, W. Roles of activation and inhibition in sex differences in cognitive abilities. *Psychological Review,* 1968, *75,* 23–50.

Buhler, C. Theoretical observations about life's basic tendencies. *American Journal of Psychotherapy,* 1959, *13,* 561–581.

Cowen, E. L. The social desirability of trait descriptive terms: Preliminary norms and sex differences. *Journal of Social Psychology,* 1961, *53,* 225–233.

Erikson, E. H. *Childhood and society.* New York: Norton, 1950.

Fernberger, S. W. Persistence of stereotypes concerning sex differences. *Journal of Abnormal and Social Psychology,* 1948, *43,* 97–101.

Kitay, P. M. A comparison of the sexes in their attitudes and beliefs about women. *Sociometry,* 1940, *34,* 399–407.

Kogan, W. S., Quinn, R., Ax, A. F., & Ripley, H. S. Some methodological problems in the quantification of clinical assessment by Q array. *Journal of Consulting Psychology,* 1957, *21,* 57–62.

Komarovsky, M. Functional analysis of sex roles. *American Sociological Review,* 1950, *15,* 508–516.

Lynn, D. B. A note on sex differences in the development of masculine and feminine identification. *Psychological Review,* 1959, *66,* 126–135.

Maslow, A. H. *Motivation and personality.* New York: Harper, 1954.

McKee, J. P., & Sherriffs, A. C. The differential evaluation of males and females. *Journal of Personality,* 1957, *25,* 356–371.

McKee, J. P., & Scherrifs, A. C. Men's and women's beliefs, ideals, and self-concepts. *American Journal of Sociology,* 1959, *64,* 356–363.

Rogers, C. R. *Client-centered therapy; Its current practice, implications, and theory.* Boston: Houghton, 1951.

Rosenkrantz, P., Vogel, S., Bee, H., Broverman, I., & Broverman, D. Sex-role stereotypes and self-concepts in college students. *Journal of Consulting and Clinical Psychology,* 1968, *32,* 287–295.

Seward, G. H. *Sex and the social order.* New York: McGraw-Hill, 1946.

Seward, G. H., & Larson, W. R. Adolescent concepts of social sex roles in the United States and the two Germanies. *Human Development,* 1968, *11,* 217–248.

White, L., Jr. *Educating our daughters.* New York: Harper, 1950.

Wiener, M., Blumberg, A., Segman, S., & Cooper, A. A judgment of adjustment by psychologists, psychiatric social workers, and college students, and its relationship to social desirability. *Journal of Abnormal and Social Psychology,* 1959, *59,* 315–321.

Wylie, R. *The self concept.* Lincoln: University of Nebraska Press, 1961.

6. *The Psychiatrist and Tests of Criminal Responsibility*

RONALD LEIFER

The primary tests of criminal responsibility in this country are based on two well-known rules, the McNaughten Rule[1] and the Durham Decision.[2] The effect of both of these rules has been to thrust the psychiatrist into increasing courtroom prominence as an expert witness in cases of challenged responsibility. Although these rules have been criticized on various grounds the psychiatrist's capacity as an expert witness has, with few exceptions (Szasz, 1957), been taken for granted. The purpose of this essay is to demonstrate that psychiatric testimony fails to meet certain scientific standards on two grounds: First, in the case of the McNaughten Rule, it answers questions put in ordinary language by ordinary means; second, in the case of the Durham Rule, it serves the same ethical function as the jury, namely the ascription of responsibility.

In Western society, prior to the seventeenth century, the guilt of an accused criminal was often determined by tests which were believed to express the will of God, and punishment was prescribed according to a prevalent principle, such as the Law of Talion. In 1724, Judge Tracey formulated the"wild beast" test according to which an offender was not held responsible for his actions if he could not distinguish good from evil more than a wild beast.[3] This test held that it was the function of reason that distinguished man from beast. In 1760, the terms "right and wrong" were substituted for "good and evil" (Sobeloff, 1958). Like the wild beast test, the McNaughten Rule, which was formulated in England in 1843, also used a cognitive criterion for the determination of responsibility. McNaughten's acquittal on the grounds of insanity provoked a debate in Parliament which was answered by the judges of England; in that answer were embodied the rules of responsibility which bear McNaughten's name:

The jurors ought to be told in all cases that every man is to be presumed to be sane and to possess a sufficient degree of reason to be responsible for his crimes, until the contrary be proved to their satisfaction: and that, to establish a defense on the grounds of insanity, it must be clearly proved that at the time of committing the act, the party accused was labouring under such defect of reason from disease of the mind, as to not know the nature and quality of the act he was doing; or if he did know it that he did not know that what he was doing was

Ronald Leifer, The psychiatrist and tests of criminal responsibility, *American Psychologist, 19,* 1964, 825-830. Copyright © 1964 by the American Psychological Association and reproduced by permission.

[1] McNaughten's Case, 10 Cl. & Fin. 200, 8 Eng. Rep. 718 (1843).

[2] Durham v. United States, U.S. App. D.C. 214 F.2d 862 (1954).

[3] Rex v. Arnold, 16 How. St. Tr. 695 (1724).

wrong [Weihofen, 1933, p. 28, roman added].

This rule forms the basis of tests for criminal responsibility in the large majority of states in this country.

The McNaughten Rule *asserts* that responsibility is a function of the intellect: Reason is aligned with responsibility, and defect of reason is aligned with nonresponsibility. The key to the determination hinges on an evaluation of the "intellect" of the accused, specifically on whether he *knows* the nature and quality of his act and whether he *knows* that what he was doing was wrong. The job of the psychiatric expert witness is to aid the court in making this determination. For the psychiatrist to be considered an expert, he must have special skills or special knowledge which enable him to determine whether or not "Mr. Jones knows x," for which the "right and wrong" test offers specific instances.

Much like the medical pathologist or internist, the psychiatrist is considered to be a scientific expert, whose special province is the mind and the personality. Thus, it is thought that the psychiatrist has special skills and tools which enable him to penetrate the mind much as the toxicologist has special skills and tools for examining the blood. The basis for this view is the ancient notion, derived from the Greeks, that the mind is resident in the body much like the blood, and has as its defining properties knowing and reasoning which occur in a private stream of consciousness. However, there are differences between the psychiatrist and the toxicologist.

First, the determination that "Mr. Jones knows x" is an ordinary determination which most people make every day of their lives. Every day teachers determine whether their students know their work, employers determine whether their workers know their jobs, and mothers determine whether children know their manners. Such judgments do not require special skills. The difficulty in making the determination does not depend on skill, but rather depends on the seriousness of the consequences of the judgment. The more serious the consequences, the more the need is felt to justify them and the greater will be the tendency to enlarge the inquiry and to enlist the assistance of experts or arbitrators. In contrast, the toxicologist's determination of blood arsenic, for instance, requires the use of special bioanalytic tools, which requires special skills.

Second, the judgment of whether or not "Mr. Jones knows x" is an ordinary one precisely because it is based on a knowledge of language usage, which most people possess. On the other hand, the judgment about the blood level of arsenic is based on the understanding of the specialized subjects of chemistry and physiology. Some elaboration on these points will clarify the manner in which the psychiatrist makes a determination about another person's knowledge.

The applicability of the verb "to know" is based on an evaluation of the behavior of the person in question, but contrary to common belief, it is not the case that we infer behind that behavior to a private sphere of events, the mind. Rather, our evaluation of another person's knowledge is a commentary *about* his behavior, in the same way that to judge an object useful is not to remark about an additional property such as weight or shape, but to comment about its properties in relation to a certain purpose we have for them. This point has been well clarified by modern philosophers such as Ryle (1949) and Ayer (1956), and is insufficiently attended to by those who would understand psychiatric operations. Thus, we consider that a man knows geography if he can tell us the characteristics of various regions; and we can judge that a man knows what he has done if he can tell us the details, history, purposes, and consequences of his actions. We can only tell whether a man "knows" by applying conventional standards which link behavior and language. Conversely, there are conventional standards which govern the use of the phrase "He does not know." These criteria for the use of language do not require a special knowledge of language (for if it did the philologist or the philosopher would be the true expert here) nor a special knowledge of human nature. Some special techniques might be required for eliciting the behavior on which a judgment is based, i.e., asking the proper questions, but interviewing is not a skill which the psychiatrist monopolizes. A skillful lawyer, detective, or personnel manager, among others, may be equally skillful in interviewing. Although this skill requires verbal techniques beyond those used in ordinary conversation, they are techniques which are employed in a variety of occupations.[4]

It should be obvious that the determination of the proposition "Mr. Jones know x" is easy at the extremes. If when asked about the nature and quality of his act, Mr. Jones continually replies with irrelevant and disconnected phrases, we would consider him not to know the nature and quality of the act in question. Of course, considering what may lie ahead for him, he could be lying or faking, but the determination of this is an equally ordinary task. On the other hand, if he could give a detailed, coherent account of his actions, including their history and purposes, we would consider, *by convention*, that he knew their nature and quality.[5] It is in the middle ground that this determination is difficult; not because of a borderline mental state, but because the rules of the language game are imprecise and ambiguous. When we add the ambiguous terms "right and wrong" and "nature and quality" to the middle ground of "knowing," we have created linguistic difficulties which no scientific technique or theory can overcome.

The fundamental linguistic ambiguity of this test is one basis of the court's burden in ascribing responsibility (Szasz, 1956), and has led to the employment of psychiatric "experts" to aid in the determination.[6] The use of a "scientific expert" to aid in the determination of responsibility eases the burden of the court by giving the impression that the determination rests on a scientifically determined fact rather than on an ambiguous matter of semantics. It thus disguises and distracts us from the fact that the courts have to justify life and death decisions on the basis of arbitrary and ambiguous criteria and provides what appears to be a scientific justification for the court's decision. Psychiatrists have been all too eager to testify, and why not?— they have everything to gain and nothing to lose by it. In exchange for helping the court out of its difficulty, the psychiatrist's own claim to scientific status is underwritten by the courts.[7] And there are no risks. For since there are no explicit conventions describing the conditions under which "he does know" or "does not know" would be appropriate judgments, the psychiatrist is free to formulate his own rules. These rules are usually underwritten primarily by the psychiatrist's credentials rather than by an explicit method. It is the fact that the psychiatrist is using his personal judgment, and not that psychiatry is a young or inexact science, that explains the notorious disagreements between psychiatrists in courtroom procedures. These difficulties have been recognized by psychiatrists who have criticized the McNaughten Rule since its inception. In two recent polls, more than 85% of the psychiatrists questioned disapproved of this test (Guttmacher & Weihofen, 1952, p. 408). Philip Roche (1958) states:

The tests of responsibility as expressed in the McNaughten Rule . . . are untenable propositions within the discipline of scientific medical psychology [p. 407].

[4] The nontechnical task associated with the McNaughten Rule has received some mention. Thus, Davidson (1952) states: "A simple way of finding out is to ask the offender whether he now thinks his act is right or wrong [p. 7]." And Roche (1958) writes: "It must be apparent that the only direct way one can determine whether the accused has 'knowledge' of right and wrong is to place the question to him [p. 19]." However, this has never been considered a major criticism of the courtroom function of the psychiatrist. In fact, psychiatrists usually treat their task as a medical matter simply because they have medical training; then they proceed to criticize the remoteness of the legal tests from the "truths" of medical science.

[5] The terms "nature" and "quality" are equally as ordinary as the term "knowledge," and their application is similarly a matter of the use of ordinary language.

[6] Cf. Hess and Thomas (1963) who state: "Our conclusion was that the issue of the defendant's competency to be tried was most frequently raised not on the basis of the defendant's mental status but rather was employed as a means of handling situations and solving problems for which there seemed to be no other recourse under the law [p. 714]."

[7] This must be considered in the light of the fact that, in its youth, psychiatry had difficulty in achieving acceptance both within medicine and outside of it. The opportunity to gain status by performing an important sociolegal function was not without its advantages.

Gregory Zilboorg (1949) goes further:

> To force a psychiatrist to talk in terms of the ability to distinguish between right and wrong and of legal responsibility is—let us admit it openly and frankly—to force him to violate the Hippocratic Oath, even to violate the oath he takes as a witness to tell the truth and nothing but the truth, to force him to perjure himself for the sake of justice.
>
> The fact that psychiatrists have willingly testified and continue to testify in tests of responsibility in spite of these criticisms and hazards can be explained by the social advantages, in terms of money, prestige, and power, that accrue to psychiatrists and to the institution of psychiatry as a result of this activity.

Psychiatrists, having willingly engaged in a task for which they were admittedly ill suited, set about to alter the task (GAP, 1954). The first revision of the McNaughten Rule occurred in the 1869 Pike case in New Hampshire.[8] The most famous of these reformulations is the Durham Decision of 1954 (see Footnote 2) which adopts the principle of the New Hampshire ruling. The essence of this ruling is that an accused criminal will not be held responsible if his criminal act was the product of a mental disease or defect, which is made a matter of fact for the jury to decide.

This change has several implications. It acknowledges a voluble psychiatric assertion that the intentionality of human actions is not a function of the intellect alone, but rather of a complex of interrelated cognitive, emotional, and unconscious factors.[9] The Durham Decision thus changes the legal definition of responsibility from a competent intellect to a well-integrated personality. *This is to assume that the McNaughten ruling was an erroneous characterization of human nature rather than a criterion for the ascription of legal responsibility, and betrays the psychiatric tendency to redefine all hu-*man events in its own terms. By bringing the test for criminal responsibility up to date with psychiatric theory, it was assumed that the ascription of responsibility was made more scientific. In fact, however, ascriptions of any sort, although they may be based on a consideration of facts, are themselves neither facts nor scientific principles; rather, they are human actions similar to "giving" or "bestowing" and as such are neither true nor false, and, therefore, cannot be considered to be scientific (Hart, 1960).[10] The ascription of responsibility on the basis of mental health is no more scientific than the ascription of responsibility on the basis of personal wealth. The primary effect of the Durham Decision is to make the psychiatrist more comfortable with his testimony; he may now speak with the widest latitude, in his own parlance, using his own theories.[11]

Psychiatrists frankly admit this advantage and promote it, although they define it as primarily for the advantage of the court, whom they feel can now legitimately receive all of the information the psychiatrist is capable of giving. The absurdity of this euphemism is that it is the rare jurist or juror who can understand what the psychiatrist has to tell him (Wiseman, 1961). This "technicalization" of psychiatric testimony has resulted in the paradox that although one of the purposes of the Durham Decision is to insure that the moral decision is made by the jury rather than the expert, the facts on which that decision is to be based are so technical that the jury must hear the psychiatrist's conclusion as to

---

[8]State v. Pike, 49 N.H. 399 (1869).

[9]This widely held view can by no means be taken as scientific fact. For a discussion of this problem see Nagel (1959).

[10]This is why the question of whether there is such a thing as free choice is an improper question (Guttmacher, 1963). Choice, like intention, is *ascribed* to (and not described of) a human action according to the circumstances of that action; whether or not it *should* be ascribed in a given circumstance is a moral question since the answer partly depends on the desirability of the consequences of such as ascription.

[11]This change is similar to other instances of giving special concessions to those with "dirty" jobs, e.g., an arrangement whereby an executioner can avoid a face-to-face confrontation with his victim. The reciprocal relationship between law and psychiatry, where the law underwrites psychiatry and is then influenced by it, also has its counterpart in groups being influenced by agencies to whom they have delegated power, e.g., a government being "run" by a police force which has been charged with keeping the security.

whether the act was a product of mental disease or not, which is equivalent to an opinion about responsibility. Far from making their own decision the jury can only agree or disagree with one of two psychiatrists, each of whom presents technical language which the jury cannot understand. Thus, it tends to be the psychiatrist, rather than the facts, that influences the jury; the effect is that the moral decision is placed more firmly in the hands of the psychiatrist, although more subtly.

Underlying the Durham Decision is the belief that the concept of mental illness is scientifically valid. Paradoxically, at the same time that Durham-like rules are becoming increasingly popular, serious objections are being raised about the scientific validity of psychoanalytic theory (Nagel, 1959) and the concept of mental illnes (Becker, 1962; Szasz, 1961b). It is implicit in the Durham Decision that mental illness is a fact of very much the same type as a fractured leg or pneumonia. This is false, the diagnosis of mental illness is ascriptive and *implies* nonresponsibility. Forensic psychiatrists err on this crucial point. Guttmacher (1963), for example, admits this implication but does not recognize its significance. He states:

There are various factors . . . , which may greatly limit this freedom of choice, chief among which are levels of intelligence and the presence or absence of what we denominate mental disease.

The point of this discussion is to show that mental disease is not an independent variable which is inversely related to the dependent variable of free choice, but it is *by definition* inversely related to it. The relationship is tautological and not factual. Since responsibility is *by definition* a function of intention, it logically follows that responsibility is definitionally related to the diagnosis of mental illness. Since the diagnosis of mental illness is considered to be a fact on which the psychiatrist is expert, then his conclusion that an act is the product of mental illness *logically* implies lack of intention and, thus, lack of responsibility. The determination of mental illness *logically* implies lack of intention determination similar to that with which the court is charged.

In order to demonstrate this I must comment on the concept of responsibility (Szasz, 1961a).

The court is charged with determining the responsibility of the defendant in two senses. First, it must determine whether the accused is *descriptively* responsible for the crime with which he is charged. This is essentially a matter of determining and proving the fact that the accused acted in such a way as to bring about certain consequences. Thus, we may say that X is responsible for the death of Y because he pulled the trigger of the gun which discharged a bullet into Y's heart. The determination of this question outside a court of law may be considered to be a genuine scientific question, since it deals with the verification or falsification of two facts which are held to be causally connected. It is important to note that psychiatric expert testimony is not utilized to aid the court in this determination, but other medical experts, such as toxicologists or pathologists, may be called upon. This demonstrates the functional difference between scientific determinations such as the blood level of arsenic, and nonscientific ascriptions such as the diagnosis of mental illness. Second, the court must *ascribe* responsibility, that is to say, it must determine whether or not the defendant shall be punished. This is essentially decided on the basis of "defeating" circumstances, that is to say, circumstances in addition to the fact of the crime which provide a basis for excusing the crime. Descriptive and ascriptive responsibility are thus independent, and a man may be descriptively responsible in that it is proven that he did, in fact kill Y, but responsibility may not be ascribed in that additional facts demonstrate the act to be an accident which could not have been prevented by more prudent action. The primary defenses in cases of homicide are provided by *facts* which are held to demonstrate self-defense, mental disease, or an accident. Each of these defeats the ascription of responsibility. For instance, the fact that Y first came at X with a knife would demonstrate that the excusing condition of self-defense was applicable. This is a fact in addition to the descriptive fact of the crime which would negate the ascription of responsibility. Or, it might be established as a fact that X believed that Y was a part of an elaborate plot to execute him; this belief might be considered to be a delusion which is a symptom of a mental disease on the basis of which X might be judged not responsible for his act. To put it another way, criminal responsibility is ascribed if *(a)* descriptive responsibility is proven and *(b)* it is not demonstrated that there are facts which indicate self-defense, accident, or mental illness.

Mental illness is held to defeat the ascription of responsibility because it is commonly believed to be a fact which is inversely correlated with intention. *However, neither "intention" nor "mental disease" are facts, but are ascriptive terms like "responsibility."* Responsibility is ascribed unless defeating circumstances can be demonstrated which indicate, for instance, accident or self-defense. Intention is ascribed to an action unless defeating circumstances can be demonstrated, for instance, accident or coercion. Mental health is ascribed unless defeating circumstances can be demonstrated, for instance, delusions or hallucinations. It is thus a logical error to consider mental disease to be a fact which is inversely correlated with intention, since mental disease is not a fact but is, like intention, ascribed on the basis of facts. *It is thus the facts that defeat the ascription of mental health that form the genuine but cryptic basis for defeating intention and, thus, criminal responsibility.* What kinds of facts are these?

The determination that a defendant has mental illness is based on certain facts about his behavior, usually (sometimes by law) excluding the crime for which he is being tried, and is therefore, let us be clear, *not an additional fact, but a name for a class of facts* (Szasz, 1961c). For instance, the diagnosis "paranoid personality" is a name designating a type of individual who tends to demonstrate suspiciousness, ideas of reference, or ideas of persecution. Three characteristics of the designation "mental illness" deserve to be mentioned. First, it is a name which is applied only to negatively valued behavior. It therefore registers a covert disapproval of, and is an ethical judgment about, certain forms of behavior (Szasz, 1961b). Second, while we tend to give conventional explanations for "reasonable" behavior, we tend to explain "unreasonable" behavior with unconventional explanations; socially acceptable ac-

tions are explained in terms of purposes, justifications, or rules, and unacceptable actions tend to be explained in terms of causes. Thus, the ordinary act of getting married might be explained in terms of "wanting a family," or "following custom," or "being in love." However, the more deviant behavior of the homosexual bachelor tends to be explained in terms of antecedent physical or psychosocial causes. The reasons for using causal explanations for unconventional behavior are complex. One reason is that conventional explanations do not fit; no conventional explanation can be given for a woman running stark naked through the streets simply because it is not a conventional act. Freud's attribution of psychic determinism to human behavior is based upon observations of accidents, slips, and other behavioral mishaps; these events are considered "accidents" precisely because no conventional explanations can be offered for them in terms of purposes or conventions. Thus the relationship between causal explanations and unconventional actions. Another explanation is the deep-rooted Judeo-Christian belief that man does not freely choose evil or illness; thus, Eve was influenced by the Devil, Adam was influenced by Eve, and their decendants have been influenced by a succession of malevolent factors from demons to instincts to twisted molecules to mental disease. Third, since mentally ill behavior is explained causally, it cannot be considered to be free. The diagnosis of mental illness illegitimates any consideration of intention. But intention is not a fact which is discoverable; it is a designation for certain types of behavior which do not exhibit features which are defeating to the ascription of intention. *In psychiatry, the characteristic of behavior which negates its intentional nature and qualifies it for the designation "illness" is precisely that it is unconventional; that is to say, no acceptable conventional explanations can be offered by the actor. It is therefore a history of unconventional behavior of a socially disruptive nature which defeats the ascription of both mental health and intention.* The diagnosis of mental illness logically implies the absence of choice or intention because they are both defeated by the same kinds of facts.

Here we have a hidden paradox which undermines the autonomy of the courts in ascribing responsibility. For the diagnosis of mental illness, which is supposed to be a "fact" which excludes intent, is itself a judgment that implies that certain kinds of undesirable behavior shall not be considered intentional. The determination of intention and responsibility are supposed to be judgments for the court to make, but we can now see that the psychiatrist actually makes them tacitly. The dilemma has a curious twist. The formulation of the notion of mental illness is based on the idea that only that behavior which is in some way maladaptive, deviant, and undesirable shall be included, and that behavior is considered to be determined, and thus, not to be free. The criminal who displays undesirable behavior during his lifetime, or prior to his crime, is thus more likely to be excused for his crime than the man who has led an exemplary life.

In the light of this discussion we may conjecture about why psychiatrists play such a large role in the determination of criminal responsibility. Certainly the theoretical position of most contemporary psychiatrists is offered as justification for this activity.

Whether or not this position is erroneous will hopefully be decided after a vigorous consideration of arguments and evidence. In any case, there are compelling social factors which favor the perpetuation of the current point of view. The ethical question, "Ought this man be punished?" is an extremely difficult one to answer with convincing justifications. In their difficulty in solving this vital question, the courts have turned to "experts" for help, and psychiatrists, in all good faith, have been willing and eager to perform the task. Thus, a mutually beneficial partnership was established between law and psychiatry, in which, in return for their help with a difficult problem, psychiatrists were rewarded with a change in rules which made their task conform more closely with their own professional identity. Any challenge to the psychiatrist's status as an expert is not likely to be well received by either psychiatry or the law—for psychiatrists would have to abdicate from a favored function and the law would be forced into the painful search for its own formulae and justifications for the ascription of criminal responsibility.

REFERENCES

Ayer, A. J. *The problem of knowledge.* Edinburgh: Pelican Books, 1956.

Becker, E. *The birth and death of meaning.* New York: Free Press of Glencoe, 1962.

Davidson, H. A. *Forensic psychiatry.* New York: Ronald Press, 1952.

Guttmacher, M., & Weihoffen, H. *Psychiatry and the law.* New York: Norton, 1952.

Guttmacher, M. S. What can the psychiatrist contribute to the issue of criminal responsibility? *J. nerv. ment. Dis., 1963, 136, 103-117.*

Group for the Advancement of Psychiatry. *Criminal responsibility and psychiatric expert testimony.* (Report No. 26) New York: GAP, 1954.

Hart, H. L. A. The ascription of responsibility and rights. In A. Flew (Ed.), *Logic and language.* (1st series) Oxford, Eng.: Basil Blackwell, 1960.

Hess, J. H., & Thomas, H. E. Incompetency to stand trial. *Amer. J. Psychiat., 1963, 119, 713-720.*

Nagel, E. Methodological issues in psychoanalytic theory. In S. Hook (Ed.), *Psychoanalysis, scientific method and philosophy.* New York: Grove Press, 1959.

Roche, P. Q. *The criminal mind.* New York: Farrar, Straus & Cudahy, 1958.

Ryle, G. *The concept of mind.* New York: Barnes & Noble, 1949.

Sobeloff, S. E. From McNaughten to Durham and beyond. In P. W. Nice (Ed.), *Crime and insanity.* New York: Philosophical Library, 1958.

Szasz, T. S. Some observations on the relationship between psychiatry and the law. *Arch. Neurol. Psychiat., 1956, 75, 1-19.*

Szasz, T. S. Psychiatric expert testimony—its covert meaning and social functions. *Psychiatry, 1957, 20, 313-316.*

Szasz, T. S. Criminal responsibility and psychiatry. In H. Toch (Ed.), *Legal and criminal psychology.* New York: Holt, Rhinehart & Winston, 1961. (a)

Szasz, T. S. *The myth of mental illness.* New York: Hoeber, 1961. (b)

Szasz, T. S. Naming and the myth of mental illness. *Amer. Psychologist, 1961, 16, 59-65. (c)*

Weihofen, H. *Insanity as a defense in criminal law.* New York: Commonwealth Fund, 1933.

Wiseman, F. Psychiatry and the law: Use and abuse of psychiatry in a murder case. *Amer. J. Psychiat., 1961, 118, 289-299.*

Zilboorg, G. The reciprocal responsibilities of law and psychiatry. *Shingle, 1949, 12, 79-96.*

7 The Psychologists as an Expert Witness on The Issue of Insanity

RAY JEFFERY

Recent discussions of psychology and law have been concerned with certification, privileged communication, and the like, but there are little data on the subject of the psychologist as an expert on criminal cases involving the issue of insanity.

The Code of Ethics urges psychologists to behave in a responsible manner with regard to interpretation of test data. The author is aware of the fact that the interpretation of many psychological tests and reports is open to differences of opinion, that they are by no means settled issues, and that considerable research is currently going on in the area.

Nevertheless, some psychologists have behaved in the courtroom as though the issues were settled. They have made assertions that do not have the blessings of the entire professional psychological community, and these assertions have brought court opprobrium to them, and perhaps to the psychologist in general. On one occasion, following such testimony, the presiding judge literally threw a deck of projective cards onto the floor. The defense attorney then requested that the court record show that the judge had expressed his feeling toward the testimony of this expert witness, to which the judge replied that the record would also show that he (the

judge) was going even further in that he was throwing out all of the testimony of this psychologist. Quite obviously, testimony which can arouse such a reaction in a reputable court of law is, or should be, of concern to psychologists interested in the contribution they can make to society, and in the role of their professional image in the acceptance or rejection of such contributions. The data to be presented were gathered in the District Court of the District of Columbia, and the impression created in the court was that the psychologists were not poor representatives of their profession, since in the words of the Government attorney, they were men "with more degrees than a thermometer."

The testimony may also serve the function of providing psychologists who rely on projective tests with information on how such evaluations may be treated by an opposing and often hostile attorney, or how they may be interpreted in a court of law which permits cross-examination of witnesses, including expert witnesses.

The writer is a sociologist who recently was co-investigator on a National Institute of Mental Health project concerning the operation of the insanity defense in the District of Columbia.[1] He had occasion to observe psychologists in the courtroom, and to

[1] The investigation was supported in whole by Public Health Service Grant No. M-5009 from the National Institute of Mental Health.

examine in detail court transcripts of over 25 cases in which insanity was an issue. Testimony by psychologists was given in 2 of the cases, relevant excerpts from which are presented below. The other trials involved psychiatric testimony exclusively.

The writer is not an expert on personality assessment and diagnosis, and he will leave it to the psychological community to evaluate the testimony herein presented. It should be noted that the transcripts become public records open for public inspection. As will be evident from these transcripts, attorneys have available such public records as research reports on psychological tests—and may read them, even if psychologists do not. This is in contrast to hospital hearings, where the records are private and confidential.

UNITED STATES v. KENT[2]

Psychologist A: Defense

Psychologist A testified that she had administered the following tests to Kent: the Wechsler Memory Scale, the Bender-Gestalt, the Rorschach, the Thematic Apperception Test, the House-Tree-Person Test, and the Szondi Test. From this evidence she diagnosed the defendant as schizophrenic, chronic undifferentiated type, characterized by abnormal thoughts, difficulty with emotional control, deficient in common-sense judgment, and lacking in close relationships with other people. She considered these as indicative of psychosis, and that the crimes of housebreaking, robbery, and rape, of which the defendant was accused, were products of the mental disease.

Cross-Examination by Government

Q[uestion]. What did the House-Tree-Person Test reveal?

A[nswer]. The major finding was a feeling of withdrawal, running away from reality, feelings of rejection by women.

Q. And the results of the Szondi?

A. This showed a passive, depressed person who withdrew from the world of reality, with an inability to relate to others.

Q. Wasn't the Szondi Test made up around 1900, or the early 1900 period? And wasn't it made up of a number of pictures of Europeans who were acutely psychotic?

A. Yes, that is true.

Q. And this tells you something about his personality?

A. Yes, you can tell something about the person from his responses to the photos.

Q. And the House-Tree-Person Test—you handed the defendant Kent a pencil and a blank piece of paper, is that right, Doctor?

A. That is correct.

Q. And you asked him to draw a house?

A. Yes.

Q. And what did this tell you about Kent?

A. The absence of a door, and the bars on the windows, indicated he saw the house as a jail, not a home. Also, you will notice it is a side view of the house; he was making it inaccessible.

Q. Isn't it normal to draw a side view of a house? You didn't ask him to draw a front view, did you?

A. No

Q. And those bars on the window—could they have been Venetian blinds and not bars? Who called them bars, you or Kent?

A. I did.

Q. Did you ask him what they were?

A. No.

Q. What else did the drawing reveal about Kent?

A. The line in front of the house runs from left to right. This indicates a need for security.

[2]Criminal No. 798-61, District Court for the District of Columbia.

Q. This line indicates insecurity! Could it also indicate the contour of the landscape, like a lawn or something?

A. This is not the interpretation I gave it.

Q. And the chimney—what does it indicate?

A. You will notice the chimney is dark. This indicates disturbed sexual feelings. The smoke indicates inner daydreaming.

Q. Did I understand you correctly? Did you say dark chimneys indicate disturbed sex feelings?

A. Yes

Q. You then asked Kent to draw a tree. Why?

A. We have discovered that a person often expresses feelings about himself that are on a subconscious level when he draws a tree.

Q. And what does this drawing indicate about Kent's personality?

A. The defendant said it was a sequoia, 1500 years old, and that it was diseased. This indicates a feeling of self-depreciation. Also, the tree has no leaves and it leans to the left. This indicates a lack of contact with the outside world—the absence of leaves.

Q. Don't trees lose their leaves in winter, Doctor? If you look out the window now, in Washington, do you see leaves on the trees? Perhaps the defendant was drawing a picture of a tree without leaves, as they appear in the winter.

A. The important thing is, however, why did the defendant select this particular tree. He was stripped of leaves, of emotions.

Q. You then asked him to draw a person?

A. Yes.

Q. And he drew this picture of a male?

A. Yes.

Q. And what does this drawing indicate about Kent?

A. The man appears to be running. This indicates anxiety, agitation. He is running, you will notice, to the left. This indicates running away from the environment. If he had been running to the right this would indicate entering the environment.

Q. How about the hands?

A. The sharp fingers may indicate hostility.

Q. Anything else?

A. The head and the body appear to be separated by a dark collar, and the neck is long. This indicates a split between intellect and emotion. The dark hair, dark tie, dark shoes, and dark buckle indicate anxiety about sexual problems.

Q. You then asked Kent to draw a person of the opposite sex. What did this picture indicate?

A. The dark piercing eyes indicated a feeling of rejection by women, hostility toward women.

Q. Are you familiar with the occasion upon which a Veterans Administration psychologist gave this House-Tree-Person Test to 50 psychotics, and then gave 50 normal subjects the same test, and then had a group of psychologists rate them?

A. No, I am not familiar with that research.

Psychologist B: Defense

Psychologist B testified that he administered the Wechsler-Bellevue, the Graham Kendall, the Rorschach, and the Symonds Picture Story Tests. He also testified that he had diagnosed the defendant as schizophrenic, undifferentiated type, and that mental illness had produced the alleged crimes.

Cross-Examination by Government

Q. Did you administer the Szondi Test, Doctor?

A. No. I don't happen to think much of it. The test assumes a schizophrenic looks a certain way, and we have evidence this isn't so.

Q. What responses did you receive from Kent on the Rorschach, the ink-blot test?

A. Wolf, butterfly, vagina, pelvis, bats, buttocks, etc.

Q. And from this you concluded the defendant was schizophrenic?

A. Yes, that and other things.

Q. You gave him the Wechsler Adult Scale?

A. Yes

Q. On the word-information part of the test, the word "temperature" appears. What question did you ask the defendant?

A. At what temperature does water boil.

Q. You gave him a zero. Why?

A. Because he answered 190° and that is the wrong answer. The right answer is 212°F.

Q. What question did you ask about the Iliad?

A. I am not sure; I believe I asked him to identify the Iliad or who wrote the Iliad.

Q. And he answered "Aristotle"?

A. Yes.

Q. And you scored him zero?

A. That's correct.

Q. Now you asked the defendant to define blood vessels, did you not?

A. Yes.

Q. And his answer was capillaries and veins. You scored him zero. Why? Aren't capillaries and veins blood vessels?

A. I don't know. The norms don't consider that answer acceptable.

Q. What norms.

A. You see, these tests are scored on the basis of norms secured by administering the test to thousands of people.

Q. On the comprehension section you asked Kent: "If you found a sealed, addressed, stamped envelope on the street, what would you do with it?" and he answered "Turn it in." Why did you give him a 1? Why not a 2?

A. Because of the norms. A 2-answer would require more—something like "Mail it" or "Take it to the post office."

Q. You asked Kent: "What does the phrase 'Strike when the iron is hot' mean?" What was his answer?

A. "Strike when it is best to strike." I gave him a zero.

Q. Why? Doesn't "Strike when the iron is hot" mean to strike when the opportunity presents itself?

A. In terms of the norms it is not an acceptable answer.

Q. You asked Kent: "What is similar about the eye and the ear?" and he said "They are organs." You gave him a 1. Why?

A. Because a 2-answer is more precise, such as "organs of perception."

Q. You asked him: "What is winter?" and he stated "A season of the year." You gave him a 1—why not a 2? Isn't winter a season of the year, Doctor?

A. Well, again it is a matter of the norms. A 2-answer would include a "cold season of the year."

Q. You asked him: "What is a slice?" and he said "to cut." What is wrong with that? You gave him a 1.

A. A 2-answer would include "to slice thin" or "cut into thin pieces."

Q. You asked him to define "conceal" and he said "to get rid of." What score did you give him?

A. A zero.

Q. You asked him to define "sentence" and he said: "A group of words, as a noun and a verb." Why did you give him a 1?

A. A 2-answer would include the notion that a sentence expresses an idea.

Q. You asked him "What is a sanctuary?" and he said "Protection." Why did you give him a 1?

A. According to the norms, a 2-answer includes the notion of a place or a building.

Q. You asked Kent to define "calamity," and he said "a bad thing." You gave him a zero. Isn't a calamity a bad thing, Doctor?

A. Bad is not an acceptable answer in terms of the norms.

Psychologist C: Defense

The witness testified he administered the Wechsler Intelligence Scale, the Rorschach, the Human Figure Drawing, the Kohn, the Porteus Maze, and the Thematic Apperception Tests.

Cross-Examination by Government

Q. You asked the defendant to draw a human figure?

A. Yes.

Q. And this is the figure he drew for you? What does it indicate to you about his personality?

A. You will note this is a rear view of a male. This is very rare, statistically. It indicates hiding guilt feeling, or turning away from reality.

Q. And this drawing of a female figure, does it indicate anything to you; and, if so, what?

A. It indicates hostility towards women on the part

of the subject. The pose, the hands on the hips, the hard-looking face, the stern expression.

Q. Anything else?

A. The size of the ears indicates a paranoid outlook, or hallucinations. Also, the absence of feet indicates feelings of insecurity.

Q. On the Wechsler, you asked him: "What would you do if you found a sealed, addressed, stamped envelope?" and he answered: "Open it and find out who it belongs to. I will show you I know right from wrong." [This is the same subject who answered "Turn it in" to the previous psychologist.]

Psychologist D: Defense

Psychologist D testified he saw the subject once at jail or the receiving home for an hour and a half; that he administered the Rorschach and started the Human Figure Drawing Test. The testing was interrupted when the defendant's father was announced, and Kent became very upset, highly emotional.

He diagnosed the defendant as schizophrenic, undifferentiated type. He thought productivity existed; that is, the schizophrenia produced the housebreakings, robberies, and rapes. The test showed severe thinking disturbance, an inability to control impulses, and disturbed sexual feelings.

Cross-Examination by Government

Q. Why did you see the defendant Kent?

A. Because of a call from Mr. Arens.

Q. Are you a member of the Washington School of Psychiatry?

A. No.

Q. The defendant made one drawing for you, right, Doctor?

A. Yes, that is right.

Q. After the announced arrival of his father?

A. Yes.

Q. Do you use the House-Tree-Person Test?

A. Never.

Q. Does it have validity?

A. Yes.

Q. Do you use the Szondi?

A. Five or six times.

Q. When did you stop using it?

A. At the fifth administration, about nine years ago.

Q. What does this drawing that Kent made for another psychologist indicate to you?

A. The transparency of the picture—that is, seeing through the figure to something beneath—suggests pathology.

Q. Do you usually use an extensive battery of tests before reaching a diagnosis?

A. Yes.

Q. Do you usually arrive at the diagnosis on the basis of one Rorschach administered twice within an hour?

A. Frequently.

Q. What else in the drawing is significant psychologically?

A. The irregularity or sketchiness of the lines may suggest tension and anxiety. The attention paid to details—to the belt-bow-tie, and pockets—indicate a little-boy-like quality about the defendant.

Q. Is it significant that the figure is running to the left, and not to the right?

A. To some people, yes. I don't place any significance on it.

Q. What about this drawing, made by Kent for another psychologist? What is significant about it?

A. The minimization of the breasts and the three lines across the genital area indicate tension in the sexual area. Breasts are symbolic of motherhood and early infant experiences. By minimizing the breasts the defendant indicates he has not received the satisfaction from women he had hoped to.

Q. Now, I will show you the picture Kent drew for you on September 9, 1961. What is significant about it?

A. The overemphasis of the breasts indicates how upset the defendant was because his father had been announced.

Q. You showed the defendant a series of Rorschach cards, right? And what responses did you get to Card 1, Card 2, etc.?

A. Cat, flying bird, a house, people, crab, wolf, pinchers, wings, clouds, blood, "like a vagina," menstrual blood, buckets, hip-bones, breast, apes, butterflies, jet airplane.

Q. On the basis of these responses, you concluded

the defendant was a schizophrenic?

A. Yes.

UNITED STATES v. JENKINS[3]

Psychologist A: Defense

Psychologist A testified that he had administered the following tests to the defendant: Wechsler Adult Intelligence Scale, Bender-Gestalt, Rorschach, and Szondi. The IQ rating was 74, a dull normal.

Direct Examination by Defense

Q. Why do you give these tests?

A. To get at personality functioning—to get a sample of behavior. It is assumed that the sample is representative of how a person deals with other life situations.

COURT. Do you say you can conclude that a person is suffering from schizophrenia from answers to a Rorschach?

A. Yes. For example, if somebody looked at this card and described it as a church with a steeple with three men standing there and the Virgin Mary descending, with the Devil hiding behind the house, I would feel confident in thinking that person is suffering from disordered thinking.

Q. As a result of your tests, what is your diagnosis?

A. Schizophrenia.

Q. And productivity?

A. I cannot fail to see how a man's mental condition is unrelated to his behavior. I would expect there is a relationship, yes. I cannot say definitely that one thing is a product of another.

Cross-Examination by Government

Q. Doctor, do you agree with this statement: "It is well established that psychiatrists and psychol-

ogists freely concede there is no absolute accuracy and reliability of tests in the measurement of intelligence."

A. I do not agree.

Q. How about this statement: "Two persons of substantially the same mental capacity may test with materially different scores or rating depending on education, training, environment, etc."

A. Well, environment includes so much that I would think this would affect the performance on intelligence tests.

Q. You can tell from responses to Rorschach cards what his personality is like?

A. From a global picture.

Q. What response did he give to Card 4?

A. He saw a frog.

Q. And what significance do you attach to this answer, Doctor?

A. This is not the response normal people give. People often see two boots.

Q. And Card 5?

A. He saw a butterfly. This is a perfectly acceptable response. Many normal people see butterflies in this card.

Q. Card 6?

A. He said: "Don't see nothing—don't look like nothing."

Q. What things about the defendant's responses to the Rorschach led you to your diagnosis of schizophrenia?

A. The poor quality of his responses, the lack of seeing other kinds of responses, more typical responses you would expect from an adult.

Q. You also administered the Draw-a-Person test?

A. Yes.

Q. And what did it indicate?

A. The defendant drew the figure on the upper left-

[3]Criminal No. 614-59, District Court for the District of Columbia.

hand corner of the page. This indicated explosive feelings, insecurity, in a sense, holding onto the edges of the paper. This indicates anxiety and insecurity.

Q. What if he had placed the drawing in the middle of the page—what would that indicate?

A. It would mean he is a little less insecure.

Q. Do you believe in free will?

A. I believe it means complete control over one's actions and thoughts. I believe one's environment and heredity affect one's ability to exercise choice. Man has ability to make choices, but this is affected by other factors.

Q. Do you come from the so-called behavioristic school?

A. No, I am an eclectic.

Q. Do you believe all crime is a product of mental illness?

A. No.

Q. Any category of crimes?

A. I would expect bizarre crimes are often a product of mental illness.

Q. On the Wechsler, you asked him, "What color is the flag?" What did the defendant answer?

A. He answered, "Red, white, blue"—a 1, or perfect score. The test is scored 1-0.

Q. The second question?

A. "What shape is a ball?" He answered, "Round" —a 1 response.

Q. The fifth question?

A. "What does rubber come from?" His answer was "wood." I gave him a zero.

Q. Why a zero—aren't trees wood?

A. Yes, but it doesn't follow that rubber comes from wood.

COURT. You know where we get wood other than trees?

A. No.

[Other questions, similar to Kent material used, not recorded here because of repetition.]

Q. Why do you use pictures of insane people on the Szondi? Why not normal subjects?

A. We know penicillin works; we don't know why it works. It's the same thing here. We know that certain kinds of tests work; we don't understand why they work.

Q. You stated he was a chronic, undifferentiated schizophrenic. Can he also be an undifferentiated psychotic?

A. No. Undifferentiated psychosis is not a recognized classification.

Q. Do you know whether or not these schizophrenia symptoms were in remission on June 10, 1959?

A. No, I do not.

Q. You cannot state an opinion as to whether or not the schizophrenia caused the crime?

A. Yes, that is right.

Psychologist B: Defense

This psychologist testified that she gave one part of the Szondi Test. She made a diagnosis of schizophrenia on the basis of the increase in the IQ scores.

Direct Examination by Defense

Q. What background factors confirmed your diagnosis of schizophrenia?

A. He was a withdrawn person who had few friends. He didn't associate with other children. He couldn't control his behavior.

Cross-Examination by Government

Q. What do you mean by adequate controls?

A. When the tensions build up in him to a state of anxiety, anger, frustration, his emotions explode into behavior over which he has no control.

Q. Do you believe in free will?

A. That is a philosophic, not a psychological, problem. Free will is an arbitrary, sudden explosion without cause. I don't believe that. If I am free to choose, why is it I choose one thing and you choose another? It is because of the structure of the nervous system, and the influence of the environment.

Q. You believe in God?

A. Yes, certainly.

COURT. You believe in free will, don't you?

A. I believe I can make a free choice, based on what I am.

COURT. Any individual is free to make a choice, isn't he?

A. Yes.

Q. Why did you use photographs of mentally ill persons—why not normal persons?

A. Because photographs of mentally ill persons are supposed to accentuate the needs or drives or deprivations or frustrations that human beings experience. Normal people have managed to resolve their frustrations. I don't know why it works. It is something underneath. It is difficult to explain and understand. Doctors use digitalis for heart disease without knowing why it acts as it does.

[On questioning concerning the Szondi Test, the witness testified that a psychologist could diagnose illness by the pictures a subject selected as those he liked or disliked. At this point the judge threw the cards down. At a Bench conference the defense attorney asked: "May the record reflect that after the last question the Court slammed the cards down?"]

COURT. The record may reflect it but the record may show I am throwing it all out. That will take care of that session.

SECTION 2 NEUROSIS, PSYCHOSOMATIC DISEASE, AND DEPRESSION

This section includes a series of articles dealing with neurosis, asthma, depression, and suicide. These problems share the characteristic of disordered behavioral or bodily functioning with by and large unimpaired intellectual functioning.

Neurosis refers to emotional and behavioral dysfunctions. Its emotional hallmark is the feeling of overwhelming and often debilitating anxiety. In order to protect himself, the neurotic often adopts behavioral strategies designed to shield himself from the stimuli that provoke his feelings of anxiety. While such strategies often succeed, they may also create disruption and discomfort in other areas of his life. For example, a person with a neurotic fear of flying may protect himself from the terror that flying would generate by never setting foot in an airplane; however, this could also considerably disrupt his life if his occupation demanded cross-country travel. Similarly, a person may so fear rejection by the opposite sex that he never dates. He protects himself from intolerable anxiety, yet by this very avoidance he also denies himself satisfactory heterosexual relationships.

As is the case with most psychological disorders, the first modern theory of the etiology and treatment of neurosis must be credited to Sigmund Freud. He distinguished between fear that normal people feel in the face of objective danger and anxiety that neurotics experience in response to presumably unrealistic dangers. He hypothesized that the origins of neurosis lie in intrapsychic conflicts resulting from childhood experiences and speculated about the unconscious coping strategies (e.g., repression) that neurotics use to deal with their anxieties.

Freud relied heavily on case studies both to suggest hypotheses and to provide evidence for his theories. The case of little Hans is one of the most celebrated of Freud's case histories, all the more remarkable because Freud saw the patient only once and relied on the boy's father for the rest of the clinicical information. Nevertheless, it is considered a landmark case report, providing what is considered evidence for some of the basic concepts of psycho-

71

analysis, such as the Oedipal conflict.

Selection 8, by Wolpe and Rachman, is a lively critique of the case of little Hans. It infuriates analysts almost as much as it delights their opponents. Their principle argument is that interpretations of events made by Hans's father and by Freud are treated as facts, rather than as interpretations of the actual events. Furthermore, when the facts themselves are considered, they often contradict the interpretations made. Wolpe and Rachman provide what they consider a more accurate and parsimonious explanation of the facts of Hans's phobia in terms of learning principles. Hans became afraid of horses and of leaving his house immediately after seeing a horse-drawn cart tip over. Freud ignored this connection, emphasizing instead the symbolic relationship between the horse and Hans's father. Freud believed that Hans wanted to sexually possess his mother and replace his father-rival, whom he feared. Wolpe and Rachman, on the other hand, see the traumatic incident with the horse as the key to Hans's disorder. They propose that the fright that Hans felt on witnessing the accident was associated with horses through a process of one-trial classical conditioning.

Although Wolpe and Rachman's analysis of Hans's phobia is assuredly more parsimonious than that of Freud (and parsimony is indeed one goal of scientific explanation), their hypothesis is not necessarily more accurate. It, too, relies on retrospective report by father and son as filtered through Freud's pen. And their learning hypothesis is based on experimental data largely collected from research with animals. Demonstrating that phobias can be produced in a laboratory through classical conditioning is not conclusive evidence that the same phenomenon arises similarly in the natural world. At the present time, the etiology of phobias is still an open question. The article by Wolpe and Rachman is valuable as an example of the paradigm clash between the psychoanalytic and the behavioral schools.

Selection 9 found its way into this section because asthma, along with a variety of other physical disorders (e.g., ulcers, anorexia nervosa, ulcerative colitis, essential hypertension, migraine, and neurodermatitis) have long been thought to involve psychological processes. Psychoanalysts have variously interpreted such psychosomatic disorders as symbolically related to underlying intrapsychic conflicts or as expressions of blocked emotional impulses. Other investigators have sought to correlate specific disorders with neurotic personality traits. Still others have related the disorders to overreactions to stress or to adventitious or disordered classical or operant conditioning.

Luparello and his colleagues report an excellent, well-controlled study of the effects of suggestion on the breathing efficiency of asthmatics. They found that when asthmatics inhaled a nonirritating mist that was described to them as an irritant, full-blown asthmatic attacks were produced in 12 out of 40 subjects. Given the same mist to inhale afterwards, but told that it was Isuprel, a bronchodilator that would make breathing easier, the asthmatics responded with improved breathing, thus demonstrating the power of suggestion over physiological responding. The experiment also partly confirms the work of other investigators who have found that asthmatics can be subdivided into two groups: those with a large somatic component to asthma, and those with a smaller somatic and larger psychological component, and therefore, presumably more amenable to suggestion and psychotherapeutic intervention. Additional research of this caliber will go far in helping to elucidate the mechanisms of psychosomatic disorders.

In selection 10, Seligman suggests a novel theory to account for depression. He bases his theory primarily on laboratory experiments with animals, extrapolating his results to humans by analogy, although there is some recent laboratory work with humans that confirms the animal data. Seligman suggests that if an individual learns early in life that he has no control over his environment, that whatever he does has no effect on anything or anybody else, then he gives up trying to act upon his environment. He withdraws and allows himself to be acted upon by others. Helplessness leads to hopelessness. Seligman's theory is very exciting because it holds out the promise for innovative therapy of a disorder notoriously difficult to treat. Future research will determine how useful this experimentally based conceptualization is.

Severe depression is one factor that can lead to suicide. Seiden describes some of the attributes that characterize college student suicides and dispels some of the myths about their causes in selection 11. As the second most common cause of student death, suicide merits the closest study and attention.

SUGGESTED READINGS

Beck, A. T. *Depression: Clinical, experimental and theoretical aspects.* New York: Harper and Row, 1967.

Purcell, K. & Weiss, J. H. Asthma. In C. G. Costello (Ed.) *Symptoms of psychopathology.* New York: Wiley, 1970.

Wolf, S. & Goodell, H. *Harold G. Wolff's stress and disease.* Springfield, Illinois: Charles Thomas, 1968.

8. Psychoanalytic Evidence: A Critique Based on Freud's Case of Little Hans

JOSEPH WOLPE & STANLEY RACHMAN

Beginning with Wohlgemuth's trenchant monograph (13), the factual and logical bases of psychoanalytic theory have been the subject of a considerable number of criticisms. These have generally been dismissed by psychoanalysts, at least partly on the ground that the critics are oblivious of the "wealth of detail" provided by the individual case. One way to examine the soundness of the analysts' position is to study fully-reported cases that they themselves regard as having contributed significantly to their theories. We have undertaken to do this, and have chosen as our subject matter one of Freud's most famous cases, given in such detail that the events of a few months occupy 140 pages of the *Collected Papers*.

In 1909, Freud published "The Analysis of a Phobia in a Five-year old Boy" (2). This case is commonly referred to as "The case of Little Hans." Ernest Jones, in his biography of Freud, points out that it was "the first published account of a child analysis" (8, p. 289), and states that "the brilliant success of child analysis" since then was "indeed inaugurated by the study of this very case" (8, p. 292). The case also has special significance in the development of psychoanalytic theory because Freud believed himself to have found in it "a more direct and less roundabout proof" of some fundamental psychoanalytic theorems (p. 150). In particular, he thought that it provided a direct demonstration of the essential role of sexual urges in the development of phobias. He felt his position to have been greatly strengthened by this case and two generations of analysts have referred to the evidence of Little Hans as a basic substantiation of psychoanalytic theories (e.g., 1, 5, 7). As an example, Glover (5, p. 76) may be quoted.

In its time the analysis of Little Hans was a remarkable achievement and the story of the analysis constitutes one of the most valued records in psychoanalytical archives. Our concepts of phobia formation, of the positive Oedipus complex, of ambivalence, castration anxiety and repression, to mention but a few, were greatly reinforced and amplified as the result of this analysis.

In this paper we shall re-examine this case history and assess the evidence presented. We shall show that although there are manifestations of sexual behavior on the part of Hans, there is no scientifically acceptable evidence showing any connection between this behavior and the child's phobia for horses; that the assertion of such connection is pure assumption; that the elaborate discussions that follow from it are pure speculation; and that the case affords no factual support for any of the concepts listed by Glover above. Our examination of this case exposes in considerable detail patterns of think-

Joseph Wolpe & Stanley Rachman, Psychoanalytic evidence: A critique based on Freud's case of little Hans, *Journal of Nervous and Mental Disease, 130.* Copyright © 1960, The Williams & Wilkins Co. Reproduced by permission.

ing and attitudes to evidence that are well-nigh universal among psychoanalysts. It suggests the need for more careful scrutiny of the bases of psychoanalytic "discoveries" than has been customary; and we hope it will prompt psychologists to make similar critical examinations of basic psychoanalytic writings.

The case material on which Freud's analysis is based was collected by Little Hans's father, who kept Freud informed of developments by regular written reports. The father also had several consultations with Freud concerning Little Hans's phobia. During the analysis, Freud himself saw the little boy only once.

The following are the most relevant facts noted of Hans's earlier life. At the age of three, he showed "a quite peculiarly lively interest in that portion of his body which he used to describe as his widdler." When he was three and a half, his mother found him with his hand to his penis. She threatened him in these words, "If you do that, I shall send for Dr. A. to cut off your widdler. And then what will you widdle with?" Hans replied, "with my bottom." Numerous further remarks concerning widdlers in animals and humans were made by Hans between the ages of three and four, including questions directed at his mother and father asking them if they also had widdlers. Freud attaches importance to the following exchange between Hans and his mother. Hans was "looking on intently while his mother undressed."

Mother: "What are you staring like that for?"
Hans: "I was only looking to see if you'd got a widdler, too."
Mother: "Of course. Didn't you know that?"
Hans: "No, I thought you were so big you'd have a widdler like a horse."

When Hans was three and a half his sister was born. The baby was delivered at home and Hans heard his mother "coughing," observed the appearance of the doctor and was called into the bedroom after the birth. Hans was initially "very jealous of the new arrival" but within six months his jealousy faded and was replaced by "brotherly affection." When Hans was four he discovered a seven-year old girl in the neighborhood and spent many hours await-

ing her return from school. The father commented that "the violence with which this 'long-range love' came over him was to be explained by his having no play-fellows of either sex." At this period also, "he was constantly putting his arms round" his visiting boy cousin, aged five, and was once heard saying, "I *am* so fond of you" when giving his cousin "one of these tender embraces." Freud speaks of this as the "first trace of homosexuality."

At the age of four and a half, Hans went with his parents to Gmunden for the summer holidays. On holiday Hans had numerous playmates including Mariedl, a fourteen year old girl. One evening Hans said "I want Mariedl to sleep with me." Freud says that Hans's wish was an expression of his desire to have Mariedl as part of his family. Hans's parents occasionally took him into their bed and Freud claims that, "there can be no doubt that lying beside them had aroused erotic feelings in him,[1] so that his wish to sleep with Mariedl had an erotic sense as well."

Another incident during the summer holidays is given considerable importance by Freud, who refers to it as Hans's attempt to seduce his mother. It must be quoted here in full.

"Hans, four and a quarter.[2] This morning Hans was given his usual daily bath by his mother and afterwards dried and powdered. As his mother was powdering round his penis and taking care not to touch it, Hans said "Why don't you put your finger there?"

Mother: "Because that'd be piggish."
Hans: What's that? Piggish? Why?
Mother: "Because it's not proper."
Hans (laughing): "But it's great fun."

Another occurrence prior to the onset of his phobia was that when Hans, aged four and a half, laughed while watching his sister being bathed and was asked why he was laughing, he replied, "I'm laughing at Hanna's widdler." "Why?" "Because

[1]This is nothing but surmise—yet Freud asserts "there can be no doubt" about it.
[2]Earlier his age during the summer holidays is given as four and a half. Unfortunately, there is no direct statement as to the length of the holiday.

her widdler's so lovely." The father's comment is, "Of course his answer was a disingenuous one. In reality her widdler seemed to him funny. Moreover, this is the first time he has recognized in this way the distinction between male and female genitals instead of denying it."

In early January, 1908, the father wrote to Freud that Hans had developed "a nervous disorder." The symptoms he reported were: fear of going into the streets; depression in the evening, and a fear that a horse would bite him in the street. Hans's father suggested that "the ground was prepared by sexual over-excitation due to his mother's tenderness" and that the fear of the horse "seems somehow to be connected with his having been frightened by a large penis." The first signs appeared on January 7th, when Hans was being taken to the park by his nursemaid as usual. He started crying and said he wanted to "coax" (caress) with his mother. At home "he was asked why he had refused to go any further and had cried, but he would not say." The following day, after hesitation and crying, he went out with his mother. Returning home Hans said ("after much internal struggling"), *"I was afraid a horse would bite me"* (original italics). As on the previous day, Hans showed fear in the evening and asked to be "coaxed." He is also reported as saying, "I know I shall have to go for a walk again tomorrow," and "The Horse'll come into the room." On the same day he was asked by his mother if he put his hand to his widdler. He replied in the affirmative. The following day his mother warned him to refrain from doing this.

At this point in the narrative, Freud provided an interpretation of Hans's behavior and consequently arranged with the boy's father "that he should tell the boy that all this nonsense about horses was a piece of nonsense and nothing more. The truth was, his father was to say, that he was very fond of his mother and wanted to be taken into her bed. The reason he was afraid of horses now was that he had taken so much interest in their widdlers." Freud also suggested giving Hans some sexual enlightenment and telling him that females "had no widdler at all.[3]

"After Hans had been enlightened there followed a fairly quiet period." After an attack of influenza which kept him in bed for two weeks, the phobia got worse. He then had his tonsils out and was indoors for a further week. The phobia became "very much worse."

During March, 1908, after his physical illnesses has been cured, Hans apparently had many talks with his father about the phobia. On March 1, his father again told Hans that horses do not bite. Hans replied that white horses bite and related that while at Gmunden he had heard and seen Lizzi (a playmate) being warned by her father to avoid a white horse lest it bite. The father said to Lizzi, *"Don't put your finger to the White horse"* (original italics). Hans's father's reply to this account given by his son was, "I say, it strikes me it isn't a horse you mean, but a widdler, that one mustn't put one's hand to." Hans answered, "But a widdler doesn't bite." The father: "Perhaps it does, though." Hans then "went on eagerly to try to prove to me that it was a white horse." The following day, in answer to a remark of his father's, Hans said that his phobia was "so bad because I still put my hand to my widdler every night." Freud remarks here that, "Doctor and patient, father and son, were therefore at one in ascribing the chief share in the pathogenesis of Hans's present condition to his habit of onanism." He implies that this unanimity is significant, quite disregarding the father's indoctrination of Hans the previous day.[4]

On March 13, the father told Hans that his fear would disappear if he stopped putting his hand to his widdler. Hans replied, "But I don't put my hand to my widdler any more." Father: "But you still want to." Hans agreed, "Yes, I do." His father suggested that he should sleep in a sack to prevent him from wanting to touch his widdler. Hans accepted this view and on the following day was much less afraid of horses.

Two days later the father again told Hans that

[4]The mere fact that Hans repeats an interpretation he has heard from his father is regarded by Freud as demonstrating the accuracy of the interpretation; even though the child's spontaneous responses noted earlier in the paragraph point clearly in the opposite direction.

[3]Incidentally contradicting what Hans's mother had told him earlier (p. 171).

girls and women have no widdlers. "Mummy has none, Anna has none and so on." Hans asked how they managed to widdle and was told "They don't have widdlers like yours. Haven't you noticed already when Hanna was being given her bath." On March 17 Hans reported a phantasy in which he saw his mother naked. On the basis of this phantasy and the conversation related above, Freud concluded that Hans had not accepted the enlightenment given by his father. Freud says, "He regretted that it should be so, and stuck to his former view in phantasy. He may also perhaps have had his reasons for refusing to believe his father at first." Discussing this matter subsequently, Freud says that the "enlightenment" given a short time before to the effect that women really do not possess a widdler was bound to have a shattering effect upon his self-confidence and to have aroused his castration complex. For this reason he resisted the information, and for this reason it had no therapeutic effect.[5]

For reasons of space we shall recount the subsequent events in very brief form. On a visit to the Zoo Hans expressed fear of the giraffe, elephant and all large animals. Hans's father said to him, "Do you know why you're afraid of big animals? Big animals have big widdlers and you're really afraid of big widdlers." This was denied by the boy.

The next event of prominence was a dream (or phantasy) reported by Hans. "In the night there was a big giraffe in the room and a crumpled one; and the big one called out because I took the crumpled one away from it. Then it stopped calling out; and then I sat down on the top of the crumpled one."

After talking to the boy the father reported to Freud that this dream was "a matrimonial scene transposed into giraffe life. He was seized in the night with a longing for his mother, for her caresses, for her genital organ, and came into the room for that reason. The whole thing is a continuation of his fear of horses." The father infers that the dream is related to Hans's habit of occasionally getting into his parents' bed in the face of his father's disapproval. Freud's addition to "the father's penetrating observation" is that sitting down on the crumpled giraffe means taking possession of his mother. Confirmation of this dream interpretation is claimed by reference to an incident which occurred the next day. The father wrote that on leaving the house with Hans he said to his wife. "Goodbye, big giraffe." "Why giraffe?" asked Hans. "Mummy's the big giraffe," replied the father. "Oh, yes, " said Hans, "and Hanna's[6] the crumpled giraffe, isn't she?" The father's account continues, "In the train I explained the giraffe phantasy to him, upon which he said 'Yes, that's right,' And when I said to him that I was the big giraffe and that its long neck reminded him of a widdler, he said 'Mummy has a neck like a giraffe too. I saw when she was washing her white neck'."

On March 30, the boy had a short consultation with Freud who reports that despite all the enlightenment given to Hans, the fear of horses continued undiminished. Hans explained that he was especially bothered "by what horses wear in front of their eyes and the black round their mouths." This latter detail Freud interpreted as meaning a moustache. "I asked him whether he meant a moustache," and then, "disclosed to him that he was afraid of his father precisely because he was so fond of his mother." Freud pointed out that this was a groundless fear. On April 2, the father was able to report "the first real improvement." The next day Hans, in answer to his father's inquiry, explained that he came into his father's bed when he was frightened. In the next few days further details of Hans's fear were elaborated. He told his father that he was most scared of

<hr>

[5]It is pertinent at this point to suggest that Hans "resisted" this enlightenment because his mother had told him quite the opposite and his observations of his sister's widdler had not been contradicted. When he was four, Hans had observed that his sister's widdler was "still quite small" (p. 155). When he was four and a half, again while watching his sister being bathed, he observed that she had "a lovely widdler" (p. 164). On neither occasion was he contradicted.

[6]Hans's baby sister, *not* his mother. Again, the more spontaneous response directly contradicts Freud's interpretation. Thus Freud's subsequent comment that Hans only confirmed the interpretation of the two giraffes as his father and mother and not the sexual symbolism, transgresses the facts.

horses with "a thing on their mouths," that he was scared lest the horses fall, and that he was most scared of horse-drawn buses.

Hans: "I'm most afraid too when a bus comes along."
Father: "Why? Because it's so big?"
Hans: "No. Because once a horse in a bus fell."
Father: "When?"

Hans then recounted such an incident. This was later confirmed by his mother.

Father: "What did you think when the horse fell down?"
Hans: "Now it will always be like this. All horses in buses'll fall down."
Father: "In all buses?"
Hans: "Yes. And in furniture vans too. Not often in furniture vans."
Father: "You had your nonsense already at that time?"
Hans: "*No* (italics added). I only got it then. When the horse in the bus fell down, it gave me such a fright really: That was when I got the nonsense."

The father adds that, "all of this was confirmed by my wife, as well as the fact that *the anxiety broke out immediately afterwards*" (italics added).

Hans's father continued probing for a meaning of the black thing around the horses' mouths. Hans said it looked like a muzzle but his father had never seen such a horse "although Hans asseverates that such horses do exist."[7] He continues, "I suspect that some part of the horse's bridle really reminded him of a moustache and that after I alluded to this the fear disappeared." A day later Hans observing his father stripped to the waist said, "Daddy you are lovely! You're so white."

Father: "Yes. Like a white horse."
Hans: "The only black thing's your moustache. Or perhaps it's a black muzzle."[8]

Further details about the horse that fell were also

[7]Six days later (p. 211) the father reports, "I was at last able to establish the fact that it was a horse with a leather muzzle."
[8]A good example of the success of indoctrination.

elicited from Hans. He said there were actually two horses pulling the bus and that they were both black and "very big and fat." Hans's father again asked about the boy's thoughts when the horse fell.

Father: "When the horse fell down, did you think of your daddy?"[9]
Hans: "Perhaps. Yes. It's possible."

For several days after these talks about horses Hans's interests, as indicated by the father's reports "centered upon lumf (feces) and widdle, but we cannot tell why." Freud comments that at this point "the analysis began to be obscure and uncertain."

On April 11 Hans related this phantasy. "I was in the bath[10] and then the plumber came and unscrewed it.[11] Then he took a big borer and stuck it into my stomach." Hans's father translated this phantasy as follows: "I was in bed with Mamma. Then Pappa came and drove me away. With his big penis he pushed me out of my place by Mamma."

The remainder of the case history material, until Hans's recovery from the phobia early in May, is concerned with the lumf theme and Hans's feelings towards his parents and sister. It can be stated immediately that as corroboration for Freud's theories all of this remaining material is unsatisfactory. For the most part it consists of the father expounding theories to a boy who occasionally agrees and occasionally disagrees. The following two examples (pp. 209 and 214) illustrate the nature of most of this latter information.

Hans and his father were discussing the boy's slight fear of falling when in the big bath.

Father: "But Mamma bathes you in it. Are you afraid of Mamma dropping you in the water?"
Hans: "I am afraid of her letting go and my head going in."

[9]One of many leading questions, the positive answer to which of course proves nothing. It is worth noticing how the same question, differently phrased, elicits contrasting answers from Hans. When asked earlier what he thought of when the horse fell, Hans replied that he thought it would always happen in future.
[10]"Hans's mother gives him his bath" (Father's note).
[11]"To take it away to be repaired" (Father's note).

Father: "But you know Mummy's fond of you and won't let you go."
Hans: "I only just thought it."
Father: "Why?"
Hans: "I don't know at all."
Father: "Perhaps it was because you'd been naughty and thought she didn't love you anymore?"
Hans: "Yes."
Father: "When you were watching Mummy giving Hanna her bath perhaps you wished she would let go of her so that Hanna should fall in?"[12]
Hans: "Yes."

On the following day the father asks, "Are you fond of Hanna?"

Hans: "Oh, yes, very fond."
Father: "Would you rather that Hanna weren't alive or that she were?"
Hans: "I'd rather she weren't alive."

In response to close, direct questioning Hans voiced several complaints about his sister. Then his father proceeded again:

Father: "If you'd rather she weren't alive, you can't be fond of her, at all."
Hans: (assenting[13]) "Hm, well."
Father: "Thats why you thought when Mummy

was giving her her bath if only she's let go, Hanna would fall in the water . . . . . ."
Hans: (taking me up) ". . . and die."
Father: "and then you'd be alone with Mummy. A good boy doesn't wish that sort of thing, though."

On April 14, the following conversation was recorded.

Father: "It seems to me that, all the same, you do wish Mummy would have a baby."
Hans: "But I don't want it to happen."
Father: "But you wish for it?"
Hans: "Oh, yes, *wish*."[14]
Father: "Do you know why you wish for it? It's because you'd like to be Daddy."
Hans: "Yes. How does it work?"
Father: "You'd like to be Daddy and married to Mummy; you'd like to be as big as me and have a moustache; and you'd like Mummy to have a baby."
Hans: "And Daddy, when I'm married I'll have only one if I want to, when I'm married to Mummy, and if I don't want a baby, God won't want it either when I'm married.
Father: "Would you like to be married to Mummy?"
Hans: "Oh yes."

THE VALUE OF THE EVIDENCE

Before proceeding to Freud's interpretation of the case, let us examine the value of the evidence presented. First, there is the matter of selection of the material. The greatest attention is naturally paid to material related to psychoanalytic theory and there is a tendency to ignore other facts. The father and mother, we are told by Freud, "were both among my closest adherents." Hans himself was constantly encouraged, directly and indirectly, to relate material of relevance to the psychoanalytic doctrine.

Second, we must assess the value to be placed on the testimony of the father and of Hans. The father's account of Hans's behavior is in several instances suspect. For example, he twice presents his own interpretations of Hans's remarks as observed facts. This is the father's report of a conversation with Hans about the birth of his sister Hanna.

Father: "What did Hanna look like?"

[12] Leading question.
[13] A very questionable affirmation.

[14] Original italics suggest a significance that is unwarranted, for the child has been maneuvered into giving an answer contradicting his original one. Note the induced "evidence" as the conversation continues.

Hans (hypocritically): "All white and lovely. So pretty."

On another occasion, despite several clear statements by Hans of his affection for his sister (and also the voicing of complaints about her screaming), the father said to Hans, "If you'd rather she weren't alive, you can't be fond of her at all." Hans (assenting): "Hmn . . well." (See above).

The comment in parenthesis in each of these two extracts is presented as observed fact. A third example has also been quoted above. When Hans observes that Hanna's widdler is "so lovely" the father states that this is a "disingenuous" reply and that "in reality her widdler seemed to him funny." Distortions of this kind are common in the father's reports.

Hans's testimony is for many reasons unreliable. Apart from the numerous lies which he told in the last few weeks of his phobia, Hans gave many inconsistent and occasionally conflicting reports. Most important of all, much of what purports to be Hans's views and feelings is simply the father speaking. Freud himself admits this but attempts to gloss over it. He says, "It is true that during the analysis Hans had to be told many things which he could not say himself, that he had to be presented with thoughts which he had so far shown no signs of possessing and that his attention had to be turned in the direction from which his father was expecting something to come. This detracts from the evidential value of the analysis but the procedure is the same in every case. For a psychoanalysis is not an impartial scientific investigation but a therapeutic measure" (p. 246).[15] To sum this matter up, Hans's testimony is subject not only to "mere suggestion" but contains much material that is not his testimony at all!

From the above discussion it is clear that the "facts of the case" need to be treated with considerable caution and in our own interpretation of Hans's behavior we will attempt to make use only of the testimony of direct observation.

FREUD'S INTERPRETATION

Freud's interpretation of Hans's phobia is that the boy's oedipal conflicts formed the basis of the illness which "burst out" when he underwent "a time of privation and the intensified sexual excitement." Freud says, "These were tendencies in Hans which had already been suppressed and which, so far as we can tell, had never been able to find uninhibited expression: hostile and jealous feelings against his father, and sadistic impulses (premonitions, as it were, of copulation) towards his mother. These early suppressions may perhaps have gone to form the predisposition for his subsequent illness. These aggressive propensities of Hans's found no outlet, and as soon as there came a time of privation and of intensified sexual excitement, they tried to break their way out with reinforced strength. It was then that the battle which we call his 'phobia' burst out" (pp.279-280).

This is the familiar oedipal theory, according to which Hans wished to replace his father "whom he could not help hating as a rival" and then complete the act by "taking possession of his mother." Freud refers for confirmation to the following. "Another symptomatic act, happening as though by accident, involved a confession that he had wished his father dead; for, just at the moment that his father was talking of his death-wish Hans let a horse that he was playing with fall down—knocked it over, in fact" (p. 272). Freud claims that, "Hans was really a little Oedipus who wanted to have his father 'out of the way' to get rid of him, so that he might be alone

[15] Nevertheless, both the theory and practice of psychoanalysis are built on these "not . . impartial scientific investigations." For Freud to admit this weakness has some merit, but the admission is neither a substitute for evidence nor a good reason for accepting conclusions without evidence.

with his handsome mother and sleep with her" (p. 253). The predisposition to illness provided by the oedipal conflicts are supposed to have formed the basis for "the transformation of his libidinal longing into anxiety." During the summer prior to the onset of the phobia, Hans had experienced "moods of mingled longing and apprehension" and had also been taken into his mother's bed on occasions. Freud says, "We may assume that since then Hans had been in a state of intensified sexual excitement, the object of which was his mother. The intensity of this excitement was shown by his two attempts at seducing his mother (the second of which occurred just before the outbreak of his anxiety); and he found an incidental channel of discharge for it by masturbating . . . . . Whether the sudden exchange of this excitement into anxiety took place spontaneously, or as a result of his mother's rejection of his advances, or owing to the accidental revival of earlier impressions by the 'exciting cause' of his illness . . . this we cannot decide. The fact remains that his sexual excitement suddenly changed into anxiety" (p. 260).[16]

Hans, we are told, "transposed from his father on to the horses." At his sole interview with Hans, Freud told him "that he was afraid of his father because he himself nourished jealous and hostile wishes against him." Freud says of this, "In telling him this, I had partly interpreted his fear of horses for him: the horse must be his father—whom he had good internal reasons for fearing" (p. 264). Freud claims that Hans's fear of the black things on the horses' mouths and the things in front of their eyes was based on moustaches and eye-glasses and had been "directly transposed from his father on to the horses."[17] The horses "had been shown to represent his father."

Freud interprets the agoraphobic element of Hans's phobia thus. "The content of his phobia was such as to impose a very great measure of restriction upon his freedom of movement, and that was its purpose . . . After all, Hans's phobia of horses was an obstacle to his going into the street, and could serve as a means of allowing him to stay at home with his beloved mother.[18] In this way, therefore, his affection for his mother triumphantly achieved its aim" (p. 280).

Freud interprets the disappearance of the phobia as being due to the resolution by Hans of his oedipal conflicts by "promoting him (the father) to a marriage with Hans's grandmother . . . instead of killing him." This final interpretation is based on the following conversation between Hans and his father.

On April 30, Hans was playing with his imaginary children.

Father: "Hullo, are your children still alive? You know quite well a boy can't have any children."
Hans: "I know. I was their Mummy before, *now I'm their Daddy*" (original italics).
Father: "And who's the children's Mummy?"
Hans: "Why, Mummy, and you're their *Grandaddy*" (original italics).
Father: "So then you'd like to be as big as me, and be married to Mummy, and then you'd like her to have children."
Hans: "Yes, that's what I'd like, and then my Lainz Grandmamma" (paternal side) "will be their Grannie."

CRITIQUE OF FREUD'S CONCLUSIONS

It is our contention that Freud's view of this case is not supported by the data, either in its particulars or as a whole. The major points that he regards as demonstrated are these: 1) Hans had a sexual desire

---

[16] Thus a theoretical statement, beginning with "We may assume" ends up as a "fact." The only fact is that the assumed sexual excitement is assumed to have changed into anxiety.

[17] But in fact the child was thinking of a muzzle (see above).
[18] It should be noted, however, that Hans's horse-phobia and general agoraphobia were present even when he went out with his mother (p. 167).

for his mother, 2) he hated and feared his father and wished to kill him, 3) his sexual excitement and desire for his mother were transformed into anxiety, 4) his fear of horses was symbolic of his fear of his father, 5) the purpose of the illness was to keep near his mother and finally 6) his phobia disappeared because he resolved his oedipus complex.

Let us examine each of these points.

1. That Hans derived satisfaction from his mother and enjoyed her presence we will not even attempt to dispute. But nowhere is there any evidence of his wish to copulate with her. Yet Freud says that, "if matters had lain entirely in my hands . . I should have confirmed his instinctive premonitions, by telling him of the existence of the vagina and of copulation," (see p. 286). The "instinctive premonitions" are referred to as though a matter of fact, though no evidence of their existence is given.

The only seduction incident described (see above) indicates that on *that particular occasion* Hans desired contact of a sexual nature with his mother, albeit a sexual contact of a simple, primitive type. This is not adequate evidence on which to base the claim that Hans had an oedipus complex which implies a sexual desire for the mother, a wish to possess her and to replace the father. The most that can be claimed for this "attempted seduction" is that it provides a small degree of support for the assumption that Hans had a desire for sexual stimulation by some other person (it will be recalled that he often masturbated). Even if it is assumed that stimulation provided by his mother was especially desired, the two other features of an Oedipus complex (a wish to possess the mother and replace the father) are not demonstrated by the facts of the case.

2. Never having expressed either fear or hatred of his father, Hans was told by Freud that he possessed these emotions. On subsequent occasions Hans denied the existence of these feelings when questioned by his father. Eventually, he said "Yes" to a statement of this kind by his father. This simple affirmative obtained after considerable pressure on the part of the father and Freud

is accepted as the true state of affairs and all Hans's denials are ignored. The "symptomatic act" of knocking over the toy horse is taken as further evidence of Hans's aggression towards his father. There are three assumptions underlying this "interpreted fact"—first, that the horse represents Hans's father; second that the knocking over of the horse is not accidental; and third, that this act indicates a wish for the removal of whatever the horse symbolized.

Hans consistently denied the relationship between the horse and his father. He was, he said, afraid of horses. The mysterious black around the horses' mouths and the things on their eyers were later discovered by the father to be the horses' muzzles and blinkers. This discovery undermines the suggestion (made by Freud) that they were transposed moustaches and eye-glasses. There is no other evidence that the horses represented Hans's father. The assumption that the knocking over of the toy horse was meaningful in that it was prompted by an unconscious motive is, like most similar examples, a moot point. Freud himself (3) does not state that *all* errors are provoked by unconscious motives and in this sense "deliberate." This is understandable for it is easy to compile numerous instances of errors which can be accounted for in other, simpler terms[19] without recourse to unconscious motivation or indeed motivation of any kind. Despite an examination of the literature we are unable to find a categorical statement regarding the frequency of "deliberate errors." Furthermore, we do not know how to recognize them when they do occur. In the absence of positive criteria the decision that Hans's knocking over of the toy horse was a "deliberate error" is arbitrary.

As there is nothing to sustain the first two assumptions made by Freud in interpreting this "symptomatic act," the third assumption (that this act indicated a wish for his father's death) is untenable; and it must be reiterated that there is no independent evidence that the boy feared or hated his father.

[19] See for example the experiments on learning and habit interference (11, 16).

3. Freud's third claim is that Hans's sexual excitement and desire for his mother were transformed into anxiety. This claim is based on the assertion that "theoretical considerations require that what is today the object of a phobia must at one time in the past have been the source of a high degree of pleasure" (p. 201). Certainly such a transformation is not displayed by the facts presented. As stated above, there is no evidence that Hans sexually desired his mother. There is also no evidence of any change in his attitude to her before the onset of the phobia. Even though there is some evidence that horses were to some extent previously a source of pleasure, in general the view that phobic objects must have been the source of former pleasures is amply contradicted by experimental evidence. Apart from the numerous experiments on phobias in animals which disprove this contention, (4, 10, 15) the demonstrations of Watson and Rayner (12) and Jones (9) have clearly shown how phobias may be induced in children by a simple conditioning process. The rat and rabbit used as the conditioned stimuli in these demonstrations can hardly be regarded as sources of "a high degree of pleasure," and the same applies to the generalized stimulus of cotton wool.

4. The assertion that Hans's horse phobia symbolized a fear of his father has already been criticized. The assumed relationship between the father and the horse is unsupported and appears to have arisen as a result of the father's strange failure to believe that by the "black around their mouths" Hans meant the horses' muzzles.

5. The fifth claim is that the purpose of Hans's phobia was to keep him near his mother. Aside from the questionable view that neurotic disturbances occur for a purpose, this interpretation fails to account for the fact that Hans experienced anxiety even when he was out walking *with his mother*.

6. Finally, we are told that the phobia disappeared as a result of Hans's resolution of his oedipal conflicts. As we have attempted to show, there is no adequate evidence that Hans had an oedipus complex. In addition, the claim that this assumed complex was resolved is based on a single conversation between Hans and his father (see above). This conversation is a blatant example of what Freud himself refers to as Hans having to "be told many things he could not say himself, that he had to be presented with thoughts which he had so far *shown* no signs of possessing, and that his attention had to be turned in the direction that his father was expecting something to come" (p.246).

There is also no satisfactory evidence that the "insights" that were incessantly brought to the boy's attention had any therapeutic value. Reference to the facts of the case shows only occasional coincidences between interpretations and changes in the child's phobic reactions. For example, "a quiet period" early followed the father's statement that the fear of horses was a "piece of nonsense" and that Hans really wanted to be taken into his mother's bed. But soon afterwards, when Hans became ill, the phobia was worse than ever. Later, having had many talks without effect, the father notes that on March 13 Hans, after agreeing that he still *wanted* to play with his widdler, was "much less afraid of horses." On March 15, however, he was frightened of horses, after the information that females have no widdlers (though he had previously been told the opposite by his mother). Freud asserts that Hans resisted this piece of enlightenment because it aroused castration fears, and therefore no therapeutic success was to be observed. The "first real improvement" of April 2 is attributed to the "moustache enlightenment" of March 30 (later proved erroneous), the boy having been told that he was "afraid of his father precisely because he was so fond of his mother." On April 7, though Hans was constantly improving, Freud commented that the situation was "decidedly obscure" and that "the analysis was making little progress."[20]

Such sparse and tenuous data do not begin to justify the attribution of Hans's recovery to the bringing to consciousness of various unacceptable unconscious repressed wishes. In fact, Freud bases

[20] By Freud's admission Hans was improving despite the absence of progress in the analysis.

his conclusions entirely on deductions from his theory. Hans's latter improvement appears to have been smooth and gradual and unaffected by the interpretations. In general, Freud infers relationships in a scientifically inadmissible manner: if the enlightenments or interpretations given to Hans are followed by behavioral improvements, then they are automatically accepted as valid. If they are not followed by improvement we are told the patient has not accepted them, and not that they are invalid. Discussing the failure of these early enlightenments, Freud says that in any event therapeutic success is not the primary aim of the analysis,[21] thus sidetracking the issue; and he is not deflected from claiming an improvement to be due to an interpretation even when the latter is erroneous, *e.g.,* the moustache interpretation.

No systematic follow-up of the case is provided. However, fourteen years after the completion of the analysis, Freud interviewed Hans, who "declared that he was perfectly well and suffered from no troubles or inhibitions" (!). He also said that he had successfully undergone the ordeal of his parents' divorce. Hans reported that he could not remember anything about his childhood phobia. Freud remarks that this is "particularly remarkable." The analysis itself "had been overtaken by amnesia!"

AN ALTERNATIVE VIEW OF HANS'S PHOBIA

In case it should be argued that, unsatisfactory as it is, Freud's explanation is the only available one, we shall show how Hans's phobia can be understood in terms of learning theory, in the theoretical framework provided by Wolpe (14). This approach is largely Hullian in character and the clinical applications are based on experimental findings.

In brief, phobias are regarded as conditioned anxiety (fear) reactions. Any "neutral" stimulus, simple or complex, that happens to make an impact on an individual at about the time that a fear reaction is evoked acquires the ability to evoke fear subsequently. If the fear at the original conditioning situation is of high intensity or if the conditioning is many times repeated the conditioned fear will show the persistence that is characteristic of *neurotic* fear; and there will be generalization of fear reactions to stimuli resembling the conditioned stimulus.

Hans, we are told, was a sensitive child who "was never unmoved if someone wept in his presence" and long before the phobia developed became "uneasy on seeing the horses in the merry-go-round being beaten" (p. 254). It is our contention that the incident to which Freud refers as merely the exciting cause of Hans's phobia was in fact the cause of the entire disorder. Hans actually says, "No. I only got it [the phobia] then. When the horse in the bus fell down, it gave me such a fright, really! That was when I got the nonsense" (p. 192). The father says, "All of this was confirmed by my wife, as well as the fact that the anxiety broke out immediately afterwards" (p. 193). The evidence obtained in studies on experimental neuroses in animals (e.g. 14) and the studies by Watson and Rayner (12), Jones (9) and Woodward (15) on phobias in children indicate that it is quite possible for one experience to induce a phobia.

In addition, the father was able to report two other unpleasant incidents which Hans had experienced with horses prior to the onset of the phobia. It is likely that these experiences had sensitized Hans to horses or, in other words, he had already been partially conditioned to fear horses. These incidents both occurred at Gmunden. The first was the warning given by the father of Hans's friend to avoid the horse lest it bite, and the second when another of Hans's friends injured himself (and bled) while they were playing horses.

Just as the little boy Albert (in Watson's classic

---

[21] But elsewhere (p. 246) he says that a psychoanalysis is a therapeutic measure and not a scientific investigation!

demonstration, 12) reacted with anxiety not only to the original conditioned stimulus, the white rat, but to other similar stimuli such as furry objects, cotton wool and so on; Hans reacted anxiously to horses, horse-drawn buses, vans and features of horses, such as their blinkers and muzzles. In fact he showed fear of a wide range of generalized stimuli. The accident which provoked the phobia involved two horses drawing a bus and Hans stated that he was more afraid of large carts, vans or buses than small carts. As one would expect, the less close a phobic stimulus was to that of the original incident the less disturbing Hans found it. Furthermore, the last aspect of the phobia to disappear was Hans's fear of large vans or buses. There is ample experimental evidence that when responses to generalized stimuli undergo extinction, responses to other stimuli in the continuum are the less diminished the more closely they resemble the original conditional stimulus.

Hans's recovery from the phobia may be explained on conditioning principles in a number of possible ways, but the actual mechanism that operated cannot be identified, since the child's father was not concerned with the kind of information that would be of interest to us. It is well known that especially in children many phobias decline and disappear over a few weeks or months. The reason for this appears to be that in the ordinary course of life generalized phobic stimuli may evoke anxiety responses weak enough to be inhibited by other emotional responses simultaneously aroused in the individual. Perhaps this process was the true source of Little Hans's recovery. The interpretations may have been irrelevant, or may even have retarded recovery by adding new threats and new fears to those already present. But since Hans does not seem to have been greatly upset by the interpretations, it is perhaps more likely that the therapy was actively helpful, for phobic stimuli were again and again presented to the child in a variety of emotional contexts that may have inhibited the anxiety and in consequence diminished its habit strength. The *gradualness* of Hans's recovery is consonant with an explanation of this kind (14).

CONCLUSIONS

The chief conclusion to be derived from our survey of the case of Little Hans is that it does not provide anything resembling direct proof of psychoanalytic theorems. We have combed Freud's account for evidence that would be acceptable in the court of science, and have found none. In attempting to give a balanced summary of the case we have excluded a vast number of interpretations but have tried not to omit any material facts. Such facts, and they alone, could have supported Freud's theories. For example, if it had been observed after Gmunden that Hans had become fearful of his father, and that upon the development of the horse phobia the fear of the father had disappeared, this could reasonably have been regarded as presumptive of a displacement of fear from father to horse. This is quite different from observing a horse phobia and then asserting that it must be a displaced father-fear without ever having obtained any direct evidence of the latter; for then that which needs to be demonstrated is presupposed. To say that the father-fear was repressed is equally no substitute for evidence of it.

Freud fully believed that he had obtained in Little Hans a direct confirmation of his theories, for he speaks towards the end of "the infantile complexes that were revealed behind Hans's phobia" (p. 287). It seems clear that although he wanted to be scientific Freud was surprisingly naive regarding the requirements of scientific evidence. Infantile complexes were not *revealed* (demonstrated) behind Hans's phobia: they were merely hypothesized.

It is remarkable that countless psychoanalysts have paid homage to the case of Little Hans, without being offended by its glaring inadequacies. We shall not here attempt to explain this, except to point to one probable major influence—a tacit belief among analysts that Freud possessed a kind of unerring insight that absolved him from the obligation to obey rules applicable to ordinary men. For example, Glover (6), speaking of other analysts who arrogate to themselves the right Freud claimed to subject his material to "a touch of revision," says, "No doubt when someone of Freud's calibre appears in our midst he will be freely accorded . . . this privilege." To accord such a privilege to anyone is to violate the spirit of science.

It may of course be argued that some of the conclusions of Little Hans are no longer held and that there is now other evidence for other of the conclusions; but there is no evidence that in general psychoanalytic conclusions are based on any better logic than that used by Freud in respect of Little Hans. Certainly no analyst has ever pointed to the failings of this account or disowned its reasoning, and it has continued to be regarded as one of the foundation stones on which psychoanalytic theory was built.

SUMMARY

The main facts of the case of Little Hans are presented and it is shown that Freud's claim of "a more direct and less roundabout proof" of certain of his theories is not justified by the evidence presented. No confirmation by direct observation is obtained for any psychoanalytic theorem, though psychoanalysts have believed the contrary for 50 years. The demonstrations claimed are really interpretations that are treated as facts. This is a common practice and should be checked, for it has been a great encumbrance to the development of a science of psychiatry.

REFERENCES

1. Fenichel, O. *The Psychoanalytical Theory of Neurosis.* Norton, New York, 1945.
2. Freud, S. *Collected Papers,* Vol. *3.* Hogarth Press, London, 1950.
3. Freud, S. *Psychopathology of Everyday Life.* Pelican Books, Harmondsworth, 1938.
4. Gantt, W. H. *Experimental Basis for Neurotic Behavior.* Hoeber, New York, 1944.
5. Glover, E. *On the Early Development of Mind.* International Universities Press, New York, 1956.
6. Glover, E. Research methods in psychoanalysis. *Int. J. Psychoanal., 33:* 403-409, 1952.
7. Hendrick, I. *Facts and Theories of Psychoanalysis.* Knopf, New York, 1939.
8. Jones, E. *Sigmund Freud: Life and Work*, Vol. *2.* Hogarth Press, London, 1955.
9. Jones, M. C. Elimination of childrens' fears. *J. Exp. Psychol., 7:* 382-390,

1924.

10. Lidell, H. S. Conditioned reflex method and experimental neurosis. In *Personality and the Behavior Disorders*, Hunt, J. McV., ed. Ronald, New York 1944.

11. McGeoch, J. and Irion, A. *The Psychology of Human Learning*. Longmans, New York, 1952.

12. Watson, J. B. and Rayner, P. Conditioned emotional reactions. *J. Exp. Psychol., 3:* 1-14, 1920.

13. Wohlgemuth, A. *A Critical Examination of Psychoanalysis*. Allen Unwin, London, 1923.

14. Wolpe, J. *Psychotherapy by Reciprocal Inhibition*. Stanford. Univ. Press, Stanford, 1958.

15. Woodward, J. Emotional disturbances of burned children. *Brit. Med. J., 1:* 1009-13, 1959.

16. Woodworth, R. and Schlosberg, H. *Experimental Psychology*. Methuen, London, 1955.

9 Influences of Suggestion on Airway Reactivity in Asthmatic Subjects

THOMAS LUPARELLO, HAROLD A. LYONS,
EUGENE R. BLEECKER, & E. R. McFADDEN

The effect of suggestion on bronchomotor tone was evaluated in a setting in which accurate, rapid, and reproducible measurements of airway resistance (Ra) could be made. Subjects with asthma, emphysema, and restrictive lung disease, as well as normal subjects, were studied. All subjects were led to believe that they were inhaling irritants or allergens which cause bronchoconstriction. The actual substance used in all instances was nebulized physiologic saline solution. Nineteen of 40 asthmatics reacted to the experimental situation with a significant increase in Ra. Twelve of the asthmatic subjects developed full-blown attacks of bronchospasm which was reversed with a saline solution placebo. The 40 control nonasthmatic subjects did not react.

The investigation of bronchial asthma has been concerned with the role of allergic, infectious, psychological, social, endocrinous, and hereditary factors.[1] Up to now, no single causative determinant has been isolated, and it appears that a variety of factors may be involved in the development and continuance of asthma and in the precipitation of any given acute attack. The effect of psychological stimuli on the precipitation of asthma attacks has been evaluated sporadically over the years. MacKenzie[2] noted bronchospasm in a patient with an "allergy" to roses, when he presented to her an artificial rose. More recently, Dekker and Groen[3] exposed asthmatic subjects to "meaningful emotional

Thomas Luparello, Harold A. Lyons, Eugene R. Bleecker & E. R. McFadden, Influences of suggestion on airway reactivity in asthmatic subjects, *Psychosomatic Medicine, 30,* 1968, 819-825. Copyright © 1968 by the American Psychosomatic Society and reproduced by permission.

From the Departments of Psychiatry and Medicine, State University of New York, Downstate Medical Center, Brooklyn, N. Y.

Supported in part by National Institute of Mental Health

Research Career Development Award K3MH 15,620 and Grants MH-13439, National Institute of Mental Health, and 5T1-HE 5485, National Heart Institute, U. S. Public Health Service.

Presented in part at the Annual Meeting of the American Psychosomatic Society, Mar. 30, 1968.

The authors wish to thank Mrs. Frances Klugman for her help in the preparation of the manuscript and Miss Eileen Abramoff for her help with the statistics.

stimuli" and were able to measure a decrease in vital capacity in some of the subjects. Each stimulus in that study was specific for a particular subject and represented historical events in the individual's disease process. For example, one subject reported developing asthma attacks at the sight of goldfish in a bowl. When shown an artificial representation of this by the experimenters, the subject developed bronchospasm. Another individual, who had indicted dust as a trigger substance for asthma, reacted with bronchospasm when presented with a sealed glass container filled with dust. Those experiments have demonstrated that certain asthmatics are sensitive to perceptual cues which are capable of affecting bronchomotor tone. However, the heterogeneity of the stimuli employed was such that it was not possible to make meaningful comparisons within the group of subjects. In addition, the respiratory end point chosen was an indirect and relatively insensitive measure of airway obstruction.

The present study was undertaken to overcome these problems and to gain an impression of the prevalence of psychological stimuli as factors in the precipitation of asthma attacks. The independent variable chosen was suggestion, since it could be clearly defined, uniformly applied to all subjects, and easily controlled in a laboratory setting. Changes in airway resistance (Ra) were measured directly by body plethysmography. In addition, it became possible to determine whether the effects of suggestion on bronchomotor tone were unique for asthmatics or were shared by subjects with other lung diseases.

METHODS

The data were obtained from 40 asthmatic subjects. The diagnosis of asthma was based on a characteristic history of episodic attacks of reversible bronchospasm associated with a family or personal history or both of allergy, and on an absence of irreversible mechanical defects within the lungs. The subjects were told that they were cooperating in a study related to the control of air pollution and that the experimenters were trying to determine the concentrations at which a variety of substances in the atmosphere would induce attacks of wheezing. It was indicated to each subject that he would be inhaling five different concentrations of an irritant or allergen which the subject had previously indicted as being associated with his asthmatic attacks. The subject was led to believe that he would be exposed to progressively increasing concentrations of this substance, whereas the material actually presented to him, in all instances, was physiologic saline solution. Ra and thoracic gas volume (TGV) were measured in a Collins body plethysmograph, prior to the onset of any test inhalation.[4] Ra and TGV were calculated as the mean of five successive measures of each variable. Resistance was converted to its reciprocal or conductance (Ga) and was expressed as a conductance–thoracic gas volume ratio (Ga/TGV) in order to correct for a variation in lung volume during testing.[5] The normal range for this ratio is 0.13 to 0.35 L.sec./cm. H_2O/L.

After baseline data were obtained, the subjects inhaled over a 30-sec. period ten deep breaths of the suggested "allergen" or "irritant" from a DeVilbiss nebulizer. Following this, Ra and TGV were measured at 1-min. and 4-min. postinhalation intervals, with each measurement representing the mean of 5 determinations at each interval. This procedure was repeated for each new suggested "increased concentration" of the bogus allergen or irritant given to the subject. In the event the subject experienced dyspnea or wheezing, the inhalations were stopped and a placebo in the form of nebulized physiologic saline solution was administered; the subjects were told that they were receiving Isuprel. The Ga/TGV ratios were then determined 3 min. after administering the placebo.

As control subjects, 10 normal individuals, 15 subjects with sarcoid or with tuberculosis (restrictive lung diseases), and 15 individuals with chronic bronchitis were investigated in the same manner, except that they were told the inhalants were 5 different concentrations of industrial air pollutants which cause bronchial irritation and difficulty in breathing.

RESULTS

The data are summarized in Table 1. The mean age of the asthmatic subjects was 25.8 years with a standard deviation (S.D.) of 7.4 years. There were 26 women and 14 men. The mean baseline Ra was 2.22 ± 0.27 cm. H_2O/L./sec. This was associated with a TGV of 2.79 ± 0.49 L. which produced a Ga/TGV ratio of 0.18 ± 0.05 L./sec./cm. H_2O/L. Following exposure to the suggested allergen or irritant (i.e., saline solution), the Ga/TGV ratios of the entire group fell to an abnormal level (mean Ga/TGV ratio 0.12 ± 0.05; $p = 0.001$ by t test). This change was effected by an increase in the Ra to 3.43 ± 1.35 cm. H_2O/L./sec., while the TGV only increased to 3.00 ± 0.74 L. This clearly indicated that the Ga/TGV ratios fell because of a disproportionate rise in Ra.

Correlation between baseline values and postinhalation Ga/TGV ratios in the entire group of asthmatics indicated that the changes produced in this ratio were not a function of the initial value ($r = 0.05$).

Twelve of the 40 subjects developed full-blown clinical attacks of asthma with dyspnea and wheezing. The mean Ga/TGV ratio of these 12 individuals dropped from a baseline ratio of 0.18 ± 0.03 to 0.07 ± 0.03 L./sec./cm. H_2O/L. following inhalation of the supposed noxious substance (Table 2). Following the administration of a placebo, the Ga/TGV ratio rose to 0.13 ± 0.04 L./sec./cm. H_2O/L. (Fig. 1). An analysis of variance for correlated means reveals significant differences between the baseline values and the lowest Ga/TGV ratios following inhalation of the supposed irritant or allergen, and between this lowest value and that obtained 3 min. following the giving of a placebo. Further analysis by Duncan's New Multiple Range Test showed that there was a significant difference between the baseline levels and the lowest ratio values ($p < 0.001$)

TABLE 1. *Plethysmographic Responses of Test Subjects to the Inhalation of Suggested Bogus Allergens or Irritants*

Subjects	No.	M	F	Age*	Ra*† (cm. H_2O/L./sec.)		TGV*‡ (L.)		Ga/TGV* § (L./sec./cm. H_2O/L.)	
					B‖	PI¶	B	PI	B	PI
Asthmatic	40	14	26	25.8 ± 7.4	2.22 ± 0.27	3.43 ± 1.35	2.79 ± 0.49	3.00 ± 0.74	$0.18 \pm .05$	$0.12 \pm .05$
Normal	10	4	6	23.7 ± 1.8	1.22 ± 0.36	1.39 ± 0.37	2.86 ± 0.41	2.85 ± 0.41	$0.32 \pm .11$	$0.28 \pm .09$
Restrictive	15	4	11	30.0 ± 9.8	2.77 ± 0.82	3.12 ± 0.89	2.12 ± 0.70	2.04 ± 0.64	$0.20 \pm .07$	$0.18 \pm .05$
Bronchitic	15	10	5	51.8 ± 14.8	3.59 ± 1.44	3.95 ± 1.28	3.91 ± 1.02	4.03 ± 1.05	$0.09 \pm .03$	$0.08 \pm .03$

*Values given are the mean and standard deviation.
†Airway resistance.
‡Thoracic gas volume.
§Conductance–thoracic gas volume ratio.
‖Baseline measurements.
¶Postinhalation measurements.

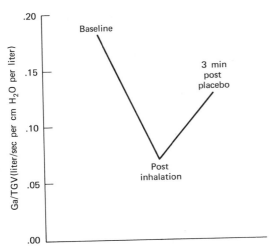

FIG. 1.
Mean Ga/TGV ratio values of 12 asthmatic subjects developing clinical signs and symptoms of bronchospasm in response to the inhalation of a supposed allergen or irritant, and the subsequent response following the administering of a placebo.

and between the pre- and post placebo administration values ($p < 0.001$).

Seven of the 40 subjects responded with an increased Ra (Table 2) so that their Ga/TGV ratios fell below accepted normal levels. However, the degree of airway obstruction associated with these changes was not of sufficient magnitude to induce signs and symptoms of acute bronchospasm (Ga/TGV ratio baseline value s, 0.18 ± 0.05; Ga/TGV postinhalation values, 0.10 ± 0.01). The remaining

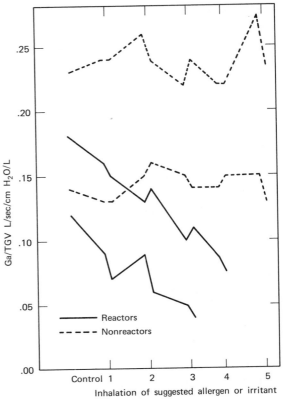

FIG. 2.
Solid lines represent the responses of 2 asthmatic subjects who reacted to the inhalation of suggested allergens with bronchospasm (expressed as a fall in the Ga/TGV ratio value). Broken lines represent the responses of 2 asthmatic subjects who did not react to the same test stimulus.

TABLE **2.** *Effect of Suggestion on Airway Reactivity in Asthmatic Subjects*

Asthmatic Subjects	No.	Ra (cm. H_2O/L./sec)		TGV (L.)		Ga/TGV (L./sec./cm. H_2O/L.)	
		B	PI	B	PI	B	PI
Clinical asthma attacks	12	2.29 ± 0.60	4.97 ± 0.87	2.71 ± 0.69	3.10 ± 0.85	0.18 ± 0.03	0.07 ± 0.03
Increased Ra with no symptoms	7	2.26 ± 0.35	3.72 ± 0.41	2.57 ± 0.38	2.83 ± 0.67	0.18 ± 0.05	0.10 ± 0.01
No reactions	21	2.16 ± 0.51	2.44 ± 0.49	2.90 ± 0.73	2.99 ± 0.72	0.18 ± 0.05	0.15 ± 0.05

Abbreviations and measurement values are the same as in Table 1.

INFLUENCES OF SUGGESTION ON AIRWAY

21 asthmatic subjects did not respond to the experimental manipulation (Table 2), and there was minimal change in their Ra (Ga/TGV ratio baseline values, 0.18 ± 0.05; Ga/TGV ratio postinhalation values, 0.15 ± 0.05; p = N.S.). Figure 2 shows the characteristic responses of 2 subjects who reacted to the inhalation of bogus allergens with bronchospasm and the responses of 2 asthmatic subjects who, under similar test conditions, did not reach with bronchospasm.

No changes were found in the Ra or Ga/TGV ratios of the normal, restrictive, or bronchitis subjects studied (Table 1). It is of interest to note that the mean baseline Ga/TGV ratio of the bronchitic group was in the abnormal range (Ga/TGV ratio value, 0.09 ± 0.03 L./sec./cm. $H_2O/L.$, and it might be argued that significant changes in the Ra of this population would be missed because of the large baseline TGV. However, several asthmatic subjects were observed who had equivalently abnormal baseline Ga/TGV ratio values but who still responded to the experimental situation with a marked fall in Ga/TGV ratio values (e.g., a baseline Ga/TGV ratio value of 0.12, followed by a postinhalation Ga/TGV ratio value of 0.04, observed in one subject).

DISCUSSION

The data demonstrate that an appropriately supplied suggestion is capable of influencing the airway caliber of 47.5% of the asthmatic subjects investigated. Bronchoconstriction or dilatation could be accomplished, depending upon the suggestion supplied. This phenomenon was not observed in normal subjects or in subjects with bronchitis or restrictive lung diseases. It cannot be argued that the asthmatics developed their attacks by chance alone under the stresses of the experimental situation, since this would not account for the dramatic reversal of the bronchospasm in those subjects who received a placebo under the same test conditions. The following observation illustrates that the response of the subjects was related specifically to the suggestion. One subject, who was given the suggestion that she was inhaling pollen, developed hay fever as well as bronchospasm. As part of another experiment, she was given the suggestion that the inhalant was dust and the subject then had only an asthma attack without hayfever. On a third occasion, following exposure to supposed "pollen," she once more reacted with hayfever as well as asthma.

Although the independent variable in the present study has been referred to as suggestion, it may be that such a designation is an over simplification. It is possible that certain elements of conditioning may also be operating. If an individual has repeatedly associated the onset of asthma attacks with the presence of a specific agent, it is possible that contiguous stimuli may assume a conditional stimulus value. The present study, however, does not provide sufficient information to permit a distinction to be made about the various types of learning which could be instrumental in bringing about the phenomenon observed in this investigation.

With the demonstration that asthmatics can be divided into two populations—namely, those who react to suggestion with changes in lung mechanics and those who do not, it becomes relevant to inquire about other possible differences between these two populations. For example, are there differences between the two groups in personality, duration of illness, frequency of attacks, or allergic diathesis? These questions cannot be answered on the basis of the available information, and further studies are required before any meaningful comparisons of the two asthmatic populations can be made along these parameters.

The changes in the Ga/TGV ratio observed in the present study occurred primarily because of a fall in airway conductance. The rapidity of both the responses and their reversibility point to a change in smooth-muscle tone as the most likely explanation.[6] In another study, we have demonstrated that atropine is capable of blocking the broncho-constriction induced by suggestion,[7] indicating that the response of airways to this stimulus is mediated through cholinergic efferent pathways. This hypothesis is in keeping with the observations of Simonsson *et al.*[8] Those authors have shown that stimulation of subepithelial receptors will trigger reflex airway constriction, which is eliminated by atropine blockade of the efferent limb of the reflex arc. The present study indicates that activation of efferent fibers can occur at a central level without direct stimulation of the afferent side. The exact site of stimulation of the efferent fibers and the mechanism by which they are activated is unknown.

Asthma is a complex disease process, the pathogenesis of which remains unknown. In the light of the present findings, a meaningful assessment of the precipitants of asthma and the treatment of any given asthmatic patient must necessarily include an appraisal of the role played by suggestion. If an individual associates a specific agent with the onset of his asthmatic attacks, there is a likelihood that contact with that substance when the asthmatic is aware of it will induce an asthma attack, regardless of whether that agent at that time is physiologically active. Subsequent provocative tests for diagnostic purposes, if done with the subject's knowledge of the test substance, will probably only enhance the asthmogenic potential of that substance. Similarly, the expectations of the patient will have a marked influence on the efficacy of any given therapeutic regimen.

Research related to the psychophysiology of asthma must necessarily institute suitable controls for the influence of suggestion. In such experiments, it often becomes extremely difficult to provide adequate controls for the large number of complex, interacting psychological variables presumed to be operating. In those instances, it is especially important to be sure that the subject is not responding to subtle cues being communicated by the experimenter. Such cues could operate as a suggestion for a particular response, which would then confound rather than clarify the psychophysiology of asthma.

SUMMARY

The effect of suggestion on the pulmonary mechanics of subjects with bronchial asthma, of subjects with restrictive lung diseases, of emphysematous subjects, and of normal individuals was studied by whole-body plethysmography. Following baseline measurements of Ra, each subject was told that he would be inhaling progressively increasing concentrations of an allergen or irritant which would induce bronchospasm. The substance actually given was nebulized physiologic saline solution. After inhalation of the bogus allergen or irritant, the mean Ra of the entire group of asthmatic subjects rose significantly. This was brought about by a marked rise in the Ra of 19 of the 40 asthmatic subjects. Of those 19 asthmatic subjects who reacted, 12 developed full-blown attacks of asthma with wheezing and dyspnea. All asthma attacks were successfully treated with a saline solution placebo, and 3 min. after the inhalation of the placebo, the Ra had returned to baseline levels. The normal subjects and those subjects with restrictive and nonasthmatic, obstructive lung diseases did not react to the inhalation of suggested bogus irritants or allergens with significant changes in Ra.

REFERENCES

1. Stein, M. "Etiology and mechanisms in the Development of Asthma." In *The First Hahnemann Symposium on Psychosomatic Medicine.* Lea,

Philadelphia, 1962, p. 149.

2. MacKenzie, J. N. The production of "rose asthma" by an artificial rose. *Amer J Med Sci 91*:45, 1886.

3. Dekker, E., and Groen, J. Reproducible psychogenic attacks of asthma. *J Psychosom Res 1*:58, 1956.

4. DuBois, A. B., Botelho, S. Y., and Comroe, J. H., Jr. A new method for measuring airway resistance in man using a body plethysmograph: Values in normal subjects and in patients with respiratory disease. *J Clin Invest 35:327*, 1956.

5. Briscoe, W. A., and DuBois, A. B. The relationship between airway resistance, airway conductance and lung volume in subjects of different age and body size. *J Clin Invest 37:1279*, 1958.

6. Widdicombe, J. G. Regulation of tracheobronchial smooth muscle. *Physiol Rev 43:1*, 1963.

7. McFadden, E. R., Jr., Luparello, T., Lyons, H. A., and Bleecker, E. R. The mechanisms of action of suggestion in the induction of acute asthma attacks. In preparation.

8. Simonsson, B. G., Jacobs, F. M., and Nadel, J. A. Role of autonomic nervous system and the cough reflex in the increased responsiveness of airways in patients with obstructive airway disease. *J Clin Invest 46: 1812*, 1967.

10. *Fall into Helplessness*
MARTIN E. P. SELIGMAN

Depression is the common cold of psychopathology, at once familiar and mysterious. Most of us have suffered depression in the wake of some traumatic event—some terrible loss—in our lives. Most of these depressions, like the common cold, run their course in time.

Serious forms of depression afflict from four to eight million Americans. Many of these depressive Americans will recover. Some of them won't; they'll just give up, becoming like T.S. Eliot's hollow men, a '. . .shape without form, shade, without color. Paralyzed force, gesture without motion . . .". Many of those who are hospitalized will simply turn their heads to the wall. Others, at least once out of 200, will take their own lives. Yet we know there are some individuals who *never* succumb to depression, no matter how great their loss.

The *Wall Street Journal* has called depression the "disease of the '70s," and perhaps it is part of the character of our times. It is not a new malady, however. Physicians have been describing depression since the days of Hippocrates; he called it melancholia. The 2,500 years since Hippocrates have added little to our knowledge of the cure and prevention of depression. Our ignorance is due not to lack of research on the problem, but, I believe, to a lack of clearly defined and focused theory. Without a theory to organize what is known about the symptoms and cause, predictions about the cure and prevention of depression are, at best, haphazard.

A COGENT THEORY

I think such a theory is possible, and my belief is based on the phenomenon known as "learned helplessness." [See "For Helplessness: Can We Immunize the Weak?," by Martin E. P. Seligman, PT, June 1969.] There are considerable parallels between the behaviors that define learned helplessness and the major symptoms of depression. In addition, the types of events that set off depression parallel the events that set off learned helplessness. I believe that cure for depression occurs when the individual comes to believe that he is not helpless and that an individual's susceptibility to depression depends on the success or failure of his previous experience with controlling his environment.

So the focus of my theory is that if the symp-

Reprinted from *Psychology Today* magazine, June 1973. Copyright © Communications/Research/Machines, Inc.

toms of learned helplessness and depression are equivalent, then what we have learned experimentally about the cause, cure and prevention of learned helplessness can be applied to depression.

INESCAPABLE SHOCK

A few years ago, Steven F. Maier, J. Bruce Overmier and I stumbled onto the behavioral phenomenon of learned helplessness while we were using dogs and traumatic shock to test a particular learning theory. We had strapped dogs into a Pavlovian harness and given them electric shock—traumatic, but not physically damaging. Later the dogs were put into a two-compartment shuttlebox where they were supposed to learn to escape shock by jumping across the barrier separating the compartments.

A nonshocked, experimentally naive dog, when placed in a shuttlebox, typically behaves in the following way: at the onset of the first electric shock, the dog defecates, urinates, howls, and runs around frantically until it accidentally scrambles over the barrier and escapes the shock. On the next trial, the dog, running and howling, crosses the barrier more quickly. This pattern continues until the dog learns to avoid shock altogether.

But our dogs were not naive. While in a harness from which they could not escape, they had already experienced shock over which they had no control. That is, nothing they did or did not do affected their receipt of shock. When placed in the shuttlebox, these dogs reacted at first in much the same manner as a naive dog, but not for long. The dogs soon stopped running and howling, settled down and took the shock, whining quietly. Typically, the dog did not cross the barrier and escape. Instead, it seemed to give up. On succeeding trials, the dog made virtually no attempts to get away. It passively took as much shock as was given.

After testing alternative hypotheses, we developed the theory that it was not trauma per se (electric shock) that interfered with the dog's adaptive responding. Rather, it was the experience of having *no control* over the trauma. We have found that if animals can control shock by any response—be it an active or a passive one—they do not later become helpless. Only those animals who receive uncontrollable shock will later give up. The experience in the harness had taught the dog that its responses did not pay, that his actions did not matter. We concluded that the dogs in our experiments had learned that they were helpless.

Our learned-helplessness hypothesis has been tested and confirmed in many ways with both animal and human subjects. Tests with human beings revealed dramatic parallels between the behavior of subjects who have learned helplessness and the major symptoms exhibited by depressed individuals.

REACTIVE DEPRESSION

Depression, like most clinical labels, embraces a whole family of disorders. As a label it is probably no more discriminating than "disease of the skin," which describes both acne and cancer. The word "depressed" as a behavioral description explicitly denotes a reduction or depression in responding.

The reactive depressions, the focus of this article are most common. As distinguished from process depression, reactive depression is set off by some external event, is probably not hormonally based, does not cycle regularly in time, and does not have a genetic history. The kind of depression experienced by manic-depressives is process depression.

Some of the events that may set off reactive depression are familiar to each of us: death, loss, rejection by or separation from loved ones; physical disease, failure in work or school, financial setback, and growing old. There are a host of others, of course, but those capture the flavor. I suggest that what all these experiences have in common—what depression is—is the belief in one's own helplessness.

GOODIES FROM THE SKY

Many clinicians have reported an increasing pervasiveness of depression among college students. Since this is a generation that has been raised with more reinforcers—more sex, more intellectual stimulation, more buying power, more cars, more music, etc.— than any previous generation, why should they be depressed? Yet the occurrence of reinforcers in our affluent society is so independent of the actions of the children who receive them, the goodies might as well have fallen from the sky. And perhaps that is our answer. Rewards as well as punishments that come independently of one's own effort can be depressing.

We can mention "success" depression in this context. When an individual finally reaches a goal after years of striving, such as getting a Ph.D. or becoming company president, depression often ensues. Even the disciplined astronaut, hero of his nation and the world, can become depressed after he has returned from walking on the Moon.

From a learned-helplessness viewpoint, success depression may occur because reinforcers are no longer contingent on present responding. After years of goal-directed activity, a person now gets his reinforcers because of who he is rather than because of what he is *doing*. Perhaps this explains the number of beautiful women who become depressed and attempt suicide. They receive abundant positive reinforcers not for what they do but for how they look.

SYMPTOMS IN COMMON

Consider the parallels between depression and learned helplessness: the most prominent symptom of depression, passivity, is also the central symptom of learned helplessness. Joseph Mendels describes the slowdown in responding associated with depression: ". . .Loss of interest, decrease in energy, inability to accomplish tasks, difficulty in concentration, and the erosion of motivation and ambition all combine to impair efficient functioning. For many depressives the first signs of illness are in the area of their increasing inability to cope with their work and responsibility. . ." Aaron T. Beck describes "paralysis of the will" as a striking characteristic of depression:

. . . In severe cases, there often is complete paralysis of the will. The patient has no desire to do anything, even those things which are essential to life. Consequently, he may be relatively immobile unless prodded or pushed into activity by others. It is sometimimes necessary to pull the patient out of bed, wash, dress and feed him . . .

Experiments in learned helplessness have produced passivity in many kinds of animals, even the lowly cockroach, and in human subjects. Donald Hiroto subjected college students to loud noise. He used three groups: group one could not escape hearing the loud noise; group two heard the loud noise but could turn it off by pressing a button; group three heard no noise.

In the second part of the experiment, Hiroto presented the students with a finger shuttlebox. Moving one's fingers back and forth across the shuttlebox turned off the loud noise. The students in group two, who had previously learned to silence the noise by pushing a button, and those in group three, who had no experience with the loud noise, readily learned to move their fingers across the shuttlebox to control the noise. But the students in group one, whose previous attempts to turn off the noise had been futile, now merely sat with their hands in the shuttlebox, passively accepting the loud noise. They had learned that they were helpless.

Hiroto also found out that "externals" [see "External Control and Internal Control," by Julian B. Rotter, PT, June 1971] were more susceptible to learned helplessness than "internals." Externals are persons who believe that reinforcement comes from outside themselves; they believe in luck. Internals believe that their own actions control reinforcement.

BORN LOSERS

Depressed patients not only make fewer responses, but they are "set" to interpret their own responses, when they do make them, as failures or as doomed to failure. Each of them bears an invisible tattoo: "I'm a Born Loser." Beck considers this negative cognitive set to be the primary characteristic of depression:

"... The depressed patient is peculiarly sensitive to any impediments to his goal-directed activity. An obstacle is regarded as an impossible barrier, difficulty in dealing with a problem is interpreted as a total failure. His cognitive response to a problem or difficulty is likely to be an idea such as 'I'm licked,' 'I'll never be able to do this,' or 'I'm blocked no matter what I do' ..."

This cognitive set crops up repeatedly in experiments with depressives. Alfred S. Friedman observed that although a patient was performing adequately during a test, the patient would occasionally reiterate his original protest of "I can't do it," "I don't know how," etc. This is also our experience in testing depressed patients.

Negative cognitive set crops up in both depression and learned helplessness. When testing students, William Miller, David Klein and I found that depression and learned helplessness produced the same difficulty in seeing that responding is successful. We found that depressed individuals view their skilled actions very much as if they were in a chance situation. Their depression is not a general form of pessimism about the world, but pessimism that is specific to their own actions. In animal behavior this is demonstrated by associative retardation: animals don't catch on even though they make a response that turns off shock; they have difficulty in learning what responses produce relief.

Maier and I found in separate experiments, that normal aggressiveness and competitiveness become deficient in the subjects who have succumbed to learned helplessness. In competition, these animals lose out to animals who have learned that they control the effects of their responses. Further, they do not fight back when attacked.

Depressed individuals, similarly, are usually less aggressive and competitive than nondepressed individuals. The behavior of depressed patients is depleted of hostility and even their dreams are less hostile. This symptom forms the basis for the Freudian view of depression. Freud claimed that the hostility of depressed people was directed inward toward themselves rather than outward. Be this as it may, the *symptom* corresponds to the depleted aggression and competitiveness of helpless dogs and rats.

THE BALM OF TIME

Depression also often dissipates with time. When a man's wife dies he may be depressed for several days, several months, or even several years. But time usually heals. One of the most tragic aspects of suicide is that if the person could have waited for a few weeks, the depression might well have lifted.

Time is also an important variable in learned helplessness. Overmier and I found that the day after they received one session of inescapable shock, dogs behaved helplessly in the shuttlebox. However, if two days elapsed between the inescapable shock and testing, the dogs were not helpless; their helplessness like the widower's depression, had run its course.

Unfortunately, helplessness does not always respond so well to the elixir of time. We found that multiple sessions of inescapable shock made the animals' learned helplessness virtually irreversible. We also found that animals that had been reared from birth in our laboratories with a limited history of controlling reinforcers also failed to recover from learned helplessness over time.

Often when we are depressed we lose our appetites and our zest for life. Jay M. Weiss, Neal E. Miller and their colleagues at Rockefeller University found that rats that had received inescapable shock lost weight and ate less than rats who had been able

	Learned Helplessness	Depression
SYMPTOMS	1 passivity	1 passivity
	2 difficulty learning that responses produce relief	2 negative cognitive set
	3 lack of aggression	3 introjected hostility
	4 dissipates in time	4 time course
	5 weight loss and under-eating, anorexia, sexual deficits (?)	5 loss of libido
	6 norepinephrine depletion	6 norepinephrine depletion
	7 ulcers and stress	7 ulcers (?) and stress
		8 feelings of helplessness
CAUSE	learning that responding and reinforcement are independent	belief that responding is useless
CURE	1 directive therapy forced exposure to responding producing reinforcement	1 recovery of belief that responding produces reinforcement
	2 electroconvulsive shock	2 electroconvulsive shock (?)
	3 pharmacological agents (?)	3 pharmacological agents (?)
	4 time	4 time
PREVENTION	inoculation with mastery over reinforcement	inoculation (?)

to escape from shock. In addition, the brains of the rats subjected to inescapable shock are depleted of norepinephrine, an important transmitter substance in the central nervous system. Joseph J. Schildkraut and Seymour S. Kety have suggested that the cause of depression may be a deficiency of norepinephrine at receptor sites in the brain. This is because reserpine, a drug that depletes norepinephrine, among other things, produces depression in man. Moreover, antidepressant drugs increase the brain's supply of norepinephrine. Therefore, there may be a chemical similarity between depression and learned helplessness.

Weiss found that rats subjected to uncontrollable shock got more stomach ulcers than rats receiving no shock or shock they could control.

No one has done a study of ulcers in depression, so we don't know if human experience will correspond to ulceration in helpless rats. However, anxiety and agitation are sometimes seen along with depression. It is my speculation, however, that anxiety persists as long as the depressed person believes there might still be something he can do to extract himself from his dilemma. When he finally comes to believe that no response will work, depression wholly displaces anxiety.

THE CHANCES FOR CURE

As arrayed above, there are considerable parallels between the behaviors which define learned helplessness and the major symptoms of depression. We have also seen that the cause of learned helplessness and reactive depression is similar: both occur when important events are out of control. Let me now speculate about the possibility of curing both.

In our animal experiments, we knew that only when the dog learned to escape the shock, only when it learned that it could control its environment, would a cure for its learned helplessness be found.

At first, we could not persuade the dog to move to the other side of the box, not even by dropping meat there when the dog was hungry. As a last resort, we forcibly dragged the dog across the barrier on a leash. After much dragging, the dog caught on and eventually was able to escape the shock on its own. Recovery from helplessness was complete and lasting for each animal. We can say with confidence that so far only "directive therapy"—forcing the animal to see that it can succeed by responding—works reliably in curing learned helplessness. However, T. R. Dorworth has recently found that electroconvulsive shock breaks up helplessness in dogs. Electroconvulsive shock is often used as a therapy for depression and it seems to be effective about 60 percent of the time.

Although we do not know how to cure depression, there are therapies that alleviate it, and they are consonant with the learned helplessness approach. Successful therapy occurs when the patient believes that his responses produce gratification, that he is an effective human being.

AGAINST THE GRAIN

In an Alabama hospital, for instance, E.S. Taulbee and H.W. Wright have created an "antidepression room." They seat a severely depressed patient in the room and then abuse him in a simple manner. He is told to sand a block of wood, then is reprimanded because he is sanding against the grain of the wood. After he switches to sanding with the grain, he is reprimanded for sanding with the grain. The abuse continues until the depressed patient gets angry. He is then promptly led out of the room with apologies. His outburst, and its immediate effect on the person abusing him, breaks up his depression. From the helplessness viewpoint, the patient is forced to vent his anger, one of the most powerful responses people have for controlling others. When anger is dragged out of him, he is powerfully reinforced.

Other methods reported to be effective against depression involve the patient's relearning that he controls reinforcers.

Expressing strong emotions is a therapy that seems to help depressed patients, as self-assertion does. In assertive training, the patient rehearses asserting himself and then puts into practice the responses he has learned that bring him social reinforcers.

Morita therapy puts patients in bed for about a week to "sensitize them to reinforcement." Then the patients progress from light to heavy to complicated work [see "Morita Therapy," by Takehisa Kora and Kenshiro Ohara, PT, March 1973].

THE LIFT OF SUCCESS

Other forms of graded-task assignments also have been effective. Elaine P. Burgess first had her patients perform some simple task, such as making a telephone call. As the task requirements increased, the patient was reinforced by the therapist for successfully completing each task. Brugess emphasized how crucial it is in the graded-task treatment that the patient succeed.

Using a similar form of graded-task assignment, Aaron Beck, Dean Schuyler, Peter Brill and I began by asking patients to read a short paragraph aloud. Finally, we could get severely depressed patients to give extemporaneous speeches, with a noticeable lifting of their depression. What one patient said was illuminating: "You know, I used to be a debater in high school and I had forgotten how good I was."

Finally, there is the age-old strategy adopted by individuals to dispel their own minor depressions:

doing work that is difficult but gratifying. There is no better way to see that one's responses are still effective. It is crucial to succeed. Merely starting and giving up only makes things worse.

Dramatic successes in medicine have come more frequently from prevention than from treatment, and I would hazard a guess that inoculation and immunization have saved more lives than cure. Surprisingly, psychotherapy is almost exclusively limited to curative procedures, and preventive procedures rarely plan an explicit role.

In studies of dogs and rats we have found that behavioral immunization prevents learned helplessness. Dogs that first receive experience in mastering shock do not become helpless after experiencing subsequent inescapable shock. Dogs that are deprived of natural opportunities to control their own rewards in their development are more vulnerable to helplessness than naturally immunized dogs.

THE MASTERFUL LIFE

Even less is known about the prevention of depression than about its cure. We can only speculate on this, but the data on immunization against learned helplessness guide our speculations. The life histories of those individuals who are particularly resistant to depression or who are resilient from depression may have been filled with mastery. Persons who have had extensive experience in controlling and manipulating the sources of reinforcement in their lives may see the future optimistically. A life without mastery may produce vulnerability to depression. Adults who lost their parents when they were children are unusually susceptible to depression and suicide.

A word of caution is in order. While it may be possible to immunize people against debilitating depression by giving them a history of control over reinforcers, it may be possible to get too much of a good thing. The person who has met only success may be highly susceptible to depression when he faces a loss. One is reminded for example, of the stock market crash of 1929: it was not the low-income people who jumped to their deaths, but those who had been "super-successful" and suddenly faced gross defeat.

One can also look at successful therapy as preventative. After all, therapy usually does not focus just on undoing past problems. It also should arm the patient against future depressions. Perhaps therapy for depression would be more successful if it explicitly aimed at providing the patient with a wide repertoire of coping responses. He could use these responses in future situations where he finds his usual reactions do not control his reinforcements. Finally, we can speculate about child rearing. What kind of experiences can best protect our children against the debilitating effects of helplessness and depression? A tentative answer follows from the learned helplessness view of depression: to see oneself as an effective human being may require a childhood filled with powerful synchronies between responding and its consequences.

REFERENCES

Beck, Aaron T. *Depression Causes and Treatment.* University of Pennsylvania, 1972.

Bibring, Edward. "The Mechanism of Depression" in *Affective Disorders*, Phyllis Greenacre, ed. International Universities, 1953.

Mendels, Joseph. *Concepts of Depression.* Wiley, 1970.

Miller, Neal E. and Jay M. Weiss. "Effects of Somatic or Visceral Responses to Punishment" in *Punishment and Aversive Behavior.* Byron A. Campbell and Russell M. Church, eds. Appleton, 1969.

Seligman, Martin E. and Steven F. Maier. "Failure to Escape Traumatic Shock" in *Journal of Experimental Psychology*, Vol. 74, No. 1, pp. 1-9, 1967.

Seligman, Martin E., Steven F. Maier and James H. Geer. "Alleviation of Learned Helplessness in the Dog" in *Journal of Abnormal Psychology*, Vol. 73, (3, Pt. 1), pp. 256-262, 1968.

Seligman, M.E.P., S.F. Maier and R.L. Solomon. "Unpredictable and Uncontrollable Aversive Events" in *Aversive Conditioning and Learning*, Robert Brush, ed. Academic, 1971.

Taulbee, E.S. and H.W. Wright. "A Psychosocial-Behavioral Model for Therapeutic Intervention" in *Current Topics in Clinical and Community Psychology*, Volume III, Charles D. Spielberger, ed. Academic, 1971.

Thornton, Jerry W. and Paul D. Jacobs. "Learned Helplessness in Human Subjects" in *Journal of Experimental Psychology*, Vol. 87, No. 3, pp.

367-372, March 1971.

Weiss, Jay M. "Effects of Coping Behavior in Different Warning Signal Conditions on Stress Pathology in Rats" in *Journal of Comparative and Physiological Psychology*, Vol. 77, No. 1, pp. 1-13, October 1971.

11. *Campus Tragedy: A Study of Student Suicide*[1]
RICHARD H. SEIDEN

Prior studies of college suicides have neglected the need for an adequate comparison or control group. To remedy this situation, student suicides were compared to their nonsuicidal classmates on selected demographic variables. Suiciding students could be significantly differentiated from their fellow students on the basis of age, class standing, major subject, nationality, emotional condition, and academic achievement. The suicidal students presented similar prodromal patterns which were precipitated by scholastic anxieties, concern over physical health, and difficult interpersonal relationships. Contrary to general belief, the greatest suicidal activity occurred during the beginning, not the final, weeks of the semester. On the basis of changes transpiring in the college population, a future increase of student suicide was predicted.

The act of self-destruction rudely challenges our supposed love for life and fear of death. It is always a puzzlement, but in no case is suicide more shocking or bewildering than it is in the college student. For here are a relatively privileged group of persons enjoying valued advantages of youth, intelligence, and educational opportunity. Why should persons, seemingly so rewarded, seek to kill themselves, and, indeed, to commit suicide at a rate significantly in excess of their noncollege peers (Bruyn & Seiden, 1965, p. 76)?

This perplexing question—"Why do students suicide?"—has motivated a great deal of concern among college health authorities leading to several studies and evaluations of the problem in American universities (Braaten & Darling, 1962; Jensen, 1955; Parrish, 1957; Raphael, Power, & Berridge, 1937; Temby, 1961). Unfortunately, these studies have all had an exclusively descriptive approach. They have

Richard H. Seiden, Campus tragedy: A study of student suicide, *Journal of Abnormal and Social Psychology, 71,* 1966, 389-399. Copyright © 1966 by the American Psychological Association and reproduced by permission.

[1] Revision of a paper presented to Psi Chi colloquium, Western Psychological Association, Honolulu, June 1965.

This research was supported by Grant # 5 T1 MH-8104 from the National Institute of Mental Health.

drawn conclusions about certain characteristics of suicidal students but, seemingly, without appreciation for the degree to which these same characteristics are shared by the entire student body population. What has been conspicuously omitted is a baseline—a standard of comparison against which the diagnostic value of their findings might be judged. One is reminded of the gentleman who, when asked, "How is your wife?" astutely responded, "Compared to what?" This very question of relative comparison must also be asked in the study of student suicides.

The present study attempted to remedy this situation by applying a reasonable standard of comparison, namely, the great majority of fellow college students who do not commit suicide. By investigating what characteristics significantly differentiate suicidal students from their classmates plus examining those situational-temporal conditions associated with campus suicides, it was hoped to achieve a clearer diagnostic picture. Once the high-risk, suicide-prone student can be identified, a large and necessary step will have been taken toward the ultimate objective of effective prophylaxis.

METHOD

The approach used in the present study was one of analytic epidemiology, that is, comparing for particular characteristics the subset of student suicides with the total student body population from which they were drawn. This particular procedure meets the methodological criteria for selection of comparison groups, as stated by MacMahon, Pugh, and Ipsen (1960):

A comparison group is a group of unaffected individuals believed to reflect the characteristics of the population from which the affected group was drawn. Ideally the comparison group should not differ from the affected group in any respect (other than not being affected) which might be likely to influence the frequency of the variable or variables suspected of being casually connected. This means either that both the patient and comparison groups must be representative of the same population or that if selective factors enter into the choice of the patterns, the same factors ought to enter into the selection of the comparison group [p. 235].

The method of the present study involved a comparison of the sample of 23 University of California at Berkeley (UCB) students who committed suicide during the 10-year period 1952 through 1961, with the entire UCB student body population during this same decade. The objective of this comparison was

to determine what special characteristics differentiated the suicide-prone student from his classmates. Within this framework the following working definitions were employed: *(a) Student*—the definition of a student was established by registration on the Berkeley campus of the University of California, in either graduate or undergraduate status, during the regular college semester periods. Summer sessions were not included because of the unreliability of data for these periods and changes in the usual composition of the student body population during summer sessions. *(b) Suicide*—refers to a completed suicide, established by a death certificate stating suicide as the legal cause of death. In one instance, involving a jump from the Golden Gate bridge, this was not possible. Since the body was never recovered, a certificate was not issued; however, the case was well-documented in police and newspaper files. By keeping to this legalistic definition of suicide, one runs the very likely probability that the true number of suicides will be underenumerated. For example, cases of equivocal student deaths, such as by falls or drowning, were regarded as accidental, in keeping with the coroner's findings, even though these deaths, listed as accidents, could have been suicides which were covered up to avoid the social stigma related to suicide. Indeed, it has been estimated that only about 70% of successful suicides are ever recorded as such (Dublin, 1963, p. 3). The advantage in using this definition is that one can be quite certain that deaths recorded as suicide are bona-fide cases since the error is, almost always, in the direction of underreporting. *(c) Exposure to risk*—the period of exposure to risk comprised the 10-year span 1952-1961 inclusive, a total of 10 academic or 7½ calendar years. This important variable, the length of exposure, was to some degree controlled since both the suicidal and nonsuicidal students were exposed to the same period of risk. *(d) Population at risk*—population at risk was the total student body of UCB during the 10-year period cited. Case finding procedures were extremely painstaking, requiring several months of effort to detect and verify 23 bona-fide study cases. Numerous sources of information were used, but for the suicidal students the primary source was the standard death certificate, obtained from the state health department. Secondary sources consisted of newspaper clippings, police files, and University records. The source of materials for the baseline data for the total student body population was the UCB Office of the Registrar. Their publication, *A Ten-Year Survey of Certain Demographic Characteristics of the Student Population* (Suslow, 1963), was indispensable.

In terms of research design, the procedures consisted of collecting and analyzing data regarding selected attributes of the total student population. These data were then used as a baseline to which the sample of suicidal UCB students could be compared. Since suicide may also involve a strong volitional component, further analyses were made with respect to certain situational-temporal features of the academic environment.

RESULTS AND DISCUSSION

Results are presented in tabular and graphic form and discussed in the text by order of their appearance. The various comparisons were statistically analyzed by testing the significance of the difference between two proportions (Hill, 1961, pp. 122-132), specifically, the significance of proportional differences between the suicidal sample and expected population values as based upon knowledge of the student universe. All probability statements are two-tailed probabilities.

Incidence and Prevalence

Previous research on the UCB population (Bruyn & Seiden, 1965) investigated the general question of student suicide risk. By comparing the student suicide experience with the suicide incidence among a comparable group of non-college-age cohorts, it was established that the incidence of suicide among students was significantly greater than for non-student-age peers ($p = .004$). Conversely, the general mortality experience from all causes was significantly more favorable for students when compared to their non-academic-age peers ($p < .001$). In terms of total mortality, suicides accounted for 23 of the 68 student deaths which occurred during the 10-year study period. Proportionally, it ranked as the second leading cause of death (34%), exceeded only by accidents (37%).

Age

For the United States as a whole, there is a well-documented positive correlation between age and suicide (Dublin, 1963, p. 22). This same relationship holds for the student population. If the student body is divided on the basis of those who are above and below age 25, one finds that the percentage of suicides in the older age group is approximately twice their proportional percentage in the population (see Table 1). This distinction is graphically portrayed in Figure 1 which presents the relative frequency of suicidal and nonsuicidal students by 5-year age groups. It is notable that only about

TABLE 1. *Selected Demographic Characteristics of Suicidal and Nonsuicidal Students, UCB, 1952-61*

Demographic Characteristics	Suicidal Students		Total Student Body Population	p
	Frequency Distribution ($n = 23$)	% Distribution	% Distribution	
Age				
Under 25	9	39	70	.001
25 and above	14	61	30	
Class standing				
Undergraduate	12	52	72	.033
Graduate	11	48	28	
Sex				
Male	17	74	67	ns
Female	6	26	33	
Marital status[a]				
Married	3	14	23	ns
Never married	19	86	77	
Race				
White	20	87	89	ns
Nonwhite	3	13	11	
Religion				
Protestant	15	65	60	
Jewish	5	22	18	ns
Catholic	3	13	22	
Nationality				
U.S.A.	19	83	96	.002
Foreign	4	17	04	
Major subject[b]				
Mechanical-mathematic	10	50	64	ns
Aesthetic-social	10	50	36	
Grade-point average[c]				
Above average	14	67	50	ns
Below average	7	33	50	
Mental health service				
Psychiatric patient	8	34	10	<.001
Nonpatient	15	66	90	

[a]Excludes one divorced student.

[b]Excludes three students who had not declared majors.

[c]Excludes two students who did not complete a semester.

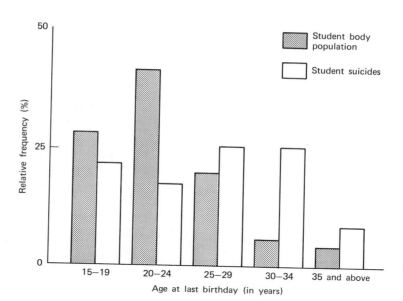

FIG. 1

Age distributions of student suicides and total student body population, UCB, 1952-1961.

6% of all students fall in the 30 to 34-year category while more than 26% of the suicidal students are found in this interval. In fact, the median age for the student body population is 22 years, 6 months, while the median age for the suicidal students, 26 years, 5 months, is greater by almost 4 years.

Class Standing

Directly correlated with, and, indeed, almost identical to, chronological age, is the class standing of individual students. Median class standing for the entire student population was the junior year, for the suicidal subset it was the senior year. When the groups are divided on the basis of graduate or undergraduate standing, one finds that graduate students committed suicide in numbers significantly greater than could be expected from their proportions in the student body at large (see Table 1).

Sex

Of the 23 student suicides, 17 were male, 6 female, a sex ratio approximating 3:1 (see Table 1). This finding accords with those sex ratios reported in previous studies of completed suicide (Dublin, 1963,

p. 23). However, an adjustment is necessary to correctly relate this information to the college population. Whereas the sexes are about equally distributed in the general United States population, they are not equally distributed on campus. For the years under study, males outnumbered females in the student body population by approximately 2:1. Accordingly, the obtained sex ratio of 3:1 must be halved to yield an adjusted student ratio of about 1.5 male suicides for each female suicide. This student sex ratio is considerably narrower than the sex ratio for the country at large. It seems to indicate a heightened risk of suicide among female students as compared to the general female population. However, this indication must remain somewhat speculative since the female suicides were considerably older (median age 30 years, 1 month) than were male suicides (median age 26 years, 1 month). As a consequence one cannot be entirely sure that the constricted ratio is not an effect of confounding between age and sex. Should further research confirm that there is, in fact, a greater risk of suicide among female students as opposed to female non-students, it would follow the predictions of Gibbs and Martin (1964). They proposed a rise in female suicides due to increasing social pressures. According to their status-integration theory, as more women enter the labor force they encounter cross-pressures from conflicting social roles. They postulate that these stresses will lead to increasing numbers of female suicides.

Marital Status

Of the 23 student suicides, it was possible to classify 22 persons into the categories of "married" or "never married," which corresponded to the available student population data. One divorced student was thereby excluded from the analysis. There was no remarkable disparity between the suicidal and nonsuicidal students on the basis of marital status (see Table 1). For the entire United States population, suicide is less common among married persons (Dublin, 1963, p. 26), but this was not the case for campus suicides. Only three of the student suicides were married, and only one of those married had children. The remaining two cases, both females, committed suicide shortly after their marriages.

Race

Of the 23 known suicides, only three were nonwhite and all three of these nonwhite students were Chinese. There were no suicides among Negro, East Indian, or American Indian students who, at any event, comprised only about 3% of the student body population. The distribution of suicides by race corresponded closely to the racial proportions found in the student population (see Table 1). It should be mentioned, however, that there is good reason to question the adequacy of these racial data. Since University records do not ask for nor indicate students' race, these breakdowns, furnished by the University Dean of Students Office, were presumably obtained from simple headcounts with all the imprecision that this method implies.

Religion

Religion was not a significant factor in differentiating suicidal students from the general campus population (see Table 1). As was the case with racial statistics, the religious data, likewise, must be re-garded with great skepticism. The University does not conduct a religious census of its students. Consequently, the religious population figures were estimated from student residence information cards on which "religious affiliation" is an optional item. Very frequently it is left unanswered.

Nationality

Only 4 of the 23 student suicides were foreign students. Nonetheless, their representation in the student body was so negligible (only 4%) that they appear among the suicides in approximately four times the magnitude one would expect from their proportions in the student population (see Table 1). As a group, these four "international student" suicides were characterized by some striking similarities. As youngsters, all of the four had known and suffered from the ravages of war, and three of them were forced to flee from their childhood homes. Two of the students, natives of mainland China, had been dispossessed by the Communist revolution; another student, born in Austria, lost his family in the horrors of the Nazi concentration camps and subsequently migrated to Israel. The fourth student, a native Israeli, had grown up amidst the Arab-Jewish war over the Palestine partition.

Moreover, they shared a similar pattern of conflicts, centering to a large degree around strong feelings of shame. These feelings were reflected in a deep dread that they would not meet expectations that others had set for them. There was some reality to these fears, in that other persons had sent them abroad, were paying their expenses, and probably did expect from them some measure of academic achievement. Still, their excessive concern about "what others would think" was unduly frenetic. All four of them were known to the Student Mental Health Service where they had been seen for psychiatric treatment. These findings, however, must be interpreted with some caution since the median age of foreign students (26 years, 1 month), exceeded the median age of American students (24 years), raising the possibility that the differences were due in some degree to age rather than nationality.

Major Subject

For this comparison, the suicidal subjects were divided into two categories, corresponding somewhat to William James' distinction between the "tough" and "tender minded." Of the 20 suicidal students who had declared majors, the breakdown was 10 students in the "tough-minded" or mechanical-mathematics group (Engineering, Professional, Physical Sciences, Biological Sciences, Agricultural majors) and 10 students in the "tender-minded" or esthetic-social group (Arts, Social Sciences, Language and Literature majors). Relative to their population proportions, there was a greater incidence of a large enough imbalance to achieve statistical significance. Further analysis, by individual subject groups, revealed that suicides were significantly more frequent among students majoring in languages and literature (five cases), especially English majors, who comprised three of the five cases (see Table 2).

Grade-Point Average

Grade-point analysis required some basic adjustments since graduate and undergraduate grading systems are not directly comparable. In practice, an undergraduate "C" is approximately equivalent to a graduate "B." For the student population, the grade-point average (GPA) for undergraduates was 2.50, while for graduates it was 3.35 (calculated to the scale: $A = 4$, $B = 3$, $C = 2$, $D = 1$, $F = 0$). Given this discrepancy, it is obviously necessary to separately compare undergraduate and graduate students with reference to their respective grade-point distributions. When the suicidal students (excluding two who did not complete a full semester at UCB) are ranked by means of achievement above or below their population GPA, we find that two-thirds of them were above average while, by definition, only half of the general student body achieved this mark. Although suggestive of a tendency toward higher grades among suicidal students, the difference, in fact, did not achieve statistical significance. However, further analysis, distributing GPA by class standing, revealed a marked discrepancy between graduate and undergraduate students. This breakdown is detailed in Table 3 and reveals that of the 11 undergraduate students who committed suicide (after one complete semester at the University), 10 of them had surpassed the undergraduate GPA. For graduate student suicides, only 4 of the 10 who had completed a semester exceeded the graduate GPA. Despite the differential grading system that rewards the graduate student with more grade points for a similar level of work, the suicidal undergraduate students received a higher overall GPA than the graduate student suicides (see Table 4).

This finding seems to indicate that undergraduate and graduate suicides differ markedly from one another in terms of academic achievement. The undergraduate suicides performed on a level well above their fellow classmates and performed considerably better than did graduate suicides. Looking at the personal histories of these undergraduate students

TABLE 2. *Suicides Among Language and Literature Majors vs All Other Subject Majors*

Major Subject Group	Suicidal Students		Total Student Body Population	p
	n	%	%	
Language and literature	5	25	9	.012
All other majors	15	75	91	

Note.—Excludes three students who had not declared major subjects.

TABLE 3. *Grade-Point Averages for Graduate and Undergraduate Student Suicides*

GPA	Suicidal Students		Student Population	p
	n	%	%	
Class standing				
Undergraduate				
Above mean	10	91	50	.006
Below mean	1	09	50	
Graduate				
Above mean	4	40	50	ns
Below mean	6	60	50	

Note.—Excludes two students; one graduate, one undergraduate, who suicided during their first semester.

one discovers an interesting paradox. To an external observer, say someone viewing their transcripts, these students achieved splendidly in their academic pursuits. They had all been A or B students in high school since a B or better average is required for undergraduate admission, a policy which is estimated to limit entrance to the top 10-12%, of graduating high school seniors. Reports from family and friends, however, reveal that self-satisfaction was not the case with these students. Rather, they seemed filled with doubts of their adequacy, dissatisfied with their grades, and despondent over their general academic aptitude. This exacerbated fear of failure was tempered somewhat by the fact that in every case of undergraduate suicide the final semester's GPA was lower ($x = 2.53$) than the previous cumulative CPA ($x = 3.34$). Another consideration is whether these students aspired to graduate school which requires a higher than average GPA (2.5-3.0 at UCB). Unfortunately, these exact data are not available; however, a check of those students in major subjects which definitely indicated future graduate work, for example, premedicine, revealed academic achievement in excess of grade requirements. Nevertheless, on balance, they were still achieving loftily above the average of their classmates. How can one explain their deep self-dissatisfaction despite contrary and objective indications of their competence? Two possible explanations suggest themselves: *(a)* The internal standards these students applied to themselves were so Olympian, the demands they imposed upon themselves so exacting, that they were destined to suffer frustration and disappointment no matter how well they fared; and/or *(b)* Whereas they had previously been crackerjack students in high school or junior college, excelling without much difficulty, the precipitous drop in grade points over the final semester threatened their feeelings of self-esteem. Thus, faced by a sudden loss of status, they may have suicided as a response to this egoistic conflict. In any case, the discrepancy between perceived self-concept and objective reality indicates that a purely objective approach often obscures more than it reveals. What one needs to try and understand is the phenomenological response of the individual

TABLE 4.
Observed and Expected GPA of Student Suicides by Class Standing

Class Standing	GPA	
	Observed	Expected
Undergraduate	3.18	2.50
Graduate	2.90	3.35

student. What is necessary to know is what inner standards, what idealized fantasy he uses to judge himself and his own personal worth. For the graduate student suicides as a group, there was no discrepancy between their academic achievements and what might be expected on the basis of the general population of graduate students. While they produced slightly below their population mean, the variation in this instance was primarily due to two students who were in considerable scholastic straits. Contrary to the undergraduates, graduate suicides showed no pattern of decline in their terminal semester GPA. Confirmation of the scholastic disparity between graduate and undergraduate suicides is further revealed by the irregular distribution of academic awards. Inspection of Table 5 indicates that undergraduate students garnered scholarship honors at a rate well beyond the general undergraduate population, while the graduate student suicides did not differ significantly from their classmates in earning academic awards. Even though graduate student awards were far more plentiful, the great majority of awards (10 of 11) were held by undergraduate student suicides.

TABLE 5.
Scholastic Awards by Class Standing

Class Standing	Suicidal Students		Student Population	
	n	%	%	p
Undergraduate				
Scholarship	7	58	05	<.001
Nonscholarship	5	42	95	
Graduate				
Scholarship	1	10	23	*ns*
Nonscholarship	10	90	77	

Mental Health

Of the 23 student suicides, 8 had been referred to the student mental health service for psychiatric treatment (of the 8 students, apparently only 2 were diagnosed as psychotic reactions). These 8 cases comprised better than one-third of the student suicides, significantly exceeding the approximately 10% of the total student body population seen at the mental health facilities (see Table 1). Besides the 8 students known to the student psychiatric service, an additional 3 students were in private psychiatric treatment, making a total of almost 50% of the suicidal group who gave this particular indication of prior mental disturbance.

Temporal-Situational Relationships

Among all causes of death, suicide allows for the greatest degree of volition. The suicidal person is in a position to choose the date, place, and method of his death, and it has long been speculated that there may be a special psychological significance to these choices. Through tracing the time, place, and method of student suicides, the following particular patterns were observed:

Time

When student suicides were charted by calendar months they formed a bimodal curve with peaks occurring during February and October. A more meaningful comparison obtained when the academic semester was used as the time interval. This distribution, as illustrated in Figure 2, challenges a frequently held belief about campus suicides. Academic folklore often explains student suicides as a response to the anxieties and stresses of final examinations. Yet, surprisingly, the data showed that almost the reverse relationship held. Only 1 of the 23 student suicides was committed during finals. (Even that single instance may be dubiously related to final exams since this student was doing well in school and had expressed satisfaction with his "finals" performance.) Most of the suicides occurred at the beginning of the semester. When the semester is divided into three equivalent parts, the vast majority of cases, 16 out of 23, are found to occur during the first 6-week segment. (Actually, the period is only 5 weeks from when instruction begins; the first week is confined to registration procedures.) No cases were found during the second 6-week period which includes the mid-term examina-

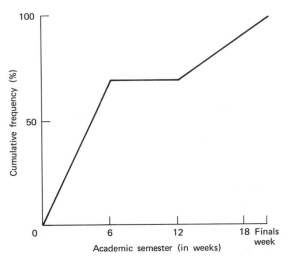

FIG. 2.
Time distribution of student suicides, UCB, 1952/1961.

tions. Over the remaining third of the semester there were seven cases, just one of which occurred during finals week itself (always the last week of the semester). This irregular time distribution of student suicides departed significantly from uniform expectations ($x^2_2 = 16.8, p < .001$). Clearly, the old saw about suicides and finals was not supported. Instead, the danger period for student suicide was found to be the start, not the finish, of the school semester. Incidentally, the day of the week departed significantly from the null hypothesis of uniformity ($x^2_1 = 4.18, p < .05$) with almost one-half the cases occurring on Monday or Friday, terminals of the school week. Unfortunately, the data were none too precise since some cases were based on coroner's estimates as to the date of death.

The unexpectedly low correspondence between final examinations and the commission of student suicide bears some resemblance to a parallel phenomenon involving student mental health during the recent free speech activities on the UCB campus. In the course of these supposedly stressful times, there was a striking drop in admissions to the student mental health service (20% below average) and no recorded student suicides during the 1965 academic

year. (Such behavior corresponds to the drop in suicides, psychosomatic illness, and neurotic conditions observed during both World Wars.) Why, in the midst of all the controversy, turmoil, and tempest was student mental health apparently enhanced? One possibility is that some students who had previously been grappling with internal problems now had the opportunity to act out, to ventilate their inner conflicts, and to displace their intrapunitive anger and hostility by redirecting it toward an external symbol, namely, the University. Perhaps it was the galvanized and heightened sense of community that facilitated mental well-being. Certainly many students felt involved in a common cause; probably, for some it imparted meaning to their lives where previously they had felt alienated and purposeless. If so, it was also a perfect antidote to the kinds of feelings that often drive people to self-destruction.

Place

Most of the students, 12 of 23, committed suicide at their residences. The next most frequent location was the University itself, upon whose grounds 4 students ended their lives. Three students were found dead in parked autos on isolated suburban roads. Another 3 suicided in out-of-town hotel rooms, and 1 student leaped from the San Francisco Golden Gate bridge. It is difficult to determine any significance to the site of these suicides, except for the 4 cases who killed themselves on the university grounds. Of these, the most symbolic suicide was the 1 student who jumped from the Campanile, an architectural landmark of the Berkeley campus.

Method

The most frequent agent of choice was firearms, followed by ingestions and asphyxiations. A comparison with the methods used by Yale student suicides (see Table 6) revealed considerable similarity in the methods employed by the two groups of students. The relatively larger number of poisonings among UCB students is most likely due to the more recent availability of tranquilizers and barbiturates.

For only two of the Berkeley cases was there the least equivocation about assigning suicide as the

TABLE 6. *Methods of Suicide Used by UCB and Yale Students*

Method	UCB (1952-1961)		Yale (1920-1955)[a]	
	n	%	n	%
Firearms	8	35	10	40
Poisonings	6	26	3	12
Asphyxiation	4	17	5	20
Hanging	2	09	6	24
Jumping from high place	2	09	1	04
Cutting instruments	1	04	—	—
Total	23	100	25	100

[a]Source: Parrish, 1957, p. 589.

cause of death. These two cases, both involving ingestions of poisonous substances, were qualified as "probably suicide" but routinely coded as "deaths due to suicide." In at least 10 instances, suicide notes were left by the decedents. These notes ranged from simple instructions concerning the disposal of personal belongings to lengthy, literary dissertations, one of which finished by tersely quoting Camus: "Life as a human being is absurd."

Psychological Factors

A statistical approach, per se, can go just so far in describing the suicide-prone student. The additional use of case history materials provides a fuller, more clinically oriented dimension to the portrayal. As such, the following inferences were derived from anecdotal reports of friends and acquaintances of the students, along with those members of the University community whose lives they touched. From a preventive standpoint, the most pertinent questions which might be asked are, "What prodromal signs, what clues to suicide could be discerned from the personal lives of these students? Specifically, were there any indications or harbingers of their ultimate destinies?" Lastly, "Was there a characteristic conflict which precipitated their self-destructive actions?" The question of prodromal indications can be flatly answered "yes." There were numerous warnings in almost every case. At least five of the

students had made past suicide attempts. Warnings of a more subtle nature could be discovered in the histories of the remaining students. For example, the pupil who went out of his way to modify an item on the medical history form. Where it had requested, "Whom shall we notify in case of emergency?" he crossed out the word "emergency" and substituted "death." Or the student who confided that he sometimes takes 10 or so nembutals because "I am an adventurer." Other students evidenced a long-standing infauation with death, often initiating "bull sessions" about the futility of life, or making wry jokes about killing themselves. Prior to their suicides a disproportionately large number of these students were involved in psychiatric treatment. As a group, they presented similar symptomatic patterns featuring symptoms of insomnia, anorexia, and extreme moodiness, especially moods of despondency; in all, it was a psychological picture compatible with the general diagnosis of agitated depression.

Although their prodromal response to stress was very similar, the particular crises that precipitated their suicides were not. Bearing in mind that each individual case was unique, for purposes of description, the main prodromal conflicts could be classified into the following three categories:

1. *Concern over studies.* In many cases acquaintances of the students made such judgments as "he pushed himself too hard," "worried over

grades," "felt his grades were not as good as he thought they should be," or similar scholastic anxieties which, they felt, triggered the suicidal crisis. It is difficult to evaluate these inferences since "worry over grades" is often seen by informants as a most likely explanation. At any event, if true, their exaggerated concern over studies contrasted vividly with generally excellent academic grades.

2. *Unusual physical complaints.* A number of the students complained of inability to eat or sleep, one student warranting a diagnosis of "avitaminosis." Others worried about possible deterioration such as the student who feared that his "failing sight" might ruin a prospective medical career. A few pupils, however, presented physical complaints of a bizarre semidelusional quality, for instance, the young man whose stomach literally persecuted him. From childhood on he had suffered from anorexia and "stomach ache." Although an exploratory laparotomy did not disclose anything, by the time he entered the University he was at least 50 pounds underweight, still wracked by chronic stomach pains. He then moved from his fraternity house, in the hope of gaining weight by selecting his own food. This plan proved to no avail, nor did extensive medical testing at the student health service, all of which proved negative. He finally ended his torment, perhaps symbolically, by ingesting cyanide.

3. *Difficulties with interpersonal relationships.* Combined under this heading were two different types of conflicts, both reflecting problems in personal relationships. First were the students involved in stormy love affairs. Here the critical stresses were feelings of rejection which had been engendered by broken romances. In the one recorded instance of double suicide, the precipitating event was parental opposition to the youngsters' marriage. Much more typical, however, was the essentially asocial, withdrawn student. These particular students were uniformly described as terribly shy, virtually friendliness individuals, alienated from all but the most minimal social interactions. Frequently they had compensated for their personal solitude by increased study and almost total absorption in schoolwork. The most calamitous example of such human isolation was the student, dead for 18 days before he was found in his lonely room. It is a tragic commentary to his existence, and perhaps a cause for his suicide, that there were no friends, no people involved enough in his life to know, or to care, that he had been missing for well over 2 weeks.

Interpretation

Reviewing the results of the present study, one can reasonably conclude that significant associations between student suicide and numerous variables, both personal and environmental, have been demonstrated. Nonetheless, one cannot, with certitude, infer that these relationships are causal ones. This type of inference would require procedures more exacting than the limited epidemiological methods herein employed. For instance, the total student body population, used as a matched control or comparison group, included a number of students who had unsuccessfully attempted suicide. Quite possibly their inclusion diluted the significance of the obtained differences between suicidal and presumably nonsuicidal students. This is a relatively minor concern, compared to other more cautionary limitations. A primary concern is to what degree the observed relationships were spuriously increased by a common variable. For example, the correlation between student suicide and declining terminal GPA may very well be due to a third factor—emotional disturbance—which both depressed scholastic grades and led to self-destruction. As a corollary, it should be recognized that not all of the selected variables were independent of one another. It is known for one that age and class standing are highly dependent, and it was observed, also, that the variable of age probably confounded to some degree the comparisons by sex and by nationality. Another area of uncertainty concerns the time-order sequence of student suicide. One is unable to state, with certainty, which comes first, the disturbed student or the stresses of student life. Are the suicides due to selection into colleges of mentally unstable individuals or are they due to competitive pressures of the academic environment? The fullest answer to these questions will only come from further research. Toward this goal some salient lines of inquiry could include: the investigation of student suicide attempters and student accident cases, postcollegiate follow-up studies, and the use of "psychological autopsy" procedures, as described by Shneidman and Farberow (1961).

Within the expressed limits of the study design, what predictions about the future suicide problem are warranted? Extrapolating from results of the present study, it appears that a future increase of student suicides may be expected. This increase should occur as a function of two variables, that is, age and academic competition, both of which are directly correlated to student suicides, and both of which are slated to increase in future student body populations. Average student age is already rising as a result of ever increasing proportions of graduate students in the American university system. For example, architects of the UCB educational master plan are considering an ultimate 50:50 graduate-undergraduate ratio. The second variable, academic competition, will likely increase as a result of mounting public demands for quasi-universal college education. As a case in point, the enrollment demands at UCB have already exceeded the available academic supply. Consequently, it has been necessary to restrict enrollment to the uppermost fraction of high school graduating classes. If accepted, the pressure on the student to achieve and maintain very high GPAs gives no indication of abatement. In fact, the situation ominously resembles a suicidal problem which prevails among the youth of Japan. In the Japanese case there are tremendous pressures to attend college, and those students who fail to gain entrance frequently turn to suicide as a solution to their dilemmas. Such conflicts, in addition to a more accepting cultural attitude, have probably helped to make Japan "a country of youthful suicides where suicide has become the number one cause of death in individuals under 30 [DeVos, 1964, p. 6]."

SUMMARY

The purpose of this study was to identify distinctive attributes of the suicidal student, and to determine those environmental conditions which heighten his susceptibility to suicide.

Using an epidemiological approach, demographic comparisons were made between the sample of 23 UCB students who committed suicide during the years 1952-1961 inclusive, and the total student body population for those years. As an additional procedure, the temporal-situational characteristics of student suicides were described and analyzed.

The main findings of the research were:

1. Suicidal students could be significantly differentiated from their classmates on the variables of age, class standing, major subject, nationality, emotional condition, and academic achievement. Compared to the student population at large, the suicidal group was older, contained greater proportions of graduates, language majors, and foreign students, and gave more indications of emotional disturbance. In addition, the undergraduate suicides fared much better than their fellow students in matters of academic achievement.

2. Contrary to the popular belief that suicides frequently occur during final examinations week, time relationships indicated that the peak danger period for student suicides was the beginning (first 6 weeks), not the midterm, nor end of the semester.

3. Most of the students gave recurrent warnings of their suicidal intent. Many of them presented a similar prodromal pattern marked by anorexia, insomnia, and periods of despondency.

4. Major precipitating factors were: Worry over schoolwork, chronic concerns about physical

health (sometimes of a decidedly bizarre nature), and difficulties with interpersonal relationships. This last category contained some students who had reacted to romantic rejections but, for the most part, comprised the emotionally withdrawn and socially isolated student.

5. A future increase of student suicides was predicted on the basis of changes taking place in the age structure of college populations and in the competitive pressures of student life.

REFERENCES

Braaten, J., & Darling, C. Suicidal tendencies among college students. *Psychiatric Quarterly,* 1962, *36*, 665-692.

Bruyn, H. B., & Seiden, R. H. Student suicide: Fact or fancy? *Journal of the American College Health Association*, 1965, *14*, 69-77.

DeVos, G. Role narcissism and the etiology of Japanese suicide. Berkeley, Calif.: Institute of International Studies, University of California, 1964. (Mimeo)

Dublin, L. I. *Suicide: A sociological and statistical study*. New York: Ronald, 1963.

Gibbs, J. P., & Martin, W. T. *Status integration and suicide.* Eugene: Oregon University Press, 1964.

Hill, A. B. *Principles of medical statistics*. New York: Oxford University Press, 1961.

Jensen, V. W. Evaluating the suicidal impulse in the university setting. *Journal Lancet*, 1955, *75*, 441-444.

MacMahon, B., Pugh, T. F., & Ipsen, J. *Epidemiological methods*. Boston: Little, Brown, 1960.

Parrish, H. M. Epidemiology of suicide among college students. *Yale Journal of Biology and Medicine*, 1957, *29*, 585-595.

Raphael, T., Power, S. H., & Berridge, W. L. The question of suicide as a problem in college mental hygiene. *American Journal of Orthopsychiatry,* 1937, *7*, 1-14.

Shneidman, E. S., & Farberow, N. L. Sample investigations of equivocal deaths. In N. L. Farberow & E. S. Shneidman (Eds.), *The cry for help*. New York: McGraw-Hill, 1961. Pp. 118-128.

Suslow, S. *A ten-year survey of certain demographic characteristics of the student population*. Berkeley: Office of the Registrar, University of California, 1963. (Mimeo)

Temby, W. D. Suicide. In G. B. Blaine & C. G. McArthur (Eds.), *Emotional problems of the student*. New York: Appleton-Century-Crofts, 1961. Pp. 133-152.

SECTION 3
SOCIOCULTURAL DEVIANCE

The disorders discussed in this section—psychopathy, alcoholism, drug use, and homosexuality—are subsumed under the heading "personality disorders and certain other nonpsychotic mental disorders" in the American Psychiatric Association's *Diagnostic and Statistical Manual II*.

Psychopathy is an especially slippery label to apply. *DSM II* labels it antisocial personality and defines it as follows: "This term is reserved for individuals who are basically unsocialized and whose behavior pattern brings them repeatedly into conflict with society. They are incapable of significant loyalty to individuals, groups, or social values. They are grossly selfish, callous, irresponsible, impulsive, and unable to feel guilt or to learn from experience and punishment. Frustration tolerance is low. They tend to blame others or offer plausible rationalizations for their behavior. A mere history of repeated legal or social offenses is not sufficient to justify this diagnosis." A related category, dyssocial behavior, is reserved for ". . . individuals who are not classifiable as antisocial personalities, but who are predatory and follow more or less criminal pursuits, such as racketeers, dishonest gamblers, prostitutes, and dope peddlers." It should be obvious that one treads on shaky ground in ascribing mental disorder *a priori* to any individual demonstrating any of the above behaviors. Describing someone as a psychopath may be only a value judgment. Although it is clear that a great number of lawbreakers exhibit many of the characteristics descriptive of a psychopath, there is probably an equal number of socially upstanding citizens who exhibit similar behavior. Indeed, in his classic work on psychopathy, Cleckley (1964) presents case studies of professionals, including doctors, who fit the psychopathic profile perfectly.

The label has probably been considerably overused by society attempting to explain behavior that is difficult to understand. On the other hand, it might prove useful to consider a more limited syndrome of psychopathy to be characterized by deviant behavior and deviant autonomic nervous system and learning responses.

The first selection (12) in this section is by one of the leading researchers in the area of psychopathy. Noting that psychopaths seem to ignore the long-term negative effects of antisocial behavior, Hare investigated the hypothesis that persons bearing the diagnosis "fear" delayed punishment less than normals. His results support the concept that psychopaths prefer immediate gratification despite the knowledge of subsequent punishment. Work such as this helps make psychopathy a more operational term and removes some ambiguity from it as a diagnostic category.

Marlatt, Demming, and Reid (Selection 13) deal with alcoholism. In our introductory remarks to Section 1 we pointed out how the insane of the nineteenth century were labeled mentally ill partly as an effort by reformers to humanize their treatment. A similar process has occurred with alcoholism. Many mental health workers have labored arduously to convince the public that alcoholism is not a crime but a disease, and that, therefore, alcoholics should be candidates for treatment, not jail. The argument for regarding alcoholism as a disease has been stronger, however, than the arguments for regarding many other behavioral excesses as diseases because it is generally believed that a physical addiction develops to alcohol that the alcoholic is powerless to resist. One of the corollaries of this belief is that the alcoholic is incapable of drinking moderately because his first drink sets up a physiological reaction which demands that he continue to drink. The research reported by Marlatt et al. is an ingenious test of this belief. The authors gave a group of alcoholics and social drinkers glasses of tonic with or without vodka to drink and misinformed half of them about what they were actually drinking. They found that the alcoholics' beliefs about what they were drinking were more important in determining how much they drank than the amount of alcohol they actually consumed. The conclusion of the authors is that psychological factors play a crucial role in alcoholics' inability to control their drinking. These findings have potential usefulness for redefining the nature of alcoholism and perhaps also for devising more effective treatments.

Although alcoholics far outnumber hard drug users in the United States, drug addiction occupies the public mind as one of today's most pressing health hazards and social problems. This partly stems from the fact that most psychoactive drugs are illegal (and *ipso facto* a crime) and partly from the reality that many drugs can do considerable damage to the body with prolonged use.

In contrast to the relatively small number of persons who use heroin, it has been estimated that tens of millions of Americans have smoked marijuana at least occasionally. While marijuana is outlawed along with the so-called hard drugs, there is considerable controversy surrounding the question of what somatic and psychological effects the drug has. The selection by Weil et al. (selection 14) represents one of the first well-controlled studies of the effects of marijuana. The authors confirm some of the widely held beliefs about the drug and contradict other widely held myths. One of the clear findings of the study is that (as in the Marlatt et al. study) psychological set, or expectation, plays a crucial role in determining whether or not a "high" results from ingesting the drug. One of the questions Weil et al. fail to answer relates to the observation that smaller does of the drug are required by regular users to achieve the desired effect. Is this a result of psychological sensitization to the effects of marijuana or does a chemical residue remain in the brain? If the latter is the case, can there be a potential harmful cumulative effect of prolonged heavy use of the drug?

In a recent review of the literature pertaining to the use of LSD, McWilliams and Tuttle (1973) found that lasting adverse reactions to its use did not occur in psychologically healthy individuals who took LSD under secure circumstances but did occur in persons who were already emotionally disturbed or who took the drug in situations of crisis or in insecure settings. Cohen's selection 15 is a very personal statement by an individual with extensive experience in counseling college-age students. During his graduate student years at Harvard in the early 1960s, Cohen was himself heavily involved in the Leary-Alpert psychedelic drug movement, and his disillusionment with the transitoriness of the drug experience is eloquently presented in the selection reprinted.

The final selection (16) in this section deals with female homosexuality, an area where ignorance and mythology abound. Homosexuality has been condemned as immoral or unnatural from biblical times down to our own day. The mental health establishment has considered sexual activities between members of the same sex to be pathological—basing their judgment not so much on scientific evidence as on social prejudice and ignorance. But the current *Zeitgeist* is beginning to bring about a change in conceptions of health and pathology in the area of sexual behavior. Homosexuality is gradually coming to be regarded not as a pathological life-style but as merely one of a number of possible styles of living. Even the conservative American Psychiatric Association has begun taking steps to eliminate the diagnostic category homosexuality from the next edition of the *Diagnostic and Statistical Manual of Mental Disorders*. The selection by Martin and Lyon is from their book, *Lesbian/Woman*. In it they reject the idea that a lesbian is a heterosexual reject or a counterfeit man. In fact, their book is more an essay about women than about lesbians per se. They put to rest the idea that a homosexual's all-consuming interest lies in sexual activity, showing that sexuality is merely one aspect of their lives, just as it is with heterosexuals. No more, no less.

SUGGESTED READINGS

Cleckley, H. *The mask of sanity* (4th ed.). St. Louis, Mo.: Mosby, 1964.
Hare, R. D. *Psychopathy*. New York: Wiley, 1970.
McWilliams, S. A., & Tuttle, R. J. Long-term psychological effects of LSD. *Psychological Bulletin*, 1973, *79*, 341-351.
Miller, M. What it means to be a homosexual. *New York Times Magazine*,

January 17, 1971; Discussion February 21, October 10, 1971.
Tart, C. (Ed.) *Altered states of consciousness*. New York: Wiley, 1969.

12. Psychopathy and Choice of Immediate versus Delayed Punishment[1]

ROBERT D. HARE

This study tested the hypothesis that psychopathic Ss would show less prefer-ence for immediate shock than would nonpsychopathic Ss. 12 psychopathic and 12 nonpsychopathic criminals and 19 noncriminals were presented with 6 trials in which they were required to choose between an immediate shock and 1 delayed 10 sec. The results confirmed the hypothesis ($p < .001$). The psychopaths chose immediate shock 55.5% of the time while the nonpsycho-paths chose it 82.3% of the time. The preference for immediate shock in-creased over trials for the nonpsychopathic Ss but not for the psychopathic ones. The results were interpreted in terms of a conditioned fear hypothesis.

Recent evidence indicates that normal subjects (Ss) tend to prefer an immediate punishment (electric shock) over one that is delayed (Cook & Barnes, 1964), or randomly delayed (D'Amato & Gumenik, 1960). While it is obvious that many interacting variables are involved in choice behavior of this sort,

Robert D. Hare, Psychopathy and choice of immediate versus delayed punishment, *Journal of Abnormal Psycho-logy, 71,* 1966, 25-29. Copyright © 1966 and reproduced by permission.

[1]This research was supported by the President's Research Fund, U.B.C., and by Research Grant APA-139 from the National Research Council of Canada. Appreciation is ex-tended to John Moloney, Warden of the B.C. Penitentiary and to S. A. Miller, Director of Research and Special Ser-vices for the Vancouver School Board, for making subjects and facilities available.

relatively few empirical data concerning their effects are available. Among the variables likely to be of importance are (*a*) the relative delay, intensity, and probability of punishment associated with each of the alternatives presented to the S; (*b*) the type of punishment involved and the characteristics of the situation in which it is administered; and (*c*) certain characteristics (e.g., personality and motivational) of the individual making the choice. The present study investigated what was considered to be a par-ticularly relevant example of the latter, namely, psychopathy.[2]

It is well known clinically that the psychopath

[2]The term refers to the entity described by Cleckley (1959) and to what Karpman (1961) terms the primary psycho-path.

tends to avoid immediate discomfort and that he appears to be relatively unconcerned about the long term consequences of his behavior (Cleckley, 1959; Karpman, 1961). On the basis of these and other considerations, it was expected that when faced with a choice between immediate and delayed shock, psychopaths would show less preference for immediate shock than would nonpsychopathic Ss.

METHOD

The Ss were all male volunteers and consisted of 12 psychopathic (Group P) and 12 nonpsychopathic (Group NP) inmates of the British Columbia Penitentiary, and 19 students (Group C) obtained from the university and a local adult education center. Mean age was 26.3 (*SD* = 3.6) for Group P, and 23.8 (*SD* = 3.6) for Group NP, and 23.8 (*SD* = 2.9) for Group C. Mean number of years of formal education was 10.4 (*SD* = 1.6) for Group P, 10.2 (*SD* = 1.7) for Group NP, and 11.5 (*SD* = 1.1) for Group C. Mean Revised Beta IQ was 108.1 (*SD* = 9.2) for Group P, 106.9 (*SD* = 8.9) for Group NP, and 110.8 (*SD* = 8.0) for Group C. None of these differences was significant. Selection of the psychopaths was made by the institutional psychologists on the basis of criteria outlined by Cleckley (1959).

Testing was carried out in a quiet room in the appropriate institution. The *S* was seated before a horizontal panel upon which two telegraph keys were situated 12 inches apart. A small green pilot light was mounted at about eye-level on a vertical panel placed immediately behind the keys. A Model 1A Psychological Instruments Stimulator was used to deliver a brief electric shock via finger electrodes of the zinc, zinc-sulphate type (Lykken, 1959). The level of shock used was individually determined by gradually increasing the intensity until the *S* indicated that he was not prepared to accept anything stronger. The mean intensities of shock arrived at by this procedure and subsequently used in the experiment were 3.9, 3.6, and 3.8 milliamperes for Groups P, NP, and C, respectively. These intensities did not differ significantly from one other and are approximately the same as those obtained from similar *Ss* in another study (Hare, in press).

After the intensity of shock to be used had been determined, *S* was asked to place his dominant hand in front of the keys and midway between them. He was told that his task was simply to press one of the keys whenever the light came on, and that as a result he would receive a shock either immediately or after a 10-second delay, depending upon which key had been pressed. A card placed above each key informed *S* of the delay associated with the key. In order to familiarize him with the actual shocks delivered by the keys, he was required to press each key once. Six free-choice trials were then given, with about 30 seconds between each trial. The effect of possible position preferences was controlled by having the immediate shock associated with the left key for one-half of the *Ss* and with the right key for the other half. After the experiment *Ss* were briefly questioned about their experiences.

RESULTS AND DISCUSSION

The total number and percentage of choices of immediate and delayed shock made by each group are shown in Table 1. The mean number of trials (out of six) on which immediate shock was chosen was

TABLE 1.
Total Number and Percentage of Choices of Immediate (0 Secs.) and Delayed (10 Secs.) Shock Made by Each Group

Choice	P		NP		C	
	0 secs.	10 secs.	0 secs.	10 secs.	0 secs.	10 secs.
Total	40	32	63	9	90	24
Percentage	55.5	44.5	87.5	12.5	78.9	21.1

3.33 for Group P, 5.25 for Group NP, and 4.74 for Group C. An analysis of variance indicated that these means differed significantly from one another, $F(2,40) = 7.93, p < .001$. Individual comparisons among these means (Winer, 1962, p. 100) revealed that Groups NP and C were not significantly different, $F(1,40) = 1.26, p > .10$, but that these two groups combined differed significantly from Group P, $F(1,40) = 15.86, p < .001$.

A more detailed impression of the choices made by each group can be gained from inspection of Table 2, which contains the choice of shock delay made by each S on each of the six trials. On the first trial, 67% of the nonpsychopathic Ss chose immediate shock while only 50% of the psychopaths did so. Although in the expected direction, this difference was not significant. During the next five trials however, the number of nonpsychopathic Ss who chose immediate shock increased significantly, Cochran's $Q = 9.7, df = 5, p < .05$ (Siegal, 1956), while the number of psychopaths doing so showed virtually no change.

The relatively strong overall preference for immediate shock shown by the nonpsychopathic Ss (82.3% for Groups NP and C combined) is consistent with previous research involving both human (Cook & Barnes, 1964; D'Amato & Gumenik, 1960) and animal Ss (Knapp, Kause & Perkins, 1959; Sidman & Boren, 1957), and also with the common experience that waiting for an unpleasant event to occur can be extremely distressing. The postexperimental comments made by these Ss are pertinent

here. Most stated that waiting for delayed shock produced a considerable amount of apprehension and that they wanted "to get it over with as soon as possible." The psychopaths, on the other hand, showed only a slight overall (55.5%) preference for immediate shock and reported that waiting for the

TABLE 2.
Individual Choices of Immediate (1) and Delayed (D) Shock on Each trial

				Trial			
Group P							
Subject	1	2	3	4	5	6	$\Sigma 1$
1	D	1	D	1	D	1	3
2	1	1	1	1	1	1	6
3	1	1	1	1	1	D	4
4	D	D	D	D	D	D	0
5	D	1	1	D	1	D	3
6	1	1	D	1	1	1	5
7	1	D	1	1	D	1	4
8	D	D	1	D	1	1	3
9	1	D	1	D	1	D	3
10	1	1	1	1	1	1	6
11	D	1	D	1	D	1	3
12	D	D	D	D	D	D	0
$\Sigma 1$	6	7	7	6	7	7	40
%1	50	58	58	50	58	58	55.5
Group NP							
Subject	1	2	3	4	5	6	$\Sigma 1$
1	1	1	1	1	1	1	6
2	1	1	1	1	1	1	6
3	D	1	1	1	1	1	5
4	1	1	1	1	1	1	6
5	D	1	D	1	1	1	4
6	1	D	1	1	1	1	5
7	1	1	1	1	1	1	6
8	1	1	1	1	1	1	6
9	1	1	1	D	1	1	5
10	D	D	1	1	1	1	4
11	1	1	1	1	1	1	6
12	D	1	1	D	1	1	4
$\Sigma 1$	8	10	11	10	12	12	63
%1	67	83	92	83	100	100	87.5

TABLE 2. (continued)

			Trial				
Group C							
Subject	1	2	3	4	5	6	Σ1
1	D	1	1	1	1	1	5
2	1	1	D	1	D	1	4
3	1	D	1	D	1	1	4
4	D	1	1	1	1	1	5
5	1	1	1	1	1	1	5
6	D	1	1	1	1	D	5
7	1	D	1	1	1	1	4
9	1	D	D	1	1	1	4
10	1	1	1	1	D	D	5
11	D	1	1	1	1	1	4
12	D	1	D	1	1	1	4
13	1	D	1	1	1	1	5
14	1	D	1	D	1	1	4
15	1	1	1	1	1	1	6
16	1	1	D	1	1	1	5
17	D	1	1	1	D	1	4
18	1	1	1	1	1	1	6
19	1	1	1	1	1	1	6
Σ1	13	14	14	16	16	17	90
%1	68	74	74	84	84	89	78.9

occurrence of delayed shock bothered them very little.

A basis for interpreting the differential effects of delayed shock upon psychopathic and nonpsychopathic Ss is provided by the theory that cues associated with painful stimulation acquire, through classical conditioning, the capacity to elicit fear responses (Miller, 1951). In normal persons, these cues would serve to elicit fear responses in the interval prior to anticipated pain or punishment. Presumably the aversive properties of this aroused fear (apprehension?) would summate with those of delayed shock and would be greater than the aversive properties of immediate shock alone. Since the aroused fear is a conditioned response, its magnitude and aversiveness would be expected to increase with repeated delayed shock experiences, and this would be reflected in an increased number of choices of immediate shock over trials. As Table 2 indicates, this is what happened in the case of the nonpsychopathic Ss (Groups NP and C). The choice behavior of the psychopaths can be similarly interpreted. Thus, the finding that psychopaths may acquire conditioned fear responses slowly (Hare, 1965a; Lykken, 1957) suggests that, even after a number of delayed shock experiences, relatively little fear would be generated by cues preceding the shock. This would account for the failure of the psychopaths (Group P) to show an increased number of immediate shock choices over trials (see Table 2).

The results of this study, as well as the interpretation offered, are in accord with the recent finding that psychopathic Ss showed less increase in palmar skin conductance in the interval prior to anticipated shock than did nonpsychopathic Ss (Hare, 1965b; in press). This was taken to indicate that the emotional effects and the aversive properties of future pain or punishment are relatively small for the psychopath. Whereas the normal person finds it distressing to wait for some unpleasant event, the psychopath apparently does not.

A limitation of the present study is that it is not known to what extent nonsensory variables (Swets, 1961) affected the level of shock which Ss reported to be their maximum. It is possible, for example, that some Ss, in an attempt to avoid strong shock, reported that their maximum had been reached when in fact it had not. This possibility would particularly apply to the psychopaths, whose tendency to avoid discomfort is well known (Cleckley, 1959). Unfortunately, the method employed in this study did not allow the effects of such nonsensory variables to be evaluated directly. It will be recalled, however, that all three groups received approximately the same intensity of shock. This suggests that unless psychopaths have a pain threshold for shock that differs considerably from that of normal persons, the subjective intensity of shock was probably within the same range for all three groups. In this regard, Schachter and Latané (1964) found that psychopathic and nonpsychopathic Ss did not differ significantly in their ratings of the degree of pain experienced when they were all administered the same level of shock.

While the present findings are consistent with the hypotheses that psychopaths lack the normal capacity to acquire conditioned fear responses and that the emotional significance of future punishment is of relatively little immediate concern to them, they may also be interpreted in another way. It is possible that the choice behavior of the psychopaths was determined not by the emotional consequences of delayed shock or by an inability to acquire fear responses, but by a deliberate attempt on their part to use the experimental situation to their own advantage. In the absence of any specific information about the purpose of the experiment, and knowing that it was being conducted by a psychologist who, among other things, might communicate the results to prison authorities, the psychopaths may have reasoned that any extreme or unusual pattern of responding would appear abnormal or revealing of themselves. As a result they may have intentionally employed a random or systematic distribution of choices. Thus, the advantage or payoff expected by the psychopaths for responding in a particular way (including their comments that waiting for delayed shock to occur did not bother them) may have outweighed whatever emotional effects delayed shock might have had. Inspection of Table 2 indicates that the pattern of choices of five Ss (1, 5, 8, 9, 11) in Group P conforms to this alternative explanation of the results.

This interpretation raises the additional possibility that the results of other experimental studies of psychopathy, including those involving fear (GSR) conditioning (Hare, 1965a; Lykken, 1957), may have been similarly influenced by an attempt on the part of the Ss to control the situation and to manipulate or "con" the experimenters. In other words, the psychopath may be able to control the amount of overt and autonomic emotionality displayed in a variety of social situations, perhaps because of a past history of reinforcement for such control and lack of display under similar circumstances. While this hypothesis is plausible and certainly coincides with the psychopath's well known penchant for manipulation, there is no direct experimental evidence to support it. On the other hand, the results of a number of recent studies involving avoidance learning (Lykken, 1957; Schachter & Latane, 1964), serial learning under conditions of punishment (Hetherington & Klinger, 1964), and the emotional effects of anticipated punishment (Hare, in press), are consistent with the hypothesis that psychopaths do not acquire fear responses as readily as do normal persons. As noted above, the present results are also consistent with this conditioned fear hypothesis. It is clear, however, that further research is necessary to determine the degree to which experimental findings, such as those obtained in the present study, are influenced by the psychopath's characteristic tendency to manipulate people and situations to meet his own needs. Research along these lines is currently being planned.

REFERENCES

Cleckley, H. M. Psychopathic states. In S. Arieti (Ed.), *American handbook of psychiatry*. Vol. 1. New York: Basic Books, 1959. Pp. 567-588.

Cook, J. O., & Barnes, L. W. Choice of delay of inevitable shock. *Journal of Abnormal and Social Psychology*, 1964, *68*, 669-672.

D'Amato, M. R., & Gumenik, W. E. Some effects of immediate versus randomly delayed shock on an instrumental response and cognitive processes. *Journal of Abnormal and Social Psychology*, 1960, *60*, 64-67.

Hare, R. D. Acquisition and generalization of a conditioned fear response in psychopathic and nonpsychopathic criminals. *Journal of Psychology,*

1965, *59*, 367-370. (a)

Hare, R. D. Psychopathy, fear arousal, and anticipated pain. *Psychological Reports*, 1965, *16*, 499-502. (b)

Hare, R. D. Temporal gradient of fear arousal in psychopaths. *Journal of Abnormal Psychology*, in press.

Hetherington, E. M., & Klinger, E. Psychopathy and punishment. *Journal of Abnormal and Social Psychology*, 1964, *69*, 113-115.

Karpman, B. The structure of neurosis: With special differentials between neurosis, psychosis, homosexuality, alcoholism, psychopathy, and criminality. *Archives of Criminal Psychodynamics*, 1961, *4*, 599-646.

Knapp, R. K., Kause, R. H., & Perkins, C. C. Immediate versus delayed shock in T-maze performance. *Journal of Experimental Psychology*, 1959, *58*, 357-362.

Lykken, D. T. A study of anxiety in the sociopathic personality. *Journal of Abnormal and Social Psychology*, 1957, *55*, 6-10.

Lykken, D. T. Properties of electrodes used in electrodermal measurement. *Journal of Comparative and Physiological Psychology*, 1959, *52*, 629-634.

Miller, N. E. Learnable drives and rewards. In S. S. Stevens (Ed.), *Handbook of experimental psychology*. New York: Wiley, 1951. Pp. 435-472.

Schachter, S., & Latané, B. Crime, cognition and the autonomic nervous system. In D. Levine (Ed.), *Nebraska symposium on motivation*: *1964*. Lincoln: Univer. Nebraska Press, 1964. Pp. 221-273.

Sidman, M., & Boren, J. J. The relative aversiveness of warning signal and shock in an avoidance situation. *Journal of Abnormal and Social Psychology*, 1957, *55*, 339-344.

Siegal, S. *Nonparametric statistics for the behavioral sciences*. New York: McGraw-Hill, 1956.

Swets, J. A. Is there a sensory threshold? *Science*, 1961, *134*, 168-177.

Winer, B. J. *Statistical principles in experimental design*. New York: McGraw-Hill, 1962.

13. *Loss of Control Drinking in Alcoholics: an Experimental Analogue*[1]

G. ALAN MARLATT, BARBARA DEMMING, & JOHN B. REID

Nonabstinent alcoholics and social drinkers were presented with an ad-lib supply of either alcoholic or nonalcoholic beverages in a taste-rating task. Subjects were assigned to one of two instructional set conditions in which they were led to expect that the beverage to be rated contained alcohol (vodka and tonic) or consisted only of tonic. The actual beverage administered consisted of either vodka and tonic or tonic only. The results showed that instructional set was a significant determinant of the amount of beverage consumed and posttask estimates of the alcoholic content of the drinks. The actual beverage administered did not significantly affect the drinking rates of either alcoholics or social drinkers. Loss of control drinking, in the form of increased consumption by alcoholics who were administered alcohol, did not occur during the drinking task. The results are discussed in terms of implications for treatment and for the conception of alcoholism as a disease.

The conception of alcoholism as a disease is subject to controversy, because of the apparent "voluntary"

G. Alan Marlatt, Barbara Demming, & John B. Reid, Loss of control drinking in alcoholics: An experimental analogue, *Journal of Abnormal Psychology, 81,* 1973, 233-241. Copyright © 1973 by the American Psychological Association and reproduced by permission.

[1]This research was supported, in part, by Grant MH-17982 from the National Institutes of Mental Health to the senior author.

nature of the drinking response. The concept of addiction can be introduced as a means of specifying the involuntary characteristics associated with alcoholism, thus bringing it into greater accord with the commonly accepted definition of disease (Jellinek, 1960). It is assumed that the addictive process manifests itself through subjective craving for alcohol and the subsequent inability to control intake. As such, the loss of control phenomenon, with its emphasis on involuntary drinking, is a central assumption underlying a disease theory of alcoholism.[2]

Although definitions of loss of control drinking vary in the literature, most are in essential agreement with Jellinek (1960), who described it as

that stage in the development of [the alcoholics'] drinking history when the ingestion of one alcoholic drink sets up a chain reaction so that they are unable to adhere to their intention to "have one or two drinks only" but continue to ingest more and more —often with quite some difficulty and disgust—contrary to their volition [p. 41].

Presence of the loss of control phenomenon is considered by some investigators to be the single most important symptom of alcoholism, as it denotes the existence of "helpless dependence or addiction, the essence of the disease [Keller, 1962, p. 313]." Jellinek cited loss of control as a key behavioral symptom of "gamma alcoholism," considered by him to be the predominant form of alcoholism in North America.

Various hypotheses relating to the underlying process assumed to account for loss of control drinking have been proposed. Adherents of the disease model appear to agree that the alcoholic's ingestion of relatively small amounts of alcohol acts as a "triggering mechanism" which activates the addictive process leading to subsequent involuntary consumption to the point of eventual intoxication. The specific physiological processes assumed to mediate this effect differ among theorists, ranging from the altered cellular metabolism which "becomes conditioned by the 'signal' of the 'first drink' [Jellinek, 1960, p. 149]," to paralysis of the "control cen-

ters" of the brain initiated by the first effects of alcohol (MacLeod, 1955), or activation of specific neuronal circuits located in the hypothalamus which elicit craving for alcohol (Marconi, Poblete, Palestini, Moya, & Bahamondes, 1970). These theories have in common the assumption that it is the *physical* effects of alcohol which are responsible for the elicitation of uncontrolled drinking in the alcoholic, initiated through the mediating effects of some *physiological* process. As such, loss of control drinking should be transituational in nature and would be expected to occur in both the naturalistic and controlled (laboratory) setting.

It is also possible, however, to conceive of loss of control drinking as learned behavior, differing only in rate and quantity of alcohol consumed from normal social drinking. Most behavioral theories of alcoholism (e.g., Conger, 1956) assume that alcohol has strong reinforcing properties for the alcoholic. It may be that the alcoholic has learned to expect these reinforcing effects of drinking, based on his past learning history (cf. Rotter, 1954). Expectation of these effects may lead him to the initial consumption of an alcoholic beverage in a given situation. Increased consumption may occur due to the alcoholic's greater tolerance to alcohol, requiring progressively higher dosages to obtain the desired effect.

The present experiment was an initial attempt to test the validity of the disease model assumptions related to loss of control drinking. If it could be shown that regardless of the actual content of the beverage administered (alcoholic or nonalcoholic), the individual's *expectancy* of the alcoholic content of the drink is a significant determinant of his drinking rate, doubt would be cast on the theoretical position which accounts for loss of control drinking primarily as a physiologically mediated effect. In the present study, the drinking behavior of alcoholic and social drinkers was compared under the guise of a task which directed subjects to rate the taste qualities of either alcoholic or nonalcoholic beverages. Subjects were assigned to groups which differed both in terms of the actual beverage administered and the expectancy for the type of beverage given.

---

[2]Jellinek, in a major work on the disease conception of alcoholism, has recognized the importance of this issue: "If it is assumed that certain species of alcoholism have the natures of diseases, it may be further assumed that the act which results in intoxication is outside the volitional sphere of the alcoholic. Nevertheless, the loss of control is preceded by a period in which the ground for the disease is prepared and in which the question of impaired volition does not arise [1960, pp. 45-46]."

METHOD

Selection of Placebo Beverage

It was first necessary to select a mixed beverage in which the presence or absence of alcohol could not be reliably detected on the basis of taste alone. The same beverage could then be used under instructional set conditions identifying the drink as either alcoholic or nonalcoholic in content. The use of a "floater" placebo, in which a small amount of alcohol (e.g., gin) is placed on the top of a soft-drink mix such as tonic, was deemed inappropriate, as it would not contain enough alcohol to activate the loss of control phenomenon. It was decided instead to try vodka, a relatively tasteless alcoholic beverage, which was mixed with tonic water (quinine). In the beverage pretesting procedure, 25 college students (all social drinkers) who volunteered to participate in a study involving rating the taste of alcoholic beverages were individually presented with a series of nine beverage samples. Each drink contained from 0 to 2 ounces of 80-proof Petrushka vodka (gradated at quarter-ounce increments) and from 4 to 6 ounces of Schweppes tonic water, so as to make a total of 6 ounces in each glass. The series of drinks was ordered randomly prior to each subject's taste rating. After first rinsing out his mouth with a commercial mouthwash (to equalize prior taste acuity for all subjects and to partially "dull" discriminative ability), each subject was asked to take three sips of the first drink. The subject was then told to decide whether or not the drink contained any alcohol, on a simple yes/no basis. This procedure was repeated for all nine drinks. The results showed that a mixture containing five parts tonic to one part vodka could not be rated as containing alcohol on better than a chance basis (44% of the subjects rated this mixture as containing alcohol, while 56% rated it as containing no alcohol). All other ratio mixtures were correctly or incorrectly identified by a majority of subjects. The five-one ratio of tonic to vodka was thus chosen as the alcoholic beverage for use in the experiment; the nonalcoholic beverage consisted of straight tonic.

Subjects

Alcoholic Group

An attempt was made to recruit 32 male alcoholics, between the ages of 21 and 65 years, who were currently nonabstinent. As considerable difficulty was encountered in the recruitment of these subjects, a variety of sources were tapped in and around the Madison, Wisconsin, area. The sources used included: (a) Sign-up sheets, requesting names and telephone numbers of volunteers were given to cooperating hotel desk clerks and bartenders in areas known to be frequented by alcoholics. Volunteers were asked "to participate in a taste study which may involve sampling alcohol." (b) An ex-alcoholic, previously in treatment, was asked to recruit names of local individuals believed to be alcoholics and who were currently "off the wagon." (c) Additional subjects were recruited from friends and acquaintances of potential subjects obtained through the sources described above. All subjects, both alcoholic and control, signed a consent form prior to participation in the experiment, which stated in part, "I understand that, as part of the project, I may or may not consume a quantity of alcoholic beverage." Subjects received monetary remuneration (five dollars) for their participation in the study.

Once contacted, potential subjects were given an appointment for a detailed screening interview to assess their eligibility for participation in the experiment. As far as it could be determined, no individuals knew that they had to meet the criteria for alcoholism in order to qualify as subjects. This information was kept secret so as to partially rule out the possibility that individuals would falsify the information obtained in the interview in order to take part in the study. The screening interview was applied to all subjects, following which a candidate was classified as an alcoholic or social drinker (control), or was rejected from the study. The interview, about 30 minutes in duration, obtained information concerning the subject's demographic and socioeconomic status, current drinking patterns and rates, previous hospitalizations or involvement in treatment programs for alcoholics (including Alcoholics Anonymous), and record of arrests for drunken conduct. To be assigned to the alcoholic group, a subject has to meet one or more of the following criteria: (a) at least one prior admission to an alcoholic treatment center; (b) five or more prior arrests for "drunk and disorderly conduct"; (c) previous membership in Alcoholics Anonymous or in the local Vocational Rehabilitation for Alcoholics Program. All but 7 of the 32 alcoholic subjects qualified on at least two of the above criteria. Based on the interview information, 23 subjects had been in treatment for alcoholism (X = 5.5 admissions); 21 had been arrested on charges associated with excessive drinking ($\overline{X}$ = 21.5 arrests); 18 claimed prior membership in Alcoholics Anonymous; and 10 had been involved in the Vocational Rehabilitation program.

In addition to these criteria, only those subjects who reported that they had consumed some alcoholic beverages within the prior 2 weeks and who claimed to have no immediate intentions of abstaining from alcohol were accepted for the experiment, so as to insure that the study would not involve drinkers who were trying to maintain abstinence. All prospective subjects were also administered a Breathalyzer test upon their arrival in the laboratory. Those individuals who showed a reading of greater than .06% blood-alcohol concentration were asked to return when they felt totally sober. All but a few of the eligible subjects had Breathalyzer readings of zero, as subjects were told to refrain from drinking for at least 12 hours prior to their time of appointment. Fully qualified subjects were weighed (to enable computation of postexperimental blood-alcohol concentrations), randomly assigned to a treatment condition, and then participated in the experimental procedure. For safety reasons, all subjects were transported to and from the laboratory by taxi.

Control Group

Only male social drinkers were accepted for inclusion in the control condition. A total of 32 subjects were recruited from the following sources: (a) sign-up sheets, identical in form to those used with the alcoholic sample, and distributed in local hotels, bars, and in the University physical plant, and with local taxi drivers; (b) a local newspaper ad ("Applicants must be male, 21 and over, and be social drinkers . . ."); and (c) friends of other subjects. In this context, a "social drinker" was defined as anyone who did not abstain from alcoholic beverages but was not an alcoholic as defined above. In addition, potential control subjects were screened out in the initial interview if they reported "heavy drinking" behavior and/or if they described drinking as "a problem" for them to the interviewer. Control subjects underwent identical procedures to the alcoholic group prior to their involvement in the experiment.

The age range was 24-65 years ($\overline{X}$ = 46.75) for the controls. Although an effort was made to match subjects on the basis of age, it should be noted that there is a significant difference in age between the two groups ($p < .01$). Correlations of age with the various dependent measures used in the study were conducted and are reported in a later section. The social class index (Hollingshead & Redlich, 1958), which takes into account educational background and occupation, was found to be 59.2 for the alcoholics and 52.2 for the controls; both of these mean scores fall within Social Class IV.

Procedure

Taste-Rating Task

In order to provide a rationale to the subjects which would convince them of the appropriateness of consuming alcoholic beverages in a laboratory setting, the experimental procedure was presented as a "taste-rating" task. This task was based on a procedure originally proposed by Schachter, Goldman, and Gordon (1968), in a study investigating eating behavior in normal and obese subjects. The task served no function other than to provide a legitimate setting in which either alcoholic or nonalcoholic beverages could be consumed and compared on various dimensions of taste. Subjects were asked to sample and compare three drinks on each of a series of adjectives (e.g., "bitter," "strong," "watery," "sweet," etc.). The adjectives appeared individually in the window of a memory drum, which the subject rotated manually at his own pace. The memory drum was used so that the subject could not tell how many items were on the scale, nor how long the overall task would take. In fact, the subject was terminated 15 minutes after beginning the task. More adjectives were stored on the drum tape than any one subject could complete in this time period.

Treatment Conditions

Alcoholic and control subjects were each randomly assigned to one of four cells in a 2 X 2 matrix. The main independent variables in addition to the subject population factor consisted of (*a*) actual beverage administered, either a mixture of vodka and tonic, or tonic only; (*b*) instructional set, in which subjects were told they were receiving either vodka and tonic, or tonic only. Thus, the four conditions consisted of (*a*) told alcohol/given alcohol; (*b*) told alcohol/given tonic; (*c*) told tonic/given tonic; and (*d*) told tonic/given alcohol.

Primer Dose

Assuming that loss of control is "triggered" after the consumption of a single drink (Jellinek, 1960), it was necessary to give subjects a "primer" drink prior to beginning the taste task. For this reason, subjects who were to receive alcohol in the task were administered an initial dose of 1 ounce of 80-proof vodka mixed with 5 ounces of tonic, equivalent to a single mixed drink served in most bars. Subjects who were assigned to the nonalcoholic beverage conditions also received a primer, consisting of 6 ounces of tonic only. The primer was administered approximately 20 minutes before beginning the taste rating task, so as to allow time for the drink to "take effect." The instructions providing the rationale for the primer dose also served as an introduction to the taste-rating task which would follow:

You are going to participate in a taste study. We are trying to find out how sensitive drinkers are to various types of beverage. We are using both heavy drinkers and social drinkers to see if there is any difference between the two groups in taste perception. Please listen carefully to these instructions. We are testing a new type of [tonic or vodka, depending on condition assignment] that is not yet on the market. We want to see whether people can taste any difference between this and standard types of [tonic/vodka]. You will be given three beverages, each containing a different brand of [tonic/vodka]. We want you to sample these drinks, compare them, and rate them on taste scales which I'll tell you about later. Before you do that, we would like you to have an introductory sample of each of the three types of drinks right now.

At this point, the experimenter (the second author) prepared the drinks before the subject, in accordance with the condition assignment. In the told alcohol/given alcohol condition, 4 ounces of vodka from each of three different vodka bottles (Smirnoff, Petrushka, and a third liquor bottle which was labeled "Brand X") into three respective decanters. Following this, 20 ounces of tonic from Schweppes' bottles were poured into each of the three decanters (thus each decanter contained 24 ounces of beverage, in the proportion of five parts tonic to one part vodka). In the told tonic/given tonic condition, the experimenter poured 24 ounces each of three brands of tonic (Canada Dry, Schweppes, and "Brand X") into the three decanters. In order to increase the subject's belief in the two beverage deception conditions, the actual mixtures to be used were prepared ahead of time, and poured into the "legitimate" bottles. In the told alcohol/given tonic condition, the same procedure as in the told alcohol/given alcohol condition was followed, except that *both* the vodka and tonic bottles contained only decarbonated tonic water during the mixing procedure. Similarly, in the told tonic/given alcohol condition, the ostensible tonic bottles contained mixtures of vodka and tonic in the same proportion as described above.

After the beverages were poured into the three decanters, the subject was asked to rinse out his mouth with a mouthwash solution. The mouthwash was prepared by adding 30% 100-proof alcohol to a commercially available mouthwash. The mouthwash was administered to dull the subject's sense of taste and to create a sensation of alcohol in the mouth. Subjects were told that the mouthwash was used to remove foreign tastes which might interfere with the tasting task, a rationale which was accepted by all subjects. The subject was then given the primer dose, consisting of an "introductory sample" of each of the three drinks (2 ounces from each for a total of 6 ounces), and was asked to drink each completely. Subjects began the actual taste rating task following a 20-minute waiting period.

Task Procedure

At the beginning of the taste-rating task, subjects were read further instructions explaining the procedure for rating the three beverages for each adjective presented on the memory drum. Included in the instructions was the statement "feel free to sample as much of each beverage as you need in order to arrive at a decision." The taste task took place in a small, quiet room. The subject was seated at a table on which the three decanters were arranged in a row; in front of each was an empty glass. To the right was placed the memory drum and rating sheets. On the wall facing the subject was a disguised one-way mirror containing a small translucent area that allowed for viewing. Behind the mirror was an adjoining room in which a trained rater (unaware of the subject's condition assignment) observed the subject during the task. Also present was an intercom which was left on during the task period so that the subject's spontaneous verbalizations could be monitored in the observation room.

After receiving the instructions, the subject was again asked to rinse out his mouth with mouthwash before beginning the task. The experimenter then announced that she "had to leave to set up for another experiment" and that she would return shortly. The subject was not told how long the taste task would last. During the 15-minute period, the experimenter came back into the room at the half-way point to "check the progress" of the subject and to answer any questions. At the end of the time period, the experimenter reentered and asked the subject the following question, "Did you think that there was any alcohol in any of the drinks?" If the answer was affirmative, he was asked, "From 0 to 100%, how much alcohol was in each of the drinks?" After the responses were recorded, the subject was thanked for his cooperation and was asked not to tell anyone about the experimental procedures for a fixed period of time.

Dependent Measures

Amount of Beverage Consumed

Total amount of beverage consumed (in fluid ounces) was determined by subtracting the amount of beverage left in the three decanters from the original 72 ounces allowing for the 6 ounces consumed in the primer dose sample.

Sip Rate

During the taste task, the subject's behavior was monitored by the rater through the disguised one-way mirror. Putting a glass to the mouth and drinking from it was defined as one "sip." This measure, therefore, does not necessarily reflect the number of swallows; several swallows would be recorded as only one sip if the glass remained at the subject's mouth.

Amount Consumed per Sip

In order to estimate the amount of beverage consumed per sip, the total amount of beverage consumed was divided by the total frequency of sips taken. While only an approximation, this measure does provide a rough index of consumption changes over the course of the task period, necessary to assess any increases associated with the loss of control effect.

Estimates of Alcohol Content

Percentage of alcohol in each of the three drinks was recorded in response to the experimenter's question at the end of the taste-rating task.

Blood-alcohol level following the taste task in the given alcohol conditions was calculated using a formula (American Medical Association, 1959) based on the subject's weight and the amount of absolute alcohol consumed, during the task period.

RESULTS

Amount of Beverage Consumed

Total amount of beverage consumed, in fluid ounces, constituted the main dependent variable. Up to 72 ounces were available for consumption during the 15-minute task. Means for this variable are presented in Table 1. Analysis of variance (2 X 2 X 2 fixed- effects design) revealed a significant effect for the instructional set condition ($F = 20.59$, $df = 1\%56$, $p < .01$). Regardless of whether they were alcoholics or controls, subjects drank an average of 9.12 ounces in the told tonic condition, and 17.77 ounces in the told alcohol condition. The actual beverage administered (vodka and tonic, or tonic only) was not a significant determinant of consumption ($F = .50$, $df = 1/56$). The interaction between set and beverage administered also did not attain significance. Thus, in terms of the beverage factor, the only significant determinant of the subject's consumption level was his expectation of the content of the drink. A significant main effect was also obtained for the subject population factor. Regardless of other factors, alcoholics consumed more beverage ($\overline{X} = 16.80$ ounces) than did control subjects ($\overline{X} = 11.08$, $F = 7.22$, $df = 1/56$, $p < .01$). The interaction between subject groups and set was not significant.

Sip Rate

Frequency of sips taken during the taste task was recorded in 3-minute blocks. Condition means for sip rates for the entire task period are presented in Table 2. Analysis of variance revealed that the only significant determinants of sip frequency were subject population ($F = 5.68$, $df = 1/56$, $p < .025$) and actual beverage administered ($F = 4.01$, $df = 1/56$, $p < .05$). Neither instructional set nor any interaction attained significance in this analysis. As is apparent from means in Table 2, control subjects ($\overline{X} = 29.81$) sip significantly more times than alcoholics ($\overline{X} = 21.59$), and all subjects sip more when administered tonic ($\overline{X} = 29.16$) than when administered alcohol ($\overline{X} = 22.25$).

TABLE 1. *Condition Means for Total Amount of Beverage Consumed (in Fluid Ounces)*

	Alcoholics		Social Drinkers		
	Told Tonic	Told Alcohol	Told Tonic	Told Alcohol	
Given tonic	10.94	23.87	9.31	14.62	14.69
Given alcohol	10.25	22.13	5.94	14.44	13.19
Condition $\overline{X}$	10.60	23.00	7.63	14.53	13.94a

[a]Grand $\overline{X}$.

TABLE 2. *Condition Means for Frequency of Sips Taken During Task Period*

Beverage Condition	Alcoholics		Social Drinkers		Condition $\bar{X}$
	Told Tonic	Told Alcohol	Told Tonic	Told Alcohol	
Given tonic	20.87	26.00	34.75	35.00	29.16
Given alcohol	18.87	20.62	29.12	20.37	22.25
Condition $\bar{X}$	19.87	23.31	31.94	27.69	25.70[a]

[a] Grand $\bar{X}$.

Amount Consumed Per Sip

The ratio of frequency of sips to amount of total beverage consumed for each subject gives an approximate estimate of the average amount consumed per sip. Means for this variable are presented in Table 3. Analysis of these results indicates that although alcoholics did not sip as often as controls (as described above), they did consume significantly more beverage per sip ($\bar{X}$ = .92 ounces) than control subjects ($\bar{X}$ = .48 ounces; F = 10.65, df = 1/56, $p < .01$). This finding suggests that alcoholics tended to "gulp" their drinks within individual sip periods, compared to social drinker controls. As found with the variable of total amount consumed, the instructional set factor also attained significance for amount consumed per sip (F = 11.89, df = 1/56, $p < .01$). Both alcoholic and control subjects consumed a greater quantity per sip ($\bar{X}$ =

.94 ounces) when they expected the beverage to contain alcohol than when they expected it to consist only of tonic ($\bar{X}$ = .46 ounces). Again, the nature of the actual beverage administered was not a significant determinant of this variable. No interactions attained significance in this analysis.

The number of sips taken for each subject was continuously recorded during the task period. On this basis, the ratio of sips to total beverage consumed for each subject was calculated for each 3-minute block of the taste task. Figure 1 presents the average amount consumed (in fluid ounces) for each time block for both alcoholics (left side of Figure 1) and social drinkers (right side). It should be noted that the means presented in Figure 1 represent only an approximation of consumption rates, since it was impossible to determine whether

TABLE 3. *Condition Means for Amount of Beverage Consumed per Sip (in Fluid Ounces)*

Beverage Condition	Alcoholics		Social Drinkers		Condition
	Told Tonic	Told Alcohol	Told Tonic	Told Alcohol	
Given tonic	.65	1.12	.35	.48	.65
Given alcohol	.63	1.29	.20	.85	.74
Condition	.64	1.20	.28	.67	.69[a]

[a] Grand $\bar{X}$.

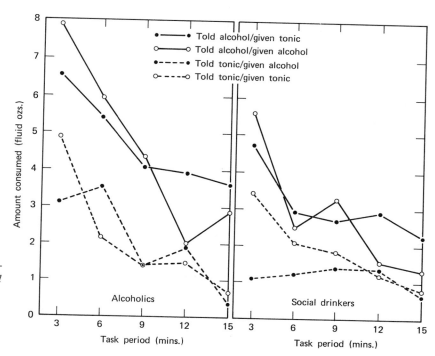

FIG. 1.

Amount of total beverage consumed by alcoholics and social drinkers during task period (based on amount consumed per sip by each subject in 3-minute blocks).

the amount consumed per sip was constant over the task period. Examination of the figure reveals that consumption declined for most groups over the duration of the task period. Highest consumption rates were obtained during the first 3-minute block, with rates decreasing during the succeeding 12 minutes. An exception to this pattern is found in the told tonic/given alcohol condition for control subjects, in which consumption is stable but consistently low during the task.

Estimates of Alcohol Content

As a partial check on the beverage deception manipulation, at the completion of the taste task all subjects were asked to estimate the percentage of alcohol, if any, in each of their three test beverages (beverages were, of course, identical within each condition). The average percentage across the three beverages was assessed and served as the basis for analysis (means are presented in Table 4). The only significant factor revealed in the analysis was instructional set ($F = 44.49$, $df = 1/56$, $p < .01$). Actual bever-

age administered and subject population factors did not attain significance. The mean estimate for all subjects in the told tonic conditions is 1% alcohol, compared to the mean of 27.6% in the told alcohol conditions.

In the conditions in which subjects received alcohol under the correct instructional set (told alcohol), estimates of alcoholic content were 21.3% for alcoholic and 23.1% for controls. When subjects were given tonic, but were told they were receiving alcohol, their estimates actually increased over the told alcohol/given alcohol condition: alcoholics estimated alcoholic content at 28.7% and controls at 37.2%. The "hidden alcohol" beverage deception (told tonic/given alcohol) seemed to be effective, in that estimates of percentage alcohol content were minimal (alcoholics = 0%; controls = 3.5%).

Postexperimental Blood-Alcohol Concentrations

Estimates of blood-alcohol concentrations were obtained for subjects who actually received alcohol,

TABLE 4. *Condition Means for Subjects' Estimates of Percentage Alcohol in Beverage Conditions (Percentage of Alcohol)*

Beverage Condition	Alcoholics		Social Drinkers		Condition $\overline{X}$
	Told Tonic	Told Alcohol	Told Tonic	Told Alcohol	
Given tonic	<1	28.7	.0	37.2	16.6
Given alcohol	.0	21.3	3.5	23.1	12.0
Condition X	<1	25.0	1.8	30.2	14.3[a]

[a]Grand $\overline{X}$.

based on their weight and the amount of pure alcohol consumed in the task. These estimates revealed that alcoholic subjects attained a mean concentration of .093% in the told alcohol condition, and .056% in the told tonic condition. The respective figures for control subjects are .044% and .031%. Most authorities consider concentrations of from .05% to .15% to constitute borderline levels of intoxication (American Medical Association, 1959). Alcoholic subjects fall within this range, whereas control subjects fall below this range.

Because of the significant difference in the ages of the alcoholic and control groups, coefficients of correlation were obtained in which age was related to all major dependent variables described above. In no case was age significantly correlated with measures of beverage consumption. The mean difference of age between the two groups (alcoholics on the average being 6 years older than controls) does not seem to be related to drinking behavior in the present study.

DISCUSSION

The main finding of the present study was that beverage consumption rates for both the alcohol mixture and tonic alone were determined largely by the subject's expectancy of the content of the beverage. This finding, obtained with both alcoholic and social drinker subjects, is in marked opposition to assumptions which suggest that the physiological effects of alcohol alone are responsible for increases in the alcoholic's drinking behavior. Expectancy of beverage content manipulated by instructional set conditions was a significant factor in the determination of total amount of beverage consumed, amount consumed per sip, and subjects' estimates of the alcoholic content of each beverage. A similar expectancy effect has been reported by Merry (1966), who

found no increase in the level of self-reported "craving" when alcohol was surreptitiously placed in a "vitamin" mixture administered to alcoholics.

Rotter (1954) has defined expectancy as "the probability held by the individual that a particular reinforcement will occur as a function of a specific behavior on his part in a specific situation [p. 107]." In the present study, it was found that consumption rates were higher in those conditions in which subjects were led to believe that they would consume alcohol, regardless of the actual beverage administered. It would be of interest to know whether subjects in the told alcohol/given tonic group showed a high level of consumption because they began to experience the initial reinforcing effects associated with drinking alcohol (a placebo effect), or continued to drink because they believed it was necessary to increase intake to an even greater extent in order to experience any effects of alcohol. Informal observation of the subjects assigned to this condition both during and following the taste task provides some support for the former possibility: several subjects, both alcoholic and control, spontaneously volunteered the information that they were feeling a "buzz" or were "a bit tipsy" from the drinking experience. In addition, the finding that subjects in the told alcohol/given tonic conditions rated the alcoholic content of the drink at the same level as subjects in the told alcohol/given alcohol groups suggests that these subjects may have experienced effects which served as a basis for subsequently estimating the strength of the drink. This hypothesis could be assessed in future investigations by including additional measures, such as rating the behavior of subjects for objective signs of intoxication, and by obtaining systematic self-reports of the effects of alcohol and degree of "craving" experienced by subjects at the completion of the task period.

Use of such additional measures would provide further information as to the validity of the expectancy effect obtained. The present findings do not rule out the possibility, for example, that subjects in the told alcohol conditions sampled more beverage because of the increased difficulty that would be involved in discriminating the taste of vodka in the mixed drink, relative to the taste of tonic alone. If the taste discrimination factor alone were a significant determinant of consumption, it would follow that alcoholics and social drinkers would consume an equal amount in the told alcohol conditions. The results show, however, that alcoholics who were told that the drink contained alcohol consumed significantly more beverage than control subjects, a finding which probably reflects the alcoholic's greater expectation of reinforcing effects. Social drinkers may have responded more than the alcoholics to the taste discrimination factor, as indicated by their significantly higher sip rate. Frequency of sips, rather than overall consumption rate, would seem to be a more appropriate measure of the extent to which subjects are attempting to make difficult taste discriminations.

Loss of control drinking, in the form of progressive increases in consumption during the task by subjects who actually received alcohol, was not demonstrated in the study. Rather, as is clear from inspection of Figure 1, drinking rates actually *decreased* over the task period. The finding of decreased consumption during the task may be accounted for in part by the limiting effects of situational factors in the task. The taste task required subjects to make a variety of discriminations and comparisons of the quality of the beverages presented. Subjects may have acquired adequate information about the qualities of the drinks in the early stages of the task, so that fewer sips were needed in the later stages to make the required taste ratings. A second factor which may have contributed to decreases in consumption involves the possibility that subjects believed that a state of intoxication would interfere with their ability to successfully complete the task requirements. A desire to be successful in the task, and/or to please the experimenter, may have led subjects to decrease their intake.

Although the findings reported are viewed as strong support for the role of cognitive factors in the determination of loss of control drinking, the limitations inherent in the present experimental situation should be systematically examined in order to assess the generalizability of these conclusions for drinking in more natural settings. First, the duration of the task period might be extended to allow for consumption of greater quantities of alcohol. In the present study, it is possible that the task duration was too short, and/or that loss of control drinking does not occur until blood alcohol concentrations reach a higher level than that reported for the alcoholic subjects (cf. Glatt, 1967). Second, the demand characteristics of the experimental situation might be altered so as to encourage subjects in all conditions to drink as much as possible (e.g., by telling them that it is an experiment to determine the physiological effects of excessive intake of alcohol or tonic, instead of telling them that it is a taste test).

A different and potentially exciting approach would be the actual observation of loss of control drinkers in the natural drinking environment. It would be of interest to observe the temporal patterning of consumption as it is affected by the presence or absence of social companions, and other situational determinants. A related approach has been recently reported by Sobell, Sobell, and Christelman (1972), who studied the drinking behavior of hospitalized alcoholics. In real-life drinking situations, the loss of control phenomenon is probably determined by a variety of factors, including the expectation of reinforcing consequences. Rather than discounting the relevance of physiological factors in loss of control drinking, the present study highlights the need for a further examination of the cognitive factors which may determine this phenomenon.

REFERENCES

American Medical Association, Committee on Medicolegal Problems. *Chemical tests for intoxication, manual.* Chicago: Author, 1959.

Conger, J. J. Reinforcement theory and the dynamics of alcoholism. *Quarterly Journal of Studies on Alcohol*, 1956, *17*, 296-305.

Glatt, M. M. The question of moderate drinking despite "loss of control." *British Journal of Addiction*, 1967, *62*, 267-274.

Hollingshead, A. B., & Redlich, R. F. *Social class and mental illness.* New York: Wiley, 1958.

Jellinek, E. M. *The disease concept of alcoholism.* New Haven, Conn.: College and University Press, 1960.

Keller, M. The definition of alcoholism and the estimation of its prevalence. In D. J. Pittman & C. R. Snyder (Eds.), *Society, culture, and drinking patterns.* New York: Wiley, 1962.

MacLeod, L. D. The "craving" for alcohol. A symposium by members of the W.H.O. Expert Committee on Mental Health and Alcoholism. *Quarterly Journal of Studies on Alcohol*, 1955, *16*, 34-66.

Marconi, J., Poblete, M., Palestini, M., Moya, L., & Bahomondes, A. Role of the dorsomedial thalamic nucleus in "loss of control" and "inability to abstain" during ethanol ingestion. In R. E. Popham (Ed.), *Alcohol and alcoholism.* Toronto: University of Toronto Press, 1970.

Merry, J. The "loss of control" myth. *Lancet*, 1966, *1*, 1257-1258.

Rotter, J. B. *Social learning and clinical psychology.* New York: Prentice-Hall, 1954.

Schachter, S., Goldman, R., & Gordon, A. Effects of fear, food deprivation, and obesity on eating. *Journal of Personality and Social Psychology*, 1968, *10* 91-97.

Sobell, L. C., Sobell, M. B., & Christelman, W. C. The myth of "one Drink." *Behavior Research and Therapy*, 1972, *10*, 119-123.

14. *Clinical and Psychological Effects of Marihuana in Man*
ANDREW T. WEIL, NORMAN E. ZINBERG,
& JUDITH M. NELSEN

In the spring of 1968 we conducted a series of pilot experiments on acute marihuana intoxication in human subjects. The study was not undertaken to prove or disprove popularly held convictions about marihuana as an intoxicant, to compare it with other drugs, or to introduce our own opinions. Our concern was simply to collect some long overdue pharmacological data. In this article we describe the primitive state of knowledge of the drug, the research problems encountered in designing a replicable study, and the results of our investigations.

Marihuana is a crude preparation of flowering tops, leaves, seeds, and stems of female plants of Indian hemp *Cannabis sativa* L.; it is usually smoked. The intoxicating constituents of hemp are found in the sticky resin exuded by the tops of the plants, particularly the females. Male plants produce some resin but are grown mainly for hemp fiber, not for marihuana. The resin itself, when prepared for smoking or eating, is known as "hashish." Various *Cannabis* preparations are used as intoxicants throughout the world; their potency varies directly with the

Andrew T. Weil, Norman E. Zinberg, & Judith M. Nelsen, *Science, 162*, 1234-1242, 13 December 1968. Copyright © 1968 by the American Association for the Advancement of Science.
This work was conducted in the Behavioral Pharmacology Laboratory of the Boston University School of Medicine, sponsored and supported by its division of psychiatry, and at the Boston University Medical Center, Boston, Massachusetts.

amount of resin present (*1*). Samples of American marihuana differ greatly in pharmacological activity, depending on their composition (tops contain most resin; stems, seeds, and lower leaves least) and on the conditions under which the plants were grown. In addition, different varieties of *Cannabis* probably produce resins with different proportions of constituents (*2*). Botanists feel that only one species of hemp exists, but work on the phytochemistry of the varieties of this species is incomplete (*3*). Chronic users claim that samples of marihuana differ in quality of effects as well as in potency; that some types cause a preponderance of physical symptoms, and that other types tend to cause greater distortions of perception or of thought.

Pharmacological studies of *Cannabis* indicate that the tetrahydrocannabinol fraction of the resin is the active portion. In 1965, Mechoulam and Gaoni (*4*) reported the first total synthesis of (−). $\triangle^1$-*trans*-tetrahydrocannabinol (THC), which they called "the psychotomimetically active constituent of hashish (marihuana)." Synthetic THC is now available for research in very limited supply.

In the United States, the use of *Cannabis* extracts as therapeutics goes back to the 19th century, but it was not until the 1920's that use of marihuana as an intoxicant by migrant Mexican laborers, urban Negroes, and certain Bohemian groups caused public concern (*3*). Despite increasingly severe legal penalties imposed during the 1930's, use of marihuana continued in these relatively small populations without great public uproar or apparent changes in numbers or types of users until the last few years. The fact that almost none of the studies devoted to the physiological and psychological effects of *Cannabis* in man was based on controlled laboratory experimentation escaped general notice. But with the explosion of use in the 1960's, at first on college campuses followed by a spread downward to secondary schools and upward to a portion of the established middle class, controversy over the dangers of marihuana generated a desire for more objective information about the drug.

Of the three known studies on human subjects performed by Americans, the first (see 5) was done in the Canal Zone with 34 soldiers; the consequences reported were hunger and hyperphagia, loss of inhibitions, increased pulse rate with unchanged blood pressure, a tendency to sleep, and unchanged performance of psychological and neurological tests. Doses and type of marihuana were not specified.

The second study, known as the 1944 LaGuardia Report (6), noted that 72 prisoners, 48 of whom were previous *Cannabis* users, showed minimum physiological responses, but suffered impaired intellectual functioning and decreased body steadiness, especially well demonstrated by nonusers after high doses. Basic personality structures remained unchanged as subjects reported feelings of relaxation, disinhibition, and self-confidence. In that study, the drug was administered orally as an extract. No controls were described, and doses and quality of marihuana were unspecified.

Williams *et al.* in 1946 (7) studied a small number of prisoners who were chronic users; they were chiefly interested in effects of long-term smoking on psychological functioning. They found an initial exhilaration and euphoria which gave way after a few days of smoking to indifference and lassitude that somewhat impaired performance requiring concentration and manual dexterity. Again, no controls were provided.

Predictably, these studies, each deficient in design for obtaining reliable physiological and psychological data, contributed no dramatic or conclusive results. The 1967 President's Commission on Law Enforcement and the Administration of Justice described the present state of knowledge by concluding (3): ". . . no careful and detailed analysis of the American experience [with marihuana] seems to have been attempted. Basic research has been almost nonexistent. . . ." Since then, no other studies with marihuana itself have been reported, but in 1967 Isbell (8) administered synthetic THC to chronic users. At doses of $120 \mu g/kg$ orally or $50 \mu g/kg$ by smoking, subjects reported this drug to be similar to marihuana. At higher doses (300 to 400 $\mu g/kg$ orally or 200 to 250 $\mu g/kg$ by smoking), psychotomimetic effects occurred in most subjects. This synthetic has not yet been compared with marihuana in nonusers or given to any subjects along with marihuana in double-blind fashion.

Investigations outside the United States have been scientifically deficient, and for the most part have been limited to anecdotal and sociological approaches (9-12). So far as we know, our study is the first attempt to investigate marihuana in a formal double-blind experiment with the appropriate controls. It is also the first attempt to collect basic clinical and psychological information on the drug by observing its effects on marihuana-naive human subjects in a neutral laboratory setting.

RESEARCH PROBLEMS

That valid basic research on marihuana is almost nonexistent is not entirely accounted for by legislation which restricts even legitimate laboratory investigations or by public reaction sometimes verging on hysteria. A number of obstacles are intrinsic to the study of this drug. We now present a detailed description of our specific experimental approach, but must comment separately on six general problems confronting the investigator who contemplates marihuana research.

1. Concerning the route of administration, many pharmacologists dismiss the possibility of giving marihuana by smoking because, they say, the dose cannot be standardized (13). We consider it not only possible, but important to administer the drug to humans by smoking rather than by the oral route for the following reasons. (i) Smoking is the way nearly all Americans use marihuana. (ii) It is possible to have subjects smoke marihuana cigarettes in such a way that drug dosage is reasonably uniform for all subjects. (iii) Standardization of dose is not assured by giving the drug orally because little is known about gastrointestinal absorption of the highly water-insoluble cannabinols in man. (iv) There is considerable indirect evidence from users that the quality of the intoxication is different when marihuana or preparations of it are ingested rather than smoked. In particular, ingestion seems to cause more powerful effects, more "LSD-like" effects, longer-lasting effects, and more hangovers (12, 14). Further, marihuana smokers are accustomed to a very rapid onset of action due to efficient absorption through the lungs, whereas the latency for onset of effects may be 45 or 60 minutes after ingestion. (v) There is reported evidence from experiments with rats and mice that the pharmacological activities of natural hashish (not subjected to combustion) and hashish sublimate (the combustion products) are different (14).

2. Until quite recently, it was extremely difficult to estimate the relative potencies of different samples of marihuana by the techniques of analytical chemistry. For this study, we were able to have the marihuana samples assayed spectrophotometrically (15) for THC content. However, since THC has not been established as the sole determinant of marihuana's activity, we still feel it is important to have chronic users sample and rate marihuana used in research. Therefore, we assayed our material by this method as well.

3. One of the major deficiencies in previous studies has been the absence of negative control or placebo treatments, which we consider essential to the design of this kind of investigation. Because marihuana smoke has a distinctive odor and taste, it is difficult to find an effective placebo for use with chronic users. The problem is much less difficult with nonusers. Our solution to this dilemma was the use of portions of male hemp stalks (16), devoid of THC, in the placebo cigarettes.

4. In view of the primitive state of knowledge about marihuana, it is difficult to predict which psychological tests will be sensitive to the effects of the drug. The tests we chose were selected because, in addition to being likely to demonstrate effects, they have been used to evaluate many other psychoactive drugs. Of the various physiological parameters available, we chose to measure (i) heart rate, because previous studies have consistently reported increases in heart rate after administration of marihuana (for example, 5); (ii) respiratory rate, because it is an easily measured vital sign, and depression has been reported (11, 17); (iii) pupil size, because folklore on effects of marihuana consistently includes reports of pupillary dilatation, although objective experimental evidence of an effect of the drug on pupils has not been sought; (iv) conjunctival appearance, because both marihuana smokers and eaters are said to develop red eyes (11); and (v) blood sugar, because hypoglycemia has been invoked as a cause of the hunger and hyperphagia commonly reported by marihuana users, but animal and human evidence of this effect is contradictory (6, 10, 11). [The LaGuardia Report, quoted by Jaffe in Goodman and Gilman (18) described hyperglycemia as an effect of acute intoxication.] We did not measure blood pressure because previous studies have failed to demonstrate any consistent effect on blood pressure in man, and we were unwilling to subject our volunteers to a nonessential annoyance.

5. It is necessary to control set and setting. "Set" refers to the subject's psychological expectations of what a drug will do to him in relation to his general personality structure. The total environment in which the drug is taken is the setting.

All indications are that the form of marihuana intoxication is particularly dependent on the interaction of drug, set, and setting. Because of recent increases in the extent of use and in attention given this use by the mass media, it is difficult to find subjects with a neutral set toward marihuana. Our method of selecting subjects (described below), at the least, enables us to identify the subjects' attitudes. Unfortunately, too many researchers have succumbed to the temptation to have subjects take drugs in "psychedelic" environments or have influenced the response to the drug by asking questions that disturb the setting. Even a question as simple as, "How do you feel?" contains an element of suggestion that alters the drug-set-setting interaction. We took great pains to keep our laboratory setting neutral by strict adherence to an experimental timetable and to a prearranged set of conventions governing interactions between subjects and experimenters.

6. Medical, social, ethical, and legal concerns about the welfare of subjects are a major problem in a project of this kind. Is it ethical to introduce people to marihuana? When can subjects safely be sent home from the laboratory? What kind of follow-up care, if any, should be given? These are only a few specific questions with which the investigator must wrestle. Examples of some of the precautions we took are as follows. (i) All subjects were volunteers. All were given psychiatric screening interviews and were clearly informed that they might be asked to smoke marihuana. All nonusers tested were persons who had reported that they had been planning to try marihuana. (ii) All subjects were driven home by an experimenter; they agreed not to engage in unusual activity or operate machinery until the next morning and to report any unusual, delayed effects. (iii) All subjects agreed to report for follow-up interviews 6 months after the experiment. Among other things, the check at 6 months should answer the question whether participation in the experiment encouraged further drug use. (iv) All subjects were protected from possible legal repercussions of their participation in these experiments by specific agreements with the Federal Bureau of Narcotics, the Office of the Attorney General of Massachusetts, and the Massachusetts Bureau of Drug Abuse and Drug Control (*19*).

SUBJECTS

The central group of subjects consisted of nine healthy, male volunteers, 21 to 26 years of age, all of whom smoked tobacco cigarettes regularly but had never tried marihuana previously. Eight chronic users of marihuana also participated, both to "assay" the quality of marihuana received from the Federal Bureau of Narcotics and to enable the experimenters to standardize the protocol, using subjects familiar with their responses to the drug. The age range for users was also 21 to 26 years. They all smoked marihuana regularly, most of them every day or every other day.

The nine "naive" subjects were selected after a careful screening process. An initial pool of prospective subjects was obtained by placing advertisements in the student newspapers of a number of universities in the Boston area. These advertisements sought "male volunteers, at least 21 years old, for psychological experiments." After nonsmokers were eliminated from this pool, the remaining volunteers were interviewed individually by a psychiatrist who determined their histories of use of alcohol and other intoxicants as well as their general personality types. In addition to serving as a potential screening technique to eliminate volunteers with evidence of psychosis, or of serious mental or personality disorder, these interviews served as the basis for the psychiatrist's prediction of the type of response an individual subject might have after smoking marihuana. (It should be noted that no marihuana-naive volunteer had to be disqualified on psychiatric grounds.) Only after a prospective subject passed the interview was he informed that the "psychological experiment" for which he had volunteered was a marihuana study. If he consented to participate, he was asked to sign a release, informing him that he would be "expected to smoke cigarettes containing marihuana or an inert substance." He was also required to agree to a number of conditions, among them that he would "during the course of the experiment take no psychoactive drugs, including alcohol, other than those drugs administered in the course of the experiment."

It proved extremely difficult to find marihuana-naive persons in the student population of Boston, and nearly 2 months of interviewing were required to obtain nine men. All those interviewed who had already tried marihuana volunteered this information quite freely and were delighted to discuss their use of drugs with the psychiatrist. Nearly all persons encountered who had not tried marihuana admitted this somewhat apologetically. Several said they had been meaning to try the drug but had not got around to it. A few said they had no access to it. Only one person cited the current laws as his

reason for not having experimented with marihuana. It seemed clear in the interviews that many of these persons were actually afraid of how they might react to marihuana; they therefore welcomed a chance to smoke it under medical supervision. Only one person (an Indian exchange student) who passed the screening interview refused to participate after learning the nature of the experiment.

The eight heavy users of marihuana were obtained with much less difficulty. They were interviewed in the same manner as the other subjects and were instructed not to smoke any marihuana on the day of their appointment in the laboratory.

Subjects were questioned during screening interviews and at the conclusion of the experiments to determine their knowledge of marihuana effects. None of the nine naive subjects had ever watched anyone smoke marihuana or observed anyone high on marihuana. Most of them knew of the effects of the drug only through reports in the popular press. Two subjects had friends who used marihuana frequently; one of these (No. 4) announced his intention to "prove" in the experiments that marihuana really did not do anything; the other (No. 3) was extremely eager to get high because "everyone I know is always talking about it very positively."

SETTING

Greatest effort was made to create a neutral setting. That is, subjects were made comfortable and secure in a pleasant suite of laboratories and offices, but the experimental staff carefully avoided encouraging any person to have an enjoyable experience. Subjects were never asked how they felt, and no subject was permitted to discuss the experiment with the staff until he had completed all four sessions. Verbal interactions between staff and subjects were minimum and formal. At the end of each session, subjects were asked to complete a brief form asking whether they thought they had smoked marihuana that night; if so, whether a high dose or a low dose; and how confident they were of their answers. The experimenters completed similar forms on each subject.

MARIHUANA

Marihuana used in these experiments was of Mexican origin, supplied by the Federal Bureau of Narcotis (20). It consisted of finely chopped leaves of *Cannabis*, largely free of seeds and stems. An initial batch, which was judged to be of low potency by the experimenters on the basis of the doses needed to produce symptoms of intoxication in the chronic users, was subsequently found to contain only 0.3 percent of THC by weight. A second batch, assayed at 0.9 percent THC, was rated by the chronic users to be "good, average" marihuana, neither exceptionally strong nor exceptionally weak compared to their usual supplies. Users consistently reported symptoms of intoxication after smoking about 0.5 gram of the material with a variation of only a few puffs from subject to subject. This second batch of marihuana was used in the experiments described below; the low dose was 0.5 gram, and the high dose was 2.0 grams.

All marihuana was administered in the form of cigarettes of standard size made with a hand-oper-

ated rolling machine. In any given experimental session, each person was required to smoke two cigarettes in succession (Table 1).

Placebo material consisted of the chopped outer covering of mature stalks of male hemp plants; it contained no THC. All cigarettes had a tiny plug of tobacco at one end and a plug of paper at the other end so that the contents were not visible. The length to which each cigarette was to be smoked was indicated by an ink line. Marihuana and placebos were administered to the naive subjects in double-blind fashion. Scented aerosols were sprayed in the laboratory before smoking, to mask the odor of marihuana. The protocol during an experimental session was as follows. The sessions began at approximately 5.30 p.m.

TABLE 1.
Composition of the Dose. The Placebo Cigarette Consisted of Placebo Material, Tobacco Filler, and Mint Leaves for Masking Flavor. The Low Dose was Maee Up of Marihuana, Tobacco Filler, and Mint Leaves. The High Dose Consisted of Marihuana and Mint Leaves.

Dose	Marihuana in Each Cigarette (g)	Total Dose Marihuana (2 Cigarettes) (g)	Approximate Dose THC
Placebo	—	—	
Low	0.25	0.5	4.5 mg
High	1.0	2.0	18 mg

Time	Procedure
0:00	Physiological measurements; blood sample drawn
0:05	Psychological test battery No. 1 (base line)
0:35	Verbal sample No. 1
0:40	Cigarette smoking
1:00	Rest period
1:15	Physiological measurements; blood sample drawn
1:20	Psychological test battery No. 2
1:50	Verbal sample No. 2
1:55	Rest period (supper)
2:30	Physiological measurements
2:35	Psychological test battery No. 3
3:05	End of testing

EXPERIMENTAL SESSIONS

Chronic users were tested only on high doses of marihuana with no practice sessions. Each naive subject was required to come to four sessions, spaced about a week apart. The first was always a practice session, in which the subject learned the proper smoking technique and during which he became thoroughly acquainted with the tests and the protocol. In the practice session, each subject completed the entire protocol, smoking two hand-rolled tobacco cigarettes. He was instructed to take a long puff, to inhale deeply, and to maintain inspiration for 20 seconds, as timed by an experimenter with a stopwatch. Subjects were allowed 8 to 12 minutes to smoke each of the two cigarettes. One purpose of this practice smoking was to identify and eliminate individuals who were not tolerant to high doses of nicotine, thus reducing the effect of nicotine on the variables measured during subsequent drug sessions (21). A surprising number (five) of volunteers who had described themselves in screening interviews as heavy cigarette smokers, "inhaling" up to two packs of cigarettes a day, developed acute nicotine reactions when they smoked two tobacco cigarettes by the required method. Occurrence of such a reaction disqualified a subject from participation in the experiments.

In subsequent sessions, when cigarettes contained either drug or placebo, all smoking was similarly supervised by an experimenter with a stopwatch. Subjects were not permitted to smoke tobacco cigarettes while the experiment was in progress. They were assigned to one of the three treatment groups listed in Table 2.

TABLE 2. *Order of Treatment*

Group	Drug Session		
	1	2	3
I	High	Placebo	Low
II	Low	High	Placebo
III	Placebo	Low	High

PHYSIOLOGICAL AND PSYCHOLOGICAL MEASURES

The physiological parameters measured were heart rate, respiratory rate, pupil size, blood glucose level, and conjunctival vascular state. Pupil size was measured with a millimeter rule under constant illumination with eyes focused on an object at constant distance. Conjunctival appearance was rated by an experienced experimenter for dilation of blood vessels on a 0 to 4 scale with ratings of 3 and 4 indicating "significant" vasodilatation. Blood samples were collected for immediate determinations of serum glucose and for the serum to be frozen and stored for possible future biochemical studies. Subjects were asked not to eat and not to imbibe a beverage containing sugar or caffeine during the 4 hours preceding a session. They were given supper after the second blood sample was drawn.

The psychological test battery consisted of (i) the Continuous Performance Test (CPT)—5 minutes; (ii) the Digit Symbol Substitution Test (DSST) —90 seconds; (iii) CPT with strobe light distraction —5 minutes; (iv) self-rating bipolar mood scale—3 minutes; and (v) pursuit rotor—10 minutes.

The Continuous Performance Test was designed to measure a subject's capacity for sustained attention (22). The subject was placed in a darkened room and directed to watch a small screen upon which six letters of the alphabet were flashed rapidly and in random order. The subject was instructed to press a button whenever a specified critical letter appeared. The number of letters presented, correct responses, and errors of commission and omission were counted over the 5-minute period. The test was also done with a strobe light flickering at 50 cycles per second. Normal subjects make no or nearly no errors on this test either with or without strobe distraction; but sleep deprivation, organic brain disease, and certain drugs like chlorpromazine adversely affect performance. Presence or absence of previous exposure to the task has no effect on performance.

The Digit Symbol Substitution Test is a simple test of cognitive function (see Fig. 1). A subject's score was the number of correct answers in a 90-second period. As in the case of the CPT, practice should have little or no effect on performance.

The self-rating bipolar mood scale used in these

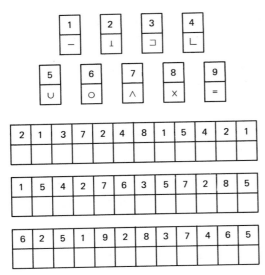

FIG. 1.

This is a sample of the Digit Symbol Substitution Test as used in these studies. On a signal from the examiner the subject was required to fill as many of the empty spaces as possible with the appropriate symbols. The code was always available to the subject during the 90-second administration of the test. [This figure appeared originally in Psychopharmacologia 5. 164 (1964).]

experiments was one developed by Smith and Beecher (23) to evaluate subjective effects of mor-

phine. By allowing subjects to rate themselves within a given category of moods, on an arbitrary scale from +3 to -3, it minimizes suggestion and is thus more neutral than the checklists often employed in drug testing.

The pursuit rotor measures muscular coordination and attention. The subject's task was to keep a stylus in contact with a small spot on a moving turntable. In these experiments, subjects were given ten 30-second trials in each battery. The score for each trial was total time in contact with the spot. There is a marked practice effect on this test, but naive subjects were brought to high levels of performance during their practice session, so that the changes due to practice were reduced during the actual drug sessions. In addition, since there was a different order of treatments for each of the three groups of naive subjects, any session-to-session practice effects were minimized in the statistical analysis of the pooled data.

At the end of the psychological test battery, a verbal sample was collected from each subject. The subject was left alone in a room with a tape recorder and instructions to describe "an interesting or dramatic experience" in his life until he was stopped. After exactly 5 minutes he was interrupted and asked how long he had been in the recording room. In this way, an estimate of the subject's ability to judge time was also obtained.

RESULTS

1. *Safety of marihuana in human volunteers.* In view of the apprehension expressed by many persons over the safety of administering marihuana to research subjects, we wish to emphasize that no adverse marihuana reactions occurred in any of our subjects. In fact, the five actute nicotine reactions mentioned earlier were far more spectacular than any effects produced by marihuana.

In these experiments, observable effects of mari-

huana were maximum at 15 minutes after smoking. They were diminished between 30 minutes and 1 hour, and they were largely dissipated 3 hours after the end of smoking. No delayed or persistent effects beyond 3 hours were observed or reported.

2. *Intoxicating properties of marihuana in a neutral setting.* With the high dose of marihuana (2.0 grams), all chronic users became "high" (24) by their own accounts and in the judgment of experimenters who had observed many per-

sons under the influence of marihuana. The effect was consistent even though prior to the session some of these subjects expressed anxiety about smoking marihuana and submitting to tests in a laboratory.

On the other hand, only one of the nine naive subjects (No. 3) had a definite "marihuana reaction" on the same high dose. He became markedly euphoric and laughed continuously during his first battery of tests after taking the drug. Interestingly, he was the one subject who had expressed his desire to get high.

3. *Comparison of naive and chronic user subjects.* Throughout the experiments it was apparent that the two groups of subjects reacted differently to identical doses of marihuana. We must caution, however, that our study was designed to allow rigorous statistical analysis of data from the naive group—it was not designed to permit formal comparison between chronic users and naive subjects. The conditions of the experiment were not the same for both groups: the chronic users were tested with the drug on their first visit to the laboratory with no practice and were informed that they were to receive high doses of marihuana. Therefore, differences between the chronic and naive groups reported below—although statistically valid—must be regarded as trends to be confirmed or rejected by additional experiments.

4. *Recognition of marihuana versus placebo.* All nine naive subjects reported that they had not been able to identify the taste or smell of marihuana in the experimental cigarettes. A few subjects remarked that they noticed differences in the taste of the three sets of cigarettes but could not interpret the differences. Most subjects found the pure marihuana cigarettes (high dose) more mild than the low dose or placebo cigarettes, both of which contained tobacco.

The subjects' guesses of the contents of cigarettes for their three sessions are presented in Table 3. It is noteworthy that one of the two subjects who called the high dose a placebo was the subject (No.

TABLE 3. *Subjects' Appraisal of the Dose*

Actual Dose	Guessed Dose			Fraction Correct
	Placebo	Low	High	
Placebo	8	1		8/9
Low	3	6		6/9
High	2	6	1	1/9

4) who had told us he wanted to prove that marihuana really did nothing. There were three outstanding findings: (i) most subjects receiving marihuana in either high or low dose recognized that they were getting a drug; (ii) most subjects receiving placebos recognized that they were receiving placebos; (iii) most subjects called their high dose a low dose, but none called his low dose a high dose, emphasizing the unimpressiveness of their subjective reactions.

5. *Effect of marihuana on heart rate.* The mean changes in heart rate from base-line rates before smoking the drug to rates at 15 and 90 minutes after smoking marihuana and placebo (Table 4) were tested for significance at the .05 level by an analysis of variance: Tukey's method was applied for all possible comparisons (Table 5). In the naive subjects, marihuana in low dose or high dose was followed by increased heart rate 15 minutes after smoking, but the effect was not demonstrated to be dose-dependent. The high dose caused a statistically greater increase in the heart rates of chronic users than in those of the naive subjects 15 minutes after smoking.

Two of the chronic users had unusually low resting pulse rates (56 and 42), but deletion of these two subjects (No. 11 and No. 15) still gave a significant difference in mean pulse rise of chronic users compared to naives. Because the conditions of the sessions and experimental design were not identical for the two groups, we prefer to report this difference as a trend that must be confirmed by further studies.

6. *Effect of marihuana on respiratory rate.* In the

TABLE 4. *Change in Heart Rate (Beat/Min) After Smoking the Best Material. Results are Recorded as a Change from the Base Line 15 Minutes and 90 Minutes After the Smoking Session*

Subject	15 Minutes			90 Minutes		
	Placebo	Low	High	Placebo	Low	High
			Naive Subjects			
1	+16	+20	+16	+20	- 6	- 4
2	+12	+24	+12	- 6	+ 4	- 8
3	+ 8	+ 8	+26	- 4	+ 4	+ 8
4	+20	+ 8			+20	- 4
5	+ 8	+ 4	- 8		+22	- 8
6	+10	+20	+28	- 20	- 4	- 4
7	+ 4	+28	+24	+12	+ 8	+18
8	- 8	+20	+24	- 3	+ 8	-24
9		+20	+24	+ 8	+12	
Mean	+7.8	+16.9	+16.2	+0.8	+7.6	-2.9
S.E.	2.8	2.7	4.2	3.8	3.2	3.8
			Chronic Subjects			
10		+32			+ 4	
11		+36			+36	
12		+20			+12	
13		+ 8			+ 4	
14		+32			+12	
15		+54			+22	
16		+24				
17		+60				
Mean		+33.2			+15.0	
S.E.		6.0			5.0	

naive group, there was no change in respiratory rate before and after smoking marihuana. Chronic users showed a small but statistically significant increase in respiratory rate after smoking, but we do not regard the change as clinically significant.

7. *Effect of marihuana on pupil size.* There was no change in pupil size before and after smo-

TABLE 5. *Significance of Differences (at the .05 Level) in Heart Rate. Results of Tukey's Test for All Possible Comparisons*

Comparison	15 Minutes	90 Minutes
Low dose versus placebo	Significant	Significant
High dose versus placebo	Significant	Not significant
Low dose versus high dose	Not significant	Significant
Chronic users versus high dose	Significant	Significant

TABLE 6. *Significance of Differences (at the .05 Level) for the Digit Symbol Substitution Test. Results of Tukey's Test for All Possible Comparisons*

Comparison	15 Minutes	90 Minutes
Low dose versus placebo	Significant	Significant
High dose versus placebo	Significant	Significant
Low dose versus high dose	Significant	Significant
Chronic users versus high dose	Significant	Not significant
	Significant	Significant

king marihuana in either group.

8. *Effect of marihuana on conjunctival appearance.* Significant reddening of conjunctivae due to dilatation of blood vessels occurred in one of nine subjects receiving placebo, three of nine receiving the low dose of marihuana, and eight of nine receiving the high dose. It occurred in all eight of the chronic users receiving the high dose and was rated as more prominent in them. The effect was more pronounced 15 minutes after the smoking period than 90 minutes after it.

9. *Effect of marihuana on blood sugar.* There was no significant change in blood sugar levels after smoking marihuana in either group.

10. *Effect of marihuana on the Continuous Performance Test.* Performance on the CPT and on the CPT with strobe distraction was unaffected by marihuana for both groups of subjects.

11. *Effect of marihuana on the Digit Symbol Substitution Test.* The significance of the differences in mean changes of scores at the .05 level was determined by an analysis of variance by means of Tukey's method for all possible comparisons. Results of these tests are summarized in Tables 6 and 7.

The results indicate that: (i) Decrements in performance of naive subjects following low and high doses of marihuana were significant at 15 and 90 minutes after smoking. (ii) The decrement following marihuana was greater after high dose than after low dose at 15 minutes after taking the drug, giving preliminary evidence of a dose-response relationship. (iii) Chronic users started with good base-line per-

formance and improved slightly on the DSST after smoking 2.0 grams of marihuana, whereas performance of the naive subjects was grossly impaired. Experience with the DSST suggests that absence of impairment in chronic users cannot be accounted for solely by a practice effect. Still, because of the different procedures employed, we prefer to report this difference as a trend.

12. *Effect of marihuana on pursuit rotor performance.* This result is presented in Table 8. Again applying Tukey's method in an analysis of variance, we tested differences in mean changes in scores (Table 9). Decrements in performance of naive subjects after both low and high doses of marihuana were significant at 15 and 90 minutes. This effect on performance followed a dose-response relation on testing batteries conducted at both 15 minutes and 90 minutes after the drug was smoked.

All chronic users started from good baselines and improved on the pursuit rotor after smoking marihuana. These data are not presented, however, because it is probable that the improvement was largely a practice effect.

13. *Effect of marihuana on time estimation.* Before smoking, all nine naive subjects estimated the 5-minute verbal sample to be 5 ± 2 minutes. After placebo, no subject changed his guess. After the low dose, three subjects raised their estimates to 10 ± 2 minutes, and after the high dose, four raised their estimates.

14. *Subjective effects of marihuana.* When ques-

TABLE 7. *Digit Symbol Substitution Test. Change in Scores from Base Line (Number Correct) 15 and 90 Minutes After the Smoking Session*

Subject	15 Minutes			90 Minutes		
	Placebo	Low	High	Placebo	Low	High
Naive Subjects						
1	- 3	—	+ 5	- 7	+ 4	+ 8
2	+10	-8	- 17	- 1	- 15	- 5
3	- 3	+6	- 7	-10	+ 2	- 1
4	+ 3	-4	- 3		- 7	
5	+ ·4	+1	- 7	+ 6		- 8
6	- 3	-1	- 9	+ 3	- 5	- 12
7	+ 2	-4	- 6	+ 3	- 5	- 4
8	- 1	+3	+ 1	+ 4	+ 4	- 3
9	- 1	-4	- 3	+ 6	- 1	- 10
Mean	+0.9	- 1.2	-5.1	+ 0.4	-2.6	- 3.9
S.E.	1.4	1.4	2.1	1.9	2.0	2.0
Chronic Users						
10			- 4			- 16
11			+ 1			+ 6
12			+11			+ 18
13			+ 3			+ 4
14			- 2			- 3
15			- 6			+ 8
16			- 4			
17			·+ 3			
Mean			+ 0.25			+ 2.8
S.E.			1.9			4.7

tioned at the end of their participation in the experiment, persons who had never taken marihuana previously reported minimum subjective effects after smoking the drug, or, more precisely, few effects like those commonly reported by chronic users. Nonusers reported little euphoria, no distortion of visual or auditory perception, and no confusion. However, several subjects mentioned that "things seemed to take longer." Below are examples of comments by naive subjects after high doses.

Subject 1: "It was stronger than the previous time (low dose) but I really didn't think it could be marihuana. Things seemed to go slower."

Subject 2: "I think I realize why they took our watches. There was a sense of the past disappearing as happens when you're driving too long without sleeping. With a start you wake up to realize you were asleep for an instant; you discover yourself driving along the road. It was the same tonight with eating a sandwich. I'd look down to discover I'd just swallowed a bite but I hadn't noticed it at the time."

Subject 6: "I felt a combination of being almost-drunk and tired, with occasional fits of silliness—

TABLE 8. *Pursuit Rotor (Naive Subjects). Changes in Scores (Averages of Ten Trials) from Base Line (Seconds)*

Subject	15 Minutes			90 Minutes		
	Placebo	Low	High	Placebo	Low	High
1	+1.20	-1.04	-4.01	+1.87	-1.54	-6.54
2	+0.89	-1.43	-0.12	+0.52	+0.44	-0.68
3	+0.50	-0.60	-6.56	+0.84	-0.96	-4.34
4	+0.18	-0.11	+0.11	+0.06	+1.95	-1.37
5	+3.20	+0.39	+0.13	+2.64	+3.33	+0.34
6	+3.45	-0.32	-3.46	+2.93	+0.22	-2.26
7	+0.81	+0.48	-0.79	+0.63	+0.16	-0.52
8	+1.75	-0.39	-0.92	+2.13	+0.40	+1.02
9	+3.90	-1.94	-2.60	+3.11	-0.97	-3.09
Mean	+1.18	-0.6	-2.0	+1.6	+0.3	-1.9
S.E.	0.5	0.3	0.8	0.4	0.5	0.8

not my normal reaction to smoking tobacco."

Subject 8: "I felt faint briefly, but the dizziness went away, and I felt normal or slightly tired. I can't believe I had a high dose of marihuana."

Subject 9: "Time seemed very drawn out. I would keep forgetting what I was doing, especially on the continuous performance test, but somehow every time an "X" (the critical letter) came up, I found myself pushing the button."

After smoking their high dose, chronic users were asked to rate themselves on a scale of 1 to 10, 10 representing "the highest you've ever been." All subjects placed themselves between 7 and 10, most at 8 or 9. Many of these subjects expressed anxiety at the start of their first battery of tests after smoking the drug when they were feeling very high. Then they expressed surprise during and after the tests when they judged (correctly) that their performance was as good as or better than it had been before taking the drug.

15. The effect of marihuana on the self-rating mood scale, the effect of marihuana on a 5-minute verbal sample, and the correlation of personality type with subjective effects of marihuana will be reported separately.

DISCUSSION

Several results from this study raise important questions about the action of marihuana and suggest directions for future research. Our finding that subjects who were naive to marihuana did not become subjectively "high" after a high dose of marihuana in a neutral setting is interesting when contrasted with the response of regular users who consistently reported and exhibited highs. It agrees with the reports of chronic users that many, if not most, people do not become high on their first exposure to marihuana even if they smoke it correctly. This puzzling phenomenon can be discussed from either a physiological or psychosocial point of view. Neither interpretation is entirely satisfactory. The physiological

TABLE 9. *Significance of Differences (at the .05 Level) for the Pursuit Rotor. Results of Tukey's Test for All Possible Comparisons, 15 and 90 Minutes After the Smoking Session*

	15 Minutes	90 Minutes
Low dose versus placebo	Significant	Significant
High dose versus placebo	Significant	Significant
Low dose versus high dose	Significant	Significant

hypothesis suggests that getting high on marihuana occurs only after some sort of pharmacological sensitization takes place. The psychosocial interpretation is that repeated exposure to marihuana reduces psychological inhibition, as part of, or as the result of a learning process.

Indirect evidence makes the psychological hypothesis attractive. Anxiety about drug use in this country is sufficiently great to make worthy of careful consideration the possibility of an unconscious psychological inhibition or block on the part of naive drug takers. The subjective responses of our subjects indicate that they had imagined a marihuana effect to be much more profoundly disorganizing than what they experienced. For example, subject No. 4, who started with a bias against the possibility of becoming high on marihuana, was able to control subjectively the effect of the drug and report that he had received a placebo when he had actually gotten a high dose. As anxiety about the drug is lessened with experience, the block may decrease, and the subject may permit himself to notice the drug's effects.

It is well known that marihuana users, in introducing friends to the drug, do actually "teach" them to notice subtle effects of the drug on consciousness (25). The apparently enormous influence of set and setting on the form of the marihuana response is consistent with this hypothesis, as is the testimony of users that, as use becomes more frequent, the amount of drug required to produce intoxication decreases—a unique example of "reverse tolerance." (Regular use of many intoxicants is accompanied by the need for increasing doses to achieve the same effects.)

On the other hand, the suggestion arising from this study that users and nonusers react differently to the drug, not only subjectively but also physiologically, increases the plausibility of the pharmacological-sensitization hypothesis. Of course, reverse tolerance could equally well be a manifestation of this sensitization.

It would be useful to confirm the suggested differences between users and nonusers and then to test in a systematic manner the hypothetical explanations of the phenomenon. One possible approach would be to continue to administer high doses of marihuana to the naive subjects according to the protocol described. If subjects begin reporting high responses to the drug only after several exposures, in the absence of psychedelic settings, suggestions, or manipulations of mood, then the likelihood that marihuana induces a true physiological sensitization or that experience reduces psychological inhibitions, permitting real drug effects to appear, would be increased. If subjects fail to become high, we could conclude that learning to respond to marihuana requires some sort of teaching or suggestion.

An investigation of the literature of countries where anxieties over drug use are less prominent would be useful. If this difference between responses of users and nonusers is a uniquely American phenomenon, a psychological explanation would be indicated, although it would not account for greater effects with smaller doses after the initial, anxiety-reducing stage.

One impetus for reporting the finding of differences between chronic and naive subjects on some of the tests, despite the fact that the experimental designs were not the same, is that this finding agrees with the statements of many users. They say that the effects of marihuana are easily suppressed—much more so than those of alcohol. Our observation, that the chronic users after smoking marihuana performed on some tests as well as or better than they did before taking the drug, reinforced the argument advanced by chronic users that maintaining effective levels of performance for many tasks—driving, for example (26)—is much easier under the influence of marihuana than under that of other psychoactive drugs. Certainly the surprise that the chronic users expressed when they found they were performing more effectively on the CPT, DSST, and pursuit rotor tests than they thought they would is remarkable. It is quite the opposite of the false sense of improvement subjects have under some psychoactive drugs that actually impair performance.

What might be the basis of this suppressibility? Possibly, the actions of marihuana are confined to higher cortical functions without any general stimulatory or depressive effect on lower brain centers. The relative absence of neurological—as opposed to psychiatric—symptoms in marihuana intoxication suggests this possibility (7).

Our failure to detect any changes in blood sugar levels of subjects after they had smoked marihuana forces us to look elsewhere for an explanation of the hunger and hyperphagia commonly reported by users. A first step would be careful interviewing of users to determine whether they really become hungry after smoking marihuana or whether they simply find eating more pleasurable. Possibly, the basis of this effect is also central rather than due to some peripheral physiological change.

Lack of any change in pupil size of subjects after they had smoked marihuana is an enlightening finding especially because so many users and law-enforcement agents firmly believe that marihuana dilates pupils. (Since users generally observe each other in dim surroundings, it is not surprising that they see large pupils.) This negative finding emphasizes the need for data from carefully controlled investigations rather than from casual observation or anecdotal reports in the evaluation of marihuana. It also agrees with the findings of others that synthetic THC does not alter pupil size (8, 27).

Finally, we would like to comment on the fact that marihuana appears to be a relatively mild intoxicant in our studies. If these results seem to differ from those of earlier experiments, it must be remembered that other experimenters have given marihuana orally, have given doses much higher than those commonly smoked by users, have administered potent synthetics, and have not strictly controlled the laboratory setting. As noted in our introduction, more powerful effects are often reported by users who ingest preparations of marihuana. This may mean that some active constituents which enter the body when the drug is ingested are destroyed by combustion, a suggestion that must be investigated in man. Another priority consideration is the extent to which synthetic THC reproduces marihuana intoxication—a problem that must be resolved before marihuana research proceeds with THC instead of the natural resin of the whole plant.

The set, both of subjects and experimenters, and the setting must be recognized as critical variables in studies of marihuana. Drug, set, and setting interact to shape the form of a marihuana reaction. The researcher who sets out with prior conviction that hemp is psychotomimetic or a "mild hallucinogen" is likely to confirm his conviction experimentally (10), but he would probably confirm the opposite hypothesis if his bias were in the opposite direction. Precautions to insure neutrality of set and setting, including use of a double-blind procedure as an absolute minimum, are vitally important if the object of investigation is to measure real marihuana-induced responses.

CONCLUSIONS

1. It is feasible and safe to study the effects of marihuana on human volunteers who smoke it in a laboratory.

2. In a neutral setting persons who are naive to

marihuana do not have strong subjective experiences after smoking low or high doses of the drug, and the effects they do report are not the same as those described by regular users of marihuana who take the drug in the same neutral setting

3. Marihuana-naive persons do demonstrate impaired performance on simple intellectual and psychomotor tests after smoking marihuana; the impairment is dose-related in some cases.

4. Regular users of marihuana do get high after smoking marihuana in a neutral setting but do not show the same degree of impairment of performance on the tests as do naive subjects. In some cases, their performance even appears to improve slightly after smoking marihuana.

5. Marihuana increases heart rate moderately.

6. No change in respiratory rate follows administration of marihuana by inhalation.

7. No change in pupil size occurs in short term exposure to marihuana.

8. Marihuana administration causes dilatation of conjunctival blood vessels.

9. Marihuana treatment produces no change in blood sugar levels.

10. In a neutral setting the physiological and psychological effects of a single, inhaled dose of marihuana appear to reach maximum intensity within one-half hour of inhalation, to be diminished after 1 hour, and to be completely dissipated by 3 hours.

REFERENCES AND NOTES

1. R. J. Bouquet, *Bull. Narcotics 2*, 14 (1950).
2. F. Korte and H. Sieper, in *Hashish: Its Chemistry and Pharmacology*, G. E. W. Wolstenholme and J. Knight, Eds. (Little, Brown, Boston, 1965), pp. 15-30.
3. Task Force on Narcotics and Drug Abuse, the President's Commission on Law Enforcement and the Administration of Justice, *Task Force Report: Narcotics and Drug Abuse* (1967), p. 14.
4. R. Mechoulam, and Y. Gaoni, *J. Amer. Chem. Soc. 67*, 3273 (1965).
5. J. F. Siler, W. L. Sheep, L. B. Bates, G. F. Clark, G. W. Cook, W. A. Smith, *Mil. Surg.* (November 1933), pp. 269-280.
6. Mayor's Committee on Marihuana, *The Marihuana Problem in the City of New York*, 1944.
7. E. G. Williams, C. K. Himmelsbach, A. Winkler, D. C. Ruble, B. J. Lloyd, *Public Health Rep. 61*, 1059 (1946).
8. H. Isbell, *Psychopharmacologia 11*, 184 (1967).
9. I. C. Chopra and R. N. Chopra, *Bull. Narcotics 9*, 4 (1957).
10. F. Ames, *J. Ment. Sci. 104*, 972 (1958).
11. C. J. Miras, in *Hashish: Its Chemistry and Pharmacology*, G. E. W. Wolstenholme and J. Knight, Eds. (Little, Brown, Boston, 1965), pp. 37-47.
12. J. M. Watt, in *Hashish: Its Chemistry and Pharmacology*, G. E. W. Wolstenholme and J. Knight, Eds. (Little, Brown, Boston, 1965), pp. 54-66.
13. AMA Council on Mental Health, *J. Amer. Med. Ass. 204*, 1181 (1968).
14. G. Joachimogly, in *Hashish: Its Chemistry and Pharmacology*, G. E. W.

Wolstenholme and J. Knight, Eds. (Little, Brown, Boston, 1965), pp. 2-10.

15. We thank M. Lerner and A. Bober of the U.S. Customs Laboratory, Baltimore, for performing this assay.

16. We thank R. H. Pace and E. H. Hall of the Peter J. Schweitzer Division of the Kimberly-Clark Corp. for supplying placebo material.

17. S. Garattini, in *Hashish: Its Chemistry and Pharmacology*, G. E. W. Wolstenholme and J. Knight, Eds. (Little, Brown, Boston, 1965), pp. 70-78.

18. J. H. Jaffee, in *The Pharmacological Basis of Therapeutics*, L. S. Goodman and A. Gilman, Eds. (Macmillan, New York, ed. 3, 1965), pp. 299-301.

19. We thank E. L. Richardson, Attorney General of the Commonwealth of Massachusetts for permitting these experiments to proceed and N. L. Chayet for legal assistance. We do not consider it appropriate to describe here the opposition we encountered from governmental agents and agencies and from university bureaucracies.

20. We thank D. Miller and M. Seifer of the Federal Bureau of Narcotics (now part of the Bureau of Narcotics and Dangerous Drugs, under the Department of Justice) for help in obtaining marihuana for this research.

21. The doses of tobacco in placebo and low-dose cigarettes were too small to cause physiological changes in subjects who qualified in the practice session.

22. K. E. Rosvold, A. F. Mirsky, I. Sarason, E. D. Bransome, L. H. Beck, *J. Consult. Psychol. 20*, 343 (1956); A. F. Mirsky and P. V. Cardon, *Electroencephalogr. Clin. Neurophysiol. 14*, 1 (1962); C. Kornetsky and G. Bain, *Psychopharmacologia 8*, 277 (1965).

23. G. M. Smith and H. K. Beecher, *J. Pharmacol. 126*, 50 (1959).

24. We will attempt to define the complex nature of a marihuana high in a subsequent paper discussing the speech samples and interviews.

25. H. S. Becker, *Outsiders: Studies in the Sociology of Deviance* (Macmillan, New York, 1963), chap. 3.

26. Although the motor skills measured by the pursuit rotor are represented in driving ability, they are only components of that ability. The influence of marihuana on driving skill remains an open question of high medico-legal priority.

27. L. E. Hollister, R. K. Richards, H. K. Gillespie, in preparation.

28. Sponsored and supported by Boston University's division of psychiatry, in part through PHS grants MH12568, MH06795-06, MH7753-06, and MH33319, and the Boston University Medical Center. The authors thank Dr. P. H. Knapp and Dr. C. Kornetsky of the Boston University School of Medicine, Department of Psychiatry and Pharmacology, for consistent support and excellent advice, and J. Finkelstein of 650 Madison Avenue, New York City, for his support at a crucial time.

15. *The Journey Beyond "Trips"*

ALLAN Y. COHEN

During three years at Harvard, I was firmly committed to LSD as a way of enhancing my life. I was deeply taken with the notion that psychedelic chemicals could lead me closer to God, to enlightenment. In 1965, after thirty "trips," I ceased using these materials and now unequivocally advise persons *not* to use LSD.

The claim is still made that a drug experience, particularly an experience with the powerful hallucinogenic or psychedelic drugs, can give one a taste of true Reality, a glimpse of God. . . . Let us examine that claim.

This is a critical time. It is a strange era in which the solidity of values seems to have disappeared especially among young people. They often confront a vacuum in purpose and raise such questions as "Who am I?" and "What is the meaning of life?" Because these are spiritual questions, and there has been a remarkable increase in serious interest about God, consciousness and the quest for enlightenment, it is not surprising that the psychedelic claims (not only for LSD, but for marijuana, hashish, STP and many new exotic drugs) fall on very receptive ears. It is a seductive cry, since the psychedelic proponents argue: "Well, so what if it causes a little physiological damage?" or "So what if some people go psychotic? Isn't it worth it? Isn't the risk worth the possibility of real awakening, true enlightenment—and in only a few hours!" After all, Western technology has bombarded us with the notion that internal states of dissatisfaction are easily changed by modern chemistry. We have pills and remedies for everything. Materialistic thinking has led us to believe that all our internal perplexities are modified by the external environment, not by what lies within.

THE FACTS

Before delving more deeply into the spiritual question, let us review the current state of scientific knowledge. There was never any question that LSD is incredibly powerful, but at one time it was thought physically harmless and non-habituating. But there is deep disagreement about that now. Even leaving aside the questions of possible physical damage, the psychological effects of psychedelics now appear

Allan Y. Cohen, The journey beyond "trips", Reprinted from *The A.R.E. Journal III*(4), Copyright © The Association for Research and Enlightenment, Inc., 1968.

extraordinarily varied. There is no question that a single dose of LSD can put one in a mental hospital for a long time. However, many people have pleasurable reactions in which they experience great sensuousness or apparent profundity. There are "neutral" trips and "bad" trips. The bad ones can create incomparable terror and mental anguish. The chronic tripster "turns on" and finally "freaks out," coming back a fragmented person. Most of these people eventually recover; some don't. A friend of mine took LSD four years ago under "perfect"

conditions and with "perfect preparation," but even today, after two murder attempts and a long stay in a mental hospital with extreme depression, he remains crippled by severe anxiety.

Actually, many of the "psychotic" symptoms produced by the various mind-altering drugs may reflect disruption of psychic centers (chakras) and mechanisms which link the physical body with the astral or more subtle sphere of consciousness, but such consequences are usually beyond the comprehension of most users.

WHAT HAPPENS UNDER PSYCHEDELICS?

I'd like to help you understand how people can believe in the spiritual qualities of LSD, no matter how intelligent or sensible they are. For those of you not personally acquainted with the psychedelic experience, I ask you to enter with me into the following fantasy: I ask you to pretend that you have been raised on a tropical island. You have had all the educational facilities we have here and possess all of our cultural sophistication with the one exception that you have *never* been exposed to the electronic media. Imagine that you have never heard of radio, television, or motion pictures and have no concept of similar phenomena. You migrate to the United States and locate in a large city. You get a job and begin to form an idea that the ordinary world isn't quite as it should be. There seems to be hypocrisy evident, much spiritual ignorance, bad feeling among people, and you are personally confused about your own life. A friend comes to you and says, "Hey, man, have you turned on to SCA?" You ask what it is. He says, "I can't describe it—it's beyond words. You've gotta experience it!" He praises its ability to produce spiritual experience, and though you remember some physicians contending that it is bad for your health, you feel you have nothing much to lose and ask your friend to "guide" you on an SCA trip.

He takes you downtown; you walk to a strange building and give a young lady two and a half dollars

for a "ticket cube," then walk through a doorway into a huge dark room. Your friend is with you. There are many people milling around, apparently relaxed. You are a bit nervous. They tell you to sit down in a chair and soft music is played; astoundingly, it seems to come from nowhere. You sit for fifteen minutes and nothing happens. Bravely, you taunt your friend: "SCA, big deal!" He replies, "Man, wait—just wait till it comes on." Suddenly the curtain opens and you are struck by a fantastic display of lights and colors and images and stereophonic sound—it seems to be coming up from all around you! Initially frightened, indeed terrified, you are saved (this time) by your friend, who takes your hand and says, "O.K., man, just cool it—relax, let it happen." So you manage to relax, and experience these amazing sensory perceptions in unbelievable vividness. You've never seen anything like this. You are simply stunned.

Gradually you get used to the sensory explosion and begin to identify with the characters. Suddenly, as they say in the psychedelic literature, you "lose your ego." You are no longer sitting in that seat. You are projected into the story, no longer conscious of your body or ordinary identity. Like most LSD users, you get totally emotionally involved in the film. The movie is a fantastic romance-adventure with a spiritual theme. The story builds up to an incredible climax; you, as the hero, win the battles and gain the love of everyone. . . . The curtain closes with you standing on top of the Alps, Handel's *Messiah* ringing in the moment of spiritual triumph.

You sit back, ecstatic, abruptly realizing that you're back in the seat—drained, exhausted, and emotionally awestruck. Your friend smiles knowingly; he's an old SCA tripster. You stumble out to the street and see funny little people with briefcases rushing along, cars honking in the nonsensical battle to get from nowhere to nowhere. You conclude that what you see just can't be reality. You think: In there, I saw visions I've never seen before, felt emotion a hundred times as powerfully, and even had a glimpse of a whole new spiritual awakening! You come to the conclusion that SCA has shown you Reality. That's where God is, inside that Magic Theater! Of course, you tell your friends the news, extolling the wonderments of the SCA experience and belittling objections to its validity. Finally, when it goes to the extreme, you quit your job—in order to catch the matinee every day.

LSD AND SPIRITUALITY

Initially, the spiritual status of chemically induced "mystical experience" is difficult to assess. It cannot be measured by electronic machines and few have the authority to make a value judgment on another's subjective consciousness. Yet two criteria stand firm: effect on ordinary life and the perspective of those enlightened souls who *know*. As for the first, in my own experience I found great psychedelic hypocrisy in myself and friends. We talked love, compassion, brotherhood, and thought of ourselves as highly developed. With open eyes the evidence was to the contrary—LSD produced neither saints nor even an increase in spiritual behavior. How many times did I hear of incidents like the one where a "beautiful, mystical, love-filled" LSD trip was immediately followed by serious fights over who was to do the dishes that morning! It has now been long enough so that we would know if psychedelics *were* the magic spiritual key. *If* LSD worked, it would have produced immensely successful human beings and subcultures. Even the diehard "acid-heads" and "potheads" must admit the failure of this utopian expectation. . . .

Now let us turn to the second facet of the debate. The early and sincere psychedelic users became aware that the esoteric teachings of all spiritual systems emphasized development of consciousness of the God Force within and that history has catalogued many techniques and approaches toward unlocking that latent Divinity. We also became aware of outstanding spiritual Oneness and Love. In the youth subculture generally, there was an upsurge in respect for the "Eastern" mystical tradition.

The result has been an increasing awareness of the possible validity of statements of "holy men," although the number of spiritual pretenders lends confusion to identification. To the serious student of spirituality, however, there are certain historical figures whose mystical Enlightenment is beyond question; e.g., Zoroaster, Rama, Krishna, Gautama the Buddha, Jesus the Christ, and Mohammed the Prophet. The spiritual status of such Divine Manifestations is referred to as Avatar, Christ, Rasool, Saviour, Messiah, or Ancient One, denoting the cyclical appearance of God in human form. (I do not mean to overlook our other favorite spiritual personalities; names such as Moses, Hafiz, Saint Francis, Sri Ramakrishna, etc., are also associated with great, if not matchless, spiritual heights.) Yet none of these had talked about LSD and psychedelic drugs.

Thus it has been left to contemporary spiritual figures to destroy the psychedelic myth. In 1965, a twenty-two-year-old friend of mine from New England set off for Asia. Although he had graduated from college and was sincerely interested in spiritual matters, he used drugs constantly and his "vision" included spending the rest of his life wandering through Nepal, feasting on inexpensive local hashish. He carried three books with him, one of which was *God Speaks* by Meher Baba, the "God-man" of India. He was very taken with this book, and once in India was able to see Baba personally. Their communication included some very provocative statements from Baba on psychedelic drugs.

The proliferation of these and later statements shocked people in the LSD movement, since many of the major figures in the spiritual psychedelic underground considered Baba the world's leading authority on consciousness. Baba pointed out that chemically induced experience is more often a roadblock rather than a spur to spiritual advancement. In the booklet *God in a Pill*, he wrote, "The experience of a semblance of freedom that these drugs (including marijuana) may temporarily give to one is in actuality a millstone round the aspirant's neck in his efforts toward emancipation from the rounds of birth and death." In a letter to one of the psychedelic leaders he explained, "Although LSD is not an addiction-forming drug, one can become attached to the experiences arising from its use, and one gets tempted to use it in increasing doses, again and again, in the hope of deeper and deeper experiences. . . ." Calling psychedelic effects a form of "perverted consciousness," Baba likened the spiritual drug trip to a mirage and reflected that "No matter how much one pursues the mirage, one will never reach water; and the search for God through drugs must end in disillusionment." He went on: "An individual may feel LSD has made a 'better' man of him socially and personally. But one will be a better man through Love than once can ever be through drugs or any other artificial aid."

Baba's views and the general thrust of his declarations have been reflected by scores of other respected contemporary spiritual figures from Yogis to Christian mystics, all of whom firmly propound that drugs are a blind alley for spiritual development. As I have personally involved myself in the approach espoused by Meher Baba, some principal differences between the chemical and authentic spiritual techniques have become clear. First, the LSD path *denies* internal worth. Using drugs creates an underlying feeling that inner happiness must somehow be enhanced from the outside. In contrast, authentic spirituality stresses the omnipresence of God Within and defines the spiritual task as uncovering that essence. The drug approach emphasizes separateness and exclusiveness—it is "We, the hip people" versus the "straight, unaware world." Yet true mysticism implies oneness and tolerance for every being. The drug orientation is passive and often leads to disengagement from active life in society. One supposedly gets results by swallowing the pill, the sum total of effort necessary. But in Reality, you don't get something for nothing. The genuine Path entails real effort, and earned progress can be retained as one's *own*. Psychedelic experience is inevitably temporary; genuine mystical experience is lasting in its impact.

Chemical insights are often irrelevant to ordinary life; traditional spiritual approaches generally stress the conversion of spiritual knowledge into spiritual *action in society*. LSD can result in apparent feelings of love, but the authentic attainment is Love *itself*. The drug orientation provides insurance of eventual dependence on the desires of the lower self; the true mystic learns to trust and surrender to a Master who is identical with his own God-self.

Some drug users say life is a game. That may be so, but to "win" the game, one must have a clear understanding of its goal. A passage from Meher Baba's *Discourses* may help to reevaluate what it is all about:

To penetrate into the essence of all being and significance and to release the fragrance of that inner attainment for the guidance and benefit of others, by expressing, in the world of forms, truth, love, purity and beauty—this is the sole game which has any intrinsic and absolute worth. All other happenings, incidents and attainments can, in themselves, have no lasting importance.

16. *The Lesbian —Myth and Reality*
DEL MARTIN & PHYLLIS LYON

So little is known about the Lesbian that even Lesbians themselves are caught up in the myths and stereotypes so prevalent in our society.

When we first started living together as a couple we knew practically nothing about female homosexuality. We only knew that we loved each other and wanted to be together. Somehow that tagged us as Lesbians and bound us to some mysterious underground "gay" society of which we were only barely aware. That was back in the days when the term "gay" was an in-group password, a means of double talk in a hostile "straight" (heterosexual) society. It was a word you could use to let someone else know you were homosexual without the fear that anyone overhearing it would understand— unless, of course, they were in the know. With increased attention of the media to the subjects of homosexuality and Gay Liberation, the term is now popular in its usage.

Del had read a few books—that's all there were in earlier days. She had been to a number of gay bars, which was always a twitchy experience, since police raids were commonplace then. She had met a few Lesbians and had one previous affair.

Phyllis had been vaguely aware of homosexuality, but, like so many other women, never heard or thought of it in terms of the female, only in terms of the male. That the reason she and her roommate had been thrown out of their college dorm was undoubtedly due to implied homosexuality never occurred to her until years later. The dean of women and the housemother had charged that Phyllis and Jane were "too close," that they engaged in double talk at the dinner table, that they did not mix socially with the other girls in the dormitory, and that they had missed "lock out" a couple of times.

Although she liked men, dated them and even once went so far as to become engaged, Phyllis still had reservations about taking that final step down the aisle. She sought a career in journalism and enjoyed her independence. She had always maintained a number of close friendships with women and recalls feeling very resentful when one of them would call up and cancel a prior engagement to go to the movies with her, just because some man had asked for a date.

That's about where we were. Hardly the ideal background from which to launch a Lesbian "marriage," which is the way we thought of our relationship. The only model we knew, a pattern that also seemed to hold true for those few Lesbians we had met, was that of mom-and-dad or heterosexual marriage. So Del assumed the role of "butch" (she was working at the time) and Phyllis, being completely brainwashed in society's role of woman anyway, decided she must be the "femme." Like her mother before her, she got up every morning to make breakfast—at least for the first week.

The closest friends we had at the time were a newly married heterosexual couple. They, too, assumed that Lesbians would adopt butch-femme roles. Sam happily encouraged Del to be a male chauvinist, slapping her, on the back and plying her with cigars, all the while telling her she had to keep Phyllis in her place and coaching her on maintaining the upper hand. Meanwhile Sue and Phyllis plotted the traditionally sneaky ways women devise to gain and maintain the upper hand. If this sounds like an arm-wrestling match, it was. Like so many heterosexual couples, we played the roles in public, and with Sue and Sam, and then we went home and fought about them. The only thing that saved our relationship was Phyllis's stubborn resolve that it would last at least a year. The fact we had known each other for more than three years and had established a basic friendship was the other thing we had going for us.

In the course of our nineteen years together we have learned that many Lesbians in our age group (late forties) went through the same kind of role playing. While a few become trapped in this butch-femme pattern, most come in time, as we did, to the realization that they are both women and that's why they are together.

Because the Lesbian is every woman. She is the college student preparing for a career that will make her economically independent and give her some measure of personal accomplishment. She is the dedicated nurse or the committed social worker. She works on the assembly line of an electronics plant, drives a taxicab, or goes to night school. The Lesbian is an attorney, an architect, or an engineer. She is the blind poet and songwriter. She serves on municipal commissions, is the author of a best seller, and is honored among the "Ten Most Distinguished Women of the Year." She is a welfare recipient, an auto mechanic, a veterinarian, an alcoholic, a telephone operator, a civil service or civil rights worker. She may be a lieutenant in the armed forces or a beauty operator. And, being a woman in western society, she is certainly a clerk-typist, secretary or bookkeeper.

The Lesbian is aboard ship traveling around the world. She resides in every country. She lives in an apartment or is paying for her own home in the city, in the suburbs, or in a small country town. She is raising goats on a farm in the Ozarks or is part of a harem in Saudi Arabia. She is in attendance at state social gatherings in the White House. She lives in the Orient, Australia, Germany. She is a Democrat in the United States or a Socialist in Italy. She is the cloistered young Catholic woman in Latin America or lives in a *kibbutz* in Israel. She is a geisha girl in Japan or a belly dancer in a night club in New York City. Or she may be the Jane Doe suicide in the city morgue.

However women are depicted in world society, so may the Lesbian be. For the Lesbian is *all* women. As you who read this have related to women personally and generally in your life, so have you become personally involved with Lesbians, whether you have been aware of it or not. For you have known, met and talked with Lesbians throughout your life—in your family, at school, on the job, at the corner cocktail lounge, at the neighborhood bowling alley, at your church. You may have known and loved a Lesbian dearly or been wary of her, sensing that, despite all appearances to the contrary, she is somehow different.

Most of you can probably recall a distant cousin or a maiden aunt about whom the family whispered vaguely. But few of you wish to admit that the Lesbian in your life was really much closer to home. For we are also your daughters, your sisters, even sometimes your mothers. The Lesbian comes from all walks of society, every economic class, every educational level, every racial and ethnic group, every religious background. She is in every type of work, of every political persuasion, and in every part of the world. The Lesbian is:

—*The divorced mother, Inez, who places her child in a day care center while she commutes to her office job in the city. barely eking out a living despite the child support minimally and grudgingly paid by her ex-husband on order of the court. Underlying her daily routine is the constant fear that she will be discovered to be a Lesbian and lose not only her job, but her child as well.*

—*A teacher in specialized education working with*

the deaf, for whose services several school districts have been competing. Yet in spite of her known expertise and talent as a teacher, should it become known that she is a Lesbian, Olga would be unemployable.

—Natalie, a likeable, adequate, very average worker in a plastics factory making wastebaskets, fired when it was made known that she was a Lesbian.

—Betty, caught up in a raid on a gay bar some years ago, who lost her job as a civil service playground director even though the charges against her were dismissed. She spent more than ten years in meaningless jobs before she once again was accepted in the civil service in an area where her education and talents could be put to use.

—A Black teenager, Bea, three months away from high school graduation, who was literally thrown out of her home when she told her mother she was gay.

—The successful business woman and socialite, Constance, active in civic affairs, who is seldom seen with her "roommate" of ten years lest the finger be pointed at her, thus destroying her "image."

These are typical of the many Lesbians we have met over the years. We mention them to show how the preference for a member of her own sex as a love or life partner—which is all that sets the Lesbian apart from any other woman—can affect her entire life and inhibit or kill dreams, ambitions, creativity. Being a Lesbian makes her a misfit in American culture and sets up a barrier which prevents her from revealing herself to you. For her own protection, learned through painful experience, the Lesbian generally maintains a dual life—one that is visible and one that is kept secret. Understandably, this can lead to emotional conflicts, and time and energy wasted on weaving a web of lies. It can lead to a loss of self and potential in the process of face-saving conformity.

Understandably, too, since the Lesbian in our society is generally hidden, her existence has generated a great deal of conjecture and intrigue, out of which a whole body of folklore has been perpetrated on the public as fact.

Once aware of the Lesbian's existence, most people tend to view her solely as a sexual being. She is seen as a sad caricature of a male, trying to dress and act in the manner she deems "masculine," and generally aping some of men's worst characteristics. Or she is conceived of as a hard sophisticated female who indiscriminately seduces innocent girls or women into the mysteries of some "perversion" they know little or nothing about. On the other hand, she is seen as an unfortunate, pitiable spinster, who, unable to catch a man, has settled for a less desirable substitute in another woman as her lover— whom, of course, she will immediately abandon when and if she meets "him." Some men fantasize the Lesbian as a voluptuous, sensuous mistress who is unscrupulous in her sexual tastes, insatiable in her sexual appetite and therefore indiscriminate in her choice of sexual partner.

These stereotypes are based upon the false assumption that the Lesbian is first and foremost *sexual* in all her thoughts, desires and actions. What people fail to realize is that being a Lesbian is not merely indulging in physical acts or lovemaking. For the woman involved it is a way of life, encompassing the structure of her whole personality, one facet of which is, of course, her sexuality. For her it is the expression of a way of feeling, of loving, of responding to other people.

Furthermore, Lesbians are no more preoccupied with sex than are other people. We don't spend all our time in bed—and neither does anyone else we know. We, too, go to work, clean house, do the shopping, watch television, go to the movies, work on hobbies, have guests in for dinner, visit friends, and do all the other ordinary humdrum things which make up life in America today.

Also contrary to popular belief, most Lesbians seek relationships with those in their own age bracket. They do not put a premium on youth, as do many male homosexuals, but prefer partners with whom they have something in common besides sex. They look for companionship, community of interests, and all those other ingredients necessary to make any relationship work over a period of time.

Yet one of the myths that seems to hang on in our society is that Lesbians molest little girls and seduce young women. In actuality, childhood homosexual experiences are usually episodes of experimentation between little girls of the same age. Del recalls engaging in such experimentation at the age of nine with a girl who may have been a year younger and who, incidentally, was the initiator. But the incident bore no particular significance for Del at the time, since most of the youngsters, male and female, were in the habit of "playing doctor" and examining each other's bodies and genitals. Instances of an adult woman molesting a small child are so rare that we have not run into even a single case.

We have known Lesbians who "came out" when they were teenagers, but their partners were schoolmates or youngsters in their peer group. We have also known eighteen- and nineteen-year olds who became involved with "older women" of twenty-two or so, above the legal age for marriage between members of the opposite sexes. But by and large, most older Lesbians, while appreciative of youthful good looks, are seeking someone more sophisticated and experienced. As forty-year-old Carmen put it, when she came to us hoping we might be able to introduce her to some older Lesbians' "What on earth would I do with a twenty-year-old? I'm not looking for a daughter to raise!"

A 1959 survey by the Daughters of Bilitis indicated a very high ratio of Lesbians in the teaching profession. In writing up the research, however, these women were lumped in with the "professional" classification which comprised 38 percent of the sampling. This particular point of information we purposely withheld at the time lest a witch hunt be initiated in the California school system. Discovery or even the mere accusation of a teacher's homosexual orientation was cause for immediate dismissal or request for one's resignation, along with revocation of one's teaching credential, until 1969. It was then that the California State Supreme Court ruled that teachers may not have their teaching credential taken away simply because they have engaged in homosexual acts not specifically spelled out in the criminal statutes.

Despite the large number of Lesbians who are teachers, there is no data available, other than in fiction, that they have seduced or become sexually intimate with their female students. Yet the myth persists. It has always mystified us that the public

remains so fearful of Lesbian teachers when criminal statistics clearly indicate that young girls who are seduced or raped are invariably victimized by men. While men are increasingly taking over the elementary classroom, there is still only concern lest they be homosexuals. We can only suppose that parents and school administrators are concerned solely with preventing the possibility of a homosexual encounter—like those police officers from Northern Station in San Francisco during a 1970 police-community relations confrontation with members of the homophile community:

"Think what a traumatic effect it would have on a young boy!" the police lieutenant cried out.

"But what about the girls? What about rape?" a young Lesbian countered.

"That's different. That's 'normal'," two patrolmen replied in unison.

Before we lay the bugaboo of homosexual child-molesting to rest, we must note that women, having found each other in the women's liberation movement, are beginning to knock down this myth themselves. In New York City during their regular Saturday Women's Liberation meetings in 1970, the women asked the men to take on the responsibility for child care. The most reliable and dependable group of men to report regularly each week for such duty was from the Gay Liberation Front. Through a pact of mutual respect and trust, women learned to leave their young sons in the care of homosexual men without compunction, without hesitation. Some were even considering adding "*gay* care centers" to their demands.

Women have always been carefully warned to shun the Lesbian; after all, the sanctity of home and family must be protected. Men, on the other hand, become increasingly fascinated by the unattainable, independent woman who is not an adjunct or appendage to a man, who does not seek nor require his approval for her existence, who even dares to compete with him not only in the job market but for "his" women as well. The predatory male heterosexual can only imagine that the poor thing just hasn't met the "right man" and, of course, is eager to lay claim to the title.

At one point, Del thought she really knew the

answer to discouraging unwanted male advances. She told her boss, who had been pestering her, that she was gay. But much to her dismay, instead of discouraging him, this bit of juicy information only enhanced his ardor. It seemed his wife wouldn't let him make love to her "that way." As time went on, we learned that many Lesbians have used the same spurning technique with the same burning results.

But this woman-to-woman relationship, because it is contrary to the accepted and expected man-woman relationship and because there is so little known about it, is regarded as something weird, mysterious—and downright "queer." By community standards anything that is different must also be wrong. Consequently some people's first reaction, on learning that someone is a Lesbian, is that there must be something wrong with her physically. She must be some kind of biological freak whose genitals are somehow malformed; or perhaps she is the unfortunate victim of some type of hormone imbalance.

Phyllis was left with her mouth hanging open in astonishment when, on a guest appearance on his television show a few years ago, she was asked by the late Louis Lomax, "What are the physiological differences between Lesbians and other women?" Susan, who more recently, as part of her "liberation," felt the need to tell her mother about her Lesbian life, was equally appalled when her mother grasped her hand and asked very solemnly, "But why don't you have an operation, dear?"

Because there is no such operation. Neither our bodies nor the way they function is different from those of other females. Like other women we come in all sizes and shapes. Some of us are tall and lanky; some of us are short and fat. We are young and old, beautiful and homely, blonde and brunette, short-haired and long-haired, fair-skinned and dark-skinned—whatever the combination or variation. And no matter how you may look at it, we are and must be recognized and dealt with as women. In order to understand the Lesbian, it is therefore necessary that you think of her as a living, feeling, thinking human being: a woman. The Lesbian looks, dresses, acts, and is like any other woman. The only thing that distinguishes her as a Lesbian is her choice of another woman as her sex, love or life partner.

Wherever you find two women living together you cannot assume, however that they are Lesbians, since many heterosexual women share apartments out of economic necessity or for companionship. Nor can you be sure that two women, because they date men, are heterosexual. It may only be a cover to protect their Lesbian relationship from gossip and innuendo. Karen recalls the time when a co-worker who was driving her home after an overtime stint at the office declared emphatically, "I can spot a 'queer' every time!" The fact that she was talking to one had completely escaped her.

Another fallacy is the assumption that "it takes one to know one": that there is some telltale sign, Morse Code signal or knowing glance exchanged between Lesbians at a mixed gathering. In all likelihood any Lesbian present at such a gathering would be very much on guard lest she give herself away—even to one of her own kind, whom she still regards as a threat in such social situations.

Appearance can also be misleading in trying to detect a woman's sexual orientation. Nancy, on return from a camping trip at Yosemite National Park, told us she had finally figured out the way you can tell the Lesbians from the straight women. The "stomping butch" types wearing men's jeans and boots usually had a husband and a number of kids trailing along behind them; the Lesbians, however wore capris or women's slacks so as to appear more "feminine" and not so obvious.

The American public puts much stock in the professional opinion of medical doctors: "They ought to know; they are the authorities." Pardon us if we disagree—and with good reason. Our "authority" is personal experience, not only with leading the life of a Lesbian, but also with reading so much of the literature that indirectly affects that life.

The August, 1957, issues of two national magazines, on the newsstands at the same time, carried articles which purported to describe and enlighten the public about Lesbians. "What Makes a Homosexual?" in a publication called *Actual Medical Cases* written by Hugh Barnes, M.D., stated: "The homosexual female is characterized by deficient fat in the shoulders and at the girdle, firm muscles, excess hair on the chest, back and legs, a tendency to over-development of the clitoris. There is also a tendency toward a shorter trunk, a contracted pelvis, under-development of the breasts, excess hair on the face and a low-pitched voice."

However, Edward Dengrove, M.D., writing on "Homosexuality in Women" for *Sexology* magazine, had this to say: "Contrary to the popular conception of the woman with homosexual tendencies, she is not necessarily, or even usually, the extremely masculine woman, aggressive, strong and muscular, mannish in physical appearance and dress, lacking all the delicacy and gentleness we associate with the feminine.... For most Lesbians are not women who are pretending to be men, but rather women who cannot express their normal sexual drive in relationship to men, but must direct it towards other females instead. Even in the sexual sphere, the Lesbian remains essentially feminine, with the natural desires and reactions of a woman. . . ."

Which one has the Toni? No wonder the public is confused! And no wonder many Lesbians who have sought therapy have found themselves explaining the whole phenomenon of homosexuality to their doctors.

Even though more is known about the Lesbian today than ever before, the stereotypes still persist, reinforced by what little has been recorded in history and by subsequent literary accounts. The history of female homosexuality is probably as old as the history of the human race itself; archaeologists have discovered prehistoric cave drawings of female figures engaging in homosexual acts together. But the term *Lesbian* is derived from the island of Lesbos, a triangular area of land in the Aegean Sea off the coast of what is now Turkey. Sappho, famous Greek lyric poetess of the early sixth century B.C., was supposed to have established a school for young girls and/or a cult for female homosexuals on the island. Historians and translators are at such variance about the details that Dr. Jeannette H. Foster, former librarian for the (Kinsey) Institute for Sex Research and author of *Sex Variant Women in Literature*, was prompted to

point out that, by Ovid's day, there was so much controversy about Sappho's personal life that it almost seemed as if two Sapphos must have flourished on Lesbos, "one the great poetess and the other the courtesan of undisciplined habits."

Born out of the Sappho controversy the Lesbian has thus been depicted as a childish romantic at best, or at worst a child molester or prostitute. Prior to the twentieth century the chronicles of history and literature were written almost exclusively by men. References to Lesbians, of course, reflected the bias of the authors, who never depicted women as wholly, or even primarily, homosexual; the male ego could never admit that a woman existed who could have sexual satisfaction without a man. Lesbian episodes depicted in literature take the form of the initiation of an innocent girl by an older woman more experienced in giving sexual pleasure to men, a diversion for the prostitute, an experiment by upper class ladies with their handmaids to alleviate boredom, or the desperate activity of nuns or prison inmates who have been isolated from men. The accounts are devoid of personal devotion in any such relations, and sexual play often involved more than two participants.

There are occasional references, however, to pairs of women who formed "strongly emotional friendships," most famous of whom were the "Ladies of Llangollen": Lady Eleanor Butler and Sarah Ponsonby, two seventeenth century Irish women who settled in a cottage in the Vale of Llangollen in north Wales. While they were sometimes called "the Platonists," it is reported that Lady Eleanor wore men's clothes, that her journal spoke of "our bed," and that neither left their cottage for a single night throughout the fifty years they lived together. Even the accounts of the more recent long-term relationship between Gertrude Stein and Alice B. Toklas have a tendency to skirt the issue of their sexuality.

History also indicates that Lesbianism was existent among certain of the royalty and their courtiers, most notable of whom were Queen Christina of Sweden, Elizabeth I of England, and Marie Antoinette. But most of our knowledge of Lesbians in history is based on innuendo, rumor, or conjecture, and cannot be considered reliable.

The first novel on female variance to be written by a woman appeared in 1788: Mary Wollstonecraft's *Mary, A Fiction.* It is said to be based upon the author's consuming attachment to Fanny Blood, which began when Mary was about fifteen and continued until Fanny's death twelve years later.

Radclyffe Hall's novel *The Well of Loneliness,* first published in England in 1928, was exceedingly daring for its time. After lengthy court hearings, the book was condemned as obscene in the British Isles, simply because of its subject matter and the sympathetic manner in which it was handled. Other books published in England at the same time on the Lesbian theme did not meet the same fate, however, apparently because in them the Lesbian association was either condemned, as in Naomi Royde-Smith's *The Tortoiseshell Cat,* or satirized, as in Compton Mackenzie's *Extraordinary Women.*

Republication of *The Well of Loneliness* in Paris was followed by translation into eleven languages, and fourteen years later the book was enjoying a steady annual sale of one hundred thousand copies in the United States alone. It became the "Lesbian bible." Unfortunately, to the uninitiated the book perpetuated the myth of the Lesbian as a pseudomale, and many young women, like Del, emulated the heroine, Stephen Gordon, only to find that their lovers, like Phyllis, were not looking for a male substitute. For Lesbians are women who are attracted to *women.*

The first nonfiction book covering Lesbianism as a whole and written by a Lesbian was *We Walk Alone,* published in 1955. While pleading with society to be more tolerant and less condemning, more understanding and less prone to pity the Lesbian as some kind of freak, the author, Ann Aldrich, led her readers "through Lesbos' lonely groves," dwelling mostly on bizarre examples and giving only fleeting reference to those women who are well-adjusted, productive citizens in society.

During the 1950s newsstands were deluged with Lesbian paperback novels which were, despite appearances to the contrary, (im)pure fiction written primarily by men. Those that were written more realistically by Lesbian authors, we have since

learned, were rejected by the publishers or altered to fit the "party line" which required either a tragic ending or the ultimate realization that heterosexuality was indeed the only avenue to true happiness.

By the 1960s the trend in Lesbian fiction had changed somewhat. Happy endings were allowed in some instances, implying that Lesbian couples might be able to establish fulfilling alliances. But the quality of the literature still left much to be desired. Of some sixteen hundred titles listed in the bibliography *The Lesbian in Literature,* prepared by Gene Damon and Lee Stuart and published by the Daughters of Bilitis in 1967, the vast majority were earmarked as "trash." And these, of course, were chiefly written by men for male readers.

Led perhaps by the onslaught of these sensational sex novels, often describing Lesbians with male sex partners, and by publicity about the existence of a Lesbian organization, many men found their way to the offices of the Daughters of Bilitis in San Francisco. Some were quite outspoken about their sexual needs; others, more shy, cloaked their desires in a shroud of vagueness. But their interest in DOB was based on the false concept that Lesbians were open and available to men who "understood" and hoped to share in mutual sexual delights.

A tall, burly young man, who could easily have been taken for a police detective, made a special trip from Los Angeles in search of a Lesbian. Object: matrimony. Cliff's problem was that his responses were "feminine" in nature and that he felt trapped in a male body. Coming from a Catholic background, the only acceptable sexual outlet for him was heterosexual marriage. He reasoned, therefore, that he needed to find and marry a woman who would act as his masculine counterpart: namely, a Lesbian.

However, as Del carefully pointed out to Cliff, the Lesbian is not necessarily a male in a woman's body. Lesbianism is not a matter of gender-role designation, but contains within it elements of psychological, emotional, and spiritual involvement between two *women.* While Cliff's immediate and pressing problem was not solved, he did find a friend who was understanding and non-judgmental about his own sexual identity and needs. Del has heard from Cliff that he has since married and is the father of two children. How he and his wife have worked out their masculine and feminine roles we do not know. But we do know that what we call "femininity" and "masculinity" is culturally defined and few people, heterosexual and homosexual alike, fit the molds.

Another young man, Roger, came to the DOB office for help. He was not as articulate as Cliff, and it took Del some time to determine that he was looking for a Lesbian partner with whom to perform cunnilingus. Again Del tried to explain that female homosexuality could not be defined simply in terms of the sex act itself, but had to do with emotional involvement between women; that Lesbians are not seeking male partners; and that, in any event, DOB was not in the business of pimping. Roger, however, was not easily dissuaded and Del, in exasperation and in need of reinforcements, suggested that, since Phyllis would be getting off work soon, perhaps they could continue their discussion over dinner at a nearby gay bar. Toward the end of the meal Del excused herself to go to the restroom. Roger took this as his cue to "come on" with Phyllis "as the date Del had fixed him up with." When Phyllis cleared up his misunderstanding, he left abruptly and indignantly.

These are only two of the many examples we could offer that Lesbians in our society are perceived by men as sexually permissive in choice of partner and sexual act. Many a Lesbian, too, has been surprised to realize that the heterosexual couple whom she has befriended, whom she believed to be sympathetic and understanding, was actually conspiring to lure her into their conjugal bed.

And so it has gone through the years. The descriptive phrases, commonplace in the literature about the Lesbian, have always been ambivalent and tend to create an aura of sexual mysticism' "the exciting, alluring and tantalizing promise of a woman's closeness"; "a strange, tempting, forbidden love"; "perverse, yet compelling attraction"; "sordid and ugly revelation of the unleashed passions of evil and of love"; "the quirk of nature that lures young women into the lonely, isolated and tragic twilight world." Although such language makes for dramatic effect in fiction and attention-getting headlines for newspaper sensation-seekers, it has little to do with the realities of Lesbian life, and has led to the existing state of confusion among the general public as well as among Lesbians themselves.

Little scientific research has been done on the Lesbian, and what has been done is based primarily upon childhood background and sexual practices. Until recently most subjects were drawn from captive samples of women in prison or in psychotherapy. And it has always bothered us that the emphasis of research has been devoted almost exclusively to causation rather than to those facets of the Lesbian life itself which could help to explode some of the myths and foster better understanding.

We have also maintained a strong objection to measuring the Lesbian in terms of happiness or unhappiness. A Lesbian who is struggling with her identity or who may be trying to repress her sexuality will, of course, be unhappy during that period of her life. The woman who has come to terms with her identity and has crossed the bridge of self acceptance may have gained self confidence but not yet a lover, and so feels lonely and unhappy for a time. The Lesbian who has hurdled the identity crisis and established a meaningful and satisfying relationship with another woman may still feel somewhat unhappy on occasion because of society's strictures. Happiness is not stationary: it is fluid; it fluctuates. As Lesbians we have experienced great joy and happiness and love. We have also known despair, conflict and unhappiness. This is the human condition. The same may be said for heterosexuals, for whose miseries Lesbians have often expressed compassion and empathy. Unfortunately the concern is not reciprocal. The fact that the Lesbian is not generally thought of in terms of her humanity, her close relationship to family, her deep involvement with society, her sameness rather than her difference, is responsible for the negative self image she often adopts or must struggle to overcome.

SECTION 4
SCHIZOPHRENIA AND AUTISM

Of all diagnostic categories of abnormal behavior, schizophrenia is the most reliable. It refers to disorders in behavior, mood, and thought. Behavioral manifestations of schizophrenia include extreme withdrawal or other bizarre activities such as remaining in one rigid position for hours at a time; disorders of mood are often marked by inappropriate affect or an almost total absence of emotional responsivity; disorders in thinking are characterized by delusions or hallucinations and disturbed use of language. Schizophrenia is usually subdivided into categories of simple, hebephrenic, catatonic, and paranoid. Although it is often difficult to reliably assign individuals to these various subcategories, the behaviors they refer to give a flavor for the variety of strange activities performed by those labeled schizophrenics. Researchers in the area of schizophrenia have used other labels to subgroup schizophrenics: acute versus chronic, referring to whether or not the onset of the disorder was sudden; and good versus poor premorbids, referring to the quality of the schizophrenic's adjustment prior to hospitalization.

Despite many years of research, the etiology of schizophrenia still remains a mystery. Many hypotheses have been proposed to account for the disorder. Psychologically oriented theorists have proposed that ambiguous communication between mother and child, inappropriate parental dominance, or parental hostility and conflict leads to schizophrenia. For biologically oriented researchers, hypotheses have indicted biochemical abnormalities, bad genes, or pregnancy and birth complications. A diathesis-stress model is currently in vogue. Some biological abnormality (diathesis) in schizophrenics predisposes them to become psychotic, and an environmental stress precipitates the break. In this way, findings in both the psychological and biological areas can be integrated in a more comprehensive and hopefully more useful theory.

Schizophrenia has been studied in many different ways: through retrospective or clinical study of schizophrenics interacting with other members of their family, through studies of twins (one schizophrenic, the other not) separated from their parents after birth, and through longitudinal studies of children of schizophrenic parents. Researchers have also investigated the performance of schizophrenics on various laboratory tasks and have studied the effects of various conditions that mimic in normals some of the signs of schizophrenia.

In selection 17 Chapman effectively criticizes the psychotomimetic technique primarily because similarities between schizophrenia and schizomimetic conditions are often more apparent than real and because researchers using this model often consider schizophrenia as a unitary condition. He especially objects to the procedure of mimicking schizophrenic behavior through operant techniques because of the paucity of evidence implicating operant conditioning in the development of schizophrenia. He also emphasizes that demonstrating that a behavior can be produced in the laboratory by contingent reinforcements does not logically mean that similar behaviors develop in the same way in the natural environment. At the same time, Chapman suggests that mimicking schizophrenic behavior can be valuable if it leads to productive research into the origin of naturally occurring states of schizophrenia, or if it suggests new methods of treatment.

The methodology of much of the research into schizophrenogenic families is criticized by Fontana in selection 18. He cites the many problems that accompany retrospective reports or clinical observations of a familial interaction. When adequate studies of familial interaction are scrutinized no evidence is provided for the concept of a schizophrenogenic mother, although there is some indication that there is more conflict and less clear communication in families with a schizophrenic member. Even in this case, however, the question remains whether such phenomena cause schizophrenia or whether they result from living with a schizophrenic.

One of the problems in demonstrating a genetic component of schizophrenia is the fact that children of schizophrenic parents usually live with them. Thus, there is no way of knowing whether an individual became schizophrenic because of his genetic inheritance or because of the environmental effects of living with schizophrenic parents. Heston (selection 19) reports on a study that he conducted where he was able to get around this problem by studying children of schizophrenic mothers who were given up to foster care shortly after birth. His results support the hypothesis that genetic inheritance plays an important role in the development of schizophrenia. One of the more interesting results of his study, however, pertains to the discovery that some of the children of schizophrenic mothers who did not subsequently become schizophrenic were more creative individuals and held more colorful jobs than a comparison group of normal children.

Mednick (selection 20) reports on his ambitious undertaking of studying longitudinally, over the course of 20 to 25 years, children of schizophrenic and children of nonschizophrenic mothers. The preliminary evidence available to him leads him to propose that pregnancy and birth complications, especially anoxia at birth, may play an important role in causing the thinking disorders associated with schizophrenia.

Maher (selection 21) reviews the research literature relating to the distorted speech of schizophrenics. He points out that the speech of schizophrenics is restricted in vocabulary, is often disorganized, and is characterized by the presence of many word associations inserted into conversation seemingly haphazardly. The hypothesis proposed by Maher to account for this phenomenon is that some defect in the autonomic nervous system produces an attentional deficit that is responsible for the word salads produced by schizophrenics and for many other symptoms as well.

Wing (selection 22) descriptively reviews infantile autism, a disorder generally not considered merely a childhood precursor or variety of adult schizophrenia. Autistic children typically exhibit severe withdrawal, shrinking from the curiosity and exploration typical of normal children, and even avoiding contact with adults. One of the most distinctive and pathetic behaviors of some autistic children is self-mutilation, which can consist of ripping pieces of flesh from their bodies or banging their heads against the wall or the bars of their crib. They appear to have difficulty understanding speech and also demonstrate abnormalities in speaking, for instance, repeating whatever is said to them (echolalia). These children do not establish normal social relationships with other children but often develop extreme attachment to inanimate objects and to a strict routine of being cared for. The etiology of childhood autism is unknown and treatment in the past has relied primarily on custodial care. Recent work by Lovaas has shown that operant techniques can sometimes bring about dramatic improvement even in severely regressed children. The effects of such a treatment appear to be restricted to the operant environment and cannot be generalized to situations where the treatment contingencies are not in effect; nevertheless, this appears to be the most promising treatment for autism at the present time.

SUGGESTED READINGS

Haley, J. The art of being schizophrenic. *Voices*, 1965, *1*, 133-147.

Kaplan, B. (Ed.) *The inner world of mental illness* New York: Harper & Row, 1964.

Lovaas, I., Koegel, K., Simmons, J. Q., & Long, J. S. Some generalization and follow-up measures in autistic children in behavior therapy.

Journal of Applied Behavior Analysis, 1973, *6*, 131-166

Rimland, B. *Infantile autism*. New York: Appleton-Crofts, 1964.

Rosenthal, D. *Genetic theory and abnormal behavior*. New York: Mc-Graw Hill, 1970.

17. Schizomimetic Conditions and Schizophrenia
LOREN J. CHAPMAN

Levitz and Ullmann have added operant reinforcement to the list of allegedly schizomimetic conditions that have been used to generate theories of schizophrenic thought disorder. The diversity of such allegedly schizomimetic conditions casts doubt on the validity of interpreting schizophrenic symptoms on the basis of any one of them. The very power of operant procedures to mimic any behavior, regardless of its origin, argues against invoking its schizomimetic power as evidence concerning the nature of schizophrenia. The potential usefulness of operant methods to alter schizophrenic symptoms need not be predicated on an operant origin of the disorder.

Levitz and Ullmann (1969) have interpreted their findings as consistent with their hypothesis that schizophrenic symptoms are caused by operant reinforcement. The present discussion is focused on their general approach to the problem of schizophrenia, that is, their citing performance of normal Ss in a schizomimetic condition as evidence concerning the origin or nature of schizophrenic thought disorder.

Levitz and Ullmann's study was well designed, and it demonstrated that an operant etiology of schizophrenic symptoms is at least plausible. The investigators concluded, with appropriate caution, that their results are "consistent with" but "not proof of" the operant origin of schizophrenic thought disorder. I agree, except in a matter of relative emphasis on the two sides of the authors' conclusions. There are additional reasons, not discussed by Levitz and Ullmann, for viewing their results as very weak support for the hypothesis that reinforcement history accounts for the origin of schizophrenic thought disorder.

Operant methods are capable of producing almost any conceivable change in voluntary behavior and even, perhaps, some involuntary (autonomic) responses. Verbal responses are simply one more kind of response that can be altered operantly.

Loren J. Chapman, Schizomimetic conditions and schizophrenia, *Journal of Consulting and Clinical Psychology, 33,* 1969, 646-650. Copyright © 1969 by the American Psychological Association and reproduced by permission.

Could anyone doubt after reviewing the successes of operant workers that one could train college students to rave as paretics, speak inadequately as motor aphasics, or even to quack as ducks? However, would anyone seriously suggest that such a demonstration of the power of operant methods would constitute support for the hypothesis that paretics, aphasics, and ducks fail to speak as normal adult human beings primarily because of unfortunate reinforcement histories? The operant method has the power to shape responses that mimic almost any behavior in its natural state, regardless of its origin. Such power rules out any one such demonstration as convincing evidence that behavior of unknown origin occurred primarily because of reinforcement contingencies.

There is a second good reason for caution in viewing the schizomimetic power of reinforcement as support for a primarily operant etiology of schizophrenic thought disorder. Many other schizomimetic conditions have been reported as producing schizophreniclike verbal behavior. Investigators of these conditions have often, like Levitz and Ullmann, argued that the similarity of schizophrenic cognition to that of *Ss* in some one schizomimetic condition is evidence that the naturally occurring schizophrenic symptom has a cause like that of the behavior elicited in the schizomimetic condition. The very multiplicity of these conditions that produce behavior at least superficially akin to schizophrenic symptoms casts doubt on the validity of the argument for any one of them. The following is at least a partial list of these allegedly schizomimetic conditions that have been invoked as evidence for some particular theory of schizophrenia.

1. *LSD, mescaline, and other drugs*. Recently, the most widely discussed schizomimetic conditions have been LSD, mescaline, and other drugs. Numerous investigators have reported schizophreniclike cognitive behaviors in response to drugs (Hoffer & Osmond, 1967). These behaviors include disturbed association, pressure of thought, neologisms, blocking, hallucinations and delusions. Several investigators have inferred from such evidence that schizophrenia is caused by substances

similar to one or another of these drugs. This hypothesis has stimulated a vast amount of research on the biochemistry of these drugs, and has led to the identification of new schizomimetic drugs (notably adrenochrome, adrenolutin, and sernyl) and, concomitantly, to revised hypotheses of the biochemical basis of schizophrenia.

2. *Sensory deprivation*. The McGill investigators, who initiated the sensory deprivation research tradition, reported that a prolonged low level of sensory variation produces a deterioration in the ability to think in an organized, goal-directed manner, as well as increased day-dreaming, hallucinations, distortion of body image, and other perceptual aberrations (Bexton, Heron, & Scott, 1954; Heron, Bexton, & Hebb, 1953). Several other investigators have reconfirmed these observations.

Rosenzweig (1959) contended that the sensory deprivation reaction more closely resembles schizophrenia than either the LSD or mescaline psychoses. He suggested that both schizophrenia and the sensory deprivation reaction are caused by a loss of meaning to stimuli. In sensory deprivation, meaning is removed from the environment by the experimental procedures, whereas in schizophrenia, it results from an internal derangement of communication between the patient's "abstract system" and his "affect system."

Gaarder (1963) also cited the similarities between schizophrenia and the cognitive disorders in sensory deprivation and suggested that schizophrenia is the result of lack of input of necessary data about the environment.

3. *Sleep deprivation*. Many investigators have noted that prolonged sleep deprivation produces cognitive disorganization, hallucinations, and occasional delusions. The suggestion that schizophrenia has its origin in a mechanism similar to that of the symptoms of sleep deprivation has been made by Tyler (1947), Luby, Grisell, Frohman, Lees, Cohen, and Gottlieb (1962), and West, Janszen, Lester, and Cornelisoon (1962). Of these writers, Luby et al. were the most specific. They found in sleep deprivation a disturb-

ance of the synthesis of adenosine triphosphate and they proposed a similar defect as the cause of schizophrenia. Bliss, Clark, and West (1959) contended that naturally occurring schizophrenic episodes are often the direct result of sleep deprivation, pointing to similarities in cognition between schizophrenics and sleep-deprived *Ss* to bolster their contention.

4. *Hypnosis.* King (1957) gave a proverbs test to normal *Ss*, both during hypnosis and in the wakeful state. Because he found that hypnosis increased concrete and bizarre answers, he concluded that schizophrenia, like hypnosis, is a manifestation of heightened suggestion.

5. *Speeded performance.* Flavell and Draguns (1957) following a lead of Schilder (1951), argued that each normal thought passes through a series of stages of development, and that schizophrenic cognition represents prematurely expressed early stages in the development of normal cognition. Flavell and Draguns (1958) offered as supportive evidence of this theory their finding of some similarities between the various idiosyncrasies of schizophrenics' responses on a word association test and those exhibited by normal *Ss* when required to respond very rapidly.

Phillips and Framo (1954) reached a similar conclusion about schizophrenic cognition by noting a similarity between the responses that schizophrenics typically gave to the Rorschach bolts and those of normal adults presented with brief (tachistoscopic) exposures of the Rorschach bolts.

6. *Distraction.* Jung (1919) studied the effects of distraction on the responses of normal *Ss* in a word association test; his manipulation of distraction consisted of requiring *S* to mark a paper with a pencil in time with the beat of a metronome. Jung found that distraction more than doubled the production of rhyme responses and more than quadrupled the production of other clang associations. Later, Jung (1936) invoked the similarity of these responses to those typically found in dementia praecox patients as evidence that the responses of the patients are deviant because of insufficient attention.

Hassol, Magaret, and Cameron (1952) found that normal *Ss* showed an increase of "scattered speech" in telling TAT stories while simultaneously listening to a recording of their own previous story of the same TAT card. "Scattered speech" included imprecise speech, the use of substitute or approximate words or phrases, and interruptions in the sequence of the material. The investigators concluded that the findings supported Cameron's hypothesis that schizophrenic disorganized speech results from the intrusion of personal fantasy material.

7. *Relaxed attention.* Jung (1936) reviewed at length a study by Stransky, who obtained samples of continuous speech from normal *Ss* under the condition of "relaxed attention." Stransky gave a stimulus word and instructed his *Ss* to speak for 1 minute, but not to pay attention to what they said. The *Ss* showed many features of speech that are commonly observed in schizophrenics, including perseverations, repetitions, sound associations, and condensations of sequences of ideas into brief phrases or into single words (neologisms). Jung interpreted these findings, and his own distraction studies, as proving that dementia praecox is characterized by a diminution of attention.

8. *Disruption of perception.* Aaronson (1964), using hypnotism, induced a disturbance in depth perception in a single normal *S*, who responded with psychotic ideation and mood changes. The author inferred that disorder in depth perception may produce schizophrenia. Aaronson (1965), again using a single *S*, reported that he produced psychotic ideation, hallucinations, and withdrawal by communicating to the hypnotized *S* that time had stopped. Aaronson concluded that "Schizophrenia seems specifically a response to the elimination of some conventional dimension of perception [p. 8]."

9. *Anoxia.* Several investigators, including Freeman (1931), have noted schizophreniclike cognitive aberrations that accompany oxygen deprivation. McFarland's (1932) study was especially thorough. He reported that normal young men with reduced oxygen intake manifest several schizophreniclike symptoms, including defective

judgment, perseveration, an abandonment of moral inhibitions, and, subsequently, partial or complete amnesia. In more severe oxygen deprivation, hallucinations and delusions were found to appear. Hinsie, Barach, Harris, Brand, and McFarland (1934) pointed to these phenomena as support for the hypothesis that schizophrenic symptoms might reflect deficient oxygen supply to brain cells. They took their hypothesis so seriously that they converted a patients' dormitory into a large oxygen chamber for three months in an attempt to find a treatment for the disorder.

10. *Brain damage*. Several influential clinicians have suggested that schizophrenic cognition resembles that of brain-damaged patients, and that schizophrenia is probably, therefore, a similar condition. Kraepelin (1919) named the disorder "dementia praecox" because he believed that these patients show a mental enfeeblement resembling in part that found in paresis, senility, and epilepsy. Many other writers have pointed out specific similarities in cognitive deficit, between schizophrenics and brain-damaged patients, and have inferred that schizophrenics also have cerebral organic malfunction. The deficit cited in common has most often been one of concept formation (Babcock, 1933; Bychowski, 1935, 1943). Goldstein (1939) also took this view, but later reversed himself (Goldstein, 1959).

11. *Childhood*. Many writers, especially psychoanalytic theorists, pointing to the "primary process" in the thinking of schizophrenics and that of young children have inferred that schizophrenia results from a regression to an early stage of development (Fenichel, 1945).

12. *"Primitive" racial development*. Another version of the regression hypothesis is that schizophrenics have regressed to an earlier stage of man's development such as that of prehistoric man or members of contemporary "primitive" societies. Storch (1924), Arieti (1955), and Werner (1948) have pointed to a number of similarities of cognitive functioning that they believe support this hypothesis.

13. *Dreams and sleep*. The ancient observation that dreams resemble madness has been exploited most fully by psychoanalytic theorists who see "primary process" in both. A number of psychoanalysts have inferred that schizophrenic thought, like that of dreams, reflects an abandonment of the regulative and censoring functions of the ego (Freud, 1953; Rosen, 1953).

Despite the current impasse reached by investigators employing the method of schizomimetic conditions, the method is not logically unsound. If two syndromes are truly identical, one must take seriously the hypothesis that they have a similar cause. However, a major difficulty faced by research workers is the crudity of most measures of schizophrenic thought disorder. Apparent similarities may vanish when specific details of two error patterns are considered. Cameron (1938a, 1938b) is well known for making this point in an attempt to refute both the contention that schizophrenic thought is regressive and that it shows organic deterioration. Chapman, Burstein, Day, and Verdone (1961) have also elaborated this argument in reference to the regression hypothesis. Writers too numerous to mention have recently made the same point in relation to the allegedly schizomimetic drugs. It must be noted that Levitz and Ullmann's measure of similarity on the word association test is one of the least specific in the literature, as they merely trained atypical responses, without any scrutiny of the nature of the atypical responses. However, their measure on the Holtzman Inkblot Test was more specific.

A second difficulty faced by research in this area is the crudity of current systems of diagnosis. Almost all investigators of schizomimetic conditions have not attempted to specify what types of schizophrenics are mimicked. If there are meaningful subdisorders within schizophrenia, one might expect the cognitive disorder of some of them, but not others, to be mimicked by one or another schizomimetic condition. Tutko and Spence's (1962) study exemplifies the promise of this approach. They found that on the passive sorting portion of the Object Sorting Test, process and reactive schizophrenics depart from normal performance by distinctly different error patterns, and that the errors of brain-damaged patients resemble only those of the process schizophrenics.

Levitz and Ullmann have added to the long list of schizomimetic conditions one more condition that produces deviant verbal behavior like that of schizophrenics. One might ask whether anything that is known about reinforcement should lead one to take it more seriously as a basis of schizophrenic thought disorder than the dozen or so other schizomimetic conditions. The contrary seems true. Reinforcement may change behavior in any direction, toward health as well as illness, while the other schizomimetic conditions almost always debilitate cognition. Moreover, some schizomimetic conditions may produce only changes that are identical to those of some variety of schizophrenia.

Many operant workers might contend that the very power of reinforcement to change behavior lends support to the presumption that in the absence of contrary evidence, any behavioral variation is a learned one. This is a hypothesis worthy of investigation. The most appropriate way to test the hypothesis in reference to schizophrenia is probably by means of longitudinal studies of family interaction. Such studies would, unfortunately, be difficult to perform.

The paucity of evidence for an operant origin of schizophrenic symptoms should not, however, discourage workers who seek to modify schizophrenic symptoms by operant methods. Promising first steps in modifying schizophrenic cognition have already been reported by several investigators, as pointed out by Ullmann and Krasner (1969).

REFERENCES

Aaronson, B. S. Hypnosis, depth perception and schizophrenia. Paper presented at the meeting of the Eastern Psychological Association, Philadelphia, April 1964.

Aaronson, B. S. Hypnosis, time rate perception, and personality. Paper presented at the meeting of the Eastern Psychological Association, Atlantic City, April 1965.

Arieti, S. *Interpretation of schizophrenia.* New York: Brunner, 1955.

Babcock, H. *Dementia praecox, a psychological study.* Lancaster, Pa.: Science Press, 1933.

Bexton, W. H., Heron, W., & Scott, T. H. Effects of decreased variation in the sensory environment. *Canadian Journal of Psychology,* 1954, *8,* 70-76.

Bliss, E. L., Clark, L. D., & West, C. D. Studies of sleep deprivation: Relationship to schizophrenia. *A.M.A. Archives of Neurology and Psychiatry,* 1959, *81,* 348-359.

Bychowski, G. Certain problems of schizophrenia in light of cerebral pathology. (Trans. by W. H. Wegrocki) *Journal of Nervous and Mental Disease,* 1935, *81,* 280-298.

Bychowski, G. Physiology of schizophrenic thinking. *Journal of Nervous and Mental Disease,* 1943, *98,* 368-386.

Cameron, N. A study of thinking in senile deterioration and schizophrenic disorganization. *American Journal of Psychology,* 1938, *51* 650-654.(a)

Cameron, N. Reasoning, regression, and communication in schizophrenics. *Psychological Monographs,* 1938, *50* (1, Whole No. 221). (b)

Chapman, L. J. Burstein, A. G., Day, D., & Verdone, P. Regression and disorders of thought. *Journal of Abnormal and Social Psychology*, 1961, *63*, 540-545.

Fenichel, O. *The psychoanalytic theory of neurosis.* New York: Norton, 1945.

Flavell, J. H., & Draguns, J. A microgenetic approach to perception and thought. *Psychological Bulletin*, 1957, *54*, 197-217.

Flavell, J. H., Draguns, J., Feinberg, L. D., & Budin, W. A microgenetic approach to word association. *Journal of Abnormal and Social Psychology*, 1958, *57*, 1-8.

Freeman, W. Psychochemistry; some physiochemical factors in mental disorders. *Journal of the American Medical Association*, 1931, *97*, 293-296.

Freud, S. The unconscious. In, *Collected papers.* Vol. 4. London: Hogarth Press, 1953.

Gaarder, K. A conceptual model of schizophrenia. *Archives of General Psychiatry*, 1963, *8*, 590-598.

Goldstein, K. The significance of special mental tests for diagnosis and prognosis in schizophrenia. *American Journal of Psychiatry*, 1939, *96*, 575-587.

Goldstein, K. Concerning the concreteness in schizophrenia. *Journal of Abnormal and Social Psychology*, 1959, *59*, 146-147.

Hassol, L., Magaret, A., & Cameron, N. The production of language disorganization through personalized distraction. *Journal of Psychology*, 1952, *33*, 289-299.

Heron, W., Bexton, W. H., & Hebb, D. O. Cognitive effects of a decreased variation in the sensory environment. *American Psychologist*, 1953, *8*, 366. (Abstract)

Hinsie, L. E., Barach, A. L., Harris, M. M., Brand, E., & McFarland, R. A. The treatment of dementia praecox by continuous oxyden administration in chambers and oxygen and carbon dioxide inhalations. *Psychiatric Quarterly*, 1934, *8*, 34-71.

Hoffer, A., & Osmond, H. *The hallucinogens.* New York: Academic Press, 1967.

Jung, C. G. *Studies in word association.* (Trans. by M. D. Eder) New York: Moffat, 1919.

Jung, C. G. The psychology of dementia praecox. *Journal of Nervous and Mental Disease*, 1936, Monograph No. 3 (Originally published, 1906).

King, P. E. Hypnosis and schizophrenia. *Journal of Nervous and Mental Disease*, 1957, *125*, 481-486.

Kraepelin, E. *Dementia praecox and parapmenia.* (Trans. by R. Mary Barclay) Edinburgh: Livingstone, 1919.

Levitz, L. S., & Ullmann, L. P. Manipulation of indications of disturbed thinking in normal subjects. *Journal of Consulting and Clinical Psychology*, 1969, *33*, 633-641.

Luby, E. D., Grisell, J. L., Frohman, C. E., Lees, H., Cohen, B. D., & Gottlieb,

J. S. Biochemical, psychological and behavioral responses to sleep deprivation. *Annals of the New York Academy of Science*, 1962, *96*, 71-79

McFarland, R. A. The psychological effects of oxygen deprivation (anoxemia) on human behavior. *Archives of Psychology*, 1935, No. 145.

Phillips, L., & Framo, J. L. Developmental theory applied to normal and psychopathological perception. *Journal of Personality*, 1954, *22*, 465-474.

Rosen, J. N. *Direct analysis*. New York: Grune & Stratton, 1953.

Rosenzweig, N. Sensory deprivation and schizophrenia: Some clinical and theoretical similarities. *American Journal of Psychiatry*, 1959, *116*, 326-329.

Schilder, P. On the development of thoughts. In D. Rapaport (Ed.), *Organization and pathology of thought*. New York: Columbia University Press, 1951.

Storch, A. The primitive archaic forms of inner experiences and thought in schizophrenia. *Journal of Nervous and Mental Disease*, 1924, Monograph No. 36.

Tutko, T. A., & Spence, J. T. The performance of process and reactive schizophrenics and brain-injured subjects on a conceptual task. *Journal of Abnormal and Social Psychology*, 1962, *65*, 387-394.

Tyler, D. B. The effect of amphetamine sulfate and some barbiturates on the fatigue produced by prolonged wakefulness. *American Journal of Physiology*, 1947, *150*, 253-262.

Ullmann, L. P., & Krasner, L. *A psychological approach to abnormal behavior*. Englewood Cliffs, N. J.: Prentice-Hall, 1969.

Werner, H. *Comparative psychology of mental development*. Chicago: Follett, 1948.

West, L. J., Janszen, H. H., Lester, B. K., & Cornelisoon, F. S., Jr. The psychosis of sleep deprivation. *Annals of the New York Academy of Science*, 1962, *96*, 66-70.

18. *Familial Etiology of Schizophrenia: Is a Scientific Methodology Possible?*[1]

ALAN F. FONTANA

The 3 major research approaches toward identifying familial etiological factors in schizophrenia are examined from a methodological viewpoint. Both the clinical observational and retrospective recall methods are judged to be inadequate. The 3rd approach, direct observation and recording of family interactions, is concluded to be free of intrinsically disqualifying inadequacies, given the limiting assumption that the variables under investigation are etiological in nature. Although the limitations of this assumption can only be overcome by a longitudinal approach, family interaction studies are considered to be an indispensable, practical precondition to the formulation of longitudinal studies. Results from a subset of methodologically adequate studies are examined and conclusions drawn. Several cautions and recommendations for future research are offered.

The functional role of the family in the development of schizophrenia[2] has been the subject of intensive investigation. Researchers have reported that several personality characteristics differentiate between parents of schizophrenics and nonschizophrenics, and

Alan F. Fontana, Familial etiology of schizophrenia: Is a scientific methodology possible? *Psychological Bulletin, 66,* 1966, 214-227. Copyright © 1966 by the American Psychological Association and reproduced by permission.

[1] The preparation of this paper was supported by Research Grant MH 08050 from the National Institute of Mental Health, United States Public Health Service. The author wishes to thank Edward B. Klein and Carmi Schooler for their critical reading of the manuscript.

[2] It is assumed that the term "schizophrenia" applies to a subset of behaviors or processes which differentiates persons so labeled from others. The reliability of psychiatric diagnosis has been a topic much discussed and argued. It is clear from the extant literature that schizophrenia, as a major category, is the most reliable of the diagnoses. The possibility exists, however, that psychiatric and psychological professionals are inconsistently "over-inclusive" or "underinclusive" in applying schizophrenia as a concept, and for this reason "schizophrenics" may be just as different from each other as they are from others. The crucial question is, of course, "What is schizophrenia?" In attempting to answer this, there seems to be little choice but to study people called schizophrenic.

that several aspects of family interaction patterns differ in the families of schizophrenics and non-schizophrenics. However, reviewers (Frank, 1965; Meissner, 1964; Rabkin, 1965; Sanua, 1961) have not shared the optimism and conclusions of the majority of researchers. The recent review by Frank (1965) states that in the last 40 years of research, *no* factors have been found which either differentiate between the families of psychopathological and normal members, or among families of pathological members who are classified according to different diagnostic categories. That author's pessimism extends to the more general issue concerning the applicability of the scientific method to the study of human behavior:

Apparently, the factors which play a part in the development of behavior in humans are so complex that it would appear that they almost defy being investigated scientifically and defy one's attempt to draw meaningful generalizations from the exploration which has already been done [p. 201].

Frank is quite correct in raising the issue of methodology. It is a truism that any body of scientific facts must rest upon a scientifically sound methodology. The conclusions from any study not so based cannot be considered scientific, no matter how scholarly they may be. Some of the previous review-ers have paid insufficient attention to the methodology of individual studies. Rather, their approach has been to tabulate positive and negative results without evaluating the methodological adequacy of individual studies. This approach may have obscured some consistent empirical trends which can be found in well-designed studies.

The purpose of this paper is to examine the scientific status of the three major research approaches, first methodologically and then in terms of empirical results. The sources of data for the approaches to be considered are: (*a*) clinical observations and psychiatric impressions of family members in treatment, (*b*) retrospective accounts of child-rearing practices and attitudes obtained from family members' responses to interviews and questionnaires, and (*c*) current patterns of interaction among family members directly recorded and systematically coded by the investigator. Rabkin (1965) and Sanua (1961) have presented excellent critiques of much of the work in this area, particularly those studies classified under the first two headings above. Their papers provide extensive coverage of inadequacies, such as the lack of control groups and nonspecification of subjects' demographic characteristics, which are not essential to the viability of the methodology itself. The present analysis will focus on issues concerning the scientific appropriateness of the methodology per se.

CLINICAL OBSERVATIONAL STUDIES

The major limitation inherent in the methodology of clinical observational studies is that the theoretical biases of the therapists tend to become inextricably interwoven with the recording and obtaining of data. Since there is no mechanical recording of the data, the therapist becomes the recording instrument. The therapist typically makes notes after the therapy session has been completed. Thus not only are his perceptions of the moment colored by his biases, but his recollections are subject to primacy-recency effects. Acquisition of the data is also likely to be affected by the therapist's preconceptions. Verbal conditioning studies have demonstrated that people's verbal productions can be shaped to a marked degree by the listener's expressions of interest. Therapists are likely to be unaware that they are selectively reinforcing certain aspects of their patients' behavior.

There is some evidence that many of the theoretical concepts that serve as a framework for therapists' descriptions of the familial characteristics of schizophrenics are not accurate (Jackson, Block,

Block, & Patterson, 1958). Jackson et al. asked 20 well-known psychiatrists, who had had considerable experience with schizophrenics and their families, to perform two Q sorts on 108 statements according to their conceptions of the schizophrenic's mother and father. Factor analysis produced three factors for each parent. The six factors were considered to represent the conceptions of mothers and fathers of schizophrenics most widely held in the field of psychiatry. The conceptions were correlated with descriptions of the parents of 20 autistic and 20 neurotic children which had been made by Q sorts of the same 108 items. None of the conceptions showed even a trend toward differentiating the two groups of parents. The results of the Jackson et al. study provide an empirical example and documentation of the inadequacies of this method. Whereas the clinical observational method is valuable as a source of provocative hypotheses and potentially fruitful insights, intrinsic difficulties make it unsuitable as a firm basis for a scientific methodology.

RETROSPECTIVE STUDIES

The validity of interviews and questionnaires for ascertaining the actual parental child-rearing practices and attitudes during the subject's childhood rests upon several assumptions: (*a*) that people conceptualize their lives in terms of the language used by the investigator so that their understanding of the questions is similar to that of the investigator; (*b*) that people can accurately recall events and feelings of many years past with minimal forgetting; (*c*) that people will report unpleasant events without selective forgetting, defensive distortion, and justification of actions by inaccurate elaboration; and (*d*) that people will report past events unaffected by social desirability or other response sets. Fortunately, there is a substantial amount of empirical data available for evaluating the tenability of these assumptions. McGraw and Molloy (1941) interviewed mothers twice concerning their retrospective accounts of the developmental history of their children. The first time, they conducted the interviews in the usual manner of an intake interviewer. One month later they interviewed the mothers again with more detailed and specific questioning, including pictorial representations of many of the developmental skills involved in the questions. The accuracy of the reports, when compared to staff examination of the children during their development, increased markedly from first to second interview for many questions, particularly for those accompanied by pictor-

ial representations. These results demonstrate the considerable lack of commonality of meaning between investigator and subject when questions are phrased in their typical, unelaborated form. Moreover, questions dealing with feelings and attitudes are not amenable to the pictorial specificity possible in other areas.

The ability of people to recall past events and feelings reliably has been investigated in wider, longitudinal research projects. Haggard, Brekstad, and Skard (1960), Robbins (1963), and Yarrow, Campbell, and Burton (1964) have compared retrospective parental reports to historical parental reports, and Jayaswal and Stott (1955), McGraw and Molloy (1941), Pyles, Stolz, and Macfarlane (1935), and Yarrow et al. (1964) have compared parental recollections to observational material obtained by a research staff during the children's development. All these studies found considerable unreliability in retrospective reports, as well as large intrasubject variability in accuracy across items.

Content of the material to be recalled has an important effect on accuracy of recall. Questions asking for recall of quantitative information and concrete events are answered more reliably than inquiries about attitudes and feelings (Haggard et al., 1960; Yarrow et al., 1964). Haggard et al. (1960) have reported, further, that the greater the initial anxiety associated with an attitude, the less accurately the attitude is recalled. In fact, recall of attitudes originally associated with great anxiety is almost completely unreliable. Kohn and Carroll (1960) found that the picture of past events varied considerably depending upon the member of the family doing the reporting. Heilbrun (1960) found no difference between the way the mothers of schizophrenic and of normal daughters described their child-rearing attitudes, but did find that schizophrenic daughters described their mothers as more pathological in their attitudes than did normal daughters. On the other hand, Jayaswal and Stott (1955) reported that young adults and their parents showed high agreement in their descriptions of the young adults as children. However, neither set of descriptions bore much relation to teachers' descriptions of the young adults obtained when they were children.

Many empirical studies have shown that social desirability and other response sets affect subjects' responses to questionnaire items. There are some data to indicate that responses to questions in an interview are subject to similar biases. McGraw and Molloy (1941) and Pyles et al. (1935) have shown that maternal inaccuracies in recall tended to be made in the direction of precocity in their children, that is, mothers tended to underestimate the age at which their children acquired developmental skills and the time taken to acquire the skills. Robbins (1963) has reported a variation on this finding. Inaccuracies tended to reflect the recommendations

of a noted contemporary child-rearing expert.

The results of studies evaluating the reliability of retrospective reports make the assumptions underlying the method untenable. Kasanin, Knight, and Sage (1934), Rabkin (1965), and Sanua (1961) have pointed out additional weaknesses in this method. Two are peculiar to the use of interview material from case history folders. These records vary widely in their completeness, with the result that many are rejected because of missing data. Overprotective mothers give more information about their children's background, so that a selective bias influences the characteristics of the records accepted. Offspring of such mothers are very likely overpresented in samples drawn on the basis of completeness. Another bias derives from the manner in which the case histories are obtained. The intake interviewer asks questions and records the data according to his theoretical biases. This same limitation was discussed in connection with the clinical observational method. There is one reservation peculiar to questionnaire data. A high and consistent relationship between current attitudes and current behavior has not yet been empirically demonstrated. It would seem to be an almost insurmountable task to demonstrate a high and consistent relationship between past attitudes and past behavior. For all the above reasons, the retrospective report method is judged to be an inadequate foundation for a body of scientific facts.

FAMILY INTERACTION STUDIES

A criticism that has been applied to each of the preceding methods of investigation is that, in many cases, the data are not recorded and coded objectively and systematically. Haley (1964) and Rabkin (1965) have extended this criticism to family interaction studies, pointing out that high interjudge reliabilities may occur as a result of two or more judges coding within the framework of the same theoretical biases. Thus, one could not be sure that the data were free of inferences from the observer. Haley

has suggested and used automatic recording and tabulating of interactional indices by electronic instruments (Haley, 1962, 1964). This insures highly reliable coding, but is purchased at a high price. In one study, Haley (1964) used a machine to tabulate automatically the number of times one person followed another in conversation. However, it is impossible to tell from the data whether the second person interrupted, asked a question, answered a question, disagreed, agreed, said something irrelevant, or was even talking to the first person. The meaningfulness of the data is questionable when they are stripped of such categories. It should be possible, however, to make increased use of instrumentation without sacrificing most of the content of the interaction. Even at best, instrumentation would not solve the problem completely, since the investigator must still program his instruments to code selected aspects of the interaction. A balance must be reached between unchecked observer contamination and such rigid control of possible contamination that essential aspects of the phenomenon under investigation are obscured. At the present time, establishment of high interjudge reliabilities seems to be a workable solution to the dilemma.

Family interaction studies that seek to discover factors which are etiologically relevant to the development of schizophrenia necessarily assume that the causal factors lie in the characteristics of the family interaction pattern. Many people have made the opposite assumption that it is the schizophrenia of the child which has caused the family to develop certain interactional characteristics. Thus, if family interaction studies could demonstrate differences between families of schizophrenics and nonschizophrenics, the question would still be moot as to the locus of cause and effect. At the present time, one assumption is as valid as the other. The assumption that the family interaction patterns are the causal factors in the development of schizophrenia is important for present purposes because it implies several other assumptions concerning methodology. The first is that the interaction patterns in the experimental setting are the usual family patterns and the subjects' usual behavior is not altered by the knowledge that they are being studied by professional experts. This assumption is particularly dubious for those studies in which a hospitalized schizophrenic group is compared to a nonhospitalized control group. The two groups of families undoubtedly have different perceptions of the meaning of the experimenter's request for participation. For the families of schizophrenics, participation is probably perceived as a way of helping their children; while for the families of nonhospitalized controls, it may well be seen as a test of their psychological

health or normality. Each family's perception of its role in the research program would probably affect its mode of interaction. For example, Cheek (1964a) has found that mothers of normals were significantly more ego defensive than mothers of schizophrenics. A similar trend was also obtained for fathers (Cheek, 1965). The problem of differential defensiveness can be largely circumvented by utilizing families of other institutionalized and stigmatized groups as controls so that all are recruited on the same basis and are likely to share the meaning of the request for participation. People could still be expected to react to being studied, but the groups would not be differentially affected. The possibility (and probability) that people's behavior will be affected by the knowledge that they are being observed is present in all areas of psychology.

A second assumption, related to the first, is that current interaction patterns are unchanged from their characteristics before the child became a patient. This means that the way family members interact is unaffected by the hospitalization, and consequent change in status. It is particularly unlikely that this assumption would be valid for chronic patients. If a person has been hospitalized for a long time or for a large number of times, the family is likely to incorporate his status as a mental patient into its image of him. Likewise, the person could be expected to modify his self-concept to include the attributes of the chronic mental patient. Institutionalization effects can be lessened by using only families of acute patients, for whom hospitalization would more likely be perceived as transitory. An even more desirable group would be families of persons on outpatient or trial visit status.

A third assumption is that current interaction patterns are essentially unchanged from their characteristics at the time the child was becoming schizophrenic. In order for this assumption to be valid, there must have been no essential change over time due to aging of the parents and maturation of the child. The crucial aspect of this position revolves around the word "essential." The extent to which basic personality and interactional characteristics are modifiable beyond the first few years of life is still an issue of considerable dispute.

186

A fourth assumption is also made that the task around which the interaction is organized does not alter the pattern in some unique way so that it is specific to that task and a circumscribed group of similar tasks. Rather, it is assumed that the families react to the experimental task as they characteristically react to most tasks.

A fifth assumption is that family interaction patterns are the same when some members are absent as they are when all members are present. This assumption appears of dubious validity, but whether different groups of families are affected differentially by missing members is unknown. Siblings of the patients or control subjects could be included in the interactions in order to investigate this possibility.

Consideration of these five assumptions highlights the tentativeness of etiological conclusions that might be drawn from family interaction studies.

Nevertheless, the study of family interaction holds promise for providing valuable guidelines for the design and hypothetical formulations of longitudinal studies, from which appropriate cause and effect statements can be made. If the inconclusiveness of the etiological assumption is granted and accepted, then there are no apparent, intrinsic methodological inadequacies to the study of family interaction which would disqualify it as a scientific endeavor. The possible limitations of method arising from the etiological assumption can be largely circumvented or minimized by careful attention to specific controls. With this in mind, let us proceed to an examination of family interaction studies, first from a methodological viewpoint and then from the perspective of empirical results from the better designed studies.

DIFFICULTIES OF INTERPRETATION AND EVALUATION

Studies employing the direct recording and systematic coding of actual family interactions have been few in number and recent in origin. This reviewer is aware of only 20 reports subsequent to the year 1950 which fall into this category, with the earliest published in 1958. The paucity of such studies is primarily due to two factors: (*a*) the recent interest in the study of interpersonal relations, and (*b*) the difficulty in conducting such studies. In view of the latter factor, it is unfortunate that the results of the labor and effort invested in the majority of studies have been negated by insufficient attention to essential controls. On the basis of considerations arising from the etiological assumption and from data demonstrating the possible confounding effects of certain variables, nine criteria were selected for evaluating the methodological adequacy of studies in this area. This reviewer's judgments of the methodological status of family interaction studies are summarized in Table 1. It is apparent from the table that there is great variability among the studies, and that much desired information is unavailable from the published reports. It is important that control and experimental groups be comparable on as many demographic variables as possible, but particularly on ages of parents and children, sex and birth order of the children, family size, and social class of the family.

Different rates of interaction and patterns of participation could be expected between parents and offspring, depending on the ages of both. All parents might plausibly be expected to be more indulgent of a small child than of a young or middle-aged adult. Similarly, adult patients and control subjects could be expected to relate somewhat differently to their parents if the latter were middle-aged than if they were close to retirement age.

The importance of keeping the sexes separate in the data analysis has been demonstrated in a number of studies. Cheek (1964b) found that schizophrenic women were more active in family interactions than were normal women, and schizophrenic men were less active than normal men. In addition, women were higher than men in acknowledgements,

TABLE 1. *Methodological Summary of Family Interaction Studies*

Author	Demographic Comparability of Control and Schizophrenic Groups	Sex of Subjects[a]	Hospital Status of Schizophrenic Group	Subdivision of Schizophrenic Group
Baxter et al. (1962)	No control group	m & f	Acute	Poor premorbid[d]
Baxter & Arthur (1964)	No control group	m	Acute	Poor & good premorbid
Behrens & Goldfarb (1958)	Questionable	m & f	Ns	—[e]
Caputo (1963)	Good	m	Chronic	—
Cheek (1964a)	Fair	m & f[b]	Convalescent	—
Cheek (1964b)	Fair	m & f[b]	Convalescent	—
Cheek (1965)	Fair	m & f[b]	Convalescent	—
Farina (1960)	Fair	m	Acute	Poor & good premorbid
Farina & Dunham (1963)	No control group	m	Acute	Poor & good premorbid
Ferreira (1963	Questionable	m & f	Ns	—
Ferreira & Winter (1965)	Good	m & f	Ns	—
Fisher et al. (1959)	Good	m	Ns	—
Haley (1962)	Fair	m & f	Ns	—
Haley (1964)	Questionable	m & f	Ns	—[e]
Lennard et al. (1965)	Fair	m	Ns	—[e]
Lerner (1965)	Good	m	Ns[c]	High & low genetic level[f]
McCord et al. (1962)	Good	m	Prehospitalization	—[e]
Meyers & Goldfarb (1961)	Fair	m & f	Ns	Organic & nonorganic
Morris & Wynne (1965)	Questionable	m & f	Ns	—
Stabenau et al. (1965)	Good	m & f	Ns	—

Note.—Ns = not stated, Vs = vaguely stated, Mt = machine tabulated.

[a] m = male, f = female.

[b] Analyzed separately.

[c] Schizophrenic and control groups were equated on length of current hospitalization

[d] Premorbidity rated according to the Phillips' (1953) scale.

[e] Included unspecified psychotics.

tension release, giving opinions, and asking for opinions, and asking for opinions. Ferreira (1963) reported a difference in frequency of coalitions with each parent in normal families, depending on the sex of the child. Same-sex coalitions were more frequent than opposite-sex coalitions. This same rela-

Control Group	"Blind" Coding of Data	Reliability of Coding	Members in Interaction[h]	Task Characteristics
—	Ns	Good	F,M,C	Joint interview
—	Ns	Good	F,M	Joint interview
Maladjusted persons	No	Fair	F(u)	Home interactions
Normals[g]	Ns	Vs	F,M	RDT[j]
Normals	Ns	Vs	F,M,C	RDT
Normals	Ns	Vs	F,M,C	RDT
Normals	Ns	Vs	F,M,C	RDT
Tubercular patients[g]	Ns	High	F,M	RDT
—	Ns	High	F,M,C	RDT
Normals, maladjusted persons	Ns	Ns	F,M,C	RDT
Normals, delinquents, maladjusted persons	Ns	Ns	F,M,C	RDT
Neurotics,[g] normals,[g] normals	Yes	High	F,M	Family discussion, TAT story construction
Normals	Mt	High	F,M,C	Game
Normals	Mt	High	F,M,C	RDT, TAT story construction
Normals	Ns	Ns	F,M,C	Family discussion
Normals[g]	Ns	High	F,M	RDT
Maladjusted persons	Yes	Good	F,M,C	Home interactions
Normals	No	Ns	F(u)	Home interactions
Neurotics[g]	Yes	Unobtained	F,M[i]	Joint therapy
Delinquents, normals	Ns	Ns	F,M,C, S	RDT

[f] According to Becker's (1956) system of Rorschach analysis.
[g] Hospitalized.
[h] F = father, M = mother, C = child, S = sib, F(u) = family (unspecified).
[i] Patient present but not a verbal contributor.
[j] Modification of the Revealed Difference Technique, after Strodtbeck (1951).

tionship was found in a subsequent study (Ferreira & Winter, 1965) in terms of the initial private agreement between parents and children, and observed to increase with increasing age of the children. Again, this relationship only occurred in normal families. Baxter, Arthur, Flood, and Hedgepeth

(1962) found that families of male and female schizophrenics differed in amount of conflict, depending on whether conflict was coded from the extent of initial, private agreement among members or from disagreements arising during family interaction. Also, families of male patients tended to have more mother-father conflict, while mother-patient conflict tended to be greater in the families of female patients. Investigators in most studies using the families of both male and female subjects have not equated their experimental and control groups for the number of each sex, while, at the same time, they have summed their interaction indices across sex. It is impossible to tell how much confounding this procedure may have introduced into the data analysis.

A control related to sex effects, which no study has considered, concerns the possible effects of birth order on interaction behavior. Schooler has used birth order as an independent variable in several studies of schizophrenia. He found that female schizophrenics disproportionately come from the last half of the birth order regardless of social class, while lastborn male schizophrenics disproportionately come from middle-class families and firstborns from lower-class families (Schooler, 1961, 1964). In two other studies, female schizophrenics born in the first half of the birth order were found to be more sociable than those born in the last half (Schooler & Scarr, 1962), and firstborn male schizophrenics were observed to perform better than middle borns who in turn performed better than lastborn patients on a task where their performance was seen as helpful to another person (Schooler & Long, 1963). These findings parallel those of Schachter (1959), obtained with normal women.

Closely allied with birth order is the issue of family size. It seems reasonable to expect that parents might have more contact with each of their children, the fewer of them there are. Also, the number of children in the family might reflect differences in parental attitudes and behavior toward their offspring.

Schooler (1964) and Cheek (1964b) have identified an important qualification which must be applied to all studies using hospitalized persons as sub-

jects. It is most appropriate to generalize only to hospitalized schizophrenics and not to all schizophrenics. Schooler noted that latter-born female schizophrenics manifested more noticeable symptomatology, such as hallucinations and suicidal tendencies, than did their counterparts born in the first half of the birth order. He has suggested that the florid character of their symptoms might lead to latter borns being hospitalized more readily, therefore being disproportionately represented in hospitals. In a similar vein, Cheek has suggested that overactive females and underactive males manifest interaction patterns deviant from societal norms, which may result in their being hospitalized more readily than those whose activity patterns are congruent with socially normative behavior. If many symptom characteristics turn out to be epiphenomena of a more basic, common schizophrenic process, the search for schizophrenic-specific factors will be somewhat confounded by society's attitudes toward different symptoms.

Social class embodies many attitude, value, knowledge, and social skill differences between people and, for this reason, is an extremely important variable to keep comparable among groups. Baxter and Arthur (1964) have provided striking evidence of how social class can interact with an independent variable to confound the results of the unwary investigator. These authors found that social class interacted with the premorbid adjustment of their male schizophrenic patients, so that middle-class parents of patients who had made a relatively adequate premorbid adjustment showed more conflict in interaction than did middle-class parents of patients who had made an inadequate premorbid adjustment, with the reverse results obtaining for lower-class groups of parents. All differences disappeared when the data were analyzed by social class or premorbidity alone. These results also argue for a subdivision of the schizophrenic sample according to some criteria such as good-poor premorbid adjustment or the process-reactive distinction. Both of these subdivisions have been empirically demonstrated to have prognostic validity (Becker, 1959; Phillips, 1953), to reduce the heterogeneity of schizophrenic performance (Garmezy & Rodnick, 1959;

Herron, 1962), and to be highly interrelated (Solomon & Zlotowsky, 1964). Thus, either subdivision makes an empirically meaningful distinction within schizophrenia, and holds promise of indicating a fruitful theoretical distinction as well.

Religion and ethnicity are two interrelated variables which have rarely been controlled. Sanua (1961) has argued that reports of contradictory results in the literature might be reconciled by closer consideration of differences in the subjects' religion and ethnicity. In an exploratory study, he (Sanua, 1963) found that parental characteristics differed widely according to the religion and social class of the families. These data are only suggestive however, since some essential methodological controls were not employed. A well-controlled study in this area has been reported by McClelland, de Charms, and Rindlisbacher (1955). These investigators questioned Protestant, Jewish, Irish-Catholic, and Italian-Catholic parents about their expectations concerning their children's mastery of several independence skills. In addition to main effects for sex of parent, level of parental education, and religion, they found a complex triple interaction of these variables with the expected age of mastery. There also tended to be a difference within religion between the expectations of Irish and Italian parents. The available evidence is sufficiently strong to warrant attention to the religious and ethnic composition of the subject sample. Certainly, it would be hazardous to ignore sizable religious and ethnic differences between experimental and control groups by assuming on an a priori basis that such differences are irrelevant to the style of family interaction.

A minority of studies specify the characteristics of their hospitalized samples in terms of the acuteness-chronicity dimension. In view of one of the assumptions of the method and the unknown effects of institutionalization on relatives and patients, it would seem to be a highly relevant variable.

Most studies have utilized some mechanical means of recording data, yet some have relied on an interviewer to manually record the interaction as it occurs or even after it has occurred. Most reports do not state whether the data were coded in a "blind" fashion or not, that is, with the coder unable to identify the group membership of the families. In many cases, the reliability of the coding procedure is not stated or is so vaguely stated as to be of unknown value.

DIFFICULTIES OF COMPARISON

Aside from differing degrees of methodological adequacy among studies, there are two factors which complicate direct comparison of results. One is the differing group membership comprising the "family." In some cases only parental interaction has been measured, while in other cases, interaction has included the contributions from the parents and the patient or control child, and in one case assessment was made of the interaction among parents, patient or control child, and another child of the family. It is difficult to assess the possible differential effects of group size, role diversity, and other factors which accompany variation in the number of members in interaction.

A second factor is the difference in task characteristics utilized in the studies. The majority have used modifications of the revealed difference technique (RDT) initially developed by Strodtbeck (1951). The RDT essentially consists of having each member of the family privately state his solutions to a number of problem situations. Then the experimenter asks the family to discuss each problem and to arrive at a group solution. The family discussion is recorded and coded for interaction indices such as agreement, yielding, interruption, and compromise. In studies employing the RDT, however, the range of problem situations extends from highly loaded interpersonal situations involving parent-child conflict to rather trivial, neutral situations. The focus of attention on the structure of family interaction has led to a neglect of the content, around which the interaction is organized, as a factor worthy of systematic study itself. It is not readily apparent that family reactions to situations involving parent-child conflict are structurally indistinguishable from reactions to differences among members concerning trivial preferences, such as choice of colors for an automobile or choice of food from a restaurant menu.

Instead of the RDT, other investigators have used joint interviews, family discussions, joint construction of TAT stories, home interactions, game playing, and joint therapy sessions. Haley (1964), using both the RDT and the construction of stories in the TAT, found that each task yielded somewhat different results, though each individually was inferior to the two combined in differentiating families of normals from those of psychiatric subjects. One must conclude that task characteristics do affect results, but that the extent of influence is currently undetermined.

EMPIRICAL RESULTS

The methodology of most family interaction studies leaves much to be desired. Several controls which are either essential or desirable have been suggested. The five most essential controls have been selected as the bases for determining the subset of studies with sufficiently sound methodology to permit comparison of results and evaluation of conclusions. Four studies have (a) utilized only schizophrenics in an experimental group, (b) analyzed the data separately by sex, (c) made some statement indicating attention to reliability of coding, (d) specified adequate comparability of control and experimental groups on demographic variables, and (e) included at least one hospitalized control group (Caputo, 1963; Farina, 1960; Fisher, Boyd, Walker, & Sheer, 1959; Lerner, 1965). The Baxter and Arthur (1964) studies did not include control groups, but are reviewed here because they were designed to test specific points concerning premorbidity differences in Farina's (1960) study. In addition, Cheek's (1964a, 1964b, 1965) reports of her study will be reviewed. Since neither the experimental nor the control group was hospitalized at the time of data collection, the extent to which this difference may have affected her data in comparison to the data of the other studies is unknown.

One of the most widespread and persistent notions concerning schizophrenic etiology is that of the "schizophrenogenic" mother (Fromm-Reich-mann, 1948). According to this notion, the family pattern of a strong, dominant mother and a weak, passive father deprives the son of an adequate model of identification. The son reacts to the stresses of this culturally atypical pattern by becoming schizophrenic. As a result of the popularity of this notion, the most frequently coded aspects of family interaction have been maternal and paternal dominance. Fisher et al. (1959) have reported that mothers of normals talked more than did mothers of neurotics or schizophrenics.[3] The latter two groups did not differ. There were no differences among the fathers of the three groups in amount of talking or initiation of conversation. Caputo (1963) found that the fathers of schizophrenics were generally more dominant than the mothers, with the fathers winning more disagreements than mothers. The parents of normals did not differ in the number of disagreements won. Lerner (1965) obtained no differences for mothers and fathers of normals and of two groups of schizophrenics in yielding to the other's position. Cheek (1964a, 1964b, 1965) found no support for the notion of the domineering "schizophrenogenic" mother. In the families of males, each

[3]All differences reported in this review have been found to be statistically significant at the .05 level or less, unless they are otherwise stated herein as tending to be the case, as trends, or as not significant.

member of the normal's family interacted in a more dominant way than each corresponding member of the schizophrenic's family. Thus all members of the schizophrenic's family were more passive than members of the normal's family when the offspring were males. The reverse tended to be true for fathers and offspring in the families of females: each of these members of the schizophrenic's family acted in a more dominant way than each corresponding member of the normal's family. On the other hand, mothers of both male and female normals were more dominant than mothers of schizophrenics. When pairs of means for indices relating to dominance are compared for mothers and fathers, the largest discrepancies between parents occur most often for the parents of normals. In other words, there tended to be a greater imbalance in dominance between parents in the families of normals than in the families of schizophrenics. The most notable exception to this trend was for the index, Total Interaction, for which fathers of both male and female schizophrenics tended to be more active relative to their wives, than fathers of normals. All of these findings are counter to what would be expected according to the schizophrenogenic mother notion.

Rodnick and Garmezy (1957; Garmezy & Rodnick, 1959) have proposed a theory which essentially states that the pattern of the schizophrenogenic mother can be found in the families of patients with a poor premorbid adjustment (Poors), while the reverse pattern can be observed in the families of schizophrenics with a relatively good premorbid adjustment (Goods). The adequacy of premorbid adjustment and degree of pathology are presumed to be causally related to the sex of the dominant parent, with the Poors being "sicker" because of the cultural atypicality of their family pattern. Discrepancy in parental dominance is held to be one of the pathognomonic factors predisposing to schizophrenia. One of the keystone studies testing the theory was conducted by Farina (1960). He found that the parents of Poors and Goods were different on all seven of his dominance indices, with Poors being mother dominated and Goods father dominated. However, enthusiasm for this finding as support for the theory must be tempered by consideration of other aspects of these and subsequent data. The parents of Poors were not different from the normals on any of the dominance indices. Goods differed from normals on four of the seven indices. However, two of the nonsignificant indices involved the extent of yielding of one parent to the other. Thus, although the parental dominance pattern for Poors is quite different from that of Goods, neither is strikingly different from the pattern for normals. It is particularly puzzling that the lesser difference from normals was found where the greater difference could have been expected from the theory, that is, in the families of Poors.

Farina also coded the interactions for conflict. It seems reasonable that initiation of conflict could be another way of viewing dominance. Inspection of the index means for conflict reveals that, in all groups, mothers tended to interrupt more and to disagree and agress more than did fathers. The parental differences are not significant, but the data indicate that the mothers in all groups initiated conflict at least as much as fathers did. A later study by Farina and Dunham (1963) investigated the interactions of mother, father, and patient for groups of Poors and Goods. Although some differences exist, this study can be considered an approximate replication of the Poor-Good comparisons in Farina's study. In the replication, the parental differences for the means of the dominance indices were not as consistent in direction as in the initial study, nor were any of the differences statistically significant. These studies neither support the proposition that the schizophrenogenic pattern is uniquely characteristic of the families of poor premorbid schizophrenics, nor do they offer strong or consistent support for the proposed interaction between parental dominance pattern and adequacy of the patients' social and sexual premorbid adjustment.

Another popular conception is that the schizophrenic's family, in many cases, is characterized by high levels of parental hostility and conflict (Lidz, Cornelison, Fleck & Terry, 1957). Fisher et al. (1959) found that the parents of schizophrenics and neurotics disagreed more than the parents of normals when they were discussing their sons. The parents of schizophrenics and neurotics did not differ in amount of disagreement. When parents worked jointly on constructing a TAT story, the parents of schizophrenics were higher in disagreement than parents of neurotics who were higher than parents of normals. Caputo (1963) reported that parents of schizophrenics disagreed more and displayed more hostility toward one another than did parents of normals. In Lerner's (1965) study, parents of normals compromised their differences more than either schizophrenic group did, although there were no significant differences among groups in lack of agreement without distortion. However, when lack of agreement with distortion was coded from the interaction, parents of the low genetic level schizophrenic group scored higher than parents of the high genetic level and normal groups. The theoretical significance of this distinction will be elaborated in the next section dealing with clarity of communication. Farina (1960) coded parental interactions on 10 indices of conflict. Parents of Poors manifested more conflict than parents of normals on seven of the indices, while parents of Goods and normals did not differ on any of the indices. Three indices showed differences within schizophrenia, with parents of Poors consistently higher than parents of Goods. The Farina and Dunham (1963) replication provided some support for the differences within schizophrenia obtained by Farina. It will be recalled that Baxter and Arthur (1964) found an interaction between social class and premorbidity affecting parental conflict scores. They suggested that Farina's Poor-Good differences in conflict may have resulted from the particular social-class characteristics of his groups and may not be attributable to premorbidity alone. In brief, the evidence consistently favors support of the contention that there is more conflict in the families of schizophrenics (particularly in the families of the more pathological patients, poor premorbids, and those with a low genetic level of development) than in the families of normals. Whether there is more conflict in the families of schizophrenics than in those of other psychiatric groups is less clear. Systematic variation of social class in this area is necessary for clarification and generalization of present trends.

A fourth theoretical position which can be evaluated in terms of the present data is that the etiological family factor pathognomonic for schizophrenia is lack of clarity in parental communication patterns. This idea has been most systematically developed by Wynne and Singer (1963a, 1963b). They have proposed that the unique characteristic of schizophrenia is disorder of the thought processes, particularly inability to focus attention on thematic material in a consistent and prolonged manner. The thought disorder is learned by imitation of parental patterns of communication, in which meanings are blurred by subtle shifts in attention to progressively tangential material. These authors have reported several successful attempts at differentiating the parents of schizophrenics from the parents of other groups on the basis of their projective test protocols (Singer & Wynne, 1963, 1965a, 1965b). Morris and Wynne (1965) have reported similar success using excerpts from joint therapy sessions. It is evident that these authors have engaged in a systematic research approach. However, before their results can be considered to be scientifically demonstrated, their research needs the introduction of some basic methodological controls such as specification of an objective coding system and establishment of acceptable interjudge reliabilities. Fortunately, the studies of Fisher et al. (1959) and Lerner (1965) provide more scientifically established evidence relevant to this theoretical position. Fisher et al. (1959) found that parents of normals were less ambiguous in their communication with each other than were the parents of neurotics and schizophrenics when they were discussing their sons, and were less ambiguous than parents of schizophrenics when jointly constructing a TAT story. It will be recalled that in the Lerner (1965) study there were no differences among parental groups of high and low genetic level schizophrenics and normals in extent of agreement without distortion of communication. When interactions were coded for lack of agreement *with* distortion, parents of the low genetic level group scored higher than parents of the high genetic level and normal groups. The latter two groups did not differ significantly. In addition, parents of the low genetic level group yielded more often than parents of the other two groups by "masking," that is, by claiming that they held a position different from the one which they had previously endorsed privately. These data lend support to Wynne and Singer's position that communication between parents of schizophrenics is less clear and comprehensible than it is between parents of normals.

CONCLUSIONS AND RECOMMENDATIONS

Studies obtaining data by clinical observation or by retrospective recall are unsuitable bases for a scientific body of etiological facts since the data are confounded by intrinsic methodological inadequacies. Interpretation of data acquired from direct recording and systematic coding of family interactions is subject to the cautions and tentativeness necessitated by the etiological assumption. *If the etiological assumption is granted and if the behavior sample is characteristic of the families' usual behavioral repertoire*, there are no apparent, intrinsic methodological inadequacies which disqualify this approach as unscientific. The greatest value of current studies of family interaction seems to lie in the guidelines the findings might provide for longitudinal research. Truly appropriate etiological conclusions can only be drawn from careful longitudinal studies. This reviewer doubts that sufficient knowledge is currently available to warrant the great expenditure involved in longitudinal research at the present time.

Four general findings are consistently supported by the few methodologically adequate research studies reviewed here: *(a)* there is no evidence for the proposed "schizophrenogenic" pattern of dominant mother—passive father, *(b)* there is little support for the proposed interaction between parental dominance pattern and premorbid adjustment of patients, *(c)* there is more conflict between the parents of schizophrenics (or a schizophrenic subgroup) than between the parents of normals, and *(d)* communication between parents of schizophrenics (or a schizophrenic subgroup) is less clear than it is between the parents of normals. These generalizations apply mainly to hospitalized white males. Future research on family interaction and schizophrenia would seem to require *(a)* use of families of recently institutionalized persons only; *(b)* comparability of control and experimental groups on social class, religion and ethnicity of the family, and sex, birth order, and premorbidity of the patients and control subjects; *(c)* inclusion of other institutionalized and stigmatized groups as controls, for example, non-schizophrenic psychiatric patients, tubercular patients, and prisoners; *(d)* investigation of the interaction of parents of schizophrenics with their non-schizophrenic children as a control condition; and *(e)* objective data recording, "blind" coding, and attainment of high interjudge reliabilities.

Handel (1965) and Haley (1962) have argued that it is premature to attempt to differentiate between the families of normal and pathological subjects or to attempt to differentiate among the families of pathological individuals. In their opinion before such differentiation is attempted, a typology of families according to dimensions and characteristics peculiar to intimate groups is needed. This reviewer believes that the most fruitful approach would direct attention to the two goals concurrently. Certainly the typology and classification of individuals according to traits and motives, independent of theoretical concerns, has not been very effective in the more traditional realms of psychology. A similar approach to family psychology could not reasonably be expected to have a different history.

REFERENCES

Baxter, J. C., & Arthur, S. C. Conflict in families of schizophrenics as a function of premorbid adjustment and social class. *Family Process,* 1964, *3,* 273-279.

Baxter, J. C., Arthur, S. C., Flood, C. G., & Hedgepeth, B. Conflict patterns in the families of schizophrenics. *Journal of Nervous and Mental Disease,* 1962, *135,* 419-424.

Becker, W. C. A genetic approach to the interpretation and evaluation of the process-reactive distinction in schizophrenia. *Journal of Abnormal and Social Psychology,* 1956, *53,* 229-236.

Becker, W. C. The process-reactive distinction: A key to the problem of schizophrenia? *Journal of Nervous and Mental Disease,* 1959, *129,* 442-449.

Behrens, M. L., & Goldfarb, W. A study of patterns of interaction of families of schizophrenic children in residential treatment. *American Journal of Orthopsychiatry,* 1958, *28,* 300-312.

Caputo, D. The parents of the schizophrenic. *Family Process,* 1963, *2,* 339-356.

Cheek, F. E. The "schizophrenogenic mother" in word and deed. *Family Process,* 1964, *3,* 155-177. (a)

Cheek, F. E. A serendipitous finding: Sex roles and schizophrenia. *Journal of Abnormal and Social Psychology,* 1964, *69,* 392-400. (b)

Cheek, F. E. The father of the schizophrenic. *Archives of General Psychiatry,* 1965, *13,* 336-345.

Farina, A. Patterns of role dominance and conflict in parents of schizophrenic patients. *Journal of Abnormal and Social Psychology,* 1960, *61,* 31-38.

Farina, A., & Dunham, R. M. Measurement of family relationships and their effects. *Archives of General Psychiatry,* 1963, *9,* 64-73.

Ferreira, A. J. Decision-making in normal and pathologic families. *Archives of General Psychiatry,* 1963, *8,* 68-73.

Ferreira, A. J., & Winter, W. D. Family interaction and decision making. *Archives of General Psychiatry,* 1965, *13,* 214-223.

Fisher, S., Boyd, I., Walker, D., & Sheer, D. Parents of schizophrenics, neurotics, and normals. *Archives of General Psychiatry,* 1959, *1,* 149-166.

Frank, G. H. The role of the family in the development of psychopathology. *Psychological Bulletin,* 1965, *64,* 191-205.

Fromm-Reichmann, F. Notes on the development of treatment of schizophrenics by psychoanalytic psychotherapy. *Psychiatry,* 1948, *11,* 263-273.

Garmezy, N., & Rodnick, E. H. Premorbid adjustment and performance in schizophrenia: Implications for interpreting heterogeneity in schizophrenia. *Journal of Nervous and Mental Disease,* 1959, *129,* 450-466.

Haggard, E. A., Brekstad, A., & Skard, A. On the reliability of the anamnestic interview. *Journal of Abnormal and Social Psychology,* 1960, *61,* 311-318.

Haley, J. Family experiments: A new type of experimentation. *Family Process,* 1962, *1,* 265-293.

Haley, J. Research on family patterns: An instrument measurement. *Family Process,* 1964, *3,* 41-65.

Handel, G. Psychological study of whole families. *Psychological Bulletin,* 1965, *63,* 19-41.

Heilbrun, A. B. Perception of maternal child rearing attitudes in schizophrenia. *Journal of Consulting Psychology,* 1960, *24,* 169-173.

Herron, W. G. The process-reactive classification of schizophrenia. *Psychological Bulletin,* 1962, *59,* 329-343.

Jackson, D. D., Block, J., Block, J., & Patterson, V. Psychiatrists' conceptions of the schizophrenogenic parent. *Archives of Neurology and Psychiatry,* 1958, *79,* 448-459.

Jayaswal, S. R., & Stott, L. H. Persistence and change in personality from childhood to adulthood. *Merrill-Palmer Quarterly,* 1955, *1,* 47-56.

Kasanin, J., Knight, E., & Sage, P. The parent-child relationship in schizophrenia. I. Overprotection-rejection. *Journal of Nervous and Mental Disease,* 1934, *72,* 249-263.

Kohn, M. L., & Carroll, E. E. Social class and the allocation of parental responsibilities. *Sociometry,* 1960, *23,* 372-392.

Lennard, H. L., Beaulieu, M. R., & Embry, N. G. Interaction in families with a schizophrenic child. *Archives of General Psychiatry,* 1965, *12,* 166-183.

Lerner, P. M. Resolution of intrafamilial role conflict in families of schizophrenic patients. I: Thought disturbance. *Journal of Nervous and Mental Disease,* 1965, *141,* 342-351.

Lidz, T., Cornelison, A. R., Fleck, S., & Terry, D. The intrafamilial environment of schizophrenic patients: II. Marital schism and marital skew. *American Journal of Psychiatry,* 1957, *114,* 241-248.

McClelland, D. C., de Charms, R., & Rindlisbacher, A. Religious and other sources of parental attitudes toward independence training. In D. McClelland (Ed.), *Studies in motivation.* New York: Appleton-Century-Crofts, 1955. Pp. 389-397.

McCord, W., Porta, J., & McCord, J. The familial genesis of psychoses. *Psychiatry,* 1962, *25,* 60-71.

McGraw, M. B., & Molloy, L. B. The pediatric anamnesis: Inaccuracies in eliciting developmental data. *Child Development,* 1941, *12,* 255-265.

Meissner, W. W. Thinking about the family-psychiatric aspects. *Family Process,* 1964, *3,* 1-40.

Meyers, D. F., & Goldfarb, W. Studies of perplexity in mothers of schizophrenic children. *American Journal of Orthopsychiatry,* 1961, *31,* 551-564.

Morris, G. O., & Wynne, L. C. Schizophrenic offspring and parental styles of communication. *Psychiatry,* 1965, *28,* 19-44.

Phillips, L. Case history data and prognosis in schizophrenia. *Journal of Nervous and Mental Disease,* 1953, *117,* 515-525.

Pyles, M. K., Stolz, H. R., & MacFarlane, J. W. The accuracy of mothers' reports on birth and developmental data. *Child Development*, 1935, *6*, 165-176.

Rabkin, L. Y. The patient's family: Research methods. *Family Process*, 1965, *4*, 105-132.

Robbins, L. C. The accuracy of parental recall of aspects of child development and of child rearing practices. *Journal of Abnormal and Social Psychology*, 1963, *66*, 261-270.

Rodnick, E. H., & Garmezy, N. An experimental approach to the study of motivation in schizophrenia. In M. R. Jones (Ed.), *Nebraska Symposium on Motivation: 1957*. Lincoln: University of Nebraska Press, 1957. Pp. 109-184.

Sanua, V. D. Sociocultural factors in families of schizophrenics. *Psychiatry*, 1961, *24*, 246-265.

Sanua, V. D. The sociocultural aspects of schizophrenia: A comparison of Protestant and Jewish schizophrenics. *International Journal of Social Psychiatry*, 1963, *9*, 27-36.

Schachter, S. *The psychology of affiliation*. Stanford, Calif.: Stanford University Press, 1959.

Schooler, C. Birth order and schizophrenia. *Archives of General Psychiatry*, 1961, *4*, 117-123.

Schooler, C. Birth order and hospitalization for schizophrenia. *Journal of Abnormal and Social Psychology*, 1964, *69*, 574-579.

Schooler, C., & Long, J. Affiliation among chronic schizophrenics: Factors affecting acceptance of responsibility for the fate of another. *Journal of Nervous and Mental Disease*, 1963, *137*, 173-179.

Schooler, C., & Scarr, S. Affiliation among chronic schizophrenics: Relation to intrapersonal and birth order factors. *Journal of Personality*, 1962, *30*, 178-192.

Singer, M. T., & Wynne, L. C. Differentiating characteristics of parents of childhood schizophrenics, childhood neurotics, and young adult schizophrenics. *American Journal of Psychiatry*, 1963, *120*, 234-243.

Singer, M. T., & Wynne, L. C. Thought disorder and family relations of schizophrenics. III. Methodology using projective techniques. *Archives of General Psychiatry*, 1965, *12*, 187-200. (a)

Singer, M. T., & Wynne, L. C. Thought disorder and family relations of schizophrenics. IV. Results and implications. *Archives of General Psychiatry*, 1965, *12*, 201-212. (b)

Solomon, L., & Zlotowski, M. The relationship between the Elgin and Phillips measures of process-reactive schizophrenia. *Journal of Nervous and Mental Disease*, 1964, *138*, 32-37.

Stabenau, J. R., Tupin, J., Werner, M., & Pollin, W. A comparative study of families of schizophrenics, delinquents, and normals. *Psychiatry*, 1965, *28*, 45-59.

Strodtbeck, F. Husband-wife interaction over revealed differences. *American Sociological Review*, 1951, *16*, 468-473.

FAMILIAL ETIOLOGY OF SCHIZOPHRENIA

Wynne, L. C., & Singer, M. T. Thought disorder and family relations of schizophrenics. I. A research strategy. *Archives of General Psychiatry,* 1963, *9,* 191-198. (a)

Wynne, L. C., & Singer, M. T. Thought disorder and the family relations of schizophrenics. II. Classification of forms of thinkings. *Archives of General Psychiatry,* 1963, *9,* 199-206. (b)

Yarrow, M. R., Campbell, J. D., & Burton, R. V. Reliability of maternal retrospection: A preliminary report. *Family Process,* 1964, *3,* 207-218.

19 *Psychiatric Disorders in Foster Home Reared Children of Schizophrenic Mothers**

LEONARD L. HESTON

INTRODUCTION

The place of genetic factors in the aetiology of schizophrenia remains disputed. Several surveys have demonstrated a significantly higher incidence of the disorder in relatives of schizophrenic persons as compared to the general population. Furthermore, the closer the relationship, the higher the incidence of schizophrenia. The studies of Kallmann (1938) and Slater (1953) are especially significant and the research in this area has been thoroughly reviewed by Alanen (1958).

Although the evidence for a primarily genetic aetiology of schizophrenia is impressive, an alternative explanation—that schizophrenia is produced by a distorted family environment—has not been excluded. A close relative who is schizophrenic can be presumed to produce a distorted interpersonal environment and the closer the relationship the greater the distortion.

This study tests the genetic contribution to schizophrenia by separating the effects of an environment made "schizophrenogenic" by the ambivalence and thinking disorder of a schizophrenic parent from the effects of genes from such a parent. This is done by comparing a group of adults born to schizophrenic mothers where mother and child were permanently separated after the first two postpartum weeks with a group of control subjects.

SELECTION OF SUBJECTS

The Experimental subjects were born between 1915 and 1945 to schizophrenic mothers confined to an Oregon State psychiatric hospital. Most of the subjects were born in the psychiatric hospital; however, hospital authorities encouraged confinement in a neighbouring general hospital whenever possible, in which case the children were delivered during brief furloughs. All apparently normal children born of such mothers during the above time span were included in the study if the mother's hospital record (1) specified a diagnosis of schizophrenia, dementia praecox, or psychosis; (2) contained sufficient de-

Leonard L. Heston, Psychiatric disorders in foster home reared children of schizophrenic mothers, *British Journal of Psychiatry, 112,* 1966, 819-826. Reproduced by permission.

*This research was supported by the Medical Research Foundation of Oregon.

scriptions of a thinking disorder or bizarre regressed behaviour to substantiate the diagnosis; (3) recorded a negative serologic test for syphilis and contained no evidence of coincident disease with known psychiatric manifestations; and (4) contained presumptive evidence that mother and child had been separated from birth. Such evidence typically consisted of a statement that the mother had yielded the child for adoption, a note that the father was divorcing the mother, the continued hospitalization of the mother for several years, or the death of the mother. In practice these requirements meant that the mothers as a group were biased in the direction of severe, chronic disease. No attempt was made to assess the psychiatric status of the father; however, none were known to be hospital patients. The 74 children ascertained as above were retained in the study if subsequent record searches or interviews confirmed that the child had had no contact with its natural mother and never lived with maternal relatives. (The latter restriction was intended to preclude significant exposure to the environment which might have produced the mother's schizophrenia.)

All of the children were discharged from the State hospital within three days of birth (in accordance with a strictly applied hospital policy) to the care of family members or to foundling homes. The records of the child care institutions made it possible to follow many subjects through their early life, including, for some, adoption. The early life of those subjects discharged to relatives was less completely known, although considerable information was developed by methods to be described.

Sixteen subjects were dropped because of information found in foundling home records; 6 children, 4 males and 2 females, died in early infancy. Ten others were discarded, 8 because of contact with their natural mother or maternal relatives, one because of multiple gastrointestinal anomalies, and one because no control subject whose history matched the bizarre series of events that complicated the Experimental subject's early life could be found. The remaining 58 subjects comprise the final Experimental group.

A like number of control subjects, apparently normal at birth, were selected from the records of the same foundling homes that received some of the Experimental subjects. The control subjects were matched for sex, type of eventual placement (adoptive, foster family, or institutional), and for length of time in child care institutions to within ±10 per cent up to 5 years. (Oregon State law prohibited keeping a child in an institution more than five years. Subjects in institutions up to this maximum were counted as "institutionalized" regardless of final placement.) Control subjects for the Experimental children who went to foundling homes were selected as follows: When the record of an Experimental subject was located, the admission next preceding in time was checked, then the next subsequent, then the second preceding and so on, until a child admitted to the home within a few days of birth and meeting the above criteria was found. Those Experimental subjects who were never in child care institutions were matched with children who had spent less than three months in a foundling home. The above method of selection was used with the record search beginning with an Experimental child's year of birth. The above restrictions regarding maternal contacts were applied to the con-

TABLE 1.

	Experimental		Control	
	Male	Female	Male	Female
Number	33	25	33	25
Died, infancy or childhood	3	6		5
Lost to follow-up		2		3
Final Groups	30	17	33	17

trol group. Oregon State psychiatric hospital records were searched for the names of the natural parents (where known) of the control subjects. In two cases a psychiatric hospital record was located and the children of these persons were replaced by others. All of the children went to families in which both parental figures were present.

Exact matching was complicated by the subsequent admission of several subjects to other child care institutions and by changes of foster or even adoptive homes. However, these disruptions occurred with equal frequency and intensity in the two groups and are considered random.

Table 1 gives the sex distribution of the subjects and the causes of further losses. Fifteen of the 74 Experimental subjects died before achieving school age. This rate is higher than that experienced by the general population for the ages and years involved, but not significantly so.

FOLLOW-UP METHOD

Starting in 1964, it proved possible to locate or account for all of the original subjects except five persons, all females. During this phase of the research, considerable background information of psychiatric import was developed. The records of all subjects known to police agencies and to the Veterans' Administration were examined. Retail credit reports were obtained for most subjects. School records, civil and criminal court actions, and newspaper files were reviewed. The records of all public psychiatric hospitals in the three West Coast States were screened for the names of the subjects and the records located were reviewed. Enquiries were directed to psychiatric facilities serving other areas where subjects were living, and to probation departments, private physicians, and various social service agencies with which the subjects were involved. Finally, relatives, friends and employers of most subjects were contacted.

In addition to information obtained from the above sources, for most subjects the psychiatric assessment included a personal interview, a Minnesota Multiphasic Personality Inventory (MMPI), and I.Q. test score, the social class of the subject's first home, and the subject's current social class. As the subjects were located, they were contacted by letter and asked to participate in a personal interview. The interview was standardized, although all promising leads were followed, and was structured as a general medical and environmental questionnaire which explored all important psychosocial dimensions in considerable depth. Nearly all of the interviews were conducted in the homes of the subjects, which added to the range of possible observations. The short form of the MMPI was given after the interview. The results of an I.Q. test were available from school or other records for nearly all subjects. If a test score was not available, the Information, Similarities, and Vocabulary subtests of the Wechsler Adult Intelligence Scale (WAIS) was administered and the I.Q. derived from the results. Two social class values were assigned according to the occupational classification system of Hollingshead (1958). One value was based on the occupation of the father or surrogate father of the subject's first family at the time of placement, and a second on the subject's present occupational status or, for married females, the occupation of the husband. The social class values move from 1 to 7 with decreasing social status.

All of the investigations and interviews were conducted by the author in 14 States and in Canada.

EVALUATION OF SUBJECTS

The dossier compiled on each subject, excluding genetic and institutional information, was evaluated blindly and independently by two psychiatrists. A third evaluation was made by the author. Two evaluative measures were used. A numerical score moving from 100 to 0 with increasing psycho-social disability was assigned for each subject. The scoring was based on the landmarks of the Menninger Mental Health-Sickness Rating Scale (MHSRS) (Luborsky, 1962). Where indicated, the raters also assigned a psychiatric diagnosis from the American Psychiatric Association nomenclature.

Evaluations of 97 persons were done. Seventy-two subjects were interviewed. Of the remaining 25 persons, six refused the interview (7.6 per cent, of those asked to participate), eight were deceased, seven are inaccessible (active in Armed Forces, abroad, etc.), and four were not approached because of risk of exposure of the subject's adoption. It did not seem reasonable to drop all of these 25 persons from the study, since considerable information was available for most of them. For instance, one man was killed in prison after intermittently spending most of his life there. His behavioural and social record was available in prison records plus the results of recent psychological evaluations. A man who refused the interview was a known, overt, practising homosexual who had a recent felony conviction for selling narcotics. All persons in the Armed Forces were known through letters from their Commanding Officers or medical officers to have been serving honourably without psychiatric or serious behavioural problems. One 21-year-old man, the least known of any of the subjects, had been in Europe for the preceding 18 months in an uncertain capacity. He is known to have graduated from high school and to have no adverse behavioural record. In a conference the raters agreed that it would be misleading to discard any cases, and that all subjects should be rated by forced choice.

The MHSRS proved highly reliable as a measure of degree of incapacity. The Intraclass Correlation Coefficient between the scores assigned by the respective raters was 0.94, indicating a high degree of accuracy. As expected, several differences arose in the assignment of specific diagnoses. In disputed cases a fourth psychiatrist was asked for an opinion and differences were discussed in conference. The only differences not easily resolved involved distinctions such as obsessive-compulsive neurosis versus compulsive personality or mixed neurosis versus emotionally unstable personality. All differences were within three diagnostic categories: psychoneurotic disorders, personality trait or personality pattern disturbances. The raters decided to merge these categories into one: "neurotic personality disorder." This category included all persons with MHSRS scores less than 75—the point on the scale where psychiatric symptoms become troublesome— who received various combinations of the above three diagnoses. In this way, complete agreement on four diagnoses was achieved: schizophrenia, mental deficiency, sociopathic personality, and neurotic personality disorder. One mental defective was also diagnosed schizophrenic and another sociopathic. Only one diagnosis was made for all other subjects.

RESULTS

Psychiatric disability was heavily concentrated in the Experimental group. Table 2 summarizes the results.

The MHSRS scores assess the cumulative psycho-social disability in the two groups. The difference is highly significant with the Experimental group, the more disabled by this measure. However, the difference is attributable to the low scores achieved

TABLE 2.

	Control	Experimental	Exact Probability*
Number	50	47	
Male	33	30	
Age, Mean	36.3	35.8	
Adopted	19	22	
MHSRS, Mean (Total group mean = 72.8, S.D. = 18.4)	80.1	65.2	0.0006
Schizophrenia (Morbid Risk = 16.6%)	0	5	0.024
Mental Deficiency (I.Q. < 70)	0	4	0.052
Sociopathic Personality	2	9	0.017
Neurotic Personality Disorder	7	13	0.052
Persons spending > 1 year in Penal or Psychiatric Institution	2	11	0.006
Total years Institutionalized	15	112	
Felons	2	7	0.054
Armed Forces, Number Serving	17	21	
Armed Forces, Number Discharges, Psychiatric or Behavioural	1	8	0.021
Social Group, First Home, Mean	4.2	4.5	
Social Group, Present, Mean	4.7	5.4	
I.Q., Mean	103.7	94.0	
Years School, Mean	12.4	11.6	
Children, Total	84	71	
Divorces, Total	7	6	
Never Married, > 30 Years Age	4	9	

One mental defective was also schizophrenic.
Another was sociopathic.
Considerable duplication occurs in the entries below Neurotic Personality Disorder.
*Fisher Exact Probability Test.

by about one-half (26/47) of the Experimental subjects rather than a general lowering of all scores.

The diagnosis of schizophrenia was based on generally accepted standards. In addition to the unanimous opinion of the three raters, all subjects were similarly diagnosed in psychiatric hospitals. One female and four males comprised the schizophrenic group. Three were chronic deteriorated patients who had been hospitalized for several years. The other two had been hospitalized and were taking antipsychotic drugs. One of the latter persons was also mentally deficient: a brief history of this person follows.

A farm labourer, now 36 years old, was in an institution for mentally retarded children from age 6-16. Several I.Q. tests averaged 62. He was discharged to a family farm, where he worked for the next 16 years. Before his hospitalization at age 32 he was described as a peculiar but harmless person who was interested only in his bank account: he saved $5,500 out of a salary averaging $900 per year. Following a windstorm that did major damage to the farm where he worked he appeared increasingly agitated. Two days later he threatened his employer with a knife and accused him of trying to poison him. A court committed him to a psychia-

tric hospital. When admitted, he talked to imaginary persons and assumed a posture of prayer for long periods. His responses to questions were incoherent or irrelevant. The hospital diagnosis was schizophrenic reaction. He was treated with phenothiazine drugs, became increasingly rational, and was discharged within a month. After discharge he returned to the same farm, but was less efficient in his work and spent long periods sitting and staring blankly. He has been followed as an out-patient since discharge, has taken phenothiazine drugs continuously, and anti-depressants occasionally. This man exhibited almost no facial expression. His responses to questions, though relevant, were given after a long and variable latency.

The age-corrected rate for schizophrenia is 16.6 per cent., a finding consistent with Kallmann's 16.4 per cent. (Weinberg's short method, age of risk 15-45 years). Hoffman (1921) and Oppler (1932) reported rates of from 7 to 10.8 per cent, of schizophrenia in children of schizophrenics. No relationship between the severity and sub-type of the disease in the mother-child pairs was evident.

Mental deficiency was diagnosed when a subject's I.Q. was consistently less than 70. All of these persons were in homes for mental defectives at some time during their life and one was continuously institutionalized. His I.Q. was 35. The other mentally deficient subjects had I.Q.s between 50 and 65. No history of CNS disease or trauma of possible causal importance was obtained for any of these subjects. The mothers of the mentally defective subjects were not different from the other mothers and none were mentally defective.

Three behavioural traits were found almost exclusively within the Experimental group. These were: (1) significant musical ability, 7 persons; (2) expression of unusually strong religious feeling, 6 persons; and (3) problem drinking, 8 persons.

The results with respect to the effects of institutional care, social group, and type of placement will be discussed in a later paper. None of these factors had measurable effects on the outcome.

DISCUSSION

The results of this study support a genetic aetiology of schizophrenia. Schizophrenia was found only in the offspring of schizophrenic mothers. The probability of this segregation being effected by chance is less than 0.025. Furthermore, about one-half of the Experimental group exhibited major psychosocial disability. The bulk of these persons had disorders other than schizophrenia which were nearly as malignant in effect as schizophrenia itself. An illustration is provided by the 8 of 21 Experimental males who received psychiatric or behavioural discharges from the armed services. If three subjects who were rejected for service for the same reasons are added, the ratio becomes 11:24, or essentially 1:2. Only three of these 11 subjects were schizophrenic and one schizophrenic served honourably. Kallmann's (1938) rate for first degree relatives and Slater's (1953) for dizygotic twins of schizophrenic persons who developed significant psycho-social disability not limited to schizophrenia are slightly lower, though in the same range, as those found in the present study.

The association of mental deficiency with schizophrenia has been reported by Hallgren and Sjogren (1959) who noted an incidence of low-grade mental deficiency (I.Q. <50-55) in schizophrenic subjects of about 10.5 per cent. Kallmann (1938) found from 5-10 per cent mental defectives among his descendants of schizophrenic persons, but did not consider the finding significant. The association of mental deficiency with schizophrenia—if such an association exists—remains uncertain.

Two sub-groups of persons within the impaired one-half of Experimental subjects exhibited roughly delineable symptom-behaviour complexes other than schizophrenia or mental deficiency. The personalities of the persons composing these groups are described in aggregate below.

The first group is composed of subjects who fit the older diagnostic category, "schizoid psychopath". This term was used by Kallmann (1938) to describe a significant sub-group of his relatives of schizophrenic persons. Eight males from the present study fall into this group, all of whom received a diagnosis of sociopathic personality. These persons are distinguished by anti-social behaviour of an impulsive, illogical nature. Multiple arrests for assault, battery, poorly planned impulsive thefts dot their police records. Two were homosexual, four alcoholic, and one person, also homosexual, was a narcotics addict. These subjects tended to live alone—only one was married—in deteriorated hotels and rooming houses in large cities, and locating them would have been impossible without the co-operation of the police. They worked at irregular casual jobs such as dishwasher, race-track tout, parking attendants. When interviewed they did not acknowledge or exhibit evidence of anxiety. Usually secretive about their own life and circumstances, they expressed very definite though general opinions regarding social and political ills. In spite of their suggestive life histories, no evidence of schizophrenia was elicited in interviews. No similar personalities were found among the control subjects.

A second sub-group was characterized by emotional lability and may correspond to the neurotic sibs of schizophrenics described by Alanen (1963). Six females and two males from the Experimental group as opposed to two control subjects were in this category. These persons complained of anxiety or panic attacks, hyper-irritability, and depression. The most frequent complaint was panic when in groups of people as in church or at parties, which was so profoundly uncomfortable that the subject was forced to remove himself abruptly. Most subjects described their problems as occurring episodically; a situation that they might tolerate with ease on one occasion was intolerable on another. The woman reported life-long difficulty with menses, especially hyper-irritability or crying spells, and depressions coincident with pregnancy. These subjects described themselves as "moody", stating that they usually could not relate their mood swings to temporal events. Four such subjects referred to their strong religious beliefs much more frequently than other respondents. Psychophysiological gastro-intestinal symptoms were prominent in five subjects. The most frequent diagnoses advanced by the raters were emotionally unstable personality and cyclothymic personality, with neurosis a strong third.

Of the 9 persons in the control group who were seriously disabled, 2 were professional criminals, careful and methodical in their work, 2 were very similar to the emotionally labile group described above, one was a compulsive phobia-ridden neurotic, and 4 were inadequate or passive-aggressiver personalities.

The 21 Experimental subjects who exhibited no significant psycho-social impairment were not only successful adults but in comparison to the control group were more spontaneous when interviewed and had more colourful life histories. They held the more creative jobs: musician, teacher, home-designer; and followed the more imaginative hobbies: oil painting, music, antique aircraft. Within the Experimental group there was much more variability of personality and behaviour in all social dimensions.

SUMMARY

This report compares the psycho-social adjustment of 47 adults born to schizophrenic mothers with 50 control adults, where all subjects had been separated from their natural mothers from the first few days of life. The comparison is based on a review of school, police, veterans, and hospital, among several other records, plus a personal interview and MMPI which were administered to 72 subjects. An I.Q. and social class determination were also available. Three psychiatrists independently rated the subjects. The results were:

1. Schizophrenic and sociopathic personality disorders were found in those persons born to schizophrenic persons in an excess exceeding chance expectation at the 0.05 level of probability. Five of 47 persons born to schizophrenic mothers were schizophrenic. No cases of schizophrenia were found in 50 control subjects.

2. Several other comparisons, such as persons given other psychiatric diagnoses, felons, and persons discharged from the Armed Forces for psychiatric or behavioural reasons, demonstrated a significant excess of psycho-social disability in about one-half of the persons born to schizophrenic mothers.

3. The remaining one-half of the persons born to schizophrenic mothers were notably successful adults. They possessed artistic talents and demonstrated imaginative adaptations to life which were uncommon in the control group.

ACKNOWLEDGMENTS

The author is greatly indebted to Drs. Duane D. Denney, Ira B. Pauly, and Arlen Quan who evaluated the case histories and provided invaluable advice and encouragement. Drs. Paul Blachly, John Kangas, Harold Osterud, George Saslow, and Richard Thompson provided advice and/or facilities which greatly contributed to the success of the project. All of the above are faculty or staff members of the University of Oregon Medical School.

This research could not have been completed without the splendid co-operation of numerous officials of various agencies who provided indispensable information. I am especially indebted to the following: Dean R. Mathews, Waverly Baby Home; Elda Russell, Albertina Kerr Nurseries; Stuart R. Stimmel and Esther Rankin, Boys' and Girls' Aid Society of Oregon; Reverend Morton E. Park, Catholic Charities; George K. Robbins, Jewish Family and Child Services; Miss Marian Martin, State of Oregon, Department of Vital Statistics, all of Portland, Oregon. Drs. Dean K. Brooks, E. I. Silk, Russel M. Guiss, J. M. Pomeroy, Superintendents of Oregon State Hospital, Eastern Oregon State Hospital, Dammasch State Hospital, and Oregon Fairview Home, respectively. David G. Berger, Research Coordinator, Oregon State Board of Control; Stewart Adams, Research Director, Los Angeles County Probation Department; Robert Tyler, Research Information Director, California Bureau of Corrections; Evan Iverson, State of Washington, Department of Institutions; Anthony Hordern, Chief of Research, California Department of Mental Hygiene; Captain George Kanz, Oregon State Police; J. S. Gleason, Administrator, Veterans' Administration; and Lt.-General Leonard D. Heaton, Rear-Admiral E. C. Kenney, and Major-General R. L. Bohannon, Chief Medical Officers of the Army, Navy and Air Force respectively.

Renate Whitaker, University of Oregon Medical School, and Eliot Slater and James Shields of the Psychiatric Genetics Research Unit, Maudsley Hospital, London, reviewed the manuscript and made many helpful suggestions.

Finally, I wish gratefully to acknowledge the contribution made by the subjects of this research project, most of whom freely gave of themselves in the interest of furthering medical science.

REFERENCES

Alanen, Y. O. (1958). "The mothers of schizophrenic patients." *Acta psychiat. neurol. scand.,* Suppl. 1227.

—, Rekola, J., Staven, A., Tlovinen, M., Takala, K., and Rutanen, E. (1963). "Mental disorders in the siblings of schizophrenic patients." *Acta psychiat. scand.,* Suppl. 169, *39,* 167.

Hallgren, B., and Sjogren, T. (1959). "A clinical and genetico-statistical study of schizophrenia and low grade mental deficiency in a large Swedish rural population." *Acta psychiat. neurol. scand.,* Suppl. 140. Vol. *35.*

Hoffman, H. (1921). "Studien uber Vererbung und Entstehung geistiger Storungen. II. Die Nachkommenschaft bei endogenen Psychosen." Berlin: Springer.

Hollingshead, A. B., and Redlich, F. C. (1958). *Social Class and Mental Illness: A Community Study.* New York: J. Wiley.

Kallmann, F. J. (1938). *The Genetics of Schizophrenia.* New York: J. J. Augustin.

Luborsky, L. (1962). "Clinicians' judgements of mental health: a proposed scale." *Arch. gen. Psychiat. (Chic.), 7,* 407.

Oppler, W. (1932). "Zum Problem der Erbprognosebestimmung." *Z. Neurol., 141,* 549-616.

Slater, E., with Shields, J. (1953). *Psychotic and neurotic illnesses in twins.* Medical Research Council Special Report Series No. 278. London: H. M. Stationery Office.

20. Breakdown in Individuals at High Risk for Schizophrenia: Possible Predispositional Perinatal Factors

SARNOFF A. MEDNICK

The investigators observed a distinctive premorbid pattern of behavior in a group of adolescents who suffered psychiatric breakdown. This pattern was found to be closely associated with pregnancy and birth complications which could have produced anoxic states likely to damage certain areas of the brain. One such area is the hippocampus. The adolescents who suffered complications exhibit a pattern of behavior analogous to the behavior of rats with surgically-inflicted hippocampal lesions. Neurophysiological and biochemical mechanisms are described which could mediate the hypothesized relationship between a damaged or weakened hippocampus and the pattern of behavior of the breakdown group.

In 1962-63 in Copenhagen, Denmark, Dr. Fini Schulsinger and I intensively examined 207 "normally functioning" children with a high risk of becoming schizophrenic. (They have chronic and severely schizophrenic mothers.) We also examined 104 controls. The study is prospective and longitudinal. We intend to follow these 311 subjects for 20-25 years. During the course of these years we estimate that approximately 100 of the high-risk children will succumb to some form of mental illness, twenty-five to thirty should become schizophrenic.

Figure 1 presents a schematic picture of the research design of this type of study. There are certain research advantages in the longitudinal study of such high-risk populations.

1. They have not yet experienced many aspects of the schizophrenic life such as hospitalizations and drugs. Thus, these factors do not yet color their reactions.

Sarnoff A. Mednick, Breakdown in individuals at high risk for schizophrenia: possible predispositional perinatal factors, *Mental Hygiene,* 1970, *54,* 50-63. Reproduced by permission.

This article is adapted from an address delivered at the annual meeting of the Society for Research in Child Development in Santa Monica, Calif. on March 27, 1969.

The author wishes to express his appreciation to Drs. Donald Kenefick, Daniel Kimble, Neal Miller, Fini Schulsinger and Peter Venables for their advice and criticism. This research project has been supported in part by the National Association for Mental Health and the Scottish Rite Committee for Research in Schizophrenia.

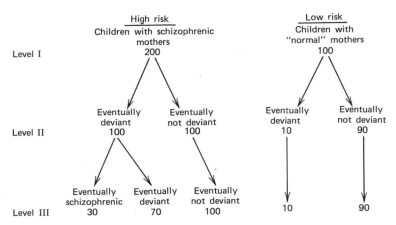

FIG. 1.

The design can be conceptualized as developing at three levels. At the first level we can study the distinguishing characteristics of children with schizophrenic mothers in comparison with children with no familial psychiatric background. At the second level we can estimate that about 50% of the high-risk children will become seriously socially deviant. Rather good controls for these deviants are the children with schizophrenic mothers who do not become deviant. At the third level we can estimate that perhaps 30 of the 100 high-risk deviants will be diagnosed schizophrenic. The remaining 70 high-risk deviants may be considered appropriate controls for these 30 schizophrenics, as may the nondeviant, high-risk children and the low-risk children.

Such a study may not be readily or at least easily replicated. Others using even the same design may not be attracted to the same variables. In view of this fact a form of replication can be built into the design. At level II the 100 eventually deviant individuals may be conceived of as suffering breakdown in five waves of 20 subjects each. Thus, there are four potential replications of the first data analysis. (It should be mentioned that the precision of the replication might be attenuated if the waves differ in age of breakdown or diagnosis.) At level III the 30 schizophrenics may be conceived of as suffering breakdown in two waves of 15 subjects each.

2. The researchers, relatives, teachers and the subject himself do not know that he will become schizophrenic. This relieves the data of a certain part of the burden of bias. The bias is certainly greater for the future schizophrenic than for other high-risk subjects who do not succumb.
3. The information we gather is current, not retrospective. That part of our inquiry which is retrospective is less so than it would be if the subjects were adults.

I will briefly summarize the 1962 premorbid characteristics that distinctly differentiated these 20 sick children from controls.

METHODS

The high- and low-risk samples were matched, individual for individual, for certain variables. (Table 1).

As may be seen, the average age of the sample was 15.1 years (range was 9-20 years). There would

TABLE 1. *Characteristics of the Experimental and Control Samples*

	Control	Experimental
Number of cases	104	207
Number of boys	59	121
Number of girls	45	86
Mean age	15.1	15.1
Mean social class†	2.3	2.2
Mean years education	7.3	7.0
Per cent of group in children's homes (5 years or more)	14%	16%
Mean number of years in children's homes (5 years or more)	8.5	9.4
Per cent of group with rural residence ϕ	22%	26%

Defined as age to the nearest whole year.

†The scale runs from 0 (low) to 6 (high) and was adapted from Svalastoga (1959). We only considered experience in children's homes of 5 years or greater duration. Many of the Experimental children had been to children's homes for brief periods while their mothers were hospitalized. These experiences were seen as quite different from the experience of children who actually had to make a children's home their home until they could go out and earn their own living.

ϕ A rural residence was defined as living in a town with a population of 2500 persons or fewer.

have been some advantage in testing a younger group; however, it will take 20-25 years for the present sample to pass through the major risk period for schizophrenia. The subjects' mean age was selected so as to maximize the probability that the investigators would still be alive at the conclusion of this risk period. Studies of three-year-old and ten-year-old high-risk samples are being undertaken. A study of prenatal high-risk children is being planned.

PROCEDURES

In addition to weight and height the following measures were taken in the intensive 1962 examination:

1. Physiological-conditioning-extinction testing. Continuous recording was made of heart rate, muscle tension, respiration, and galvanic skin response (GSR) during rest, conditioning, generalization and extinction procedures. The CS was a 54 db tone of 1000 cps. The UCS (also considered the stress stimulus) was a very irritating, loud (96 db) noise presented via earphones.

2. *Wechsler Intelligence Scale for Children.* (Danish adaptation). All subtests were administered.

3. *Personality Inventory.* This consisted of a group of items translated from the MMPI.

4. *Word Association Test.* This was a translation of the Kent-Rosanoff list.

5. *Continuous Association Test.* We observed the flow of the subject's associations to a single word over a one-minute period. Thirty stimulus words were used.

6. *Adjective Check List.* A list of 241 items was used by professional personnel to describe the

subject. The subject also described himself using the same list.

7. *Psychiatric Interview.* A pre-coded psychiatric interview was included for diagnostic purposes and to elicit reports from the subject on his current social and interpersonal functioning. A rating of Level of Adjustment was made for each subject.

8. *Parent Interview.* A pre-coded interview was conducted with the individual with major responsibility for the child's rearing.

9. *School Report.* A questionnaire was obtained from the teacher that knew each subject best.

10. *Midwife's Report.* This is a detailed, legally required, standard form prepared by the midwife attending the subject's birth.

More detailed statements of methodology may be found in Mednick and Schulsinger.[29,30,31]

RESULTS

As of last year, the first wave of 20 breakdowns (which we call the Sick Group) had been identified. Their clinical status is described very briefly in Table 2. Thirteen have been admitted to psychiatric hospitals with many diagnoses including schizophrenia. The seven not admitted include some who are clearly schizophrenic. The clinical status of these individuals was ascertained by our follow-up procedures. To each of these 20 we have matched another high-risk subject (Well Group) of the same age, sex, social class, and institutional rearing status. In addition we have matched these subjects for the psychiatrist's 1962 Level of Adjustment rating. We tried as much as possible to select individuals for the Well Group who, since 1962, had shown some improvement in Level of Adjustment. Also, 20 Controls were selected from the low-risk group for comparison purposes. This matching yielded two groups of high-risk subjects. In 1962, both were judged to be equal in Level of Adjustment. Yet

TABLE 2. *Descriptions of Conditions of Sick Group*

1. Male, born 16 March 1953. Extremely withdrawn, no close contacts, 2 months' psychiatric admission following theft, currently in institution for boys with behavior difficulties, still performing petty thieveries.

2. Female, born 19 January 1943. Married, one child, extremely withdrawn, nervous. Evidence of delusional thinking, pulls her hair out, has large bald area.

3. Female, born 29 March 1946. Promiscuous, highly unstable in work, no close contacts, confused and unrealistic, psychiatric admission for diagnostic reasons, recent abortion, some evidence of thought disorder.

4. Male, born 1 July 1946. Under minor provocation had semipsychotic breakdown in Army, expresses strange distortions of his body image, thought processes vague, immature.

5. Male, born 2 May 1944. Severe difficulties in concentrating, cannot complete tasks, marked schizoid character, marginally adjusted.

6. Male, born 3 June 1947. Lonely in the extreme, spends all spare time at home. Manages at home only by virtue of extremely compulsive routines. No heterosexual activity, marked schizoid character.

TABLE 2. (continued)

7. Male, born 1 October 1953. No close contact with peers, attends class for retarded children, abuses younger children, recently took a little boy out in the forest, undressed him, urinated on him and his clothes, and sent him home.

8. Male, born 17 January 1954. Has history of convulsions, constantly takes antiseizure drug (Dilantin), nervous, confabulating, unhappy, sees frightening "nightmares" during the day, afraid of going to sleep because of nightmares and fear that people are watching through the window, feels teacher punishes him unjustly.

9. Female, born 18 March 1944. Nervous, quick mood changes, body image distortions, passive, resigned. Psychiatric admission, paranoid tendencies revealed, vague train of thought.

10. Male, born 14 March 1952. Arrested for involvement in theft of motorbike. Extremely withdrawn, difficulties in concentration, passive, disinterested, father objected to his being institutionalized, consequently he is now out under psychiatric supervision.

11. Male, born 19 October 1947. Level of intellectual performance in apprenticeship decreasing, private life extremely disorderly, abreacts through alcoholism.

12. Male, born 20 January 1944. Severe schizoid character, no heterosexual activity, lives an immature, shy, anhedonic life, thought disturbances revealed in TAT.

13. Female, born 25 May 1947. Psychiatric admission, abortion, hospital report suspect pseudoneurotic or early schizophrenia, association test betrays thought disturbance, tense, guarded, ambivalent. Current difficulties somewhat precipitated by sudden death of boy friend.

14. Male, born 13 August 1950. Sensitive, negativistic, unrealistic. Recently stopped working and was referred to a youth guidance clinic for evaluation. Is now under regular supervision of a psychologist.

15. Male, born 28 May 1947. History of car stealing, unstable, drifting, unemployed, sensitive, easily hurt, one year institutionalization in a reformatory for the worst delinquents in Denmark.

16. Female, born 1 June 1945. Psychotic episode, one year of hospitalization. Diagnoses from 2 hospitals: (1) schizophrenia, (2) manic psychosis.

17. Male, born 3 September 1946. Severe schizoid character, psychotic breakdown in Army, preceded by arrest for car thievery. Now hospitalized.

18. Male, born 28 January 1953. Perhaps border-line retarded. Psychiatric admission for diagnostic reasons, spells of uncontrolled behavior.

19. Male, born 23 June 1948. Repeatedly apprehended for stealing, severe mood swings, sensitive, restless, unrealistic, fired from job because of financial irregularities.

20. Female, born 5 July 1941. Highly intelligent girl with mystical interests. Very much afflicted by mother's schizophrenia. TAT reveals thought disorder. Receiving psychotherapy.

since 1962 one group has improved in level of mental health, the other group has suffered severe psychiatric breakdown. Why? Part of the answer could lie with the predisposing characteristics measured in 1962 at the time of the intensive examination.

The most important characteristics distinguishing the Sick Group from the Well and Control Group were:

1. The Sick Group lost their schizophrenic mother to psychiatric hospitalization much earlier in their lives than did the other two groups. These early-hospitalized mothers were also more severely schizophrenic. The Well Group lost their mothers at approximately the same time as did the Control Group. In view of the greater severity of illness of the mothers who left their home early, these data may be interpreted in relatively genetic or environmental terms.

2. The teachers' reports indicate that the Sick subjects tended to be disturbing to the class. They were disciplinary problems, domineering, aggressive, created conflicts and disrupted the class with their talking. This was true of 53% of the Sick Group, 18% of the Well Group, and 11% of the Control Group.

3. On the Continual Association Test, where the subject is asked to give, in one minute, as many single-word associations as he can to a stimulus word, the Sick Group showed two distinctive patterns. They had a strong tendency to rattle off a whole series of words which were interrelated but contextually relatively irrelevant, "Opremsning", in Danish. Their associations also tended to "drift" away from the stimulus word. Contrary to instructions and cautions they might begin responding to their own responses; for example to the stimulus word "Table" they might respond "Chair, top, leg, girl, pretty, sky . . ." Those in the Sick Group who do not evidence drifting can apparently manage to avoid this only by restricting themselves to one or two responses per stimulus word for the entire one-minute period.

4. Some of the variables most sharply differentia-

ting the Sick Group from the Well and Control Groups were the electrodermal measures taken during the psychophysiological testing. These measures largely reflect the functioning of the body's stress mobilization mechanisms.

(a) The latency of the GSR was substantially faster for the Sick Group than for either of the other two groups.

(b) The GSR latency for the Sick Group did not show any signs of habituation. This was especially marked in their responses to nine UCS stress stimulus trials. The Control and Well Groups' rapid habituation of latency was seen in the progressive increase of their response latencies from the first to the last of the stress trials. The latencies of the Sick Group progressively decrease suggesting a negative habituation or even increasing irritability. Moving from UCS trials I-IX, 69% of the Well Group exhibit a slowing of response latency (habituation); 75% of the Sick Group actually increase the speed of their response.

(c) A well-documented characteristic of conditioned GSR behavior is the rapidity with which it demonstrates experimental extinction and/or adaptation. In both the Well and Control Groups electrodermal responsiveness was already dropping off by the end of the stress stimulus trials. Following those stress trials we presented a series of nine non-reinforced test trials for generalization and speed of extinction of the conditioned response. The Well and Control Groups evidenced very rapid extinction, i.e. they responded to only one or two of the extinction test trials. The Sick Group exhibited great resistance to extinction, in many cases responding with tenacity until the very end of the extinction series.

(d) The Sick Group showed remarkably fast recovery from momentary states of autonomic imbalance. Once a GSR was made we measured the rate at which recovery to basal level proceeded. (This measure and its theoretical significance has been reported previously in this Journal[33].) On some trials rate of recovery almost perfectly separated the Sick and Control Groups. The pooled Sick and Well Groups' distributions for rate of recovery typically found 70% of the Sick and 30% of the Well Group above the median.

The above material may be found discussed in greater detail in Mednick and Schulsinger[31].

5. In a previous report of the differences between the Sick, Well and Control Groups we pointed out that while in our analyses of data on birth complications "there was a slight general tendency for the Sick Group to have had a more difficult birth, none of the differences reached statistical significance"[31]. Subsequent, more careful, examination of these data revealed that while it was true that no single complication significantly differentiated the groups, 70% of the members of the Sick Group had suffered one or more serious pregnancy or birth complication (PBC). This contrasted sharply with the 15% of the Well Group and 33% of the Control Group with PBCs. The PBCs included anoxia, prematurity, prolonged labor, placental difficulty, umbilical cord complication, mother's illness during pregnancy, multiple births, and breech presentations. Careful perusal of these data brought out an additional striking relationship within the Sick Group (and the entire high-risk group). There is a marked correspondence between PBC and the anomalous electrodermal behavior reported above.

All the GSR differences between the Sick and Well Groups could be explained by the PBCs in the Sick Group. In the Control Group and low-risk group the PBCs were not strongly associated with these extreme GSR effects. This suggests that the PBCs trigger some characteristic which may be genetically predisposed. The PBCs seem to damage the modulatory control of the body's stress-response mechanisms. PBCs are associated with rapid response onset, poor habituation of the response, poor extinction of the conditioned electrodermal response, and very rapid recovery from the response. In terms of the theoretical orientation guiding this project (Mednick,[27,28,32]) this lack of modulation may be viewed as an important etiological factor in the development of mental illness, especially schizophrenia.

The finding that immediately raised fertile questions was the high frequency of PBCs in the Sick Group. What damage might these PBCs have done and where? We first sought for inklings of brain sites particularly sensitive to being damaged by PBCs. We then examined animal studies in which analogous damage had been inflicted by surgical lesion to particularly sensitive brain sites. The reports of the behavior of animals suffering surgically inflicted lesions to these same areas were then searched for instances of behavior similar to that which we observed in our PBC-Sick subjects. We hoped in this manner to generate hypotheses regarding specific sites of brain lesions in our PBC subjects.

BRAIN SITES OF SELECTIVE VULNERABILITY

PBCs result in future difficulties for the fetus chiefly because of the great sensitivity of neural tissue to anoxia. (Mechanical damage probably plays a less significant role, although through vascular obstruction it can also lead to anoxia.) Researchers have singled out particular brain structures as being "selectively vulnerable" to the effects of anoxia.

These areas include most prominently, the hippocampus, and Purkinje cells of the cerebellum.[2] Of these two areas, Spector[46] singles out the hippocampus as being the most vulnerable. He evaluates the effects of anoxia by studying "biochemical lesions", i.e. "the initial chemical changes in tissues following the application of harmful agents and preceding anatomical evidence of damage". The chemical changes he has studied as a function of anoxia have been losses in certain enzymes which precede "histological evidence of cell injury by approximately 10 hours. It is noteworthy that chemical changes appear in the hippocampus immediately after anoxia, whilst the other areas show earliest loss of enzymes after 1-6 hours. The enzyme loss in the hippocampus involved the neurones and was not apparent in the glia or neuropil. This observation suggests that, in this site at least, the neurones are more succeptible than are the surrounding cells to oxygen lack" (552-553).

Friede[12] also indicates that the hippocampus (Ammons Horn) represents one of "the most striking examples of selective vulnerability in the brain and in particular Sommer's Sector, H 1 is known to be a characteristic site for anoxic damage". (Friede links this vulnerability of H 1 to relatively low levels of lactate dehydrogenase in Sommer's Sector).

ANIMAL ABLATION LITERATURE

Thus, with the hippocampus as our chief, and most likely suspect, and the amygdaloid and the cerebellum (Purkinje cells) as an additional suspect we next turned to the animal ablation literature. The strategy here was to see if we could find any similarity between the behavior of our Sick subjects with PBCs and the behavior of animals with circumscribed lesions to each of these suspect areas. Conditioning and extinction behaviors are frequent dependent variables in animal ablation studies. This facilitated comparisons with our data since our subjects have gone through a conditioning and extinction session.

Briefly stated, the literature on the Purkinje cells did not strongly relate to the conditioning data of our PBC subjects. On the other hand the behavior of hippocampal animals was in some surprising ways like that of our PBC-Sick subjects. At this point we must sound a strong note of caution; below we will be relating rat, instrumental, and human, classical conditioning data. It is doubtless a questionable procedure to draw analogies across two species and two types of conditioning. In this case it has proven of great value for hypothesis formation. These ideas are presented in this spirit.

There are several aspects of the behavior of hippocampal rats which are of interest to us in the present context.

1. Rats with hippocampal lesions manifest relatively fast response latency [19,41,45].

2. Rats with hippocampal lesions evidence very poor habituation of the latency of their responses. While normal and cortically damaged control groups exhibit habituation by responding with increasing latencies across a series of test trials, the response latencies of the hippocampal rats do not slow down. They continue to respond as though they were experiencing the stimulus for the first time[17].

3. Rats with hippocampal lesions evidence great resistance to the experimental extinction of conditioned behavior[15,37].

4. Rats with hippocampal lesions are hyperactive[16,45].

5. Rats with hippocampal lesions acquire a conditioned avoidance response in a shuttle box more quickly than control or cortically damaged rats[15,18,45].

In comparing these characteristics with the characteristics described above for the Sick Group we can detect some considerable similarity. Both the Sick subjects with PBCs and the hippocampal rats evidence fast response latency, very poor habituation and poor extinction of a conditioned response. We can also tentatively link the hyperactivity of the hippocampal rats to the unruly classroom behavior of our Sick Subjects. The two points that do not immediately relate to each other are the fast avoidance conditioning of the hippocampal rats and the fast GSR recovery of the Sick Group with PBCs. In terms of some of the components of a theory of schizophrenia advanced earlier[31,32] these seemingly independent points may actually be closely related. Thus, if we assume that the fast GSR recovery of the Sick Group with PBCs is also characteristic of the hippocampal rats we can postulate some basis for the puzzling and consistent finding of unusually fast avoidance learning on the part of the hippocampal rats. Whether one takes a reinforcement or contiguity position, one crucial variable influencing speed of avoidance conditioning in a shuttle box is the rapidity and amount of fear reduction following a successful avoidance response. After the avoidance response has been made, the speed and the amount of reinforcement depends in large part, on the speed of fear reduction and hence on the rate of recovery from the stress response[57]. Any rat who recovers unusually rapidly from a stress response will receive a correspondingly rapid reward of fear reduction when he leaps from the shuttle box' electrified grid floor into the safe compartment. His reinforcement will be greater than that of a rat with normal recovery rate or slow recovery rate. Fast recovery from stress response could conceivably explain the otherwise rather mysterious rapid avoidance learning of hippocampal rats. If such fast recovery were directly demonstrated, the similarity of hippocampal rats to our PBC-Sick subjects would be striking. In the light of the sensitivity of the human hippocampus to the anoxic effects of PBCs, this similarity would suggest the hypothesis that the PBCs in our high-risk children have resulted in damage to their hippocampus. What is further suggested is the possibility that the resultant behavioral anomalies are in some way predispositional to psychiatric breakdown and schizophrenia in individuals with schizophrenic mothers.

IMPLICATIONS

In summary:

1. The most likely site of brain damage resulting from PBCs seems to be the hippocampus, especially Sommer's Sector, H 1.
2. High-risk children who have suffered PBCs exhibit a specific and unique pattern of conditioning, habituation, extinction and GSR behavior. (This pattern is also exhibited by low-risk children with PBCs but at a diminished level).
3. This pattern is strikingly similar to the conditioning, habituation and extinction behavior of rats who have experienced surgical lesions to the hippocampus. These surgical lesions encompass what in the human would be Sommer's Sector H 1.[19]

Another important aspect of behavior which is characteristic of hippocampal rats has been observed in infants who may have suffered anoxia and hence hippocampal damage at birth. Kimble[17] indicates that "damage to the hippocampus should impair the process of habituation to novel stimuli, as has been reported (Leaton, 1965)". This same failure of habituation to novel stimuli has been reported for infants at the ages of two days, five days and 30 days in those cases where the mother had undergone heavy anaesthesia during delivery. Controls were infants of the same age where the mothers had undergone mild or no anaesthesia.[6] Maternal heavy anaesthesia during delivery can affect the fetus, producing retarded respiration and anoxia.[36]. In the context of this general discussion it is tempting to postulate that in this study anaesthesia-induced anoxia produced some hippocampal damage in these children which, in turn, manifested itself in the form of a failure of habituation.

We are suggesting the existence of a relationship between a pattern of observed habituation-conditioning-extinction findings in our PBC-Sick Group and hypothesized hippocampal damage. It is tempting to consider what biochemical and neurophysiological mechanisms could possibly be at the basis of this hypothesized relationship. One interesting lead is recent evidence of a link between hippocampal functioning and ACTH secretion. Damage to the hippocampus has been shown to result in a failure of inhibition of ACTH released by the pituitary gland.[20],[21] Weiss, McEwen and DeSilva (personal communication) have evidence that this inhibitory influence is only called into play during states of stress reaction. During such stress states a damaged hippocampus does not provide an adequate inhibitory influence on the pituitary gland and thus permits an oversecretion of ACTH. Interestingly enough, such ACTH oversecretion may be expected to prolong the extinction of a conditioned response.[7],[8],[9] Such prolonged extinction effects were, of course, observed in our PBC-Sick subjects and are observed in hippocampal rats. It may be suggested that one basis for this failure of extinction was an oversupply of circulating ACTH due to the failure of a damaged hippocampus to sufficiently inhibit ACTH-pituitary secretion during the stressful psychophysiological session.

This failure to inhibit ACTH secretion because of hippocampal inadequacy may also partially explain the state of hyperarousal that seems characteristic of the schizophrenic.[1,5,14,25,35,42,52,53,56] The explanation of the state of hyperarousal may also follow a relatively non-biochemical, neurophysiological route. On the basis of a series of studies observing cortically evoked potentials to visual and auditory stimuli, while concurrently stimulating the hippocampus, Redding[43] concluded that the hippocampus exerts an inhibitory influence on the brain stem reticular formation. An inadequate hippocampus exerting a less than normal inhibitory influence on the reticular formation could contribute to the existence of a chronic state of hyperarousal in an individual. Mechanisms by means of which this hyperarousal and fast GSR recovery and latency could translate themselves into the clinical symptoms and life condition of schizophrenia have been elaborated in detail in earlier publications including this Journal and need not be repeated here[27,28,31,32].

We are, perhaps, now at a point where we can hypothesize that PBC factors lead to defective hip-

pocampal functioning which in combination with genetic and environmental factors could conceivably play a vital predispositional role in at least some forms of schizophrenia. This linking of hippocampal functioning and schizophrenia is not an entirely new idea. Necrosis of neural tissue in Sommer's Sector of the hippocampus has been very regularly found in neuropathological studies of the epileptic.[2] Chapman[3] and Slater, Beard and Glithero[47] among others have pointed to the great similarity of epileptic states of consciousness, especially psychomotor epilepsy, to the disturbances of consciousness in the schizophrenic. Roberts[44] conceptualized schizophrenia "as a disordering of an entire brain system . . . correlated with malfunction in the dorsal hippocampal limbic system." There has also been a considerable amount of research linking PBCs with serious behavioral disturbances and schizophrenia in children[22,39,40,50] and adults.[23,49] There are studies in the literature which have demonstrated "typical" hippocampal-lesion behavior in the schizophrenic. Milstein, Stevens and Sachdev[34] demonstrated very poor habituation and very fast latency of the alpha attenuation response for chronic adult schizophrenics. As early as 1937, Cohen and Patterson reported poor habituation of the cardiac response in schizophrenics. Zahn[56] has reported poor habituation of the GSR in chronic schizophrenics. Vinogradova[55] has demonstrated that chronic schizophrenics take an unusually large number of trials to extinguish a conditioned plethysmograph response.

The adjective "chronic" has been used above to modify the noun "schizophrenia". It may well be that hippocampal dysfunction is an important contributing predispositional factor in only some types of schizophrenia. These may be the more typical, process, chronic, or poor premorbid types. Our Sick subjects tend to be "early onset" cases suggesting that many of them may have a relatively poor prognosis. It is also possible that degree of hippocampal dysfunction will relate to degree of seriousness of illness.

The emphasis on neurophysiological, biochemical and traumatic variables and materials in this paper should not be read as a denigration of the capability of genetic forces to produce identical hippocampal insufficiency or a disregard for the necessity of an appropriate environment to cultivate the learning of schizophrenic modes of behavior and thought. The emphasis on PBCs should not be read as denying the possibility that postnatal injury or high fever could also produce similar brain damage. Finally we have dealt exclusively with the possible impact of hippocampal injury. We could have also brought the septum and other limbic areas into the discussion. The functioning of the entire temporal lobe is also not irrelevant in this area. However, for reasons that are made evident above, the hippocampus seems the best candidate for our attention.

IMPLICATIONS FOR FUTURE STUDY

In terms of the theoretical orientation of the author, the condition of schizophrenia (predisposed by a variety of conditions and circumstances) is a pattern of well-learned avoidance responses. In terms of treatment considerations, such well-learned avoidance responses are difficult to extinguish. Every time an avoidance response is successfully made it is automatically and immediately reinforced. In animal research a shuttle-box-avoidance response can be extinguished by physically preventing the rat or dog from performing the avoidance response in the presence of the avoidance stimulus and not delivering the punishment. However, the bulk of the schizophrenics' avoidance responses are thoughts. These are difficult if not truly impossible to prevent or control. Thus, for theoretical as well as practical and humane reasons our research thinking centers on primary prevention rather than treatment. In view of our findings, one potentially useful field of intervention that suggests itself is the pregnancy and birth process. If a sound hippocampus is a prerequisite for sound mental health and if we can avoid PBCs in high-risk populations, we may avert hippocampal damage and hence reduce the probability of mental illness. A research project on this very matter is currently being planned. Secondly, in view of the possible involvement of poorly modulated hormonal secretions, research on psychopharmacological intervention at an early premorbid age would seem indicated. Such a study is now in its early stages. We are also conducting further prospective studies on the longterm consequences of PBCs in children with schizophrenic parents.

REFERENCES

1. Ax, A. F., Beckett, P. G. S., Cohen, B. D., Frohman, C. E., Tourney, G., and Gottlieb, J. S., Physiologic patterns in chronic schizophrenia. In Wortis, B. (Ed.), *Recent advances in biological psychiatry,* Vol. IV, New York, Plenum Press, 1962.
2. Blackwood, W., McMenemey, W. H., Meyer, A., Norman, R. M., and Russell, D. S., *Greenfield's Neuropathology,* Baltimore, Williams & Wilkins, 1967.
3. Chapman, J., The early symptoms of schizophrenia, *British Journal of Psychiatry, 112*:225-251, 1966.
4. Cohen, L. H. and Patterson, M., Effect of pain on the heart rate of normal and schizophrenic individuals, *Journal of General Psychology, 17*:273-

289, 1937.

5. Conn, J. W., Aldosteronism in man, *Journal of the American Medical Association, 183*:775-781, 1963.

6. Conway, R. and Brackbill, Y., Effects of obstetrical medication on infant sensorimotor behavior. Paper presented at meeting, Society for Research in Child Development, Santa Monica, 1969.

7. De Weid, D., Inhibitory effect of ACTH and related peptides on extinction of conditioned avoidance behavior in rats, *Proceedings of the Society of Experimental Biological Medicine, 122*:28-32, 1966.

8. De Weid, D., The influence of the posterior and intermediate lobe of the pituitary and pituitary peptides on the maintenance of a conditioned avoidance response in rats, *International Journal of Neuropharmacology, 4*:157-167, 1965.

9. De Weid, D., and Bohus, B., Long term and short term effects on retention of a conditioned avoidance response in rats by treatment with long acting pitressin and MSH, *Nature, 212*:1484-1486, 1966.

10. Fowles, D. C. and Venables, P. H., Endocrine Factors in palmar skin potential, *Psychonomic Science, 10*:387-388, 1968.

11. Fowles, D. C. and Venables, P. H., The effects of epidermal hydration and sodium reabsorption on palmar skin potential, *Psychological Bulletin,* In press.

12. Friede, R., The histochemical architecture of Ammons Horn as related to its selective vulnerability, *Acta Neuropathologica, 6*:1-13, 1966.

13. Ganong, W. F., Biglieri, E. G., and Mulrow, P. J., Mechanisms regulating adrenocortical secretion of aldosterone and glucocorticoids, *Recent Progress in Hormone Research, 22*:381-430, 1966.

14. Goldstein, L., Sugerman, A. A., and Stolberg, H., Electro-cerebral activity in schizophrenic and nonpsychotic subjects: *Quantitative EEG Amplitude analysis, Electroencephalography and Clinical Neurophysiology, 19*: 350-361, 1965.

15. Isaacson, R. L., Douglas, R. J., and Moore, R. Y., The effect of radical hippocampal ablation on acquisition of an avoidance response, *Journal of Comparative and Physiological Psychology, 54*:625-628, 1961.

16. Kimble, D. P., The effects of bilateral hippocampal lesions in rats, *Journal of Comparative and Physiological Psychology, 56*:273-283, 1963.

17. Kimble, D. P., Hippocampus and internal inhibition, *Psychological Bulletin, 70*:285-295, 1968.

18. Kimble, D. P., and Gostnell, D., Role of the cingulate cortex in schock avoidance behavior of rats, *Journal of Comparative and Physiological Psychology, 65*:290-294, 1968.

19. Kimble, D. P., Personal communication, 1969.

20. Knigge, K. M., and Hays, M., *Proceedings of the Society for Experimental Biological Medicine, 114*:67-69, 1963.

21. Knigge, K. M., Abstracts, 2nd international Congress on Hormonal Steroids, Milan, 1966.

22. Knobloch, H. and Pasamanick, B., Etiological factors in early infantile

autism and childhood schizophrenia, paper presented International Congress of Pediatrics, Lisbon, Portugal, 1962

23. Lane, E. and Albee, G. W., Comparative birth weights of schizophrenics and their siblings. *The Journal of Psychology, 64*:227-231, 1966.

24. Leaton, R. N., Exploratory behavior in rats with hippocampal lesions, *Journal of Comparative and Physiological Psychology, 59*:325-330, 1965.

25. Malmo, R. B., Shagass, C. and Smith, A. A., Responsiveness in chronic schizophrenia, *J. Personality, 19*:359-375, 1951.

26. McEwen, B. S., Weiss, J. M. and Schwartz, L. S., Selective retention of corticosterone by limbic structures in rat brain, *Nature, 220*:911-912, 1968.

27. Mednick, S. A., A learning theory approach to research in schizophrenia, *Psychological Bulletin, 55*:316-327, 1958.

28. Mednick, S. A., Schizophrenia: a learned thought disorder, in G. Nielsen (Ed.) *Clinical Psychology,* Proceedings of the XIV International Congress of Applied Psychology, Copenhagen: Munksgaard, 1962.

29. Mednick, S. A. and Schulsinger, F., A longitudinal study of children with a high risk for schizophrenia: a preliminary report, in S. Vandenberg (Ed.) *Methods and goals in human behavior genetics,* New York, Academic Press, 1965.

30. Mednick, S. A. and Schulsinger, F., Children of schizophrenic mothers, *Bulletin of the International Association of Applied Psychology, 14*:11-27, 1965.

31. Mednick, S. A. and Schulsinger, F., Some premorbid characteristics related to breakdown in children with schizophrenic mothers, *Journal of Psychiatric Research, 6*: (supplement 1), 267-291, 1968.

32. Mednick, S. A., A longitudinal study of children with a high risk for schizophrenia, *Mental Hygiene, 50*:522-535, 1966.

33. Mednick, S. A. and McNeil, T. F., Current methodology in research on the etiology of schizophrenia, *Psychological Bulletin, 70*:681-693, 1968.

34. Milstein, V., Stevens, J., and Sachdev, K., Habituation of the alpha attenuation response in children and adults with psychiatric disorders, *Electroencephalography and Clinical Neurophysiology, 26*:12-18, 1969.

35. Mirsky, A. F., Neuropsychological bases of schizophrenia, *Annual Review of Psychology, 20*:321-348, 1969.

36. Moya, F. and Thorndike, V., The effects of drugs used in labor on the fetus and newborn. *Clinical Pharmacology and Therapeutics, 4*:628-638, 1963.

37. Mulrow, P. J., Metabolic effects of adrenalmineralocorticoid hormones, in A. B. Eisenstein (Ed.). *The adrenal cortex*, Boston, Little, Brown, 1967.

38. Niki, H., The effects of hippocampal ablation on the inhibitory control of operant behavior in the rat, *Japanese Psychological Research, 7*:126-137, 1965.

39. Pasamanick, B., Rogers, M. and Lilienfed, A. M., Pregnancy experience and the development of childhood behavior disorder, *American Journal*

of Psychiatry, 112:614-618, 1956.

40. Pollack, M. and Woerner, M. G., Pre- and perinatal complication and "childhood schizophrenia": A comparison of 5 controlled studies, *Journal of Child Psychology and Psychiatry, 7*:235-242, 1966.

41. Rabe, A. and Haddad, R. K., Acquisition of 2-way shuttle box avoidance after selective hippocampal lesions, *Physiology & Behavior, 4*:319-323, 1969.

42. Ray, T. S., Electrodermal indications of levels of psychological disturbance in chronic schizophrenics, *American Psychologist, 18*:393, 1963.

43. Redding, F. K., Modification of sensory cortical evoked potentials by hippocampal stimulation, *Electroencephalography and Clinical Neurophysiology, 22*:74-83, 1967.

44. Roberts, D. R., Functional organization of the limbic systems, *International Journal of Neuropsychiatry, 2*:279-292, 1966.

45. Roberts, W. W., Dember, W. N. and Brodwick, M., Alternation and exploration in rats with hippocampal lesions, *Journal of Comparative and Physiological Psychology, 55*:695-700, 1962.

46. Silveira, J. M., The deficit in the disinhibition of attention after bilateral hippocampal lesions: Brightness discrimination and reversal in the hippocampectomized rat, unpublished master's thesis, University of Oregon, 1967.

47. Slater, E., Beard, A. W. and Glithero, E., Schizophrenia-like psychoses of epilepsy, *International Journal of Psychiatry, 1*:6-30, 1965.

48. Spector, R. G., Enzyme chemistry of anoxic brain injury, in C. W. M. Adams (Ed.), *Neurohistochemistry,* New York, Elsevier, 1965.

49. Stabenau, J. R. and Pollin, W., Early characteristics of monozygotic twins discordant for schizophrenia, *Archives of General Psychiatry, 17*:723-734, 1967.

50. Taft, L. and Goldfarb, W., Prenatal and perinatal factors in childhood schizophrenia, *Developmental Medicine and Child Neurology, 6*:32-43, 1964.

51. Venables, P. H., Input dysfunction in schizophrenia. In B. A. Maher (Ed.), *Progress in Experimental Personality Research,* Academic Press, Vol. 1, New York, 1964.

52. Venables, P. H., Psychophysiological aspects of schizophrenia, *British Journal of Medical Psychology, 39*:289-297, 1966.

53. Venables, P. H. and Wing, J. K., Level of arousal and the subclassification of schizophrenia, *Archives of General Psychiatry, 7*:114-119, 1962.

54. Venables, P. H., Personal communication, 1969.

55. Vinogradova, N. V., Protective and stagnant inhibition in schizophrenics, *Zhurnal Vysshei Nervnoi Deaietelnostni,* Imeni L. P. Pavlova, 1962.

56. Zahn, T. P., Autonomic reactivity and behaviour in schizophrenia, *Psychiatric Research Reports, 19*:156-171, 1964.

57. Zeaman, D. and Wegner, N., The role of drive reduction in the classical conditioning of an autonomically mediated response, *Journal of Experimental Psychology, 48*:349-354, 1954.

21. The Language of Schizophrenia: A Review and Interpretation

BRENDAN A. MAHER

Psychopathologists have tended to regard the phenomena of schizophrenic language as reflections of a more basic disturbance of thought. Writings on these topics generally link them together (e.g., Kasanin's *Language and Thought in Schizophrenia*, 1944). Critchley (1964), from his survey of major aspects of psychotic speech, concluded that the "causation of schizophrenic speech affection lies in an underlying thought disorder, rather than in a linguistic inaccessibility". Differences of opinion are evident as to what the nature of this thinking disorder might be. Regression (Gardner, 1931; Kasanin, 1944), excessive concreteness of thought (Goldstein, 1944; Milgram, 1959) and deficiency in logical deductive reasoning (Von Domarus, 1944) are some of the more prominent hypotheses to be found in the literature relating to this problem.

Most of these hypotheses share a set of implicit assumptions about the kind of model that is appropriate to conceptualizing the relationship between language and thought. The model might be likened to a typist copying from a script before her. Her copy may appear to be distorted because the script is distorted although the communication channel of the typist's eye and hand are functioning correctly. Alternatively, the original script may be perfect, but the typist may be unskilled, making typing errors in the copy and thus distorting it. Finally, it is possible for an inefficient typist to add errors to an already incoherent script. Unfortunately, the psychopathologist can observe only the copy (language utterances): he cannot examine the script (the thought). In general most theorists concerned with schizophrenic language have accepted the first of the three alternatives, namely that a good typist is transcribing a deviant script. The patient is correctly reporting a set of disordered thoughts. As Critchley put it: "Any considerable aberration of thought or personality will be mirrored in the various levels of articulate speech—phonetic, phonemic, semantic, syntactic and pragmatic." The language is a mirror of the thought.

In this paper the writer will review the present state of knowledge about language disturbances in schizophrenia and will suggest a theoretical formulation that may serve to encompass many reported empirical findings. Excluded from the review will be those disorders of thought in which no accompanying disturbance of language occurs. Thus delusional thinking, in which the chief evidence of the thought disorder lies in the *implausibility* of the patient's statements rather than in any aberration of his language usage, will be omitted.

As a propaedeutic to the discussion of empirical findings it will be useful to review briefly some techniques and concepts from linguistics, communi-

Brendan A. Maher, The language of schizophrenia: A review and interpretation, *British Journal of Psychiatry, 120*, 1972, 3-17. Reproduced by permission.

cation and information theory and from the psychology of language.

Information, Redundancy and Transitional Probabilities

Communications engineers, notably Shannon (1948, 1951), have introduced a technical concept of *information* which has significance for the study of schizophrenic communication. It has, however, a highly specialized meaning differing from the normal connotation of "information." A unit of communication may be said to convey information when its occurrence cannot be predicted with complete accuracy from knowledge of the previous units in the message. Obversely, when it can be predicted from the prior elements in the message the unit is defined as *redundant*. The difference between this meaning of the term redundant and the more common meaning of semantic redundancy may be shown by a relatively simple illustration. Let us take a situation in which a listener receives the following incomplete message: *The title of a popular old song is "Boys and girls come out to..."* The listener can guess with a high degree of certainty what the missing word is. In this sense, the word *play* is redundant. Its occurrence at the appropriate point in the sentence can be predicted with considerable assurance simply from the previous elements in the message. However, it is not redundant in the sense that it duplicates a unit already included in the message. The contrast can be seen from a different example where a complete message might have been *"Parents are requested to bring their children and offspring,"* but the final word is omitted. It would be very difficult to predict that the word *offspring* was the missing unit. In this sense it is not redundant but conveys information. On the other hand *offspring* is a synonym for *children* in ordinary usage and is thus semantically redundant.

These technical concepts of information and redundancy depend in turn upon the existence of *transitional probabilities* in language usage. At the level of single letters in words, the transitional probability, in English, that the letter Q will be followed by the letter U is close to 1.0, i.e., almost certain. The probability that the letter N will be followed by the letter X is quite low but that it will be followed by G is quite high, and so on. When the transitional probability that one unit will be followed by another specific unit is very high, then the actual occurrence of the second unit is relatively redundant.

In the normal English sentence, the predictability of one word's following another may be estimated at two levels, either syntactic or lexical. Given the message: *The beggar's coat was very...* it is quite probable that the missing final word is an adjective, such as *ragged, worn, tattered,* etc., thus predicting the syntax class of the missing word would be relatively easy. On the other hand, predicting the specific word used, the lexical unit, is more difficult.

Measurement of redundancy in language samples has been made possible by the use of a rather simple procedure, the technique of *Cloze Analysis* (Taylor, 1953). In this procedure, the text to be measured is prepared with every nth word (usually every fifth) omitted. Normal readers are then given copies of the text and asked to enter their estimates of the missing words in the appropriate spaces. The redundancy of passages may be compared in terms of the accuracy with which normal readers estimate the identity of the missing words. Percentage comparisons permit quantification of the differences between passages.

Edgar Rubin*, the Danish psychologist, suggested that redundancy in the language might be viewed as a safety margin for the understanding of communication under the many difficult conditions that this may be necessary—noise, fatigue of the listener and the like. A language that had little or no redundancy would be subject to easy misunderstanding under all but ideal conditions of reception. Military voice codes of the "A-Able, B-Baker, C-Charlie" variety are good examples of this principle. Noise on a

---

*Although the major development of the concepts of information and redundancy was achieved by the work of Shannon, Rubin had already performed studies and reported his ideas on these problems in the late 1920s at the University of Copenhagen. For a published version of his writings on redundancy the reader is referred to Rubin (1956).

radio channel may obliterate a single letter, such as "C", but would have less probability of obliterating all of the word "Charlie." If the receiver hears "— —arlie" he can estimate the missing part of the word fairly easily and hence receive the message correctly.

Statistical Properties of Language: Zipf's Law

Some years ago G. K. Zipf (1949) advanced the *Principle of Least Effort* to account for some statistical regularities in human behaviour. Summarized crudely the principle states that human behaviour (like the activity of many physical systems) develops towards the conservation of energy. However, the most that is possible in the planning of effort is that the average amount of work required is reduced. Thus when Morse was designing the telegraphic code he gave the shortest symbol (the dot) to the most used letter in English, E. Assignment of other transmission symbols to letters of the alphabet was also guided, albeit approximately, by their frequency of use, the least used letters being assigned the longest transmission symbols. Any one telegraph message might happen to require long transmission symbols, but the average of messages sent with this code would be efficiently brief.

The details of Zipf's theory may be omitted here, but we should note the nature of his findings regarding the relationship between *word frequency* and *rank of frequency* in language usage. In any passage of language we may count the total number of words used ("tokens") and the total number of kinds of words used ("types"). For example, in the sentence immediately preceding this one there are 26 words, but owing to the repetition of words such as "the" and "of," "used," etc., there are only 19 different types. In long passages we may, rather laboriously, tabulate the frequency of use of each type that appears in the passage and derive a rank order (Rank 1 being assigned to the type used most often, and so on) and then plot the rank order of types against the actual numbers of their frequencies. Thus, the type assigned Rank 1 might have occurred 50 times, Rank 2, 25 times and so forth.

When this kind of plot is conducted, Zipf discovered that there appears to be a regularity in the relationship which can be expressed by the statement "Rank X Frequency is a constant." When the two scales (rank and frequency) are made logarithmic the resulting graphic plot is linear, sloping down from left to right.

Zipf studied this phenomenon in many languages and from diverse sources within English. He was able to demonstrate considerable stability of the relationship in all of these sources. This relationship has been termed *Zipf's Law*. A more sophisticated exposition of it has been made by Mandelbrot (1953) in which the nature of the cost-conservation (or effort-conservation) basis of the law is demonstrated mathematically.

However, a much simpler use of the type-token frequencies has been used by many investigators through the *Type-Token Ratio*. This is computed by dividing the number of tokens in a sample into the number of types, the resulting ratio being reported as a decimal. Over several years the TTR has been computed for samples of schizophrenic writers by different investigators, with results to be discussed later in this paper.

Measures derived from the study of informational or statistical regularities in normal language provide a somewhat limited basis for the study of psychotic utterances. If we find that the language of some schizophrenic patients deviates from normal patterns of redundancy or from normal rank-frequency relations we have established the deviancy in relation to a quantifiable criterion of normalcy. We have not, however, discovered the nature of the processes that produce the deviancy—we can only say that the language was *not produced* in accordance with some of the usual principles governing language utterances. Redundancy measures and Zipf constants might be likened to oral body temperatures. When the reading deviates from the norm we know that something has occurred to interfere with a normal bodily process: the kind of thing that might have happened cannot be inferred from the temperature deviations. However, we can use shifts in these readings either towards or away from normalcy as crude indices of the shifting of the pathological process in the direction of improvement or deterioration. Thus measures derived from the techniques of linguistic analysis described above may have considerable clinical usefulness even though they do not yet contribute directly to our knowledge of the aetiology of psychopathology.

Generative Grammar

Many linguists, including especially Chomsky (cf. Chomsky, 1965), have been working on problems concerned with establishing the basic grammars for a language. The complexity of the linguistic principles that they have derived prevents adequate description here. However, a considerable share of their effort has been devoted to the question of transitional principles in sentences, i.e. the discovery of the rules whereby a sentence in one form ("John is wearing a hat") may be transformed to some other form ("A hat is worn by John") while preserving the semantic meaning of the original sentence. There would appear to be a *prima facie* possibility that the grammatical principles of a language might have psychological significance. It is possible that they are learned, or, as some linguists have suggested (cf. Lenneberg, 1967), that they may be influenced by innate structural limitations of the information-processing capacities of the central nervous system. However, although there have been suggestions by others (e.g. Pavy, 1968) that generative grammars may help unravel the problem of grammatical deviations in schizophrenic language nothing has yet been forthcoming along these lines.

With these concepts and terms in mind we may now turn to review the data so far obtained by research into schizophrenic language. Let us consider first the results of inquiries into the formal characteristics of psychopathological utterances.

FORMAL CHARACTERISTICS

Information-Redundancy

Several investigations have been made into the redundancy of schizophrenic speech and writing using the Cloze procedure. Salzinger, Portnoy and Feldman (1964) report that the speech of schizophrenic patients is less redundant (i.e. is harder to predict on the basis of partial samples) than that of normals, and this decreasing redundancy is associated with increasing stay in hospital (correlation—.47). Rice (1970) reports that redundancy is related to psychiatrists' clinical impressions of the degree of disorganization revealed by written language utterances in patients: the two measures correlated—.71 (low redundancy being found in the highly disorganized and vice versa). Nor were these measures affected by chlorpromazine medication. Speech emitted under the influences of small doses of chlorpromazine communicates less well than speech emitted without the drug, the redundancy decreasing with increasing dosages (Salzinger, Pisoni, Feldman and Bacon, 1961). Redundancy scores for speech uttered under the influence of LSD are lower than normal values (Check and Amarel, 1967), but under adrenaline redundancy increases (Honigfeld, 1965).

In a rather complex study of redundancy in schizophrenics Bertoch (1966) found that those patients who exhibited the most severe thinking disorder—on the basis of interview—were least redundant when composing verbal responses to ambiguous pictorial stimuli but most redundant when composing responses to relatively unambiguous stimuli. It is possible to interpret these results to mean that when the patient with thought disorder is faced with the necessity of talking about events that are clearly defined, he does so in a more conventional and stereotyped manner than the normal control; when required to communicate about ambiguous events, he is more disorganized and hence less redundant than the normal.

All in all, we can summarize this area of investigation by concluding that in general severity of schizophrenic disorder as judged by clinical interview and observation is reliably related to unpredictability of language utterance (low redundancy). However, as already mentioned, this kind of finding does not of itself shed direct light on the underlying aetiology of the language disturbances; it simply demonstrates it in quantitative terms. The findings with regard to drugs raise the rather interesting question of the relationship of biological variables to language production, a matter that we shall discuss later.

Redundancy and the Perception of Language

There is a solid body of evidence to the effect that redundancy in language utterance aids in later recall of what was uttered (Miller and Selfridge, 1950), and how easily it may be read (Weaver and Kingston, 1963). Presumably the greater efficiency of processing highly redundant utterances reflects the fact that words that are missed in perception or forgotten in the recall task are interpolated on the basis of the probabilities provided by perception or recall of the surrounding words. In this sense, perception and recall include processes very similar to those by which a reader decides what words to enter when completing a language sample that has been mutilated for Cloze analysis. Lawson, McGhie and Chapman (1964) report that whereas normal subjects benefit in a recall task from an increase in the redundancy of the passage to be recalled, schizophrenic subjects improve much less. From this we might conclude that redundancy in the language does not do as much to help the schizophrenic to process it.

However, the method used by Lawson *et al.* to create redundancy was to construct passages based upon increasingly long strings of words with suitable transitional probability orderings. They did not manipulate syntactic rules as well, and thus their data leave unanswered the question of whether or not the schizophrenic patient is able to utilize syntactic rules in his perception of speech. Lewinsohn and Elwood (1961) found contrary results to those of Lawson *et al.*, using the same method. Levy and

Maxwell (1968), and Raeburn and Tong (1968), used the transitional probability procedure also, and found that acute schizophrenic patients were impaired in their ability to benefit from the increased contextual cues.

Gerver (1967) introduced the factor of grammatical constraint into a further study of this problem in order to investigate the effect of linguistic rules on the perception of speech by schizophrenic patients. Subjects were required to listen to sentences that were (a) grammatical and meaningful, (b) grammatical but meaningless, and (c) ungrammatical, meaningless strings of words. They were presented against a background of white noise, there being six different signal-to-noise ratios. Immediately after hearing each sentence the subject was required to repeat it aloud to the experimenter. The results showed that schizophrenic subjects were inferior in performance to normals, but that their scores were significantly aided by syntactic and semantic organization within the material to be recalled.

Most recently, Truscott (1970) has reported a highly systematic investigation of this problem. She employed four classes of verbal material (a) normal sentences, e.g., *Snug rings bind chubby fingers*, (b) anomalous sentences, *Snug olives spread splintered subdivisions*, (c) anomalous but semantically related word strings, *Rings snug fingers chubby bind*, and (d) random word strings, *Olives snug subdivisions splintered spread*. Schizophrenic subjects were inferior to normal controls on all of these classes of language, the greatest difference being in the case of the normal sentences, where normal controls showed dramatically improved recall while the schizophrenic subjects were only a little better than they were with semantically-related and random word strings.

Salmon, Bramley and Presly (1967) report data on the Word-in-Context technique applied to thought-disordered and non-thought-disordered schizophrenics. In this technique, developed by Heim and Watts (1958), the subject is required to infer the meaning of unfamiliar words from clues provided by the context of sentences in which the words are embedded. Although the test has been regarded by its authors as a useful tool in research on thought processes and concept formation, we might note that it presents a task similar to that of the Cloze procedure—namely that of guessing what word or definition should be entered in a sequence of words on the basis of the redundancy of the previous words in the sequence. Salmon *et al.* (1967) report that thought-disordered patients were inferior to non-thought-disordered patients on this test. Their obtained differences were not statistically significant but were in the predicted direction. Unfortunately they did not obtain comparable data from normal controls and it is not possible to be certain that their patients were absolutely less competent at this task than non-schizophrenic subjects might be.

SUMMARY

All in all, however, the empirical data available strongly support the view that the schizophrenic is not able to gain as much advantage from the redundancy of language (both semantic and syntactic) as the normal does. Several theoretical possibilities exist as explanations of this and will be taken up later in this paper.

STATISTICAL PROPERTIES OF SCHIZOPHRENIC LANGUAGE

Several studies have been conducted to evaluate the nature of the Type-Token Ratio in schizophrenic utterances. For the sake of convenience the results of these studies are presented in Table 1. As will be evident from the Table, TTRs of schizophrenic utterances tend to be lower than those from normal samples, but the range of differences in both sources is rather wide. These results, if taken as reliable, would suggest that schizophrenic language is characterized by a tendency to repetition of words, and perhaps also of phrases or other verbal units, and that these repetitions will occur at shorter intervals than will be found in the usage of words by normal individuals. Detailed analysis of repetition patterns in language has been conducted by Mittenecker (1951, 1953). He has tabulated repetition of words, parts of words and syllables in German language samples. A repetition is counted whenever it occurs within 35 syllables of its previous appearance. His data indicate that frequent repetitions at smaller intervals is characteristic of both schizophrenic subjects and schizothymic normal individuals. Paranoid patients resembled normals generally more than they did schizophrenics in these measures.

A direct study of the relationship between word frequency and rank (Zipf's Law) has been reported by dal Bianco (1957). Unfortunately it is based upon very limited data, and it is not possible to draw statistically reliable conclusions. However, the schizophrenic language samples deviate from the normal linearity of the rank-frequency relationship in a manner consistent with the notion that the patient uses a more restricted vocabulary. In this respect they replicate the single-case analysis reported by Whitehorn and Zipf (1943) in which the rank frequency distribution of words in the letters of a paranoid patient showed a steeper slope of the curve, and hence more repetition, than was the case with normal adults.

The interpretation of repetitions is a matter for debate. Several plausible hypotheses may be offered. Mittenecker has suggested that repetition arises in language because the utterance of words activates them "submentally," and this activation persists for some time afterwards, increasing the probability that they will be uttered again. Individ-

TABLE 1. *Type-Token Ratios Obtained from Schizophrenic Patients*

Reference	Subjects and Controls	TTR
Fairbanks (1944)	Schizophrenics, speech	.57
	College freshmen, speech	.64
Mann (1944)	Schizophrenics, written	.66
	Freshmen, written	.71
Pavy, Grinspoon and Shader (1969)	Chronic schizophrenics, written	.39—.57
	Chronic schizophrenics, written, under medication	.58
	Acute schizophrenics, written	.66—.70
	Acute schizophrenics, written, under medication	.69
Critchley (1964)	(1) Schizophrenic patient, written	.26
	(2) Schizophrenic patient, written	.65
Maher, McKean and McLaughlin (1966)	Thought-disordered schizophrenics, written	.71
	Non-thought-disordered schizophrenics, written	.74

ual differences in the intensity of this process will be reflected by differing tendencies to repeat words. Persons with fluctuating high intensities will produce very frequent repetitions, and some such process might be inferred to be happening in the case of schizophrenia (Mittenecker, 1951). Bobon (1967), following a discussion of language aberrations in French-speaking schizophrenics, suggests that repetition is evidence of excessive rigidity and need for security and should be interpreted as an anxiety-reducing symptom. A third possibility is that the patient's inability to profit from the redundancies of his own language means that the utterance of a word does not reduce the probability that it will be repeated soon afterwards (a reduction of probability that should influence utterances by a normal speaker). It is as if the patient has "forgotten" what he just said or wrote and thus repeats himself. Such an interpretation may be made from the hypotheses of short-term memory deficit or of deficit in the processing of incoming sensory input (Venables, 1964; Yates, 1966). Finally, we should note that repetition might arise not because of some process of increased activation of previously uttered words but because low-frequency words in the patient's vocabulary have dropped out of usage; this might be due either to a general depression of infrequently practised activities or to the saving in effort resulting from doing without less immediately available vocabulary resources.

SUMMARY

The sum and substance of the data available from statistical measures such as frequency counts, repetition indices and the like is that the schizophrenic tends to use a restricted vocabulary, and that this restriction necessarily involves the frequent repetition of the same words in passages of utterance. Mittenecker's observation that the patient also tends to repeat at the level of syllables suggests that the problem is not one of the limited availability of vocabulary as such, but an active tendency for words or parts of words, once uttered, to intrude into the utterance again soon.

ASSOCIATIONAL PROPERTIES OF SCHIZOPHRENIC LANGUAGE

Clinical reports have abounded with descriptions of the tendency of schizophrenic language to be disrupted by irrelevant associations. Examples are plentiful, and a few will suffice here. A patient writes, "I like coffee, cream, cows, Elizabeth Taylor" (Maher, McKean and McLaughlin 1966). One of Bleuler's patients, when asked with whom she had been walking the previous day, enumerated the members of her family, listing "father, son" and adding "and the Holy Ghost." Mittenecker (1951) quotes a patient as saying in German, ". . . Das ist vom Kaiserhaus, sie haben es von den Voreltern, von der Vorwelt, von der Urwelt. Frankfurt-am-Main, das sind die Franken, die Frankfurter Wurstchen, Frankenthal, Frankenstein . . ." ["It is from the Imperial House, they have it from ancestors, from the ancestral world, from the pre-world. Frankfort-on-Main, there are the Franks, Frankfurter sausages, Frankenthal, Frankenstein . . ."]

This well-established phenomenon has given rise to several hypotheses. The first of these is that the manner in which the patient forms associations is deviant. In its simplest form this hypothesis leads to the prediction that the responses of schizophrenic patients to word association tests will differ significantly from those of normal individuals. Many studies have been undertaken on this point, but a large percentage of them must be regarded with caution because of a failure to ensure that the patients heard the stimulus words correctly. Moon, Mefford, Wieland, Porkorny and Falconer (1968) showed that schizophrenics had significantly more auditory misperceptions of stimulus words than normal controls with whom they were matched for auditory acuity (the misperceptions not being due, presumably, to difficulties in auditory acuity but to difficulties in recognition). When these misperceptions were controlled, schizophrenic and normal samples were similar in the pattern of associations produced. Findings of difficulty in auditory perception in schizophrenia have been reported quite frequently in the literature but not taken into serious account by most experimenters studying word association patterns. A very thorough study of the structure of associations in normal and schizophrenic subjects was reported by Moran, Mefford and Kimble (1964), with the conclusion that both groups shared a common associative structure. Additional reports by Lang and Luoto (1962) and by Spence and Lair (1964) suggest that the associational mediations of schizophrenics are similar to those of normal subjects.

As against these data may be set the many studies reporting that schizophrenic patients give idiosyncratic responses to word association test words. Several of these have been reviewed by Pavy (1968). None of them controlled for possible misperception of the stimulus words by the subject. In the circumstances it seems that there is no solid reason to suppose that the associative processes (that is to say the principles by which words become associated with each other) are different in schizophrenic patients from those operating in normals. On the other hand there is good reason to hypothesize that perceptual inaccuracy is not uncommon in schizophrenia and should lead to occasional misperception of the stimulus words. A consequence would be that the associative response may be normal in terms of the stimulus as misperceived, but will appear irrelevant or idiosyncratic to the experimenter. In this connection we may note that the basis for the associative chaining in the examples given above is generally fairly obvious—the associations between *coffee* and *cream*, between *father, son* and *Holy Ghost*, and between *Frankfurter* and *Frankenstein* do not appear difficult to fathom. What seems to be bizarre is not the nature of the associations that intrude into the utterance, but the fact that they intrude at all.

Competing Associations

Clinicians have frequently remarked on the tendency of schizophrenic patients to exhibit "punning" confusions in their language usage. Puns made deliberately by normal individuals depend for their humorous effect upon the fact that both the speaker and the listener can keep the several meanings of the word in mind at the same time. Schizophrenic punning, on the other hand, may appear as a pun only to the listener—there being no awareness of the double meanings on the part of the speaker. Chapman, Chapman and Miller (1964) have reported investigations of the hypothesis that the schizophrenic is particularly incapable of inhibiting from consciousness the 'dominant' meaning of a multiple-meaning word. In a double-meaning word, for instance, both of the meanings may not be equally frequent in normal usage. The word "date" referring to a day of the year might occur more often than "date" meaning the fruit of the date-palm. Because of differential frequency of use the associations to the more common meaning may develop in greater number and more strength than those to the less common meaning. Being vulnerable to associative intrusion, the schizophrenic may be peculiarly liable to the intrusion of associations to the dominant meaning on those occasions when his intention was to use the word in its least common meaning. In their investigations, Chapman *et al.* (1964) were able to demonstrate that schizophrenics were indeed liable to this kind of confusion when required to interpret the meanings of words in sentences. A typical sentence would be as follows: *"The tennis player left the court because he was tired."* Three alternative explanations of this sentence were provided, one

referring to a tennis-court, another referring to a court of law and a third referring to an irrelevant topic. Their findings clearly support the view that intrusions of dominant meanings occur in the responses of schizophrenics but that intrusions of weaker meanings are much less common.

It is worth noting that this tendency to select the stronger meanings of double-meaning words can be understood as a predictable consequence of the failure of the context to influence the patient's perception of an utterance. In the context of "tennis-player," the intended meaning of "court" should be clear. If the context is ignored or ineffective in determining the perception of meaning, the patient is likely to interpret it as if there were no context at all. This will influence his perception towards the most usual meaning of the word when it is presented alone—i.e., the "strongest" meaning.

Salzinger's Immediacy Hypothesis

Salzinger (1966) and his colleagues (e.g., Salzinger, Portnoy, Pisoni and Feldman, 1970) have presented an hypothesis of schizophrenic behaviour generally under the term "the immediacy hypothesis." Stated in simple form it hypothesizes that schizophrenic behaviour is primarily controlled by stimuli which are immediate in the environment. In the case of language it can be deduced from this that any specific word in a schizophrenic utterance is more likely to be a response to some immediately proximate word than to words that had occurred much earlier in the utterance. Or, put more briefly, schizophrenic utterance is less influenced by the context provided by the patient's own prior utterance than is the case with the language of normal subjects. An investigation of this (Salzinger *et al.*, 1970) showed that with increasing context it was increasingly possible for normal judges to predict which word had been omitted from the language of a normal speaker, whereas the provision of longer samples of context from schizophrenic utterance was less helpful. However, the judges were not able to do better in estimating the word omitted from schizophrenic utterances, given only a brief context, than they were with normal utterances. In short, the data do not support the view that schizophrenic language is more predictable from the immediately surrounding words than is normal language. It does support the position that longer contexts of schizophrenic languages are less influential in determining utterance than is the case in normal utterance. This latter finding, of course, is in line with the earlier reports of Lawson, McGhie and Chapman (1964) about the inability of the patient to use context in perceiving the speech of others. It extends this to include the inferred inability of the schizophrenic to be guided by the contextual restraints of his own initial utterances.

Literal—Figurative Confusion

Double-meaning words sometimes divide their meanings between literal and figurative usage. Thus the word "blue" has the literal (colour) meaning and the figurative (depressed mood) meaning. There are at the moment no data on the relative dominance of these two classes of meaning in normal usage. *Prima facie* it seems probable that the literal meaning will tend to be dominant inasmuch as the figurative meaning represents a later extension of an existing meaning to another class of phenomenon. However, this is an empirical question and requires investigation. For the present we may wish to point out that the distinction between figurative and literal meanings of words may be confounded by differences in the dominance of one kind of meaning over the other in general usage. Although a study by Chapman (1960) reported that schizophrenics made more errors of literal misinterpretation of words than did normals, an attempt at replication by Eliseo (1963) with control for vocabulary level of all subjects failed to find such a difference. All in all, it is difficult to support the conclusion that the schizophrenic is specifically troubled by confusion between literal and figurative meanings of words, and more probable that seeming instances of this kind of confusion are reflections of the inappropriate intrusion of dominant meanings.

The Concrete—Abstract Hypothesis

Several psychopathologists have suggested that the changes occurring in schizophrenia include a tendency to shift to more concrete and less abstract modes of thought and language (Goldstein and Scheerer, 1941; Flavell, 1956; Milgram, 1959). While the notion of impairment of abstracting ability as defined by Goldstein includes a rather heterogeneous collection of difficulties, it involves the assumption that the patient would have a greater likelihood of using concrete words and difficulty in distinguishing between the concrete and abstract meanings of a word that possessed both kinds of meaning. Benjamin and Watt (1968) studied the liability of patients to two kinds of confusion; concrete-abstract and dominant-meaning versus weak-meaning as in the Chapman usage. Controls were used in the selection of words, ensuring that meaning strength and concreteness were unrelated in this experiment. Their findings, although inconclusive on the point, tend to support the view that it is meaning strength rather than concreteness that influences the patient in his response to words. As this is the only reported study in which appropriate controls were used it provides the only reliable data on the problem. Demonstrations of a tendency to concreteness are unconvincing if this kind of control is not applied. While the Chapman hypothesis accounts for the difficulty the patient has with double-meaning words it leaves unmentioned the other kinds of associational intrusion that are found in schizophrenic utterances. It may perhaps then be incorporated into a summary statement that schizophrenic language is disrupted by associations; that these associations are essentially normal in content; that they appear to intrude more easily at some points of a sentence than at others, and that intrusion is more likely by associations that are dominant than by those that are weak. This last effect produces particular confusions surrounding the use of double-meaning words.

This summary of some of the pertinent research leads us to consider the possible aetiology of associational disturbances in general. In the paragraphs that follow an explanatory hypothesis will be advanced, drawing on data from studies of language, but also from investigations of other kinds of schizophrenic pathology. Before outlining this hypothesis, it may be useful to consider the logical and strategic specifications for an explanatory hypothesis of this kind. As far as possible it seems preferable to seek explanations of language symptoms by assuming that they are most likely to be aspects of a unitary pathological process. This means that *(ceteris paribus)* we would prefer explanations which manage to relate the language disturbance to other schizophrenic disturbances of perception, motor activity, etc.; we would eschew explanations which assume special pathological processes operating in the case of schizophrenic language differing from those used to account for the other anomalies of behaviour in these patients.

Secondly, a satisfactory explanation should permit *predictions* about the character and location of language disruptions: it should not be confined to *post hoc* interpretation of particular anomalies, varying in form from case to case. This does not mean that an explanation is unsatisfactory if it cannot predict precisely where the patient will have trouble in producing a clear utterance, but it does mean that the gross probabilities of difficulty with different types of utterance should be predictable from the explanatory hypothesis.

At the present time, these requirements are expressions of hope rather than descriptions of contemporary attainments. It is with these hopes that the following hypothesis is presented.

ASSOCIATIVE INTRUSION AND ATTENTIONAL DEFICIT: AN HYPOTHESIS

It is proposed here that the language disturbances seen in some schizophrenic patients might be understood as the consequences of an inability to maintain attentional focusing. This deficiency is probably mediated biologically, although the mediating processes may fluctuate with varying conditions of environmental stress. The central feature of this hypothesis is that the attentional disturbances believed to affect the processing of sensory input (cf. Venables, 1964; Shakow, 1963) also underlie the failure to inhibit associations from intruding into language utterance. Intrusion of associations into language may be regarded as similar in character to the "intrusions" of background auditory and visual stimuli into the perceptual processes of the schizophrenic patient. Attentional focusing of the patient is assumed to fluctuate so that vulnerability to distraction varies from moment to moment. Intrusions occur when attentional focusing is broad and are absent when it is narrow.

From this point of view, the utterance of normal, coherent speech may be seen as the result of the successful and instantaneous inhibition of associations to elements in the utterance. Each element of the utterance (syllable, word or phrase) may automatically activate associated elements in much the same way that single words activate associations when given in the Word Association Technique. These activated associations do not enter consciousness during the course of organized utterance. They do not enter consciousness because they are inhibited: the utterance of a sentence is thus an extremely complex act which involves amongst other things the continuous inhibition of distracting associations. In this respect it resembles successful continuous focusing of attention on a changing visual stimulus field, inasmuch as the latter is also accomplished via the "tuning out" of other elements of the visual field.

The inhibitory or "tuning out" process is assumed to be an active one. It will fluctuate as a function of several variables. In states of relaxation inhibitory efficiency will be low, and language should tend to be looser and more associative in nature. By the same token, it should be helpful to arrange for a speaker to be relaxed if we wish him to produce utterances along associational lines, as in some psychotherapeutic techniques. Under conditions of high motivational arousal, such as exist, for example, when conversing during an important employment interview, attention will be focused narrowly, and language should be organized and free from associational looseness.

Where an intrusion will occur, and what kind of intrusion it is likely to be, appear to be the resultants of several factors working in combination. Some of these may be discussed here, although it is far from clear that we can do more than indicate some of the major factors at this time. Firstly, terminal points in an utterance, such as commas, full stop or period points seem to be points of particular vulnerability. It is less common to find associations intruding in the middle of a clause than to find them between clauses. It might be that attention is organized to utter relatively coherent units, and resistance to intrusion is therefore high while the unit is in the course of being uttered.

Although clinical cases of gross disturbance of syntax are reported, they appear to be less common than semantic disturbances. Associational intrusions generally fit in with the syntactical structure of the preceding utterance. For example, a patient asked to explain the meaning of the word *fable*, replied "Trade good sheep to hide in the beginning." If we ignore the meaning of the individual words, but examine the grammar of the answer it appears acceptable in form. We do not know what the original intent of the patient's utterance might have been, but the disruptions of associations have not led to a disturbance of syntax. This suggests that where there are syntactical rules determining the word-class (noun, verb, etc.) that may be uttered next, these rules will tend to govern the probability that an association will intrude. If an association is of the correct word-class it will more readily intrude than an association which is of an inappropriate word-class. We would assume that inappropriate word-class items could only intrude when attentional focusing was very severely impaired; and that the presence of disrupted syntax in a patient's utterances would be a sign of greater clinical gravity than the semantic disturbances alone. It is quite possible that some syntactical rules are more vulnerable to disruption than others, and that a sophisti-

cated analysis of syntactically disturbed utterances would reveal this. At the moment, however, there are no data bearing on this question and it remains a matter for research.

What seems to be quite clear is that many, and perhaps most of the disturbances of language found amongst schizophrenic patients do not involve syntactic errors, but are almost entirely a matter of semantic or lexical error. We have already discussed one kind of semantic weakness—susceptibility to punning confusions. A second form of intrusion appears to occur as a kind of "clang" association to the initial syllable of a previous word (in contrast to the more usual "clang" association to the terminal syllables). For example, in a document in the writer's possession a patient wrote: "The subterfuge and the mistaken planned substitutions for that demanded American action can produce nothing but the general results of negative contention and the impractical results of careless application, the natural results of misplacement, of mistaken purpose and unrighteous position, the impractical serviceabilities of unnecessary contradictions."

In this passage we can notice the following repetitions: *Subterfuge—substitution; unrighteous—unnecessary: mistaken—misplacement; contention—contradiction.*

A third kind of associational intrusion appears in the form of associational pairings between separated words or clauses in a sentence. Critchley (1964) presented a passage from a patient reading in part as follows:

"See the Committee about me coming home for Easter my twenty-fourth birthday. I hope all is well at home, how is Father getting on. Never mind, there is hope, heaven will come, time heals all wounds, Rise again Glorious Greece and come to Hindoo Heavens, the Indian Heavens. . ." (p. 361).

We might speculate here that the initial sentence of the passage was a relatively clear statement of an intended utterance—a desire to come home for Easter. However, Easter has associations of "rising again" and eventually, of "rising to Heaven" and fragments of these now intrude later in the passage, in the form of phrases such as "Rise again Glorious

Greece" and, elsewhere, "heaven will come." These intrude in a manner which, though giving a disjointed character to the passage, does not violate syntactical rules. The intrusions occur at points where a comma separates one syntactical unit from another, much as some of our earlier examples showed associational intrusions at the full stop or period point. From the point of view advanced here, the repetition of words in schizophrenic utterance is also a case of associative intrusion. When a speaker (or writer) has uttered a word, we might suggest that there arises a state of activation of the network of associations to the uttered word. This network includes not only the associations but also the word itself. In normal language usage the content of these networks never enters consciousness but is inhibited instantaneously. Any failure of inhibition leaves open the possibility of intrusion of any strong member of the network, including, of course, the "stimulus" word itself. If the subsequent syntax permits, this stimulus word might well intrude into the utterance, producing the effect of repetition. These repetitions will be subject to the same general principles of vulnerability that apply to any other intrusion. Hence we should expect them to occur more often at the end of a sentence or at the end of a clause. From a document in this writer's possession the following example will serve:

"Kindly send it to me at the hospital. Send it to me Joseph Nemo, in care of Joseph Nemo and me who answers by the name of Joseph Nemo will care for it myself. Thanks everlasting and Merry New Year to Metholatum Company for my nose, for my nose, for my nose, for my nose, for my nose, for my nose."

This example includes several different repetitions, one of which involves a slight change of meaning ("care" as in the postal address "in care of" and later in the sense of "looking after") while the others are simple repetitions. Thus, it might be argued that the findings of Mittenecker (1951), for example, mentioned previously, and the many other data bearing on the tendency to repeat language units, could be included into the fundamental process of associational intrusion. Additional support for this possibility comes from the common observation that in the standard Word Association technique schizophrenic patients frequently respond by repeating the stimulus word. When we consider that the instructions used in this technique commonly ask the respondent to reply to the stimulus word with the first word that "comes in his mind," the tendency to repeat the stimulus word may be interpreted as a prolonged activation of the first word that did enter consciousness—namely the stimulus word. The adoption of an associational intrusion hypothesis of this kind may serve the heuristic purpose of integrating several divergent anomalies of language into one single underlying process.

Smith (1970) reports an investigation directed at distinguishing between the production of deviant associations on the one hand, and on the other hand a failure by schizophrenic patients to "edit" (i.e. inhibit) associations from utterance. He concludes:

". . . schizophrenics communicated poorly, not because they produced deviant associations . . . but because they failed to edit adequately their responses by considering the relation between what they did not want to say and what they were about to say" (p. 186).

By assigning the problem to one of attentional deficiency, we have managed to suggest a continuity between these anomalies and the many other evidences of attentional deficiency in schizophrenia. However, the ultimate usefulness of this kind of integration rests upon evidence that the attentional deficiency may be understood as the consequence of some more basic process. Venables (1964) has advanced the view that the attentional deficiencies found in the processing of sensory input are a consequence of pathological states of autonomic and cortical arousal. There is not space here to review the empirical support for his position, and it has been criticized recently by Neale and Cromwell (1969). Venables' suggestion is that in the early acute stage the patient is underaroused, and that underarousal is associated with broad span of attention. Broad span of attention renders the patient liable to distraction by a wide range of stimuli, whereas under high arousal attention is narrowed and invulnerable to distraction.

However, it should be noted that the relationship between autonomic measures (GSR, heart rate, etc.) and clinical status (acute-chronic, process-reactive and paranoid-nonparanoid) is far from clear. A proper formulation of the arousal-attention mechanism is still needed, and some investigators have preferred to deal with the relationships between arousal and psychopathology without recourse to the concept of attention at all. A notable attempt along these lines has been made by Broen and Storms (1967), who prefer to relate arousal to concepts of learning and habit-strength, explaining changes in attention span as strategies learned by the patient because they serve to reduce his confusion. In spite of the difficulties in arriving at a proper formulation of the nature of the arousal-attention mechanism it seems profitable to persist in the attempt. The data of Chapman and McGhie (1962, 1964) are difficult to ignore and equally difficult to interpret without reference to concepts of broad and narrow attention. So far we have failed to develop autonomic measures of arousal that would give us uniform and unequivocal predictions of behaviour mediated via an attention mechanism; and this failure may, at least in part, be due to the fact that the crude polygraphic indices currently in use are influenced by many other sources of variance rather than to the lack of a biological process determining attentional range.

Some data relating biological processes to language phenomena are already available. Rice (1970) reports that schizophrenic patients on phenothiazine medication (and presumably in lowered states of autonomic arousal) made more of the Chapman double-meaning errors than patients not medicated, a finding consistent with the view that lowered arousal leads to wider attention and more interference. We have already noted the finding that adrenaline improves communicability in language (Honigfeld, 1967), which is what we would expect if increased arousal leads to more highly organized utterance.

Data reported by Mednick and Schulsinger (1965) indicate that children with a high genetic risk for schizophrenia (one or both parents schizophrenic) show a significant tendency to utter chain associations in a task requiring them to give single, controlled associations to stimulus words. As these children were not exhibiting pathological symptoms at the time of testing, and as many other measures of functioning gave quite normal results, it seems plausible to suppose that the inability to inhibit associations may be one of the early consequences of a biological deficiency of inhibition. From the same investigation comes a report that this group of children also showed broader gradients of stimulus generalization of the GSR than did normal controls, suggesting the early presence of autonomic differences also.

Clearly, none of these data are more than suggestive. To a large extent the relationship between biological anomalies and language anomalies in schizophrenia remains virgin territory for research. It should also be clear that the vast bulk of previous research emphasizes the need to make distinctions within the class of patient diagnosed as schizophrenic. Many patients in this diagnostic category do not exhibit language disturbance at all. Hypernormal or hyponormal autonomic reactivity are found in only a proportion of schizophrenic patients. The same is true for a wide range of other responses. Hence, when advancing the hypothesis that associational interference is a consequence of attentional deficit, and that this in turn has probable autonomic determinants, it is most correct to say that there probably exists *a group* of patients to whom this hypothesis applies. For this group, the interpretation of language disturbance as another aspect of the disturbances found in the maintenance of external attentional focus promises to provide some integration of a range of perplexing phenomena.

REFERENCES

Benjamin, T. B., and Watt, N. F. (1968). Psychopathology and semantic interpretation of ambiguous words. Unpublished manuscript: Harvard University.

Bertoch, D. J. (1966). Encoder-decoder variables, level of response uncertainty and verbal redundancy of psychiatric patients. Unpublished doctoral dissertation, University of Utah.

Bobon, J. (1967). Schizophrasie et schizoparaphasie. *Acta neurol. Belg., 67,* 924-38.

Broen, W. E., and Storms, L. H. (1967). A theory of response interference in schizophrenia. In B. A. Maher (Ed.), *Progress in Experimental Personality Research,* Vol IV. New York: Academic Press.

Chapman, J., and McGhie, A. (1962). A comparative study of disordered attention in schozphrenia. *J. ment. Sci., 108,* 487-500.

— and — (1964). Echopraxia in schizophrenia. *Brit. J. Psychiat., 110,* 365-74.

Chapman, L. J. (1960). Confusion of figurative and literal usages of words by schizophrenics and brain-damaged patients. *J. abnorm. soc. Psychol., 60,* 412-16.

—, Chapman, J. P., and Miller, G. A. (1964). A theory of verbal behaviour in schizophrenia. In *Progress in Experimental Personality Research,* Vol. I.

Check, F. E., and Amarel, M. (1967). Studies in the sources of variation in Cloze scores: II. The verbal passages. *J. abnorm. Psychol., 73,* 424-30.

Chomsky, N. (1965). *Aspects of the Theory of Syntax.* Cambridge, Mass.: M.I.T. Press.

Critchley, M. (1964). The neurology of psychotic speech. *Brit J. Psychiat., 110,* 353-64.

Dal'Bianco, P. (1957). Schizophrasie et cybernetique. *Acta neurol. Belg., 57,* 937-49.

Eliseo, T. S. (1963). Figurative and literal misinterpretation of words by process and reactive schizophrenics. *Psychol. Rep. 13,* 871-7

Fairbanks, H. (1944). The quantitative differentiation of samples of spoken language. *Psychol. Monogr., 56,* 19-38.

Flavell, J. (1956). Abstract thinking and social behaviour in schizophrenia. *J. abnorm. soc. Psychol., 52,* 208-11.

Gardner, G. E. (1931). The measurement of psychotic age: A preliminary report. *Amer. J. Psychiat., 10,* 963-75.

Gerver, D. (1967). Linguistic rules and the perception and recall of speech by schizophrenic patients. *Brit. J. soc. clin. Psychol., 6,* 204-11.

Goldstein, K. (1944). Methodological approach to the study of schizophrenic thought disorder. In J. S. Kasanin (Ed.), *Language and Thought in Schizophrenia.*

Goldstein, K., and Scheerer, M. (1941). Abstract and concrete behavior: an experimental study with special tests. *Psychol. Monog., 53,* No. 2

Heim, A. W., and Watts, K. P. (1958). A preliminary note on the word-in-context test. *Psychol. Rep., 4,* 214.

Honigfeld, G. (1965). Temporal effects of LSD-25 and epinephrine on verbal behaviour. *J. abnorm. soc. Psychol., 70,* 303-6.

– (1967). Cloze analysis in the evaluation of central determinants of comprehensibility. In K. Salzinger and S. Salzinger (Eds.), *Research in Verbal Behavior.* New York: Academic Press.

Kasanin, J. S. (1944). *Language and Thought in Schizophrenia.* Berkeley: University of California Press.

Lang, P. J., and Luoto, L. (1962). Medication and associative facilitation in neurotic, psychotic and normal subjects. *J. abnorm. soc. Psychol., 64,* 113-20.

Lawson, J. S., McGhie, A., and Chapman, J. (1964). Perception of speech in schizophrenia. *Brit. J. Psychiat., 110,* 375-80.

Lenneberg, E. (1967). *Biological Foundations of Language.* New York: John Wiley.

Levy, R., and Maxwell, A. E. (1968). The effect of verbal context on the recall of schizophrenics and other psychiatric patients. *Brit. J. Psychiat., 114,* 311-16.

Lewinsohn, P. M., and Elwood, D. L. (1961). The role of contextual constraints in the learning of language samples in schizophrenia. *J. nerv. ment. Dis., 133,* 79.

Maher, B. A., McKean, K. O., and McLaughlin, B. (1966). Studies in psychotic language. In P. J. Stone et al. (Eds.), *The General Inquirer: A Computer Approach to Content Analysis.* Cambridge, Mass.: M.I.T. Press.

Mandelbrot, B. (1953). Jeux de communication. *Publ. Inst. Stat. Univ. Paris, 2,* 1-124.

Mann, M. B. (1944). The quantitative differentiation of samples of spoken language. *Psychol. Monogr., 56,* 41-74.

Mednick, S. A., and Schulsinger, F. (1965). A longitudinal study of children with a high risk for schizophrenia. In S. Vandenberg (Ed.), *Methods and Goals in Human Behavior Genetics.* New York: Academic Press.

Milgram, N. (1959). Preference for abstract versus concrete word meanings in schizophrenic and brain-damaged patients. *J. clin. Psychol., 15,* 207-12.

Miller, G., and Selfridge, J. (1950). Verbal context and the recall of meaningful material. *Am. J. Psychol., 63,* 176-85.

Mittenecker, E. (1951). Eine neue quantitative Methode in der Sprachanalyse und ihre Anwendung bei Schizophrenen. *Monatsschrift fur Psychiatric und Neurologie, 121,* 364-75.

–(1953). Perseveration und Personlichket. *Z. f. exp. u. angew. Psychologie, 1,* 5-31.

Moon, A. F., Mefferd, R. B., Wieland, B. A., Porkorny, A. D., and Falconer, G. A. (1968). Perceptual dysfunction as a determinant of schizophrenic word associations. *J. nerv. ment. Dis., 146,* 80-4.

Moran, L. J., Mefford, R. B., and Kimble, J. P. (1964). Idiodynamic sets in word association. *Psychol. Monogr., 78,* No. 579.

Neale, J. M., and Cromwell, R. L. (1969). Attention and schizophrenia. In *Progress in Experimental Personality Research,* Vol. V.

Pavy, D. (1968). Verbal behavior in schizophrenia: a review of recent studies. *Psychol. Bull., 70,* 164-78.

—, Grinspoon, L., and Shader, R. I. (1969). Word frequency measures of verbal disorders in schizophrenia. *Dis. nerv. System, 30,* 553-5.

Raeburn, J. M., and Tong, J. E. (1968). Experiments on contextual restraint in schizophrenia. *Brit. J. Psychiat., 114,* 43-52.

Rice, J. (1970). Disordered language as related to autonomic responsivity and the process-reactive distinction. *J. abnorm. Psychology, 76,* 50-4.

Rubin, E. (1956). Om forstaaelighedsreserven og om overbestemthed. In G. Nielsen (Ed.), *Til minde om Edgar Rubin, Nordisk Psykol., 8,* 28-37.

Salmon, P. D., Bramley, J., and Presly, A. S. (1967). The Word-in-Context test as a measure of conceptualization in schizophrenics with and without thought disorder. *Brit. J. med. Psychol., 40,* 253-9.

Salzinger, K. (1966). An hypothesis about schizophrenic behaviour. Paper presented to Fourth World Congress of Psychiatry, Madrid.

Salzinger, K., Pisoni, S., Feldman, R. S., and Bacon, P. M. (1961). The effect of drugs on verbal behavior. Paper presented to American Association for the Advancement of Science, Denver, Colorado.

—, Portnoy, S., and Feldman, R. (1964). Verbal behavior in schizophrenics and some comments toward a theory of schizophrenia. Paper presented at American Psychopathological Association, Annual Meeting.

—, —, Pisoni, D. B., and Feldman, R. S. (1970). The immediacy hypothesis and response-produced stimuli in schizophrenic speech. *J. abnorm. Psychol., 76,* 258-64.

Shakow, D. (1963). Psychological deficit in schizophrenia. *Behav. Sci., 8,* 275-305.

Shannon, C. E. (1948). A mathematical theory of communication. *Bell Sys. tech. F., 27,* 379-423, 623-56.

Shannon, C. E. (1951). Prediction and entropy of printed English. *Bell Sys. tech. J., 30,* 50-64

Smith, E. E. (1970). Associative and editing processes in schizophrenic communication. *J. abnorm. Psychol., 75,* 182-6.

Spence, J. T., and Lair, C. V. (1964). Associative interference in the verbal learning performance of schizophrenics and normals. *J. abnorm. soc. Psychol., 68,* No. 2, 204-9.

Taylor, W. (1953). "Cloze" procedure: a new tool for measuring readability. *Journ. Qtrly., 30,* 415-33.

Truscott, I. P. (1970). Contextual constraint and schizophrenic language. *J. consult. clin. Psychol., 35,* 189-194.

Venables, P. (1964). Input dysfunction in schizophrenia. In B. A. Maher (Ed.), *Progress in Experimental Personality Research,* Vol. I. New York: Academic Press.

Von Domarus, E. (1944). The specific laws of logic in schizophrenia. In J. S. Kasanin (Ed.), *Language and thought in schizophrenia.* Berkeley:

University of California Press.

Weaver, W., and Kingston, T. (1963). Factor analysis of Cloze procedure and other measures of reading and language ability, *J. Comm.*, *13*, 252-61.

Whitehorn, J., and Zipf, G. (1943). Schizophrenic language. *Arch. Neurol. Psychiat.*, *49*, 831-51.

Yates, A. (1966). Psychological deficit. *Ann. Rev. Psychol.*, *17*, 111-44.

Zipf, G. K. (1949). *Human Behaviour and the Principle of Least Effort.* New York: Hafner (Macmillan).

22. *The Syndrome of Early Childhood Autism*
LORNA WING

Early childhood autism is one form of childhood psychosis. In this paper the latter term is used as a general label to cover those syndromes in which behaviour is continuously bizarre and unpredictable in relation to the child's mental age. Used in this way it is a description of behaviour and has no theoretical implications concerning regression to an earlier level of development, nor does it imply any particular aetiology. Psychotic behaviour may be the result of a known organic pathology, and it can occur in children of any level of intelligence. The most informative psychiatric diagnoses consist of three parts: first, a label indicating the overt behaviour; secondly, the underlying organic pathology, if known; and thirdly, the level of intellectual functioning (Rutter et al, 1969; Wing, 1970a).

Childhood psychosis includes many different behaviour patterns, and attempts have been made to pick out groups of children with similar symptoms. Rutter (1967) discussed the problems of classification. The best known and widely accepted subclassification in this field is Kanner's identification of the syndrome he called "early infantile autism" characterised by "profound withdrawal from contact with people; an obsessive desire for the preservation of sameness; a skilful and even affectionate relationship to objects; the retention

of an intelligent and pensive physiognomy; and mutism, or the kind of language which does not seem intended to serve interpersonal communication." (Kanner, 1943, 1949). He chose the adjective "infantile" because he at first thought that the abnormalities were always present from birth. Later, he observed the same problems in children who had had a period of apparently normal development of up to two years (Kanner and Lesser, 1958). Other writers have noted a few children in whom the onset was apparently in the third year of life (Lotter, 1966a; Rutter, 1967). For this reason I shall use the label "early childhood autism" in this paper. Kanner described his group of children in considerable detail, but since then other workers have applied the label to a variety of syndromes, many of which bear little relation to Kanner's original description. Some writers have used it to cover all psychoses of childhood, while at the other extreme, some have limited it to a tiny minority of psychotic children who exactly fit a detailed description (Laufer and Gair, 1969). In the past, various authors have used the terms "childhood autism", "psychosis", and "schizophrenia" interchangeably. It is therefore difficult to evaluate the results of studies unless the children are described in detail.

Fortunately, order is now appearing out of the chaos. A recently convened international study group (Rutter, 1970 composed of most of the

Lorna Wing, The syndrome of early childhood autism, *British Journal of Medicine,* September 1970, 381-392. Reproduced by permission.

workers who have undertaken properly conducted scientific and clinical studies of autistic children, under the chairmanship of Professor Leon Eisenberg, was able to reach a substantial measure of agreement on a number of important points, as follows:

1. Early childhood autism begins from birth or within the first three years of life.
2. Early childhood autism is not a form of schizophrenia.
3. The basic handicaps of early childhood autism are produced by organic, not emotional, pathology. They are not caused by the personalities of the parents, nor by their child-rearing practices.
4. Problems of comprehension and use of language are important aspects of early childhood autism.

These points will be expanded in the following description of the syndrome.

PREVALENCE

Descriptions of children who were probably autistic could be found in the literature long before Kanner delineated the syndrome. These include Itard's famous account, written at the end of the eighteenth century, of a boy found living wild in the woods of Aveyron in France (Itard, 1932). Witmer (1919) also wrote about a child with most of the classic features of autism.

Kanner (1949, 1957) excluded from his group those children with obvious associated organic abnormalities of the central nervous system. Subsequent experience has shown that most or all of the features of autism can be seen in some children who have obvious neurological disorders (Lotter, 1966a,b; Rutter, 1968, 1970). Kanner also stated that the children in his group were all potentially of normal or superior intelligence. More recent work has shown that the typical syndrome can occur in children of any level of intelligence, from above average to severely subnormal (Lotter, 1966a,b; Rutter, 1966).

The first detailed epidemiological study was conducted by Lotter, who screened all children aged eight, nine or 10 with home addresses in the former county of Middlesex (Lotter, 1966a,b; Wing et al, 1967). He included children with some or all of the elements of the autistic syndrome, whether or not they had additional neurological disorders, and whatever their level of intelligence. He found a prevalence of 4·5 per 10,000 children of school age, of whom approximately half had the typical syndrome (the "nuclear" group) and the rest had many but not all of the features. Nearly one-third of the children had recorded evidence suggestive of neurological abnormalities. About 70 per cent had IQ's under 55, 15 per cent scored between 55 and 79, and 15 per cent had IQ's of 80 or above. Slightly more than two-thirds had some speech by age eight, nine or 10. Two-thirds had been abnormal from birth and the rest were reported as having a set-back in development.

Boys were affected more often than girls, especially in the "nuclear" group, where the ratio was 2·75:1. Other workers have found even higher boy:girl ratios, such as 3·6:1 (Creak and Ini, 1960) 4:1 (Kanner, 1954) and 4·5:1 (Annell, 1963).

The parents, particularly of the children in the "nuclear" group, had higher occupational levels than the average for the county. Both the fathers and the mothers had higher intelligence quotients than the average. This confirms the many similar reports in the literature (Kanner, 1943, 1954; Pitfield and Oppenheim, 1964; Rimland, 1965; Rutter and Lockyer, 1967).

A similar prevalence figure was reported in a later survey in Denmark (Brask, 1967).

DESCRIPTION OF BEHAVIOUR

Autistic children vary considerably in the severity and extent of their behaviour disorders, ranging from the child who might, on superficial acquaintance, pass for a quiet normal child, to the child whose behaviour disturbance is unmanageable by all the ordinary methods of child rearing. Nevertheless, it is possible to give a description of the elements of the typical behaviour pattern.

Kanner (1943) considered that childhood autism was, basically, a disturbance of affective contact, hence his choice of the name "autism". Many writers since then have tried to explain the characteristic features of the syndrome as consequences of an emotional disturbance (see the discussion of this subject in Rutter, 1968.) This is an unsatisfactory exercise, necessitating the ignoring of some clinical observations and the distortion of others. A working party, under the chairmanship of Creak (1961), avoided this problem by giving a list of nine points without trying to relate one to the other.

In recent years, following an expansion in experimental work with autistic children, and a concurrent increase in interest in the development of language in normal and handicapped children, the classical features of early childhood autism have been re-examined (Hermelin, 1966; Pronovost et al, 1966; Rutter, 1968, 1970; Wing J. K., 1966; Wing L., 1969b.) The new formulations link the children's behaviour to underlying problems of comprehension and use of sensory input, together with lack of development of verbal *and* non-verbal language. Looked at in this way, the symptoms form a logical pattern and the similarities between autism and other kinds of childhood handicaps such as blindness, deafness and aphasia become easier to understand. There is much to be said for finding a new name for the syndrome which calls attention to the cognitive handicaps rather than the overlay of secondary emotional disturbance.

Behaviour in Babyhood

As the diagnosis of early childhood autism is rarely made before two years of age, descriptions of behaviour in babyhood have to be based on retrospective accounts. Some mothers of autistic children feel that there is something wrong with their child almost from his birth, although they cannot explain why. For others, the realisation of abnormality comes gradually and does not crystallise until the child is two or three years of age or more. In approximately one-third of cases, parents report a period of apparently normal development and then a sudden change in behaviour, sometimes following a definite event such as an infection, an accident, or the birth of a sibling.

Some autistic babies are unusually quiet and undemanding, and do not cry even when in need of food. Others are extremely difficult, and have irregular patterns of sleeping coupled with periods of intractable screaming. They may be stiff and unresponsive to cuddling, or else lie limply in their mother's arms. Feeding may be a problem, with poor sucking, and later on difficulty with chewing lumpy food.

Autistic babies do not show the behaviour which, in normal children, precedes the development of language (Sheridan, 1969). They do not show curiosity or any interest in the environment. Their play with objects does not pass beyond the stage of handling them for simple sensations and some do not handle objects at all. They do not point things out to their parents or lean out of their prams to see what is going on. Instead they lie quietly or else indulge in primitive self-stimulation such as rocking, head banging, or scratching and tapping on the nearest available surface.

They often smile at the usual age, but smiling and laughing are initiated by physical contact such as tickling and bouncing, rather than by the visible and audible approach of the mother or father. Many parents report that their child did not lift up his arms to them or show his eagerness to be picked up.

Providing the child has no obvious additional neurological problem affecting his development, motor milestones tend to be normal or only slightly delayed. A few autistic children, however, show a long delay in crawling or walking, and a few need special teaching to overcome these problems (Witmer, 1919).

Even with those children who apparently had an initial period of normal development, appropriate questioning of the parents often provides evidence that such children always lacked curiosity and exploratory behaviour, and that their play with objects never developed appropriately (Wing, 1970b).

Behaviour from 2–5 Years

This is the period during which autistic behaviour is most marked, and the children are most difficult to manage (Wing, 1969b). The elements of the syndrome can be divided into two main groups; first, the observable handicaps which are directly linked to the underlying problems of comprehension; secondly, the difficult and disturbed behaviour which is secondary to the handicaps.

Handicaps

Abnormal Response to Sounds. Young autistic children tend to have paradoxical responses to sounds. Sometimes they ignore sounds, however loud: sometimes they find certain noises painful and cover their ears or cry in distress; and sometimes they are fascinated by sounds such as that of a friction-drive toy, and will spend hours in absorbed listening. Deafness may be suspected because of the lack of response to loud sounds, but parents usually observe that the child is aware of some sounds and also that he quickly learns the meaning of a soft sound like the rustle of a sweet paper, because he links this with the reward of receiving a sweet.

Lack of Comprehension of Speech. Young autistic children characteristically show no interest when spoken to, and parents and doctors sometimes feel that the children deliberately refuse to pay attention. However, careful observation shows that they really have great difficulty in understanding spoken speech (Pronovost et al, 1966; Rutter, 1968; Wing, 1969b). There is a tendency for comprehension to improve slowly with increasing age. When this happens the children try to cooperate, and their resulting mistakes clearly demonstrate the nature of

their difficulties, which are very similar to those of children with congential receptive aphasia. One example is of the seven-year-old autistic girl whose mother said to her "Daddy will do up your buttons, because I have got my washing-up gloves on." The child looked puzzled, then smiled happily, went to a drawer, found a pair of gloves and gave them to her father.

Abnormalities in the Use of Speech. Some autistic children remain mute throughout their lives. Speech is nearly always delayed in those who do begin to speak, and shows marked abnormalities. There are four kinds of problems which appear in the speech of autistic children. These are:

1. Immediate echolalia—in some children this remains the only kind of verbal utterance;
2. Delayed echolalia, that is repetition of words and phrases heard in the past, sometimes months or years before;
3. The abnormalities seen in aphasia, such as nominal aphasia with substitution of invented phrases for nouns, confusion of words with similar sounds or meanings, muddling of the sequence of letters in words and words in sentences, distorted reproduction of words, and telegraphic speech;
4. General immaturity of level of speech development, heard in spontaneous speech, though not in the phrases copied from other people.

The relationship between these four problems is not clear, because each can occur in differing degrees of severity, and different children can show different combinations. The children tend to compensate for the difficulties in producing spontaneously generated speech, by capitalising on their ability to reproduce phrases heard in the past. Thus the typical autistic child says "Do you want a biscuit?" when he himself wants a biscuit, because this is the phrase he heard his mother say as she opened the biscuit tin. This is known as "reversal of pronouns". His language problems prevent him from forming his own sentence using the word "I" but he does the best he can. Some children use phrases learnt in one special situation inappropriately, as with the child who said "Don't throw it out of the window" to mean "No" (Cunningham, 1966; Kanner and Lesser, 1958; Wing, 1969b; Wolff and Chess, 1965.)

When the children do make up their own phrases, as opposed to repeating other people's, their asphasia becomes obvious. A child who was asked to describe an outing said "London—town zoo—doggie-bunny—ephelant—have you dinner sausage roll—pink cake—shake-milk" ("doggie-bunny" was his own invention for "kangaroo".)

The general immaturity of speech is so severe in some children that they are still using the grammatical constructions of a 2½-year-old when they are approaching adolescence (such as "bye-bye hair" meaning "I don't want my hair washed", and "No Johnny have dinner" meaning "I don't want my dinner").

A few autistic children make good progress in speaking but even the most advanced tend to be concrete and pedantic in their speech with little feeling for the subtle nuances of language.

Problems of Pronunciation and Intonation.
Some of the children have pronunciation problems which resemble those of children with congenital executive aphasia. Others pronounce words reasonably well, but almost all of the children have an odd intonation. The voice may be monotonous or else go up and down in the wrong places. They also have problems in controlling volume and may shout on some occasions, but speak very quietly on others. The children's voices are commonly described as "mechanical" in quality. When this is combined with stereotyped echoed phrases, or with jumbled aphasic speech, the result can sound very strange. It is only by disentangling the different problems which make up the whole picture that it is possible to begin to understand and to communicate with an autistic child.

Difficulties with Copying Skilled Movements.
Some autistic children appear dainty and graceful in spontaneous movement, but others are obviously clumsy. Both groups have difficulties when attempting to copy skilled movements made by other people, even when they try hard to cooperate (Elgar and Wing, 1969; Rutter, 1966; Wing, 1969b.) They learn movements required in such tasks as do-

ing up buttons, riding a tricycle, or simple dance steps, if their limbs are moved for them, but not through visual demonstration. Right-left, back-front and up-down may be confused, with consequent problems in dressing, laying the table, turning handles and identifying and writing those letters of the alphabet which are mirror images of each other.

Problems in Understanding Visual Input.
Development of recognition of two-dimensional pictures of objects may be delayed. Many young autistic children tend to pick out tiny details of a picture, or of their environment, while ignoring the whole scene. Thus, a child will run through a roomful of people as if they did not exist, to pick up a tiny piece of shiny paper in a corner.

It seems, from observations of the behaviour of young autistic children, that they make more use of the information from their peripheral than from their central visual fields. They attend to moving, in preference to stationary, objects. They seem as much at home in the near darkness as in the light. Some parents have observed that their children watch television or look at pictures "out of the corner of their eyes". They tend to twist and flick their fingers and hands near their eyes as do children with congenital cataracts. They do not look straight at objects or people for very long (Hermelin and O'Connor, 1970) but dart rapid glances at them and look away again. They walk, run downstairs or even ride a tricycle without appearing to look where they are going, which occasionally leads to a suspicion of blindness.

Use of Proximal Senses.
Autistic children also resemble partially sighted and blind children in that they tend to explore the world and make contact with people through the senses of touch, taste, smell and movement. This continues for many years past the stage when a normal baby is smelling and tasting everything he can reach. Despite this preference for the proximal senses, many young autistic children appear oblivious of pain or cold. Later on they grow out of this indifference, and they may become oversensitive to discomfort.

Abnormal Movements.
The twisting and flicking of the hands near the eyes, seen in both autistic and partially blind children, has already been mentioned. Some autistic children also flick pieces

of string or shiny materials in their fingers. Others love to watch objects spinning, or spin round and round themselves. Flapping movements of the arms and legs, jumping up and down, facial grimaces and tip-toe walking are frequent, especially when the children are excited.

Difficulty with Comprehension and Use of Gestures.

Lack of non-verbal language is one of the important aspects of the autistic syndrome, since this additional handicap means that the children are deprived of almost all ways of communicating with other people. Young autistic children are late in pointing at things, even at objects that they want, and when they do use this gesture, it tends to be a vague wave of the arm instead of a precise indication with an extended finger. They do not make up for their inability to speak by using miming, facial expressions, or demonstrating with objects. When an autistic child wants something he gets it for himself if he possibly can. If he needs help he will grab an adult by the hand and pull him along to the place where the desired object is to be found. The children typically catch hold of the back of someone else's hand or wrist, and do not hold hands in the ordinary childish way unless specifically taught.

Understanding of gesture develops slowly and most of the children never learn to understand complicated miming or the subtle gestures which accompany social conversation. However, comprehension of broad simple movements such as pointing often precedes that of verbal language, and may give the impression that the child can understand more speech than is really the case (Pronovost et al, 1966.)

Secondary Behaviour Problems

Difficulties with Social Relationships.

One of the first problems which worries parents of young autistic children is the apparent aloofness and indifference to other people. In their early years the children seem to be cut off from human contact, and to live in a world of their own. Kanner considered this to be the fundamental problem in early childhood autism, but the accumulation of evidence now suggests that the children's social withdrawal is secondary to their inability to understand or to communicate.

Children who have language problems from other causes such as receptive aphasia, deafness, and deafness combined with blindness also tend to be socially withdrawn when young (Ingram, 1959; Myklebust, 1960; Orton, 1937; Rutter et al, 1970; Wing, 1969b). Autistic children usually show normal emotional responses to physical contact and rough and tumble games (Wing, 1969a). With increasing maturity, and proper management, the children tend to become more sociable and affectionate, but there is much less change in their cognitive handicaps (Rutter et al, 1967; Wing, 1970b). The children are most relaxed and "in contact" when they are with an adult who understands the language handicaps and who adjusts his method of communication to the children's level of comprehension (Elgar and Wing, 1969).

Resistance to Change and Attachment to Objects.

Living in a world which they find confusing and unpredictable, the children tend to cling to the routines with which they are familar, or to objects which afford them simple pleasurable sensations. These are pathetic, desperate attempts to find some order in the midst of chaos. This behaviour leads to severe problems for the parents, because the children may insist on certain routines being carried out in the same way down to the last detail, and will scream for hours if there is the slightest change. If they have favourite objects they may go to any lengths, including entering other peoples' gardens and houses, to add to their collection of, to take some actual examples, tin lids, detergent packets, plastic bottles, or pieces of garden hose.

Abnormal Emotional Responses to Situations.

The children's lack of understanding of the implications of different situations makes them react in abnormal ways. One small incident may produce a lasting fear of some harmless object or activity. A child may be frightened of barking dogs, having a bath, wearing shoes, entering a special room, even of commonplace everyday things such as a sugar bowl or an electric light bulb. On the other hand, they are often regardless of real dangers, and may run in front of moving cars, or climb out onto high roofs or window-ledges.

Some of the children have fits of laughing and

giggling for no apparent reason. If language develops enough for the child to communicate, parents usually discover that the reason for the laughter is some simple experience which gives the child pleasure, such as a shiny piece of paper or a musical sound. The children who make good progress may laugh at simple slapstick comedy and enjoy watching circus clowns throw water and custard pies. As might be expected, they cannot appreciate verbal humour. At the other extreme, the children sometimes show intense misery. They weep and cannot be comforted because the world is too complicated for them to understand.

Socially Embarrassing Behaviour. Inability to communicate severely retards the learning of social skills. The children react to frustration with screaming, temper tantrums and aggression against the nearest person or object. They may grab things in shops, wander out of the house, run away when out walking, or take off their clothes in the street. They may be overactive and destructive, necessitating constant supervision.

Not all autistic children are actively difficult. A minority react to their handicaps with complete passivity. They seem reluctant to use their hands, and have to be encouraged even to pick up and handle objects. The problem with these children is to encourage rather than to restrain activity. (See Park, 1969, for an excellent description of such a child and the methods used to help her to learn.)

Self-Destructive Behaviour. Self-directed aggression occurs in response to frustration, as well as aggression against others. The children typically bite the backs of their hands or wrists when angry, often screaming and stamping at the same time. Self-destructive behaviour also occurs when the children are bored and unoccupied. This is much more common in institutionalised children than in those who are cared for at home.

Lack of Imaginative Play. Normal children develop play as they develop language, and the complexity of their imaginative games is an outward expression of their inner language. Autistic children are severely retarded in both verbal and non-verbal language so they do not have imaginative play either alone or with other children. Some of them build constructional toys, and some can learn simple games of chasing and hide and seek, but they cannot understand complex activities or enjoy fictional stories.

Special Skills

Those autistic children who do not have any associated conditions affecting their physical appearance, usually look healthy, normal and attractive, especially in their early years. They give the impression of alert intelligence, and, in some children, this may be strengthened by the fact that they perform some non-verbal activities well. They tend to love music and may be able to select their favourite records from a large collection. Some are good with jigsaws and constructional toys, but they use the sense of touch in these activities much more than would a normal child of the same age (Hermelin and O'Connor, 1970). A few can do complicated arithmetical calculations. Memory for lists of names, dates or long poems is exceptionally good in a small number of children. They may be able to read out loud, but usually have little understanding of the meaning of the words. They tend to be able to remember the position of objects, and to be able to find routes to places visited in the past. It is likely that some "idiots-savants" were autistic children with one outstanding special skill.

However, these skills can be associated with very severe retardation in understanding and meaningful use of language, and it cannot be argued that good non-verbal skills are evidence that language problems must be emotional rather than cognitive in origin.

Later Development

After five years of age there is a tendency for slow improvement to occur, particularly in the secondary behaviour problems (see section on "Prognosis"). With the lessening of the more dramatic behaviour disturbances, some of the older children may come to resemble children with severe aphasia, or those with general retardation from other causes. In these circumstances a correct diagnosis cannot be made without good history-taking. It cannot be emphasised too strongly that good affective contact in an older child is compatible with a diagnosis of early childhood autism.

THEORIES OF AETIOLOGY

The aetiology of early childhood autism is as yet unknown, but various theories have been suggested. They can best be considered under three headings.

Theories Concerning Fundamental Causes

Emotional Causes

The theories which suggest that autistic children are potentially normal at birth but are affected by an adverse emotional environment can be included here. Kanner (1949) suggested that the parents of autistic children were detached, cold and obsessional. However, Kanner did not use any method of measuring personality nor did he have a control group. Some studies have now been done using more scientific methodology and these have found no evidence of any special peculiarities in the parents apart from, first, their high intelligence, and secondly, those problems which they share with parents of any severely handicapped child. Eberhardy (1967), Kysar (1968), Pitfield and Oppenheim (1964), Rutter et al (1970), Schopler and Loftin (1969) and Park (1969) discuss these theories and the harm that they have done to the parents and families of autistic children.

Recently, some learning theorists have suggested that autistic behaviour is the result of faulty conditioning from birth (Ferster, 1961). Neither this theory, nor those which concern the parents' personalities, take into account the severe cognitive and executive problems of the children, which suggest an organic, not an emotional or psychological cause.

Organic Causes

The frequency of associated neurological problems detectable in young children with autistic behaviour has already been noted. In a few cases the under-lying organic aetiology is known because autism is associated with a diagnosable condition such as phenylketonuria, or there is a clear history of a dramatic change in behaviour following an encephalitis or meningitis. Follow-up studies have shown that EEG abnormalities, and other signs of neurological dysfunction, increase as the children grow older, even in those who appeared to have no additional handicaps when first diagnosed (Creak, 1963; Rutter et al, 1967; Rutter et al, 1970). Creak (1963) reported post-mortems on three cases, two of whom has neurolipoidosis and one who had tuberose sclerosis. Rutter et al (1970) reported the cognitive and physical deterioration, in adolescence, of a small proportion of children in a follow-up study. They also noted that 29 per cent of the cases who were not already epileptic in early childhood, developed fits by the time they were seen in adolescence or early adult life.

Genetic factors have been suggested as a possible cause. The tendency for the parents to be of high intelligence and occupational level may have a genetic explanation. The prevalence of autism among the siblings of autistic children is very slightly higher than among the general population (Rutter, 1968), but the family histories do not suggest any simple type of genetic transmission. A genetically determined oversensitivity to the effects of oxygen immediately after birth has been suggested by Rimland (1965) but no evidence has been produced in support. Chromosome studies have not as yet revealed any specific abnormality (Book et al, 1963), but the question is still open and work is continuing.

Biochemical abnormalities have also been considered. Heeley and Roberts (1965) reported abnormal tryptophan metabolism. Boullin et al (1970) found that the ability to retain serotonin was defective in the blood platelets of a group of children selected (by means of Rimland's questionnaire), as having typical Kanner's syndrome.

In some children it seems that slow development, rather than brain damage, underlies their autism, but this is not a sufficient explanation in itself—some cause must be found to account for the delay in maturation.

Theories Attempting to Locate the Affected Brain Functions or Structure

Even if a fundamental cause is identified, its method and site of action still have to be established. Many workers have concentrated their efforts on analysing the nature of the brain dysfunction, and have, so to speak, by-passed the problem of the fundamental cause.

Abnormalities of the reticular system of the brain have been suggested by, for example, Rimland (1965) and Hutt et al (1965). It is hard to explain the details of the children's handicaps from this kind of theory. In any case the reticular system seems by now to have been blamed for almost all known psychiatric illnesses. Any abnormalities that are detected may be secondary rather than primary.

Other workers (Gellner, 1959; Rutter, 1970; Wing, 1969b) have regarded the language dysfunctions as particularly important, but the lack of precise knowledge as to the brain structures and functions which underlie the development of comprehension and use of verbal and non-verbal language, inhibits speculation as to the location of the pathology in early childhood autism.

Theories Concerning Psychological or Neurological Dysfunctions

The third level of investigation includes the work which has tried to define the nature of the dysfunctions which lead to autistic behaviour by-passing both the fundamental cause, and the location of the pathology in the brain.

Psychologists have tended to search for one single dysfunction which will account for all the various cognitive and executive problems of autism. Hermelin and O'Connor (1970), for example, have suggested a defect in concept formation and symbolisation. The problem with any "single dysfunction" theory is highlighted by the clinical observation that each of the elements of the autistic syndrome can be found alone, or in any

TABLE 1.
Cognitive and Language Dysfunctions with Possible Underlying Central Abnormalities

Dysfunctions

A. Lack of comprehension of speech
B. Echolalia—immediate
C. Echolalia—delayed
D. Aphasia—(eg: nominal aphasia, confusion of words with similar sounds or meanings, muddled sequences of letters and words, distortion of words, telegraphic speech)
E. Immaturity of level of speech development
F. Problems of pronounciation and voice control
G. Difficulty in right-left, up-down and back-front orientation and clumsiness in copying skilled movements.
H. Lack of comprehension of gestures
I. Inability to use gestures
J. Attention to small details and lack of understanding of the whole scene
K. Use of peripheral rather than central vision.

The syndromes below can be represented as follows:

Dyslexia with reversal of letters — G
Congential receptive aphasia — A+D+E+F
Congential executive aphasia — E+F+G
Early childhood autism — All the above dysfunctions in combination

combination short of the full picture (Wing, 1970b.) This is difficult to explain on any "single dysfunction" theory.

One way of dealing with this problem is to suggest that autistic children suffer from a combination of dysfunctions (Wing, 1970b). Each of the handicaps listed in the section on behaviour can be regarded as resulting from one or more neurological dysfunctions. For example, the section on use of speech suggested four different kinds of dysfunction which underlie the typical speech patterns of autistic children. Some combinations of these dysfunctions occur commonly enough to be named as syndromes. Congenital receptive aphasia, congenital executive aphasia and dyslexia with reversal of letters are examples of syndromes in which some but not all of the dysfunctions are seen in combination. In early childhood autism, all or almost all of the dysfunctions listed occur together (Table 1). The problems of concept formation and symbolisation can be regarded as the resultant of the combined dysfunctions, and not their cause.

It must be emphasised that multiple dysfunctions could be due to a single pathological cause, such as a biochemical or a genetic abnormality. However, it seems most likely that the pathological causes may be different in different groups of children. The analogy with epilepsy is helpful here. Early childhood autism, like epilepsy, may be secondary to various pathological processes, such as birth trauma, infection, or metabolic disorder, but there is, apparently, an "idiopathic" group. This group may eventually be broken down into various subgroups, each of which may be found to have a single specific cause. The classic cases of Kanner's syndrome may, as Rimland (1965) suggests, form one such subgroup.

DIFFERENTIAL DIAGNOSIS

No physical or psychological tests exist which can give a positive diagnosis of early childhood autism, although some are useful in excluding other conditions. The final diagnosis rests on detailed history-taking and observation of the child's behaviour. The parents' description of his behaviour at home is of particular importance.

Other Forms of Childhood Psychosis. The age of onset is one of the important variables in differentiating between various childhood psychoses. Psychoses starting after three years of age do not show the autistic behaviour pattern.

Early childhood autism should be clearly differentiated from schizophrenia with onset in childhood. This latter condition is extremely rare and does not begin until seven years old at the earliest. The parents of autistic children do not have a raised incidence of schizophrenia (Creak and Ini, 1960; Lotter, 1966a,b; Rutter, 1968), whereas the parents of schizophrenic children show the same raised incidence as those of schizophrenic adults (Kolvin, et al, 1970). The symptoms of early childhood autism are quite different from those of schizophrenic adults, and autistic children do not become schizophrenic adults when they grow up (Rutter, 1968).

Congenital Receptive Aphasia. This can be a difficult differential diagnosis in young children, because receptive aphasia can lead to social withdrawal and retard the development of imaginative play. The most important distinguishing feature is that aphasic children use gestures and miming to assist communication, whereas autistic children do not.

Other combinations of cognitive dysfunctions which have some but not all of the features of autism (Table 1) can be diagnosed by careful examination of the nature and extent of the child's handicaps and behaviour problems, including an estimate of his skills as well as his difficulties.

Deafness. Young deaf children can have marked autistic behaviour and their hearing may be difficult to test, especially if the deafness is combined with some degree of receptive aphasia. The child's ability with non-verbal language should help to make the diagnosis. The parents' observations of their child's reaction to small sounds heard at home is also of great value in assessing hearing.

Partial Blindness Combined with Partial Deafness. Children who are partially blind plus partially deaf because of maternal rubella may have classic autistic behaviour (Wing, 1969b), with all the secondary behaviour problems. The diagnosis depends on the history of the pregnancy and physical examination for deafness, cataracts and other handicaps which may be caused by rubella.

Elective Mutism. A child with this problem will speak in one situation (perhaps at home) and not in another (perhaps at school) (Reed, 1963). He may have some speech problems, but these do not resemble those of autistic children whose language is abnormal in all situations. The general behaviour of an electively mute child is quite different from that of an autistic child.

"Mental Subnormality" is a blanket term covering a multitude of different conditions. Most mentally subnormal children do not show autistic behaviour. However, as Lotter's survey showed, the majority of autistic children have an IQ well below normal and some are severely subnormal. Many of the latter have organic neurological disorders which would cause severe mental retardation whether or not they were autistic. The handicaps of early childhood autism interfere with learning and therefore always produce some degree of retardation at least in early childhood. As mentioned before, a helpful diagnosis should describe a child's level of intellectual functioning as well as his overt behaviour, thus making allowance for the fact that autism and mental retardation can occur together or separately.

"Brain Damage" is another blanket term, covering a variety of syndromes. Some brain-damaged children show the autistic syndrome, others have some but not all of the features, but most are clearly not autistic even if their behaviour could be called psychotic. The particular behaviour associated with brain damage must, at least in part, be determined by the areas and functions of the brain which are affected, as discussed above.

Difficult Phases in Normal Children. All of the problems seen in autistic children can be seen in normal children at some stage in their early development. However, the odd behaviour passes quickly in a normal child who usually shows only a few of all the possible features. The autistic child has most or all of the problems and they last for many years, and some are life long. A normal child also has a wide repertoire of behaviour whereas the autistic child shows the autistic pattern all the time.

Consideration of the children's handicaps and of the conditions which may be mistaken for autism, should underline the fact that a description of each child's disabilities and his special skills is far more helpful than giving him a label. This should avoid sterile arguments about whether or not a child is "really autistic", and transfer attention to finding ways of helping him overcome his problems.

TREATMENT

There is no medical or psychological treatment for early childhood autism, but this does not mean that nothing can be done to help.

Medical treatment is sometimes necessary to deal with associated conditions such as fits, or to minimise secondary problems such as sleeplessness or hyperactivity. Autistic children are very resistant to sedative drugs and doses therefore need to be adjusted to obtain the desired effect. They are equally resistant to anaesthetics, and tend to be confused and disturbed on recovery.

Proper education is the most important method

of helping the children to compensate for their handicaps to some extent, and to make full use of any skills they may possess (Wing, 1969a). Techniques are rather similar to those for deaf, blind and aphasic children. Autistic children at first learn mostly through touch and movement, so Montessori equipment is particularly suitable (Elgar and Wing, 1969).

Learning theory and methods of behaviour modification have made a contribution to this field (Lovaas, 1966; Schopler and Reichler, 1970). These techniques are most useful if they are incorporated into a programme of general education, rather than being used to the exclusion of all else.

Education should begin as early as possible.

Parents are puzzled and bewildered if given no help with managing their autistic child, but if they are taught how to help him to learn social and practical skills they can become enthusiastic and successful participants in the full teaching programme (Schopler and Reichler, 1970). The fact that early childhood autism is a syndrome which may be produced by a number of different pathologies does not affect the necessity of identifying the children who have some or all of the handicaps, and providing the appropriate education. The cause of the handicaps is, in most cases, irrelevant in planning an educational programme—what matters is their nature and their severity.

PROGNOSIS

Rutter and Lockyer (1967) and Rutter et al (1967) followed up a group of 63 autistic children into adolescence and early adult life. They found that approximately 14 per cent made good progress, and, although not completely normal, would probably be able to find open employment. Another 25 per cent made fair progress but were still obviously handicapped. The rest showed a lessening of the secondary behaviour problems, but their handicaps remained unchanged, or in a few cases had beomce worse. These were mostly in institutions at follow-up. A number had developed epileptic fits.

The children with the higher intelligence quotients when first seen were those who did best on follow-up. The amount of schooling received influenced later adjustment. Improvement was often associated with particularly good individual attention in school and at home. Marked positive changes were usually seen by six or seven years but occasionally occurred later. Improvement in behaviour and in learning skills tended to continue well into adult life.

Less than half of the group had received as much as two years' schooling, and many had not had any education at all. It is to be hoped that better educational facilities for all autistic children will, in the future, improve the outcome.

SERVICES NEEDED

The services needed for autistic children and adults include diagnostic and assessment facilities, and centres to teach parents how to help their children.

A wide range of special schools is necessary so that autistic children of all levels of ability can re-

ceive the education most suited to their handicaps. The severely subnormal autistic child needs education in social and practical skills even more than the brighter child, but this group is particularly hard to place. The National Society for Autistic Children,

1A Golders Green Road, London, N.W. 11, has recently opened a unit for this type of child, as a pioneering venture.

Education should continue into adolescence and early adult life, with gradually increasing emphasis on vocational training. Sheltered workshops are necessary for the adults who cannot manage open employment. Autistic children tend to do best if they live with their own families, but hostels or sheltered communities are needed for children and adults who cannot live at home. Many are at present to be found in mental subnormality hospitals, but their difficulties in communication and comprehension make them particularly vulnerable to the understimulating conditions often to be found in these institutions.

The aims of education are modest but worthwhile. They are, first, to help the children to become socially acceptable; secondly, to help them compensate for their handicaps; thirdly, to help them learn skills and eventually to follow some useful occupation; and last but not least, to help them towards some understanding and therefore enjoyment of life.

Annell, A. L. (1963) A*cta psychiat, scand. 39*, 235.

Book, J. A., Nichtern, S., Gruenberg, E. (1963) ibid. *39, 309.*

Boullin, D. J., Coleman, M., O'Brinn, R. A. (1970) *Nature (Lond.) 226*, 372.

Brask, B. H. (1967) *Ugeskr. Laeg., 129,* 1560.

Creak, M. (Chairman) (1961) *Cerebr. Palsy Bull. 3,* 501.

— (1963) *Brit. J. Psychiat. 109,* 84.

— Ini, S. (1960) *J. Child. Psychol. 1,* 156.

Cunningham, M. A. (1966) *ibid. 7,* 143.

Eberhardy, F. (1967) *ibid. 8,* 257.

Elgar, S. (1966) *in Early Childhood Autism* (edited by Wing, J. K.) Pergamon Press, Oxford, p. 205.

—, Wing, L. (1969) Teaching Autistic Children. Guide lines for Teachers, No. 5. The College of Special Education and the National Society for Autistic Children, London.

Ferster, C. B. (1961) *Child Develop. 32,* 437.

Gellner, L. (1959) A Neurophysiological Concept of Mental Retardation and its Educational Implications. J. D. Levinson Research Foundation, Chicago.

Heeley, A. F., Roberts, G. E. (1965) *Develop. Med. Child Neurol. 7,* 46.

Hermelin, B. (1966) *in Early Childhood Autism* (edited by Wing, J. K.) Pergamon Press, Oxford. p. 159.

—, O'Connor, N. (1970) *Psychological Experiments with Autistic Children.* Pergamon Press, London, (in press).

Hutt, S. J., Hutt, C., Lee, D., Ounsted, C. (1965) *J. psychiat. Res. 3,* 181.

Ingram, T. T. S. (1959) *Brain, 82,*450.

Itard, J. M. G. (1932) *The Wild Boy of Aveyron* (translated by Humphries, G. and M.) Appleton-Century-Crofts, New York.

Kanner, L. (1943) *Nerv. Child, 2,* 217.

— (1949) *Amer. J. Orthopsychiat. 19,* 416.

—(1954) Genetics and the Inheritance of Integrated Neurological and Psychiatric Patterns (Proceedings of the Res. Publ. Ass. nerv. ment. Dis. 33) Williams and Wilkins, Baltimore. p. 378.

— (1957) *Child Psychiatry,* 3rd edn. Thomas, Springfield, Illinois.

— Lesser, L. I. (1958) *Pediat. Clin. N. Amer. 5,* 711.

— (1957) *Child Psychiatry,* 3rd. edn. Thomas, Springfield, Illinois.

—,Lesser, L. I. (1958) *Pediat. Clin. N. Amer. 5,* 711.

Kolvin, I., Ounsted, C., Richardson, L., Kidd, J.S.H., Garside, R. F., McNay, A., Humphrey, M., Roth, M. (1970) Psychoses in childhood—a comparative study. A paper given at a Study Group in Infantile Autism, arranged by the Institute for Research into Mental Retardation, June 1970. Churchill, London (in press).

Kysar, J. (1968) *Amer. J. Psychat. 125,* 103.

Laufer, M. W., Gair, D. S. (1969) *in The Schizophrenic Syndrome* (edited by Bellak, L., Loeb, L.). Grune and Stration, New York, p. 378.

Lotter, V. (1966a) *Soc. Psychiat. 1,* 124.

— (1966b) *ibid. 1,* 163.

Lovaas, I. (1966) in *Early Childhood Autism* (edited by Wing, J. K.) Pergamon Press, Oxford. p. 115.

Myklebust, H. R. (1960) *The Psychology of Deafness*. Grune and Stratton, New York.

Orton, S. T. (1937) *Reading, Writing and Speech Problems in Children*. Chapman and Hall, London.

Park, C. C. (1969) *The Seige*, Colin Smythe, Gerrards Cross, Bucks.

Pitifield, M., Oppenheim, A. N. (1964) *J. Child Psychol. 5*, 51.

Pronovost, W., Wakstein, M. P., Wakstein, D. J. (1966) *Exceptional Children, 33*, 19.

Reed, G. F. (1963) *J. Child Psychol. 4*, 99.

Rimland, B. (1965) *Infantile Autism*. Methuen, London.

Rutter, M. (1966) *in Early Childhood Autism* (edited by Wing, J. K.) Pergamon Press Oxford p. 51.

— (1967) *in Recent Developments in Schizophrenia* (edited by Coppen, A. J., Walk, A.) Headley Brothers, London. p. 133.

— (1968) *J. Child. Psychol. 9*, 1.

—, Lebovici, S., Eisenberg, L., Sneznevskij, A. V., Sadoun, R., Brooke, E., Lin, T. (1969) *ibid. 10*, 41.

— (1970) Editor, Study Group on Infantile Autism, arranged by the institute for Research into Mental Retardation, June, 1970. Churchill, London (in press).

—, Bartak, L., Newman, S. (1970) Autism—a central disorder of cognition and language? Paper given at a Study Group on Infantile Autism, arranged by the Institute for Research into Mental Retardation. June, 1970. Churchill, London (in press).

—, Lockyer, L. (1967) *Brit. J. Psychiat. 113*, 1169.

—, Greenfield, D., Lockver, L. (1967) *ibid. 113*, 1183.

Schopler, E., Loftin, J. (1969) *Arch. gen. Psychiat, 20*, 174.

—, Reichler, R. J. (1970) Developmental therapy by parents with their own autistic child. Paper given at a Study Group on Infantile Autism, arranged by the Institute for Research into Mental Retardation. June, 1970. Churchill, London (in press).

Sheridan, M. (1969) *Health Trends, 1*, 7.

Wing, J. K. (1966) in *Early Childhood Autism* (edited by Wing, J. K.) Pergamon Press, Oxford, p. 3.

—, O'Connor, N., Lotter, V. (1967) *Brit. med. J.* iii, 389.

Wing, L. (1969a) Children Apart—Autistic Children and Their Families (Family Doctor Booklet) British Medical Association and National Association for Mental Health, London.

— (1969b) *J. Child Psychol. 10*, 1.

— (1970a) *Psychological Medicine, 1,* (in press).

— (1970b) Perceptual and language development in autistic children; a comparative study. Paper given at a Study group on Infantile Autism, arranged by the Institute for Research into Mental Retardation, June, 1970. Churchill, London (in press).

Witmer, L., (1919—22) *Psychol. Clinc. 13*, 97.

Wolff, S., Chess, S. (1965) *J. Child Psychol. 6*, 29.

SECTION 5
THE THERAPEUTIC ENTERPRISE

This section deals with a small sampling of the major psychotherapies in current use: Rogerian, Gestalt, encounter group, behavior therapy, and therapeutic communities.

In his original formulation, Carl Rogers termed his system of psychotherapy "nondirective," the assumption being that the therapist did not exert (appreciable) influence on the content of what a client would say during sessions. The therapist's job was seen as reflecting the client's own feelings back to him so that he himself might find solutions to his problems. This technique was seen as enabling the client to grow and change on his own without interference by the therapist. As questions began to be raised about the subtle influences exerted even by therapists taking pains to allow the client free rein, Rogerian therapy came to be called "client-centered." The reading by Truax (selection 23) is based on a careful analysis of tapes of therapeutic sessions furnished by Rogers himself, and the findings reveal that social influence was, indeed, exerted by him and, presumably, other therapists identified with the client-centered school. This outcome weakens the criticisms leveled by client-centered therapists against behavior therapists that they are somehow antihumanist for endeavoring to overtly change clients' behavior. It appears that even therapists who maintain that they actively strive not to influence clients, do in fact, influence them without being aware of doing so. One noteworthy feature is that Rogers was instrumental in exposing his own therapy work to scientific scrutiny by others. He and his colleagues deserve continuing credit for having opened the process of psychotherapy to dispassionate observation and critical analysis.

Gestalt therapy has come out of the same *Zeitgeist* that welcomed with open arms the humanistic theories and therapies of Carl Rogers and Abraham Maslow. Loosely derived from Gestalt psychology, the Gestalt therapy of Fritz Perls holds that man has become separated from his own experiences, feelings, and emotions. The aim of Gestalt therapy is to reacquaint clients with and enhance their spontaneity, sensory awareness, creativity, and emotional responsiveness. Gestalt therapy involves an individual in specific exercises or games to facilitate expression of his immediate feelings. Levitsky and Perls (selection 24) describe some of the techniques that are used during actual therapy sessions. While Gestalt therapy may provide very intense experiences, there is, unfortunately, no research examining its effectiveness.

The encounter-group movement is derived from the same humanistic tradition as Gestalt therapy. It stresses the phenomenology of experience and utilizes a variety of verbal and nonverbal exercises and techniques to awaken participants to their own feelings. Yalom and Lieberman's (selection 25) is one of the very few reports of research into the nature of encounter groups. The authors sound a warning that such groups can do serious damage to the emotional well-being of some individuals who are emotionally labile. They studied the reactions of casualties of encounter groups and found that the personalities of the encounter-group leaders were the most significant determinant of whether or not the individuals had satisfying experiences. The leader most apt to produce casualties is described as aggressive, charismatic and unable to differentiate among the differing needs of his group's participants. Yalom and Lieberman conclude that "individuals who are psychologically vulnerable and who overinvest their hopes in the magic of salvation through encounter groups are particularly vulnerable when they interact with leaders who believe that they can offer deliverance."

Behavior therapy has developed from the efforts of clinicians to apply principles derived from experimental psychology to the therapeutic enterprise. Early efforts in behavior therapy revolved around the use of classical and operant conditioning techniques only, although behavior therapy has subsequently opened itself up to the whole field of experimental psychology.

Lang and Melamed dramatically illustrate the use of punishment in behavior therapy (selection 26). The subject of this case study is an infant who chronically vomited all his food until he was on the verge of death. He was unresponsive to all medical intervention, whereupon the authors were invited to attempt treatment with behavior therapy. The article is impressive in demonstrating the inventiveness of the therapists in their use of psychophysiological recording and in suggesting the propriety of using drastic measures to save an individual's life.

O'Connor (selection 27) illustrates the use of modeling to increase social interaction in isolate nursery school children. The idea that modeling is an effective teacher and modifier of behavior is an old one. The accomplishment of behavior therapy is in demonstrating the effectiveness of systematically applied modeling in order to achieve a desired goal.
31) reviews reports of the use of college students in programs to help hospitalized psychiartic patients, a group notoriously lacking sufficient theraueutic attention. He finds evidence that at least the college students benefit greatly from their experience, and he expresses the hope that further controlled research will demonstrate equal therapeutic gain for the patients.

Fixsen, Phillips, and Wolf's reading (selection 28) is one of a series dealing with their effort to set up a therapeutic community for predelinquent boys. They run the community along operant conditioning (token economy) lines and try to teach the youngsters principles of self-control and prosocial behavior. Their work shows that behaviorally oriented treatment programs need not be *ipso facto* authoritarian but, in fact, may foster development of democratic behavior. Their community may be seen as putting into practice on a small scale some of the ideas expressed by Skinner in his *Beyond Freedom and Dignity,* raising the possibility that behavioral management techniques can be used to facilitate humanness and create a better world.

SUGGESTED READINGS

Cohen, H. L., & Filipczak, J. *A new learning environment.* San Francisco: Jossey-Bass, 1971

Bandura, A. *Principles of behavior modification.* New York: Holt, 1969.

Lazarus, A. A. *Behavior therapy and beyond.* New York: McGraw-Hill, 1971.

Rogers, C. *On becoming a person.* Boston, Houghton Mifflin, 1961.

23. *Reinforcement and Nonreinforcement in Rogerian Psychotherapy*[1]
CHARLES B. TRUAX

Excerpts from tape recordings of a single, long-term, successful therapy case handled by Rogers were analyzed to evaluate the adequacy of the client-centered view that empathy, warmth, and directiveness are offered throughout therapy in a manner not contingent upon the patient's behavior. Findings indicate that the therapists respond in a significantly differential way to 5 of the 9 patient behavior classes studied. Concomitantly, significant increases in the emission rates of 4 of the 5 behavior classes were noted throughout therapy. Findings thus indicated significant reinforcement effects in the client-centered therapy.

The present study is aimed at exploring the possibility that important reinforcement effects occur within the transactions of nondirective therapy.

Client-centered theorists have specified the "therapeutic conditions" of empathic understanding and acceptance or unconditional positive regard as two main antecedents to constructive behavioral or personality change in the client (Dymond, 1949; Hobbs, 1962; Jourard, 1959; Rogers, 1951, 1957; Rogers & Truax, 1965; Truax, 1961; Truax & Carkhuff, 1963). Rogers, as the leading exponent of this viewpoint, holds that these "conditions" are primarily attitudinal in nature and are offered in a nonselective fashion to the patient: they are specifically not contingent upon the patients' verbalizations or behaviors. This viewpoint, in pure form, is incompatible with the behavioristic view of

Charles B. Truax, Reinforcement and nonreinforcement in Rogerian psychotherapy, *Journal of Abnormal Psychology, 71,* 1966, 1-9. Copyright © 1966 by the American Psychological Association and reproduced by permission.

[1] Appreciation is gratefully extended to Carl R. Rogers for his freely given consent to the use of the completed successful counseling case recorded at the University of Chicago Counseling Center in 1955. This particular case is perhaps of special significance since it was heavily used by Rogers and others in the development of the "process conception of psychotherapy" and the "Process Scale" developed in 1957. Thanks are also due to James C. Baxter and Leon D. Silber for their critical comments. This work was supported in part by a grant from the Vocational Rehabilitation Administration, No. RD-906-PM.

therapy and was one basis for the Rogers-Skinner debates (1956).

The basic difference between the views exemplified by Rogers and Skinner is that the latter holds that an effective therapist attempts to alter the patient's behavior while Rogers holds otherwise. Differential reinforcement is one of the procedures used in operant research *positions*. Thus, whether or not Rogers as a therapist uses differential reinforcement, thereby altering patient behavior, in a central question in the basic issue of control which philosophically differentiates the two positions.

The growing body of evidence indicates that the therapist's accurate empathy and unconditional positive regard are significant antecedents to therapeutic change (Rogers, 1962; Rogers, Kiesler, Gendlin & Truax, 1965). This evidence has been used both as support of Roger's view and as an argument against the behavioristic views of psychotherapy typified by such theorists as Krasner (1962), Wolpe (1958), Eysenck (1952, 1960), and Bandura (1961). The evidence does suggest that when patients receive high levels of empathy and warmth there is significantly more constructive personality and behavioral change then when the patients receive relatively lower levels (Barrett-Lennard, 1962; Bergin & Solomon, 1963; Cartwright & Lerner, 1963; Dickenson & Truax, 1963; Halkides, 1958; Lesser, 1961; Rogers, 1962; Strupp, 1960; Truax, 1961a, 1961b, 1963; Truax & Carkhuff, 1964; Truax, Carkhuff & Kodman, in press; Truax, Wargo, & Silber, 1965; Wargo, 1962; and Whitehorn & Betz, 1954). None of the research just cited, however, *necessarily* argues against a behavioristic view of psychotherapy.

If, in contrast to Rogers's contention, the therapist does respond differentially to different patient behaviors (i.e., more accepting of an empathic to, some patient behaviors but less accepting of and more directive in response to other patient behaviors) then a reinforcement view would not be inconsistent with the findings. It could be argued that if empathic understanding, warmth (and nondirectiveness) are therapeutic, then it may also be argued that these therapeutic conditions are reinforcing, rewarding, or somehow encouraging, and that the types of patient behavior (presumably more adaptive ones) that are followed by high levels of these therapeutic conditions will consequently increase during the course of therapy. For example, it may be that the "high conditions" therapist offers more intense levels of accurate empathy and unconditional warmth or acceptance on both a nonselective random basis at, say, a 40% rate of reinforcement for all behaviors and, say, an 85% rate for exploration of material relevant to the private self. By contrast the "low conditions" therapist may offer less intense levels of empathy and warmth, with only a 20% rate of reinforcement for all behavior emitted and only a 40% rate of reinforcement for the patient's explorations of private material.

Support for the position exemplified by Rogers, viewed from the findings on empathy and warmth, rests upon the assumption that the therapist offers levels of conditions that do not systematically covary with the verbalizations or behavior emitted by the patient. If this were true (if, say, the level of therapist empathy or warmth did not systematically covary with patient response classes) then differential reinforcement could not account for the research findings of relationships between therapist behavior and patient outcome. On the other hand, if the therapist, in this case Rogers, does systematically vary his level of warmth or his level of empathy depending on the behavior, then Rogers's position would not be supported.

In an attempt to add clarity to this theoretic controversy, an exploratory analysis of a single successful case handled by Rogers was aimed at determining whether or not important reinforcing effects are imbedded in the transactions of client-centered therapy.

Three qualities of the therapist's behavior were studied as potential reinforcers: *(a)* empathic understanding, *(b)* acceptance or unconditional positive regard, and *(c)* directiveness (a negative reinforcer). These therapist behaviors were examined in relation to nine classes of patient behavior in order to determine the presence or absence of differential therapist responding and any consequent changes in the patient behaviors.[2] The patient behaviors studied which might theoretically be of significance were: *(a)* degree of discrimination learning by the patient, *(b)* ambiguity of patient's statements, *(c)* degree of insight development by the patient, *(d)* degree of similarity of patient's style of expression to that of the therapist, *(e)* problem orientation of the patient, *(f)* degree of patient catharsis, *(g)* degree of patient blocking, *(h)* degree of patient anxiety, and *(i)* degree of patient negative versus positive feeling expression.

CASE ANALYSIS PROCEDURE

Five clinical psychologists rated an unbiased sample of 40 typewritten interaction units consisting of (a) a therapist statement, (b) a succeeding patient statement, (c) the succeeding therapist statement. These interaction units (TPT, Therapist-Patient-Therapist) were designated by code numbers prior to the ratings, and were then assigned in random order to the five clinical psychologists who served as judges. Each judge rated separately each of the nine patient scales and the three therapist scales in different order, so as to minimize rating biases. The ratings were then decoded, and the ratings of the three classes of "reinforcers" were simply correlated separately with the nine classes of patient behavior under examination. The presence of significant correlations would then be positive evidence to indicate systematic, nonrandom use of these reinforcers with particular classes of patient behavior. Thus, the question became, for example, "Does the therapist's degree of acceptance significantly covary with the patient's degree of discrimination learning?" If a positive correlation was found, this would indicate that the therapist systematically was most accepting and unconditionally warm when the patient was engaged in discrimination learning, and was least accepting when the patient engaged in very little discrimination learning.

The Interaction Unit Sample

The TPT interaction units were selected from the following interviews out of a total of 85 therapy sessions for the complete case, 1, 3, 5, 7, 10, 15, 20, 25, 30, 35, 40, 45, 50, 55, 60, 65, 70, 75, 80, and 85. Two intersection units were taken from each of the above 20 interviews for a total of 40 interaction units. Interviews from which the samples were drawn, with the exception of Numbers 3 and 7, which were added to give more weight to the earlier stages of therapy, were evenly spaced and should constitute an unbiased sample of interviews throughout the therapy case. The two interaction units from each interview were obtained by starting the playback of the recordings of approximately the end of the first and second one-third of the hour-long tape and then listening until the therapist made a statement. Transcriptions started at the therapist's first words and included the ensuing TPT interaction unit. As a result of this sampling procedure, the length of the therapist and the patient statements varied considerably. When measured to the nearest one-tenth of an 80-character type line the range was from 0.4 to 14.0 lines.

The Clinical Psychologists as Raters

Of the five raters, none was trained in client-centered psychotherapy. One was trained in analytic therapy, while the remaining four clinicians described themselves as eclectic in orientation. All five judges had a minimum of

---

[2]Thanks are due to Israel Goldiamond for critical and helpful questions which served as the stimulus for the analysis of change in patient behaviors over time.

100 hours of supervised training as therapists, and 1,000 hours of experience as therapists. All post-doctoral clinical psychologists, the judges did not know the hypothesis being investigated. Further, they wrongly assumed that some of the more "non-directive" and "directive" statements could not have come from the same therapist.

The Rating Scales

A set of graphic rating scales were prepared for each of the three therapist behaviors and nine patient behaviors, each having a brief statement of the variable to be rated and horizontal lines 170 millimeters long on which the rating was marked. The rating was made by simply placing an X along the line labeled "most." "very much," to "least," and "very little." The scales for each therapist and patient behavior class stated a bipolarity of the variable. The bipolar definitions for the three reinforcer variables were taken from Rogers's (1951) theoretic descriptions.

Although the actual therapy samples did not contain extreme examples of the scale values, examples from the present case should add meaning to the present study. Two examples of TPT samples, rated high on each of the three reinforcer variables, are presented below.

Therapist Acceptance of Unconditional Positive Regard

The first example illustrates relatively high acceptance of the patient as he is feeling disappointed in the early results of therapy. This sample was rated relatively low on both empathy and directiveness:

T: There is nothing that I can do, but I can and do hope that the person will "lift" or something.
P: Yeh, but, well, for something to happen, or things to change, or me to change . . . inside, or . . . inside or something. Talking about it . . . doesn't really . . . seem to help, this kind of feeling. I mean, well . . . well, I don't know what I mean. I mean, I guess we're just talking about it. Well I don't know what I'm doing

(he has been thumping on something—beating on the desk?—long, long pause) . . . I feel so tremendously self-conscious. I don't know, maybe it was the therapy session yesterday, and the other thing that happened yesterday, that has just thrown, so much on me, myself again. And dangerous, I don't know, not dangerous but . . . I feel so un-free today. So . . . Hmm . . . (long pause) . . . Yeh, boy I really am self-conscious . . . sure tensed up inside.
T. I can't get the feel of what you mean by "self-conscious" It's very much aware of yourself? Or something, or generally embarrassed?

The second example illustrates relatively high acceptance of the patient's feelings of inadequacy and dependency. This sample was rated slighly above average on empathy but below average on directiveness:

T: I guess you're saying "I just can't trust those weak, and helpless and inadequate parts of me. I have to have someone to . . ."
P: To really be me. (T: Mmm, mmm) Someone else, you know . . . that's so absurd . . . that would never work. It's the same thing as, as this, uh . . . being afraid of people. It ties in with being afraid; it's like . . . well, you can use any one of a number of examples. If you really want to be someone genuinely . . . or express something genuinely . . . then, all you have to do is feel the slightest tinge of fear and you won't be able to really. And it's like that with myself . . . It's kind of . . . when I am myself, it kind of echoes on me and makes me afraid. I suddenly hear myself saying that, and then know, "careful" (T: Mmm, mmm) "Hold on here! Lookout!" (T: Mmm, mmm) . . . like that. (T: Mmm, mmm) "You won't be allowed to live if you do that." (T: Mmm, mmm) "You won't be allowed to . . . *anything*" . . . just, "You'll be blown to smithereens if you try that kind of thing."
T: Mmm, So that if you sense yourself . . . being yourself . . . then my (P: I become afraid) Gosh! Lookout! You don't know what you're getting into—you'll be destroyed.

Therapist Directiveness

The first example shows the therapist making a direct request to change the topic of discussion. This sample was rated slightly below average in empathy and low in acceptance:

T: Let's talk about something closer to you than that.

P: Or closer to you. I don't understand this at all, because I was really looking forward to this all the time, and now I just don't feel very good . . . about having harmed you.

T: You anticipated coming in, and now . . . today.

A second example of directiveness involves a more subtle "leading" of the patient. This sample was rated as average in empathy but above average in acceptance or unconditional positive regard:

T: It frightens you to even start to put it into words.

P: I guess I'll have to find it with someone else . . . first.

T: You feel that what would be demanded would be . . . put it in terms of "me" and, "you" . . . uh . . . make this the sort of thing you can sort of dimly visualize. I would need to want to really relate to that fine part of you, and find that so personally rewarding that, that in an attempt I would just . . . keep after it, or something. (P. interjects: Yeh) One, one phrase that I . . . I'm bringing in my feelings rather than yours, but . . . ever read the poem "The Hound of Heaven"? It's kinda a weird thing, but, uh, the kind of persistent love of God is the whole theme, that, that won't let the person go . . . and, and, I think that's sort of what your're talking about.

Therapist Empathy

The first example illustrates an excerpt in which the therapist attempts to verbalize what he senses is the client's uncertainty; this sample received an average rating on acceptance and a slightly above average rating on directiveness:

T: I've been trying to soak up that tone, uh, I'm not sure I'm right, but does it have some meaning like this, "What is it you want with me? I'm possibly willing to, to meet that, but I don't know what you want." Does that kinda describe it?

P: Yeh, I'm sympathetic, I'll try and do what I can. "Don't be this, and this, and this way to me." What is it? Yeh, that's it.

T: "So if you want me to get in with whatever it is you expect of me, just let me know."

The second example involves a moment when the the therapist attempts to reflect the client's feelings and move one step beyond. This sample was rated average on directiveness and acceptance:

T: Seems as though all the dark things—hurting, and being hurt—and . . . decay, and corruption, ugliness, uhmmm, Death. It's all of those that (P: frightening) that you're afraid of.

P: Yeh . . . stink and corruption and . . . pus, and . . . . There's just as. . . . It's something dark that ties them all together (T: Mmm, uhuh) Something putrid and (T: Mmm, mmm) there are 10 times the words (T: Mmm, mmm) for it . . . (laughs) it scares me.

T: Just to wander into that field verbally, . . . and even name all these things that have to do with it. . . this dark side of hurting and rottenness . . . that's hurting in itself.

The patient scales measuring the degree of insight developed, the degree of similarity of the patient's style of expression to that of the therapist, the degree of problem orientation, the degree of catharsis, the degree of blocking in thought and feeling, the degree of anxiety present, and the degree of positive-versus negative-feeling expression were defined by the trained clinical psychologists who served as judges. Degree of ambiguity of the patient's statement was defined in terms of its clarity of meaning. The judges were asked to disregard speech disturbances and length of statement in rating ambiguity. Discrimination learning was defined as making new distinctions between old feelings or experiences, and thus included both cognitive and emotional discrimination learning.[3]

FINDINGS AND DISCUSSION

Qualitative Aspects

There are three qualitative aspects exemplified in this case which perhaps are worth noting. The first concerns the style of expression by the therapist: it was characteristic of the therapist to express, restate, or interpret what the patient has been saying by "quoting" what the patient *might well have said* in the first person singular—"In a sense I feel . . . ." Out of the 40 sampled interaction units, 23 involved first person singular quotes while an additional five (for a total of 28 out of 40) involved impersonal quotes of the type: "In a sense it's like feeling . . . ."

A second characteristic of this particular case was the almost total absence of psychological jargon. Few even semitechnical terms such as "anxious" or "hostile" were used by the therapist. Instead, the therapist relied heavily on everyday language that conveys effect. Thus instead of saying "depressed" the therapist says "hopeless badness." The third qualitative characteristic of this case is the tentative character of therapist statements. There is almost universal use of such prefacing remarks as "in a sense," "I guess," and "maybe." This tentative approach might tend to elicit less resistance from the patient so that actual confrontation might sound much like an attempt to agree with the patient.

The Question of Selective Responding

The reliability of each scale, which is given in parentheses under the scale label in Table 1, was estimated by the variance formula presented by Ebel (1951) for the intraclass correlation. As can be seen in Table 1, reliabilities range from .26 to .64 for the classes of patient behavior, and from .48 to .68 for levels of "reinforcement" offered by the therapist.

The low reliabilities obtained on certain classes of patient behavior would make it difficult to detect any but the strongest of relationships. For the present hypothesis of selective reinforcement the absence of particular relationships is not critical. Rather, the *presence* of selective responding (as indicated by some significant relationship between therapist and patient classes of behavior) would be evidence in support of the hypothesis.

The obtained average intercorrelations between the levels of therapist reinforcements and the levels of the selected patient behaviors are presented in Table 1. These average intercorrelations were obtained in the following manner. First a matrix of intercorrelations was generated for each of the five raters separately. The matrices were then inspected separately for correlations which were significant at or beyond the .05 level of significance. Average correlations for the five raters combined were then obtained for those intercorrelations that were significant in three out of five individual rater matrices. All other correlations were recorded as nonsignificant in the present study so that the reported correlations tend to minimize rather than maximize the possibility of obtaining significant relationships.

The significant intercorrelations presented in Table 1 show a quite different pattern than would be expected if therapist responses were not highly selective in client-centered psychotherapy. If there was no systematic selective use of empathy, acceptance, or directiveness, then all correlations would

[3] Available from the author.

TABLE 1. *Interrelationships between the Level of Therapist Reinforcement and Levels of Patient Behaviors*

Classes of Patient Behavior	Reinforcers		
	Therapist Empathy ($r = .48$)	Therapist Acceptance UPR ($r = .59$)	Therapist Directive-ness ($r = .68$)
Patient learning of discriminations ($r = .59$)	.47	.37	ns
Patient ambiguity ($r = .35$	−.35	−.38	.33
Patient insight ($r = .32$)	.46	.37	ns
Similarity of patient style of expression to that of the therapist ($r = .57$)	.48	.32	−.31
Problem orientation ($r = .64$)	ns	.35	ns
Catharsis ($r = .44$)	ns	ns	ns
Blocking ($r = .54$)	ns	ns	ns
Anxiety ($r = .26$)	ns	ns	ns
Patient negative feeling expression ($r = .29$)	ns	ns	ns

be nonsignificant and would approach zero. Such is not the case. The therapist significantly tended to respond selectively with differential levels of empathy, warmth, or directiveness to high and low levels of the following classes of patient behavior: (*a*) learning of discriminations about self and feelings, (*b*) a lack of patient ambiguity (patient clarity), (*c*) patient expressions of insight, (*d*) patient verbal expressions that were similar in style to the therapist's way of expressing himself, and (*e*) problem orientation of the patient. Thus, when the patient expressed himself in a style similar to that of the therapist, the therapist was more empathic, more warm and accepting, and less directive. When the patient expressed himself in a style quite different from that of the therapist, the therapist tended to show significantly less empathy, less acceptance or warmth, and more directiveness.

No significant relationships were obtained be-tween the therapist's use of empathy, acceptance, or directiveness, and patient behaviors described as blocking, anxiety, negative- versus positive-feeling expression, or catharsis. While it may be that the absence of these relationships might, in part, be accounted for by the relatively low reliabilities of measurement, it also seems likely that Rogers as a therapist does not tend to respond differentially to these classes of patient behavior. In particular, as a theoretician and therapist, Rogers (1957, 1961) has felt it important for the therapist *not* to re-spond selectively to negative-versus positive-feeling expression.

The Further Question of Reinforcement
The above findings are consistent with, but not direct evidence for, the view that the therapist, in this case Rogers, is consciously or uncon-

sciously using empathy, acceptance, and directiveness as reinforcers. The basic property of a reinforcer is that its use with specific classes of behavior leads to consequent changes in the probability of occurrence of these classes of behavior.

From Table 1, the nine classes of patient behavior can be ranked according to the degree of contingency between therapist "reinforcer" responses and patient responses. Now, if the therapist's systematic selective responding has the properties of reinforcement it would be predicted that, other things being equal, the five patient classes of behavior that were selectively "reinforced" would show increases over time in therapy, while the four classes of patient behavior not reinforced would show no such increase over time. Thus, for example, one would expect an increase over time in therapy of the "Similarity of the Patient's Style of Expression to that of the Therapist" and of "Patient-Learning Discriminations," and no such increase (or decrease) in patient "Blocking" or "Negative Feeling Expression."

To evaluate this the ratings of the 40 samples for each class of patient behavior were grouped into five blocks across time-in-therapy (five raters for eight samples per block or 40 ratings per block) and the Grant Orthogonal Polynomial Trend Test Analysis of Variance (Grant, 1956) was used to test for the significance of components of trend. Further, t tests were used to test for significance of differences between early and late in therapy on all nine patient behavior classes. These data are presented in Table 2.

Of the classes of patient behavior to which the therapist selectively responded (i.e., reinforced), four out of five showed changes in patient behavior over time-in-therapy. Thus the data agree with the predictions in seven out of the nine classes of patient behaviors (78% correct prediction).

Considering the probability that the therapist also used other types of rewards or reinforcers and also rewarded other related patient behavior classes, considering the unknown differential complexity levels of the patient response classes, and consider-

TABLE 2. *Analysis of Changes over Time in Patient Response Classes*

Patient Response Classes	Highest Single Correlation with Therapist "Reinforcer"	Grant Orthogonal Polynomial Analysis of Variance for Trend			t Test Between First and all Later Blocks
		F Linear Trend	F Quadratic Trend	F Cubic Trend	
Similarity of patient style of expression to that of the therapist	.48	7.89***	1.20	.85	2.84***
Patient learning of discriminations	.47	3.10	.79	1.05	2.94***
Patient insight	.46	4.73**	1.70	0.75	2.73***
Patient ambiguity	−.38	3.04	1.50	0.91	1.35
Problem orientation	.35	3.28*	1.61	2.10	1.76**
Catharsis	*ns*	6.10**	2.13	1.20	2.03**
Blocking	*ns*	1.50	6.01**	1.50	1.29
Anxiety	*ns*	2.00	0.98	1.70	0.93
Patient negative-feeling expression	*ns*	1.17	0.65	0.89	0.75

*$p \leqslant$ .07 for 1/39 *df* for trend.
**$p \leqslant$ .05 for 1/39 *df* for trend or for 38 *df* for *t*.
***$p \geqslant$ .01 for 1/39 *df* for trend or for 38 *df* for *t*.

REINFORCEMENT IN ROGERIAN PSYCHOTHERAPY

ing the crudity of measurement, the findings strongly suggest that important reinforcement effects do indeed occur even in client-centered therapy.

Toward Evaluating the Validity of the Findings

There are, of course, some difficulties in interpreting the intercorrelation matrix. One might argue that these are simply interrelationships in the "heads" of the raters, as the raters might have known what the ' "X" value was when they rated a sample of "Y". However, each of the 12 variables was rated separately and they were rated in different orders. One would think it difficult to recall the X value of a given unit when the rating of the other units intervened between the X value and its corresponding Y value (an average of 240 ratings intervening between corresponding X and Y values). It could be argued that some of this bias is removed by the procedure for averaging the five different raters, since the raters were unaware of the actual hypothesis under study.

Beyond the above considerations, tabulation of one well-known characteristic of the therapist's behavior also suggests selective differential responding. The use of "uh huh" or 'Mmm mmm" verbalizations has become, perhaps unfortunately, the hallmark of Rogerian psychotherapy. In the samples used in the present analysis, Mmm mmm's or Uh huh's occurred 23 times in a total of 12 of the 40 samples (in 30% of the samples). The Mmm mmm occurred in 9 of the 12 samples (75% of its occurrence) during high expression of negative feeling by the patient (all above the mean ratings), while 0% occurred during low "patient negative feeling expression." In the remaining three samples, they occurred during the patient's direct restatement of what the therapist had just said. This tabulation alone suggests conscious or unconscious selective responding by the therapist, and is consistent with the obtained findings based upon relationships between rated therapist and patient classes of behavior.[4]

Finally, and most importantly, the obtained data dealing with changes in patient-in-therapy behavior were consistent with the obtained findings based upon prediction from a reinforcement view. Since the raters had no knowledge of whether a given sample came from early- or late-in-therapy, those findings of a tendency for significant linear increases to occur over time in reinforced patient behaviors and not to occur in nonreinforced patient behaviors, would also argue strongly against the notion that the obtained intercorrelations were simply "in the heads" of the raters.

IMPLICATIONS

The present findings point to the presence of significant differential reinforcement effects embedded in the transactions of client-centered psychotherapy. Since differential reinforcement is one of the procedures used in operant research to alter (or control) behavior, the findings suggest that the therapist, in this case Rogers, implicitly alters (or controls) the patient's behavior in the therapeutic setting. To this extent, then, the evidence weighs in favor of the view proposed by Skinner rather than that of Rogers. The present findings are not consistent with Rogers' view that rela-

tively *uniform conditions* which are globally "facilitative of personal growth and integration," are offered to patients in a manner not contingent upon the patient's behavior.

The present data, by demonstrating the role of empathy and warmth as positive reinforcers, suggest that the available evidence relating levels of these therapeutic conditions to patient outcome in ther-

[4]It should be noted that the therapist's use of the "Uh huh reinforcer" is relatively ineffective since there is no increase over time in "patient negative feeling expression."

apy does not argue against a reinforcement interpretation of psychotherapy. On the contrary, the finding that empathy and warmth act as reinforcers suggests that the evidence relating empathy and warmth to patient outcome is open to a behavioristic interpretation, based in part on the therapist's use of differential reinforcement.

Recent studies have suggested that such humanistic qualities as empathy and warmth are antecedents to patient personality or behavioral change. In attempting to understand *how* such therapist qualities operate in producing therapeutic change, the present data suggest the potential value of studies utilizing behavioristic models. Since the available evidence relating empathy and warmth to patient outcome deals primarily with differences in *intensity levels* contaminated by differences in *rates* between therapists, it seems likely that additional and more precise understanding of the role of empathy (and hence more effective practice) might grow out of studies carried out from a reinforcement frame of reference. Considering only empathy as the type of reinforcer used in psychotherapy, it would be expected that successful and nonsuccessful therapists might differ in: (*a*) the particular patient behaviors chosen for differential reinforcement (say, self-concept statements versus historical-genetic statements); (*b*) the differential rate of reinforcement (say, 25% versus 75% for a specific class of patient behavior); (*c*) the intensity levels of the reinforcer used (say, the depth of empathy); and even the (*d*) scheduling of reinforcement (say, fixed ratio versus variable ratio).

Research aimed at identifying which patient behaviors, if reinforced at what intensity levels etc., lead to positive therapeutic outcomes would provide more specific knowledge of how such positive human qualities as empathy and warmth operate to produce personality or behavioral change in the patient.

Such an approach aims toward more specific knowledge, but not at all toward more mechanical therapy. As the communication of any "reinforcing machine" qualities would by definition mean a low level of empathy and warmth, the present viewpoint is in full agreement with Schonbar's (1964) statement that "as a therapist I am no more a 'reinforcing machine' than my patient is a 'talking pigeon.' "

REFERENCES

Bandura, A. Psychotherapy as a learning process. *Psychological Bulletin,* 1961, *58,* 143–159.

Barrett-Lennard, G. T. Dimensions of therapist response as causal factors in therapeutic change. *Psychological Monographs,* 1962, *76*(43, Whole No. 562).

Bergin, A. E., & Solomon, Sandra. Personality and performance correlates of empathic understanding in psychotherapy. Paper read at American Psychological Association, Philadelphia, September, 1963.

Cartwright, Rosalind D., & Lerner, Barbara. Empathy: Need to change and improvement with psychotherapy. *Journal of Consulting Psychology,* 1963, *27,* 138–144.

Dickenson, W. A., & Truax, C. B. Group counseling with college underachievers: Comparisons with a control group and relationship to empathy, warmth, and genuineness. University of Kentucky and Kentucky Mental Health Institute, 1965.

Dymond, Rosalind. A scale for the measurement of empathic ability. *Journal of Consulting Psychology,* 1949, *13,* 127–133.

Ebel, R. L. Estimation of the reliability of ratings. *Psychometrika,* 1951, *16,* 407–424.

Eysenck, H. J. The effects of psychotherapy: An evaluation. *Journal of Consulting Psychology,* 1952, *16,* 319–324.

Eysenck, H. J. The effects of psychotherapy. In H. J. Eysenck (Ed.), *Handbook of abnormal psychology.* New York: Basic Books, 1960. Pp. 697–725.

Grant, David A. Analysis of variance tests in the analysis and comparison of curves. *Psychological Bulletin,* 1956, *53,* 141–154.

Halkides, Galatia. An investigation of therapeutic success as a function of four variables. Unpublished doctoral dissertation, University of Chicago, 1958.

Hobbs, N. Sources of gain in psychotherapy. *American Psychologist,* 1962, *17,* 741–747.

Jourard, S. I-thou relationship versus manipulation in counseling and psychotherapy. *Journal of Individual Psychology,* 1959, *15,* 174–179.

Krasner, L. The therapist as a social reinforcement machine. In H. H. Strupp & L. Luborsky (Eds.), *Research in psychotherapy.* Vol. II. Washington, D. C.: American Psychological Association, 1962.

Lesser, W. M. The relationship between counseling progress and empathic understanding. *Journal of Counseling Psychology,* 1961, *8,* 330–336.

Rogers, C. R. *Client-centered therapy.* Cambridge, Mass.: Riverside Press, 1951. Pp. 73–74.

Rogers, C. R. The necessary and sufficient conditions of therapeutic personality change. *Journal of Consulting Psychology,* 1957, *21,* 95–103.

Rogers, C. R. *On becoming a person.* Cambridge, Mass.: Riverside Press, 1961.

Rogers, C. R. The interpersonal relationship: The core of guidance. *Harvard Educational Review,* 1962, *32,* 416–429.

Rogers, C. R., Kiesler, D., Gendlin, E. T., & Truax, C. B. *The therapeutic relationship and its impact: A study of psychotherapy with schizophrenics.* Madison: Univer. Wisconsin Press, 1965, in press.

Rogers, C. R., & Skinner, B. F. Some issues concerning the control of human behavior. *Science,* 1956, *124,* 1057–1066.

Rogers, C. R., & Truax, C. B. The therapeutic conditions antecedent to change: A theoretical view. Chapter in, *The therapeutic relationship and its impact: A study of psychotherapy with schizophrenics.* Univer. Wisconsin Press, 1965, in press.

Schonbar, Rosalea Ann. A practitioner's critique of psychotherapy research. Paper read at American Psychological Association, Los Angeles, September 1964.

Strupp, H. H. Nature of psychotherapists' contribution to the treatment process. *Archives of General Psychiatry,* 1960, *3,* 219–231.

Truax, C. B. Clinical implementation of therapeutic conditions. In Carl R. Rogers (Chm.), Therapeutic and research progress in a program of psychotherapy research with hospitalized schizophrenics. Symposium presented at the American Psychological Association, New York, September 1961. (a)

Truax, C. B. The process of group psychotherapy. *Psychological Monographs,* 1961, *75*(7, Whole No. 511). (b)

Truax, C. B. Effective ingredients in psychotherapy: An approach to unraveling the patient-therapist interaction. *Journal of Counseling Psychology,* 1963, *10,* 256–263.

Truax, C. B., & Carkhuff, R. R. For better or for worse: The process of psychotherapeutic personality change. Chapter in, *Recent advances in the study of behavioral change.* Montreal: McGill Univer. Press, 1963, Pp. 118–163.

Truax, C. B., & Carkhuff, R. R. Significant developments in psychotherapy research. In Abt & Riess (Eds.), *Progress in clinical psychology.* New York: Grune & Stratton, 1964. Pp. 124–155.

Truax, C. B., Carkhuff, R. R., & Kodman, F., Jr. Relationships between therapist-offered conditions and patient change in group psychotherapy. *Journal of Clinical Psychology, in press.*

Truax, C. B., Wargo, D. G., & Silber, L. D. Effects of high conditions group psychotherapy with female juvenile delinquents. University of Kentucky and Kentucky Mental Health Institute, 1965.

Wargo, D. G. The Barron Ego Strength and LH[4] scales as predictors and indicators of change in psychotherapy. *Brief Research Reports,* 1962, *21,* (University of Wisconsin, Wisconsin Psychiatric Institute.)

Whitehorn, J. C., & Betz, Barbara J. A study of psychotherapeutic relationships between physicians and schizophrenic patients. *American Journal of Psychiatry,* 1954, *3,* 321–331.

Wolpe, J. *Psychotherapy by reciprocal inhibition.* Stanford: Stanford Univer. Press, 1958.

24. *The Rules and Games of Gestalt Therapy*
ABRAHAM LEVITSKY & FREDERICK S. PERLS

The techniques of Gestalt therapy revolve largely around two sets of guidelines which we will call "rules" and "games." The rules are few in number and are usually introduced and described formally at the outset. The games, on the other hand, are numerous and no definitive list is possible since an ingenious therapist may well devise new ones from time to time.

If we are to do justice at all to the spirit and essence of Gestalt therapy, we must recognize clearly the distinction between rules and commandments. The philosophy of rules is to provide us with effective means of unifying thought with feeling. They are designed to help us dig out resistances, promote heightened awareness—to facilitate the maturation process. They are definitely *not* intended as a dogmatic list of *do's* and *dont's* rather, they are offered in the spirit of experiments that the patient may perform. They will often provide considerable shock value and thus demonstrate to the patient the many and subtle ways in which he prevents himself from fully experiencing himself and his environment.

When the intention of the rules is truly appreciated, they will be understood in their inner meaning and not in their literal sense. The "good boy" for instance, totally incapable of understanding the liberating intent of rules, will frequently follow them exactly but to absurdity, thus endowing them with his own bloodlessness rather than with the vitality they seek to promote.

True to its heritage in Gestalt psychology, the essence of Gestalt therapy is in the perspective with which it views human life processes. Seen in this light, any particular set of techniques such as our presently used rules and games will be regarded merely as convenient means—useful tools for our purposes but without sacrosanct qualities.

Abraham Levitsky & Frederick S. Perls, The rules and games of Gestalt therapy. In I. Shepherd & J. Fagan (Ed.)

Gestalt therapy now. Palo Alto, California: Science and Behavior Books, Inc., 1970.

THE RULES

The Principle of the Now

The idea of the now, of the immediate moment, of the content and structure of present experience is one of the most potent, most pregnant, and most elusive principles of Gestalt therapy. Speaking from my own experience [A.L.], I have been at various times intrigued, angered, baffled, and exhilarated by the implications of the seemingly simple idea "being in the now." And what a fascinating experience it is to help others become aware of the manifold ways in which they prevent themselves from having true immediate awareness.

In order to promote *now* awareness, we encourage communications in the present tense. "What is your present awareness?" "What is happening now?" "What do you feel at this moment?" The phrase "What is your *now?*" *is* an effective one from therapist to patient.

It would not be accurate to say that there is no interest in historical material and in the past. This material is dealt with actively when it is felt to be germane to important themes of the present personality structure. However, the most effective means of integrating past material into the personality is to bring it—as fully as possible—into the present. In this way we avoid the bland, intellectualized "aboutisms" and strive vigorously to give all material the impact of immediacy. When the patient refers to events of yesterday, last week, or last year, we quickly direct him to "be there" in fantasy and to enact the drama in present terms.

We are active in pointing out to the patient how easily he leaves the now. We identify his need to bring into the dialogue absent individuals, the nostalgic urge to reminisce, the tendency to get preoccupied with fears and fantasies of the future. For most of us, the exercise of remaining in present awareness is a taxing discipline that can be maintained only for short periods. It is a discipline to which we are not accustomed and which we are inclined to resist.

I and Thou

With this principle, we strive to drive home as concretely as possible the notion that true communication involves both sender and receiver. The patient often behaves as if his words are aimed at the blank wall or at thin air. When he is asked, "To whom are you saying this?" he is made to face his reluctance to send his message directly and unequivocally to the receiver, to the *other*.

Thus the patient if often directed to invoke the other's name—if necessary, at the beginning of each sentence. He is asked to be aware of the distinction between "talking to" and "talking at" the listener. He is led to discover whether his voice and words are truly reaching the other. Is he really touching the other with his words? How far is he willing to touch the other with his words? Can he begin to see that this phobic avoidance of relating to others, of making genuine contact with others is also manifested in his voice mechanisms and his verbal behavior? If he has slight or insufficient contact, can he begin to realize his serious doubts as to whether others actually exist for him in this world; as to whether he is truly *with* people or feeling alone and abandoned?

"It Language and "I" Language

This rule deals with the semantics of responsibility and involvement. It is common for us to refer to our bodies and to our acts and behaviors in distantiated, third person, *it* language:

What do you feel in your eye?
  It is blinking.

What is your hand doing?
  It is trembling.

What do you experience in your throat?
  It is choked.

What do you hear in your voice?
  It is sobbing

Through the simple—and seemingly mechanical—expedient of changing *it* language into *I* language we learn to identify more closely with the particular behavior in question and to assume responsibility for it.

Instead of "It is trembling," "*I* am trembling." Rather than "It is choked," "*I* am choked." Going one step further, rather than "I am choked," "I am choking myself." Here we can immediately see the different degree of responsibility and involvement that is experienced.

Changing *it* to *I* is an example in microcosm of many of the Gestalt game techniques. As the patient participates, he is far more likely to see himself as an active agent who does things rather than a passive creature to whom things somehow happen."

A number of other semantic games are available. If the patient says, 'I can't do that," the therapist will ask, "Can you say, I *won't* do that?" As the patient accepts and uses this formulation, the therapist will follow with "And what do you experience now?"

T.: What do you hear in your voice?
P.: My voice sounds like it is crying.
T.: Can you take responsibility for that by saying "I am crying"?

Other gambits in the semantics of responsibility are having the patient substitute verbs for nouns and frequently use the imperative mode of speech as the most direct means of communication.

Use of the Awareness Continuum

The use of the so-called awareness continuum—the *"How"* of experience—is absolutely basic to Gestalt therapy. With it we often achieve effects both striking and startling. The frequent return to and reliance on the awareness continuum is one of the major innovations in technique contributed by Gestalt therapy. The method is quite simple:

T.: What are you aware of now?
P.: Now I am aware of talking to you. I see others in the room. I'm aware of John squirming. I can feel the tension in my shoulders. I'm aware that I get anxious as I say this.

T.: How do you experience the anxiety?
P.: I hear my voice quiver. My mouth feels dry. I talk in a very halting way.
T.: Are you aware of what you eyes are doing?
P.: Well, now I realize that my eyes keep looking away—
T.: Can you take responsibility for that?
P.: —that I keep looking away from you.
T.: Can you be your eyes now? Write the dialogue for them.
P.: I am Mary's eyes. I find it hard to gaze steadily. I keep jumping and darting about.

The awareness continuum has inexhaustible applications. Primarily, however, it is an effective way of guiding the individual to the firm bedrock of his experiences and away from the endless verbalizations, explanations, interpretations. Awareness of body feelings and of sensations and perceptions constitutes our most certain—perhaps our only certain—knowledge. Relying on information provided in awareness is the best method of implementing Perls's dictum to "lose your mind and come to your senses."

The use of awareness continuum is the Gestalt therapist's best means of leading the patient away from the emphasis on the *why* of behavior (psychoanalytic interpretation) and toward the *what* and the *how* of behavior (experiential psychotherapy):

P.: I feel afraid.
T.: How do you experience the fear?
P.: I can't see you clearly. My hands are perspiring . . . .

As we help the patient rely on his senses ("return to his senses"), we also help him distinguish between the reality *out there* and the frightening goblins he manufactures in his own fantasies:

P.: I'm sure people will despise me for what I just said.
T.: Go around the room and look at us carefully. Tell me what you *see*, what your eyes—not your imaginings—tell you.
P.: *(after some moments of exploration and discovery)* Well, actually people don't *look* so re-

jecting! Some of you even look warm and
friendly!

T.: What do you experience now?

P.: I'm more relaxed now.

No Gossiping

As is the case with many Gestalt techniques, the no-
gossiping rule is designed to promote feelings and to
prevent avoidance of feelings. Gossiping is defined
as talking about an individual when he is actually
present and could just as well be addressed directly.
For example, let us say the therapist is dealing
with Bill and Ann:

P.: *(to therapist)* The trouble with Ann is she's always picking on me.

T.: You're gossiping; say this to Ann.

P.: *(turning to Ann)* You're always picking on me.

We often gossip about people when we have not
been able to handle directly the feelings they
arouse in us. The no-gossiping rule is another Gestalt technique that facilitates direct confrontation
of feelings.

Asking Questions

Gestalt therapy gives a good deal of attention
to the patient's need to ask questions. The questioner is obviously saying, "Give me, tell me. . ."
Careful listening will often reveal that the questioner does not really need information, or that
the question is not really necessary, or that it
represents laziness and passivity on the part of the
patient. The therapist may then say, 'Change that
question into a statement." The frequency with
which the patient can actually do this validates
the action of the therapist.

Genuine questions are to be distinguished
from the hypocritical questions. The latter are
intended to manipulate or cajole the other into
seeing or doing things a particular way. On the
other hand, questions in the form of "How are
you doing?" and "Are you aware that . . ." provide genuine support.

THE GAMES

Following is a brief description of a number of
"games" used in Gestalt therapy. They are proposed by the therapist when the moment—in
terms of either the individual's or the group's
needs—seems appropriate. Some of the games,
such as "I have a secret" game or the "I take
responsibility" game are particularly useful as
group warm-ups at the beginning of a session.

It is, of course, no accident that some of the
major techniques of Gestalt therapy are couched
in game form. This is evidently a basic metacom-
munication on the part of Perls, highlighting one
of the many facets of his philosophy of personality functioning. The game language (itself a
game) can be seen as a commentary on the
nature of all or most of social behavior. The
message is *not* to stop playing games, since every
form of social organization can be seen as one or
another game form. Rather the message is to be
aware of the games we play and to be free to
substitute satisfying for nonsatisfying games.
Applying this view to any two-person relationship (love, marriage, friendship), we would not
be inclined to seek out a partner who "does not
play games" but rather one whose games fit
comfortably with our own.

Games of Dialogue

In trying to effect integrated functioning, the
Gestalt therapist seeks out whatever divisions
or splits are manifested in the personality.
Naturally, whatever "split" is found is a function of the therapist's frame of reference and
his observational powers. One of the main
divisions postulated is that between the so-

called top-dog and under-dog. Top-dog is roughly the equivalent of the psychoanalytic superego. Top-dog moralizes, specializes in *shoulds,* and is generally bossy and condemning. Under-dog tends to be passively resistant, makes excuses, and finds reasons to delay.

When this division is encountered, the patient is asked to have an actual dialogue between these two components of himself. The same game of dialogue can, of course, be pursued for any significant split within the personality (aggressive versus passive, "nice guy" versus scoundrel, masculine versus feminine, etc.). At times the dialogue game can even be applied with various body parts such as right hand versus left, or upper body versus lower. The dialogue can also be developed between the patient and some significant person. The patient simply addresses the person as if he were there, imagines the response, replies to the response, etc.

Making the Rounds

The therapist may feel that a particular theme or feeling expressed by the patient should be faced vis-a-vis every other person in the group. The patient may have said, "I can't stand anyone in this room." The therapist will then say, "OK, make the rounds." Say that to each one of us, and add some other remark pertaining to your feelings about each person.

The "rounds" game is of course infinitely flexible and need not be confined to verbal interaction. It may involve touching, caressing, observing, frightening, etc.

Unfinished Business

Unfinished business is the Gestalt therapy analogue of the perceptual or cognitive incomplete task of Gestalt psychology. Whenever unfinished business (unresolved feelings) is identified, the patient is asked to complete it. Obviously all of us have endless lists of unfinished business in the realm of interpersonal relations, with, for instance, parents, siblings, friends. Perls contends that resentments are the most common and important kinds of unfinished business.

"I take Responsibility"

In this game we build on some of the elements of the awareness continuum but we consider all perceptions to be acts. With each statement, we ask patients to use the phrase, ". . . and I take responsibility for it." For example, "I am aware that I move my leg . . . and I take responsibility for it." "My voice is very quiet . . . and I take responsibility for it." "Now I don't know what to say . . . and I take responsibility for not knowing."

What seems at first blush a mechanical, even foolish procedure is soon seen as one heavily laden with meaning.

"I have a Secret"

This game permits exploration of feelings of guilt and shame. Each person thinks of a well-guarded personal secret. He is instructed *not* to share the secret itself but to imagine (project) how he feels others would react to it. A further step can then be for each person to boast about what a terrible secret he nurses. The unconscious attachment to the secret as a precious achievement now begins to come to light.

Playing the Projection

Many seeming perceptions are projections. For instance, the patient who says, "I can't trust you," may be asked to play the role of an untrustworthy person in order to discover his own inner conflict in this area. Another patient may complain to the therapist, "You're not really interested in me. You just do this for a living." He will be told to enact this attitude, after which he might be asked whether this is possibly a trait he himself possesses.

Reversals

One way in which the Gestalt therapist approaches certain symptoms or difficulties is to help the patient realize that overt behavior commonly represents the reversal of underlying or latent impulses.

We therefore use the reversal technique. For example, the patient claims to suffer from inhibition or excessive timidity. He will be asked to play an exhibitionist. In taking this plunge into an area fraught with anxiety, he makes contact with a part of himself that has long been submerged. Or, the patient may wish to work on his problem of extreme touchiness to criticism. He will be asked to play the role of listening very carefully to everything that is said to him—especially criticism—without the need to defend or counterattack. Or, the patient may be unassertive and overly sweet; he will be asked to play the part of an uncooperative and spiteful person.

The Rhythm of Contact and Withdrawal

Following its interest in the totality of life processes, in the phenomena of figure and ground, Gestalt therapy emphasizes the polar nature of vital functioning. The capacity for love is impaired by the inability to sustain anger. Rest is needed to restore energy. A hand is neither open nor closed but capable of both functions.

The natural inclination toward withdrawal from contact, which the patient will experience from time to time, is not dealt with as a resistance to be overcome but as a rhythmic response to be respected. Consequently when the patient wishes to withdraw, he is asked to close his eyes and withdraw in fantasy to any place or situation in which he feels secure. He describes the scene and his feelings there. Soon he is asked to open his eyes and "come back to the group." The on-going work is then resumed, usually with new material provided by the patient who has now had some of his energies restored by his withdrawal.

The Gestalt approach suggests that we accept withdrawal needs in any situation where attention or interest has lagged but that we remain aware of where our attention goes.

"Rehearsal"

According to Perls, a great deal of our thinking consists of internal rehearsal and preparation for playing our accustomed social roles. The experience of stage fright simply represents our fear that we will not conduct our roles well. The group therefore plays the game of sharing rehearsals with each other, thus becoming more aware of the preparatory means employed in bolstering our social roles.

"Exaggeration"

This game is closely allied to the principle of the awareness continuum and provides us with another means of understanding body language. There are many times when the patient's unwitting movement or gesture appears to be a significant communication. However, the gestures may be abortive, undeveloped or incomplete—perhaps a wave of the arm or a tap of the leg. The patient will be asked to exaggerate the movement repeatedly, usually making the inner meaning more apparent. Sometimes the patient will be asked to develop the movement into a dance to get more of his self into integrative expression.

A similar technique is used for purely verbal behavior and can well be called the "repetition" game. A patient may make a statement of importance but has perhaps glossed over it or in some way indicated that he has not fully absorbed its impact. He will be asked to say it again—if necessary a great number of times—and, where necessary, louder and louder. Soon he is really hearing himself and not just forming words.

"May I Feed you a Sentence?"

In listening to or observing the patient, the therapist may conclude that a particular attitude or message is implied. He will then say, "May I feed you a sentence? Say it and try it on for size. Say it to several people here." He then proposes his sentence, and the patient tests out his reaction to the sentence. Typically, the therapist does not simply interpret for or to the patient. Although there is obviously a strong interpretative element here, the patient must make the experience his own through active participation. If the proposed sentence is truly a key sentence, spontaneous development of the idea will be supplied by the patient.

Marriage Counseling Games

We will mention only a few of the great number of possible variations on these games.

The partners face each other and take turns saying sentences beginning with, "I resent you for . . ." The resentment theme can then be followed by the appreciation them, "What I appreciate in you is . . ." Then the spite theme, "I spite you by . . ." Or, the compliance theme, "I am compliant by . . ."

Lastly, there is the discovery theme. The partners alternate describing each other in sentences beginning with "I see . . ." Many times this process of discovery involves actually seeing each other for the first time. Since, as Perls points out, the most difficult problem in marriage is that of being in love with a concept rather than an individual, we must learn to distinguish between our fantasied image and the flesh-and-blood person.

Finally, we should mention a particular approach that does not fall under the heading of either rules or games but which can well be included at this point. It is an important gambit in Gestalt therapy and symbolizes much of Perls's underlying philosophy. We might call it the principle of "Can you stay with this feeling?" This technique is invoked at key moments when the patient refers to a feeling or mood or state of mind that is unpleasant and that he has a great urge to dispel. Let us say he has arrived at a point where he feels empty or confused or frustrated or discouraged. The therapist says, "Can you stay with this feeling?"

This is almost always a dramatic moment and a frustrating one for the patient. He has referred to his experience with some sourness and an obviously impatient desire to get on with it, to leave this feeling well behind him. The therapist however asks him deliberately to remain with whatever psychic pain he has at the omment. The patient will be asked to elaborate the *what* and *how* of his feelings. "What are your sensations?" "What are your perceptions, fantasies, expectancies?" At these moments, it is frequently most appropriate and necessary to help the patient distinguish between what he imagines and what he perceives.

The stay-with-it technique illustrates par excellence Perls's emphasis on the role of phobic avoidance in all of neurotic behavior. In his view, the neurotic has habitually avoided vigorous contact with a variety of unpleasant and dysphoric experiences. As a result avoidance has become ingrained, a phobic anxiety has been routinized, and major dimensions of experience have never been adequately mastered.

It is interesting, in this connection, to be reminded of the title of Perls's first book, *Ego, Hunger and Aggression.* The title was chosen carefully to carry the message that we must adopt toward psychological and emotional experiences the same active, coping, attitudes that we employ in healthy eating. In healthy eating we bite the food; then we effectively chew, grind, and liquify it. It is then swallowed, digested, metabolized, and assimilated. In this way we have truly made the food a part of ourselves.

The Gestalt therapist—most especially with the stay-with-it technique—encourages the patient to undertake a similar "chewing up" and painstaking assimilation of emotional dimensions of life that have hitherto been unpleasant to the taste, difficult to swallow, and impossible to digest. In this way the patient gains improved self-confidence and a far greater capacity for autonomy and for dealing energetically with the inevitable frustrations of living.

25. *A Study of Encounter Group Casualties*

IRVIN D. YALOM and MORTON A. LIEBERMAN

A total of 209 university undergraduates entered 18 encounter groups which met for a total of 30 hours. Thirty-nine subjects dropped out of the groups, while 170 completed the group experience. Of these, 16 subjects were considered "casualties"—defined as an enduring, significant, negative outcome which was caused by their participation in the group. The most reliable method of identifying casualties was to solicit the opinions of the other group members; the leader was not a valuable judge of casualty states. The frequency, severity, and mode of psychological injury varied considerably amongst the 18 groups. The highest-risk leadership style was characterized by high stimulus input, aggressivity, charisma, support, intrusiveness, individual (as opposed to interpersonal or group) focus. The most vulnerable individuals were those with low self-concept and unrealistically high expectations and anticipations of change.

How psychologically dangerous are encounter groups? For several years mental health professionals have been in the uncomfortable position of having to answer this question without the necessary information. Despite the lack of systematic information, however, there has been no dearth of polemics.

On the one hand, many, alarmed by case reports of severe psychological decompensation following an encounter group experience (so-called "encounter group casualties"), have branded the whole encounter group field as dangerous. Some medical societies have proposed that state governments legislate regulations for encounter group practice. Clinicians' views towards encounter groups are based on heavily skewed information: they often see casualties or read about them in their professional journals, but they rarely have contact with encounter group members who have had satisfying experiences. Some psychiatric associations have attempted to garner relevant evidence by polling members for a list of all

Irvin D. Yalom & Morton A. Lieberman, A study of encounter group casualties, *Archives of General Psychiatry*, *25*, 1971, 16-30. Findings reported are more fully presented in *Encounter groups: first facts*, Morton A. Lieberman, Irvin D. Yalmo, & Mathew B. Miles, New York: Basic Books, 1973.

the casualties they have seen. Such an approach can demonstrate the existence but not the frequency of danger. Knowing the number of casualties without knowing the total number of participants from which the casualties issue offers useful but severely limited information. Anecdotal case reporting has another intrinsic flaw: multiple reporting may spuriously inflate casualty rates. An untoward outcome in a group member is generally a striking event not easily forgotten by the other group members; if the other 20 members (or, in a residential laboratory, 100 members) all describe this event to colleagues or friends, the single casualty soon assumes alarming proportions.

Encounter group leaders, enthusiastic members, and administrative staff of growth centers often take an opposite position. They report few casualties and generally do not view the encounter group as a hazardous venture—a not unexpected viewpoint. Most encounter group leaders and growth centers are limited in their source of information. Their groups are generally brief; once ended, the members scatter and the leaders have little opportunity, even were they so inclined, to gather follow-up data. A psychological decompensation occurring after the end of the group would be unlikely to come to their attention.

There are, in addition to actual limitations of information, ideological sources of bias. Many encounter group leaders reject psychiatric definitions of "adverse effect"; they feel that extreme psychological discomfort, even to the degree that professional aid is required, may be not a failure but an accomplishment of the group. They view psychological decompensation, like the legendary "night journey" as a stage, even a desideratum, of personal growth. Other leaders express a lack of interest in adverse effects since their ideological base stresses the necessity and ability of each individual to assume responsibility for himself. They believe that the leader who takes responsibility for the welfare of others thus infantilizes them and impedes their growth.

The American Psychiatric Association was sufficiently concerned with these issues to commission in 1969 a task force (chaired by one of us, I.Y.) to survey the current state of knowledge. The Task Force report[1] reviewed the literature and noted that there was "distressingly little data": the available evidence consisted entirely of anecdotal reports or loosely designed studies which lacked a post-group follow-up.

With this background in mind when designing a systematic research project on encounter groups, we attempted to pay careful attention to the negative as well as to the positive outcomes of encounter groups.

METHODOLOGY

In the spring of 1969 we conducted an intensive study of a large number of encounter groups led by leaders from different ideological schools. The group members, all Stanford University undergraduates, were studied in a variety of ways. They completed a large battery of self-report questionnaires before beginning the groups, after each meeting, at the end of the group experience, and again, for a final follow-up, six months later. The groups each met for a total of 30 hours: some had spaced (ten three-hour) meetings, others a massed format in which the groups met for only a few time-extended "marathon" meetings. The encounter group participants received three academic credits; no preparation paper or examination was required; the only requirements (though not enforced) were attendance and cooperation in the research endeavor. The groups, with a few exceptions, met on or near the Stanford campus; each meeting was tape-recorded and rated by two trained observers.

Eighteen groups were conducted. We deliberately selected leaders from a wide variety of ideological schools. Our 18 groups thus had these labels:

Group Labels	
1. N.T.L. sensitivity groups (T-groups)	2 groups
2. Gestalt therapy (Esalen—Fritz Perls derivative)	2 groups
3. Psychodrama orientation	2 groups
4. Psychoanalytic	1 group
5. Transactional analysis	2 groups
6. Sensory awareness focus (Esalen derivative)	1 group
7. Marathon (rogerian; eclectic personal growth)	2 groups
8. Synanon	2 groups
9. N.T.L. West—"personal growth," black-white encounter focus	2 groups
10. Tape groups (leaderless; Bell & Howell Peer Program)[2]	2 groups

(Our results indicate that the labels or derivative schools of the leaders convey relatively little information about their actual group behavior. On the basis of observer ratings of leader behavior and member descriptions, we evolved a different typology of leader behavior which we shall use in describing outcomes. The leader style typology is described in detail elsewhere.[3])

Once we selected the "types" of groups, we then attempted to identify the most competent, senior leaders of each ideological school in Northern California. The leaders were well paid ($750 for the 30-hour groups, plus two to three hours of research interviews and questionnaires). We were fortunate enough to recruit highly experienced, well-recommended leaders. Indeed, several of the leaders have national reputations. The instructions to the leader were minimal: they were asked to lead the encounter groups in their usual manner—to "do their thing."

When students registered for the course they were randomly assigned (stratified by sex, race, and previous encounter group experience) to one of the 18 groups. A total of 209 students began the groups,

39 dropped out (ie, missed at least the last two meetings), and 170 completed the group. Seventy-five control subjects were studied: approximately one half of these came fron the ranks of students who registered for the encounter group course and then (generally because of time-scheduling conflicts) did not attend the group; the other one half were gathered by asking the experimental subjects for a list of friends who probably would have wanted to take the course but who could not because of scheduling conflicts. We drew a random sample from this list.

The goals of the project were ambitious. We attempted a thorough study of the process and outcome of experiential groups—in short "everything you ever wanted to know about groups." This article describes only that part of the project pertaining to negative outcome. The reader is referred elsewhere[4] for a complete description of the experimental methodology and the measurement of process and of positive outcome.

A study of the casualties of encounter groups posed some basic moral problems for the experimenters. We rapidly appreciated two conflicting sets of allegiances: those to our desire to conduct a well-controlled, powerful experiment and those to our sense of ethical and moral responsibility to our subjects. On the one hand, we wished to execute an in vivo study—one which was not so far removed from life that it would have no generalizability. On the other hand, however, we felt uneasy about deliberately placing our subjects in high-risk situations: this would have violated our sense of responsibility both as researchers and as clinicians.

Our final design represented a compromise between these allegiances. Our desire for experimental power had the following results: (1) There was no pre-group screening of the subjects (since growth centers and encounter group leaders almost never screen. (2) There was random assignment of subjects to groups. (3) There was no intervention by the research staff during the course of the groups. The research observers were trained never to give feedback to the leaders or to any members of the group. (4) Some aggressive and highly confrontive leaders were included. These styles of leadership were already very much in evidence on the Stanford campus. In fact, encounter groups of all types are so common that approximately 50% of the student population has been in at least one group.

Attention to our conscience and ethical sense had the following results: (1) We informed all subjects before entering the study that "participation in encounter groups sometimes results in considerable emotional upset." They were also given the names of university mental health facilities and the name of one of the principal investigators to consult should they require help. During the midst of the project one of the group members committed suicide. When this happened we informed all leaders and requested them to remind their members of the existence of the mental health facilities on campus. (This was the single intervention the research staff made during the course of the groups.) To insure that the students gave informed consent, we attempted to communicate what to expect in an encounter group by a pregroup microlab exercise. (2) We imposed research conditions which introduced some moderation in the groups. Each meeting was observed by two researchers (a different pair for each meeting); each meeting was tape-recorded; each meeting was followed by 15 to 30 minutes of questionnaire administration.

In our judgment the overall effects of the research conditions were to *reduce* risk. The leaders knew, of course, that they were being observed, evaluated, and compared with other leaders. They knew that the results would eventually be published, and we surmised that such conditions could only serve to put them, as it were, on their best behavior.

IDENTIFICATION OF CASUALTIES

A casualty, by our definition, was an individual who, as a direct result of his experience in the encounter group, became more psychologically distressed or employed more maladaptive mechanisms of defense, or both; furthermore this negative change was not a transient but an enduring one, as judged eight months after the group experience.

Since it was not possible to interview in depth all 209 subjects who began the groups, we used eight criteria to identify a potential high-risk subsample who could then be studied more intensively. (1) *Request for psychiatric aid.*—The most obvious mode of identifying a casualty, and the one used in most previous research, is the request for emergency aid during the course of the group. (2) *Dropouts from groups.*—We expected that those who dropped out of groups might have done so because of a noxious group experience. (3) *Peer evaluation.*—At the end of the group, all members were asked, "Did anyone get hurt in your group? Who? How?" (4) *Self-esteem drop.*—The Rosenberg Self-Esteem measure[5] was used as one measure of outcome. We calculated the pre-post change in self-esteem and studied the lowest ten percentiles (the 17 subjects who decreased the most in self-esteem) of the subjects. (5) *Subjects' testimony.*—At the end of the group the subjects were asked to rate their group on a number of seven-point differential scales (eg, constructive-destructive, low learning-high learning, pleasant-unpleasant, turned off-turned on). Again, the lowest 10% were included in our high risk sample. (6) *Psychotherapy.*—At the six-month follow-up subjects were asked whether they had started psychotherapy since the beginning of the group. All subjects answering positively were studied. (7) *Leaders' ratings.*—The leaders were asked at the end of the group to rate each student on the amount of progress he had made on a number of dimensions (eg, self-understanding, positive self-image, happiness, openness, sensitivity, ability to collaborate with others). The subjects (lowest 10%) who had had the lowest leader ratings were included in the high-risk population. (8) Several miscellaneous sources of information were available to us. For example, the observers occasionally reported concern about some member of a group which they observed, or subjects during an interview expressed concern about another member (*Example:* One casualty was in fact identified by a rather remarkable method. One researcher was interviewing the 30 subjects who, on the basis of self-report questionnaires, appeared to have had the most *positive* outcome. It was clear that one subject not only had *not* benefited from the group but in fact had had a very negative experience and had scored himself highly on questionnaires in a vain and self-deceptive attempt to turn a destructive experience into a constructive one. The fact that a casualty appeared on the high positive-change list suggested to us that our methods of identification were not exhaustive and might have erred on the conservative side.)

Once a list (no. = 104) of casualty suspects was compiled, the next phase of the project began. Approximately eight months after the end of the group, one of us attempted to contact each suspect by phone. If in a 15- to 20-minute telephone interview there was any suspicion that the subject had had a psychologically destructive experience, he was invited in for an in-depth personal interview. If distance did not permit a face-to-face interview, it was conducted over the telephone. The interviewer informed the subject that the investigators, in their study of the effects of the encounter groups, were interviewing a large number of students to obtain their retrospective view of the group. Did they now view the group as an overall constructive, neutral, or destructive experience? Was the group stressful to them? Had they been made uncomfortable by the group? For how long a period of time? In which ways? Specific inquiries were made about interpersonal functioning, academic effectiveness, and self-concept. If the group had a negative effect, had they by now (eight months later) recovered the level of comfort or adaptation that was present before the group? Were there concurrent life circumstances that may have also been responsible for the subject's deterioration during the period of the study? Had they sought help from professional or informal sources? To enhance the flow of information we often mentioned our mode of identification (eg, decreased self-esteem on their self-administered questionnaires or co-members citing the subject as

having been harmed by the group) and proceeded to investigate these areas. Some dropouts may have been in the group for only a couple of sessions; to refresh their memories, a tape-recording of their last meeting was played for them. In general, however, no memory refreshing was necessary; we were struck by the vivid recall eight months later of almost all subjects—even those who described the group as dull and plodding.

Our definition of casualty was fairly stringent: not only must the student have undergone some psychological decompensation but it must have been persistent and there must have been evidence that the group experience was the responsible agent. We did not consider as casualties several subjects who were shaken up and severely distressed by the group but who, a few days later, had recovered their equilibrium. Nor did we include several subjects who during the group or in the six months following had had some psychological decompensation that was due not to the encounter group but to other circumstances in the life of the individual.

Example 1. The case of this subject is illustrative. This individual was the major tragedy of the study. A few days after his second meeting he took sleeping pills and committed suicide. It would have been easy to impugn the group as being responsible. Upon careful study, however, we learned that he had a long history of psychiatric disturbance and had, during the course of the group and over the preceding three years, sought help from a number of sources. (In fact, the main reason he had recently transferred to Stanford was because he heard that the student health psychiatric service was excellent.) In the months preceding the project he had been in a number of local encounter groups. Six months before his death, he had begun both individual and group therapy in two university health facilities (without, incidentally, informing either therapist of his work with the other). Not only was he in two forms of psychotherapy while he was in the project, but we learned from a friend that he was, concurrently, in another encounter group in a nearby growth institute. We reviewed the two meetings he attended and found that they were low-affect meetings in which the subject had participated in a constructive manner. The group leader reported that he had been helpful in moving the group along by participating in an open, nondefensive manner. The questionnaires he completed at the end of these sessions also suggested optimism about the group.

It is impossible to conclude with certainty that the encounter group did not in some way contribute to his suicide. After considering all the evidence, however, we decided that his participation in the encounter group was more a manifestation than a cause of his despair and did not, therefore, consider him a "casualty." (The suicide note the subject left is an angry one which appears to indict therapy and encounter group members past and present:

"I felt great pain that I could not stop any other way. It would have been helpful if there had been anyone to understand and care about my pain, but there wasn't. People did not believe me when I told them about my problems or pain or else that it was just self pity; or if there had been someone to share my feelings with, but all they said was that I was hiding myself, not showing my true feelings, talking to myself. They kept saying this no matter how hard I tried to reach them. This is what I mean when I say they do not understand or care about my pain; they just discredited it or irgnored it and I was left alone with it. I ask that anyone who asks about me see this; it is my only last request.")

RESULTS

A total of 104 casualty suspects were identified. Of these 79 were contacted by telephone and 25 could not be located. Sixteen casualties were identified: this represents 7.5% of the 209 subjects who began the groups, or 9.4% of the 170 subjects who completed the groups.

The severity and type of psychological injury varied considerably. Three students during or immediately following the group had psychotic decompositions—one a manic psychosis, one an acute paranoid schizophrenic episode, and the third an acute undifferentiated schizophrenic-lysergic acid diethylamide episode. Several students had depressive or anxiety symptoms, or both, ranging from low grade tension or discouragement to severe crippling anxiety attacks to a major six-month depression with a 40-lb weight loss and suicidal ideation. Others suffered some disruption of their self-system: they felt empty, self-negating, inadequate, shameful, unacceptable, more discouraged about ever growing or changing. Several subjects noted a deterioration of their interpersonal life; they withdrew or avoided others, experienced more distrust, were less willing to reach out or to take risks with others.

The comparative efficiency of the various modes of identifying casualties is illustrated in Table 1. Note that the most effective method is peer evaluation. A total of 30 subjects were listed by their comembers as having been hurt by the group and of these 30, 12 were casualties. There were 11 subjects who were multiply chosen (ie, more than one member of their group listed them); of these 11, eight were casualties (and a ninth was subject 1—the subject who committed suicide). There were four casualties with only a single nomination, but three of these four were self-selected. *Therefore, if a group member is cited by more than one member of his group, or cites himself as having been hurt by the experience, it is highly probable that he represents a casualty of the group.* (In our sample, the probability is 73%). Furthermore, all of the more severe casualties were identified by this method.

Table 1 also indicates that the leaders' ratings were a highly inaccurate mode of identifying casualties. Of the 20 subjects with the lowest leader ratings, only three were casualties. Moreover, some of the severe casualties were missed by this mode.

The usual mode of counting casualties—noting the number who seek help—was an insensitive index. Only two casualties came to our attention in this

TABLE 1. *Modes of Casualty Identification*

Casualty	Request for Emergency Psychiatric Aid	Dropout	Peer Evaluation	Self-Esteem Drop	Subjects' Testimony	Psychotherapy Began During Group	Psychotherapy Began 6 Mos After Group	Leaders' Ratings	Miscellaneous
1		X	X						
2			X						
3					X				
4			X	X			X		
5			X					X	
6	X	X	X			X			
7			X	X	X	X			
8							X*		X
9									
10			X	X	X				
11					X				
12		X	X				X		
13	X		X	X	X	X			
14		X	X			X		X	
15		X	X					X	
16			X		X				
Total no. of casualties	2	5	12	4	6	4	3	3	1
Total no. of noncasualties	0	28	18	15	11	10	0	17	0

*Did not begin therapy but stated that, as a result of the group, he had been strongly considering it.

manner: one was seen in the emergency room in an anxious depression and the other in a manic psychotic state.

Table 2 indicates that the casualties were likely to have been identified by more than one of our modes of identification. Sixty-two percent of the casualties were identified by three or four different modes compared to only 3% of the casualty suspects (who in interview were not considered to be casualties). Unfortunately, two of the three suspects with three indices of suspicion could not be located for interview, thus raising again the possibility that our reported casualty rate is low.

Table 1 indicates, too, that of the 17 subjects beginning psychotherapy either during or within an eight-month period after the group, seven were casualties. Three subjects could not be located for a follow-up interview. A study of the 14 available subjects, however, revealed some interesting interrelationships between encounter group participation and psychotherapy. Table 3 indicates that it is three times more likely that a subject who is in an encounter group

TABLE 2. *Modes of Identification for Casualties and Casualty Suspects*

Subjects	Total No. of Indices				Total No.
	1	2	3	4	
Casualties	5	2	3	6	16
Casualty suspects	65	20	3	0	88

TABLE 3. *Encounter Group Members Entering Psychotherapy*

Group Members	Never	Yes: Prior to Group	Yes: During Group	Yes: Within Six Months After End of Group	Totals*
Subjects (excluding casualties)	130	20	0	10	160
Casualties	4	5	4	3	16
Controls	50	9	1	1	61

*The totals are less than the numbers of the original subject and control groups since not all subjects were available for the six-month follow-up questionnaire study.

will seek psychotherapy during the time he is in the group, or in the eight-month follow-up period, than a control subject.

Why does he enter psychotherapy? Information from interviews with the 14 subjects suggested several reasons: (1) Five sought psychotherapy for repair. They were all casualties and were so upset by the group experiences that they needed help in order to regain their equilibrium. (2) Six (including two casualties) entered psychotherapy for the same reasons they had entered the encounter group. Psychotherapy and the encounter group experiences were not causally related; both were manifestations of the individual's search for help. (3) Two had a very constructive encounter group experience and entered therapy to continue work started in the group. They credited the group with helping them to identify their problems and showing them that it was possible to obtain help by talking about them and working on them. (4) One entered therapy for reasons entirely unrelated to the encounter group, a crisis in his life which arose months after the end of the group.

Relationship Between the Type of Encounter Group and the Casualty Rate

Table 4 indicates that the casualties were not evenly distributed amongst the 18 groups. Six groups had no casualties, while three had two casualties and one group had three casualties. To understand this skewed distribution of casualties we attempted to cluster together leaders with similar style. As we

have previously indicated, the ideological school of the leader and his actual behavior were largely unrelated so that, for example, the two transactional analysis leaders were no more likely to resemble one another than they were to resemble leaders of any of the other schools. A new taxonomy of leadership style was, therefore, required—a task of no little complexity.

The entire methodology of the derivation of this taxonomy is described elsewhere[3] but, in brief, leader behavior was examined through two lenses— participant questionnaires, designed to tap the symbolic value of the leader to each member, and observer schedules. Observers rated, exhaustively, the leaders' behavior, their global style, and their primary focus in the group (group, individual, or interpersonal issues). Observers also recorded their personal reactions to the leaders. In all 48 scales of leader behavior were rated by observers and participants. By means of factor analyses, these 48 categories were reduced to four basic dimensions of leader behavior—emotional stimulation, caring, meaning attribution, and executive functions. These four dimensions accounted for 70% of the variance of total leader behavior. By means of statistical clustering, all the leaders in the study could be subsumed under seven types of leaders.

Type A Leaders: "Aggressive Stimulators"

These five leaders (the two gestalt leaders, one psychodrama leader, and the two Synanon leaders) were characterized by their extremely high stimulus input. They were intrusive, confrontive, challenging, while at the same time demonstrating high positive caring; they revealed a great deal of themselves. They were the most charismatic of the leaders. They were authoritarian and often structured the events in the group. They focused upon the individual in the group rather than upon the group, and they often provided the individual with some cognitive framework with which to understand himself and the world. They asserted firm control and took over for the participants. They seemed ready, willing, and able to guide participants forward on the road to enlightenment.

Type B Leaders: "Love Leaders"

These three leaders (NTL T-group leader, a marathon eclectic leader, and a transactional analytic leader) were caring, individually focused leaders, who gave love as well as information and ideas about how to change. They exuded a quality of enlightened paternalism; they were "good daddies"; they had an established frame of reference about how individuals learn which they used in the group but which they do not press.

Type C Leaders: "Social Engineers"

These three leaders (NTL, rogerian, and psychodrama) focused on steering the work of the group as a whole rather than on the individual or interpersonal relationships. They offered relatively low levels of stimulus input and rarely confronted or challenged individuals. They were perceived by participants as being low on authoritarianism and were not perceived as charismatic. The distance between them and the participants was psychologically felt to be small compared to, for example, the type A leaders.

Type D Leaders: "Laissez-faire"

These two leaders (psychoanalytic and transactional analytic) offered very little stimulation input, no challenging, no confrontation, and made very little use of themselves as an issue in the group; they of-fered little support and generally remained distant and cool; they were experienced by the participants as technicians and their major input to the group was the occasional communication of ideas about how people learn. They offered very little structure to the members.

Type E Leaders: "Cool, Aggressive Stimulators"

These leaders (two personal growth leaders) were aggressive stimulators, but not to the extent of the type A leaders. They offered little positive support and were nonauthoritarian in that they rarely structured the meeting; they tended to focus more on the group ("social engineering") than did most of the other leaders except, of course, the type C leaders.

Type F Leaders: "High Structure"

One leader (sensory awareness—Esalen) was so different from all others that he must be classified separately. He used a large number (an average of eight per meeting) of structured exercises—group "games." He was exceedingly controlling and authoritarian.

Type G Leaders: The Tape Leaders

These are two groups which had as their leader the Bell & Howell encounter tape (Peer Program). At the start of each meeting the members turned on a tape-recorder which gave the group instructions for the conduct of that meeting. The tape programs focused upon learning how to give and receive feedback, how to make emotional contact with others, how to self-disclose. They fostered a warm, supportive climate and deemphasized interpersonal conflict.

Table 4 presents the number of casualties in each group and each typology. The "A" (aggressive stimulators) style of leadership was the highest-risk method and the five type A leaders produced seven of the 16 casualties (44% of the total casualties). Not only were there more casualties in type A groups, but they were the more severe casualties.

TABLE 4. *Incidence of Casualties in the 18 Groups*

Leadership Style	No. of Groups	% of the 18 Groups	Casualties	Group No.	Casualties	No. of Subjects in Group	Dropouts*
A: "Aggressive stimulation" Charisma	5/18	27.8	44.0	1	0	11	0
				2	3	13	1
				3	2	13	0
				4 & 5	2	23	10
B: "Love"	3/18	16.7	6.2	6	0	13	2
				7	0	9	0
				8	1	15	1
C: "Social engineer"	3/18	16.7	17.8	9	1	10	0
				10	1	11	2
				11	1	12	0
D: "Laissez-faire"	2/18	11.0	12.5	12	0	11	4
				13	2	14	5
E: "Cool, aggressive stimulation"	2/18	11.0	12.5	14	1	9	1
				15	1	10	4
F: "High structure"	1/18	5.6	6.3	16	1	11	1
G: "Encounter tapes"	2/18	5.6	0.0	17	0	11	1
				18	0	13	3

*Excluding the five casualties who dropped out.

The "B" (love) leaders produced only one casualty, whereas type "G" (tape) leaders produced none at all.

The probable mode of injury also differed considerably amongst the 18 groups. Our interviews with the subjects uncovered several types of prototypical group events to which they attributed their negative outcome. (Table 5): (1) Attack by leader or by the group; (2) Rejection by leader or by the group; (3) Failure to attain unrealistic goals; (4) "Input overload"; (5) "Group pressure" effects.

These are, of course, arbitrary *post hoc* categories and often several modes occur for one individual. At times boundaries between them blur. Attack usually implies lack of acceptance, whereas the reverse is not necessarily the case. Some experienced such a massive attack that the lack of acceptance was, oddly, not a crucial issue: the subject either dropped out of the group or was, in a figurative sense, too concerned about survival to afford himself the luxury of asking for love.

Table 5 indicates that Attack by leader is cited only in type A groups, and is associated with some of the more severe casualties. We should note that the categories of injury mode were developed before and independently of the taxonomy of leader styles. A clinical example is illustrative:

Example 2. This subject was unequivocal in her evaluation of her group as a destructive experience. Her group, following the model and suggestions of the leader, was an intensely aggressive one which undertook to help this subject, a passive, gentle individual, to "get in touch with" her anger. Although the group attacked her in many ways, including a physical assault by one of the female members, she most of all remembers the leader's attack on her. At one point he cryptically remarked that she "was on the verge of schizophrenia." He would not elaborate on this statement and it echoed ominously within her for many months. For several months she remained extremely uncomfortable. She withdrew

TABLE 5. *Mode of Sustaining Injury*

Leadership Style	Casualty	Attack		Rejection		Failure to Attain Unrealistic Goals	Input Overload	Group Pressure Effect
		Leader	Group	Leader	Group			
A: "Aggressive	1	X						X
stimulation"	2			X				
Charisma	3	X		X	X			
	4	X	X				X	
	5	X						
	6	X	X				X	
	7	X	X					
B: "Love"	8			X	X		X	
C: "Social engineer"	9					X		
	10		X		X	X		
	11			X				
D: "Laissez-faire"	12		X			X		
	13						X	
E: "Cool, aggressive	14		X				X	
stimulation"	15			X	X			
F: "High structure"	16					X		X
G: "Encounter tapes"	0							

markedly from her family and friends, was depressed and insomniac; she was so obsessed with her leader's remark about schizophrenia that she dreaded going to bed because she knew her mind would focus on this point of terror. Often she lapsed into daydreams in which she relived, with a more satisfying ending, some event in the group. The only benefit of the experience, she said, was to help her appreciate how lonely she was; her discomfort has been so great, however, that she has been unable to make use of this knowledge. We consider this subject a severe and long-term casualty; at the interview eight months after the end of the group, she felt that she was gradually reintegrating herself but was not yet back to the point she was before the group began. Her negative experience was a function of aggressive, intrusive leadership style which attempted to change her according to the leader's own values by battering down her characterologic defenses.

The other five subjects whose negative outcome was related to attack by the leaders were similar to this subject. The type A leaders were charismatic, highly revealing of their own feelings and values, challenging, and intrusive. They were unpredictable in that they displayed both high levels of anger and of support. They focused on the individuals in the group and one by one each member was "worked out." The type A leaders loomed very large for their group members. The casualties in their groups remembered with remarkable clarity months later the leader's remarks to them. There was an intensive focus on each member as he occupied the "hot seat." There was no place to hide and in a 20-hour marathon meeting in one group members were physically prevented from leaving the group. In the two Synanon groups, this aggressive approach resulted in an exceedingly high dropout rate (ten of the 23 members [43%] dropped out of the groups.)

Attack by the group was a mode of injury that occurred either in the type A groups, in conjunction with attack by the leader, or in groups led by leaders who were distant and modelled little or no positive supportive behavior. These occurred in groups led by a "laissez-faire" leader (D), by the least caring of the "social engineers" (C), and by one of the "impersonal" leaders (E). The following case was a subject in a group led by a laissez-faire leader:

Example 3. This subject answered the question "Was anyone hurt in your group?" in the following manner: "Me. The last meeting I didn't want to come to and came out of 'responsibility.' I was not in the mood for 'encountering' and was almost forced to. I don't trust anyone in the group and felt threatened by it. I came away feeling insecure and having many self doubts without being able to resolve them within the group. I overheard another member of the group describing my actions with his roommate, and he was reinforcing my own self doubts about myself. I didn't want to participate, was forced to participate unnaturally and then was emotionally upset by the experience for several days afterwards. Our group had no cohesion, no group feeling, no real understanding and I felt pressured to "produce' and show myself at the last meeting. I shouldn't have gone to it. In fact, I should have dropped out several times before."

He depicts his group experience as a catastrophe. He was unable to trust the other members who were aggressive and dominant. The group lacked cohesiveness and a feeling of warmth and support. The leader, he felt, was "crummy" and lacked any idea of how to deal with people. The last meeting was particularly bitter for him since he was vigorously attacked for his passivity and uninvolvement. He recalls nervously picking at the carpet during the onslaught; he was criticized for that and when he stopped he was criticized for his passivity and suggestibility. He was so shaken that he soon could not interpret comments to him and perceived all statements as criticism. The group planned a post-group beach party, but he did not attend because he felt so bitter about his experience. This subject stated that were it not for the last meeting he might have escaped relatively unscathed since he had previously rationalized his failure in the group by refusing either to take the group seriously or to involve himself emotionally.

Following the group he felt deeply depressed for about a week. Following this he was left with a residue of deflation, helplessness, self-disgust, and discouragement. Even months later he continued to feel anxious, depressed, and less trustful of others. His isolation increased and he made plans for transferring to another college. He has avoided participation in any other group, but several months after the end of the group he sought individual psychiatric help.

We consider this subject a moderately severe casualty of long duration. His negative outcome was multidetermined. He entered the group with relatively severe problems including strong homosexual conflicts. He had been lonely and isolated at college and entered the group, in part, to search for friends.

He soon experienced so little support or trust in the group that he was unable to disclose any personal feelings at all, much less his homosexual inclinations. The deviant role which he thus assumed generated even more anxiety and reinforced his alienation and negative self-concept. The group, a noncohesive, low-support group led by a laissez-faire leader, whose major and almost sole mode of participation was to comment on the interpersonal process (in the language of transactional analysis), was not considered in the testimony of the members a successful one. Towards the end it attempted to salvage itself by extra-group social events and by forcibly attempting to convert this subject—one of the major deviants. The other members had little appreciation of his discomfort and first coaxed, then ignored, and finally frontally assaulted the subject.

Rejection played a role for six casualties. For some the experience of rejection overlapped so heavily with the experience of attack that the distinction was but a semantic subtlety; others, however, explicitly emphasized being rejected by the leader or group, or both. One subject, for example, stated: "I wanted some reassurance about my existence . . . to be found acceptable . . . to be told I was O.K. . . . to dig myself." He felt that he did not get that acceptance from the group and left feeling even worse about himself. Another subject, a Mexican American, entered the group especially hoping for acceptance from the white members. He was so prepared for rejection that he perceived criticism of his circumlocution and his guardedness as total, blanket rejection. Another member, the only casualty in a type B leader's group (and of minor severity), explicitly described his failure to be accepted into the group. It reminded him of rushing for a fraternity and not making it. To his eye, the leader established an in-group of individuals "who mouthed radical jargon and were in the drug culture." He felt he could not "swing" in the way the leader wished and grew increasingly uncomfortable and anxious about his peripheral membership.

Perhaps the starkest example of rejection was a white woman in a group led by a type E leader (impersonal, aggressive stimulator). She had, prior to the group, struggled with a deep sense of shame and yearned for validation from others. Having planned her agenda in advance she revealed very early in the group a great deal about herself, including such material as intimate details of her sexual liaisons with black men and her deeply held racist feelings. She was not sensitive to the state of receptivity of the group which had several black members and was at that time preoccupied with dealing with black-white tensions. The other members were not prepared for the degree of intimacy she demanded: self-disclosure by one group member places implicit demands on the others for reciprocal disclosure. They withdrew from her and regarded her as a problem, a "sex maniac" to whom they could not relate. This sequence of events was extremely noxious to her and for many months thereafter she felt great shame and self-contempt.

Failure to achieve unrealistic goals was reported by four of the casualties who entered the group with unrealistically high expectations given their existing defenses. Their needs were extreme and would have been an appropriate ticket of admission to any psychotherapy group. One of the casualties, for example, had transferred to Stanford simply because his only friend had recently done so. He had strong schizoid trends and felt emotionally restricted and unable to make emotional contact and empathize with others. He had previously sought psychotherapy for these very problems. The three others can be described in almost identical terms. They all entered the group with great expectations: to learn to relate, to break

through their restrictive schizoid straitjacket, to get in touch with their emotions. Each explicitly hoped to find friends in the encounter group. Despite their vigorous personal resolutions to do things differently (resolutions which were abetted by the current optimistic mystique surrounding encounter groups) they found, to their great dismay, that their behavior was more locked, rigid, and repetitive than they had known. They soon recreated and reexperienced in their encounter group the same interpersonal environment from which they had fled in the outside world. They were flooded with discouragement and abandoned their abortive attempts to communicate and relate differently. All of them left the group more discouraged and more pessimistic about ever changing. In general, encounter group leaders and members share the subject's unbounded initial optimism and press very hard for the ever-elusive will-of-the-wisp of the encounter group—the "breakthrough." One individual stated it explicitly: "I tried to overcome my defenses as best I could but couldn't do it. The leader kept pressuring me to express my feelings but I didn't know what I felt. When I said this I was attacked as a phoney. This reinforced my defenses so later in the sessions I just withdrew and watched."

Group pressure effects were reported by two casualties who experienced unusual reactions to the group. Both, unable to accommodate to the group pressure to experience and express feelings, ended the group with a sense of hollowness. They could not keep up with the others in a pell-mell charge to levels of deep intimacy. They grew alarmed at their failure and defined themselves as deficient or empty. If they acceded to the group pressure by feigning intimacy, they privately felt duplicitous as well.

There is a well-known experimental analogue of this sequence of events. Asch[6] and Sherif[7] have demonstrated that it is difficult and anxiety-provoking to oppose group pressure. Individuals will misperceive or misrepresent their perceptions to align themselves with the remainder of the group. If, in a group which demands a vigorous display of emotions (like leadership styles A or F), there are experienced groupers who begin to express deep feelings in the opening minutes of the first meeting, then some real problems are posed for group beginners. This is especially stressful for individuals who are not labile, are already concerned about the texture of their feeling tone, and, in addition, lack the opportunity or confidence to seek consensual validation.

Input overload was experienced by several casualties who seemed to have suffered from "overstimulation"—a mode of injury as vague as it is inferential. Three of the five subjects involved had had psychotic episodes beginning during or shortly after the end of the group. Six months later they were still too disturbed to cooperate in the research interview and our evidence for input overload derives from their therapists and the group leaders. For example, one member had a severe manic psychosis which erupted during the fourth week of his group. The leader (a psychiatrist, type D, laissez-faire) felt strongly that the subject would have had a psychotic episode even were he not in a group, but that events in the group ("the intense stimulation, feedback, and pressure to open up") all hastened and perhaps intensified the course of his illness.

Another subject (in a type E group) was briefly hospitalized for an acute paranoid schizophrenic psychosis approximately one month after the end of the group. Her psychiatrist notified us that, in his opinion, her encounter group experience contributed to her illness. He thought that the group overstimulated her and imposed values of freedom on her which she could ill manage. Rather, she needed at that time reinforcement of order, structure and suppression.

Another subject in a type B group had a far less severe reaction, but he too was "stirred up" in a manner not constructive for him. His group, because of members with severe sexual problems, had dealt at great length with homosexuality. Although he denied homosexual concerns, he remained rather vaguely troubled by his memories of the meetings and less confident of himself in social and especially heterosexual situations. The interviewers concluded that some poorly understood sexual conflicts had been awakened but not resolved. Similarly his hierarchy of life values was strongly challenged as the leader and the group questioned his "success orientation." Here too, however, he remained only shaken as he did not have, or make, the opportunity to work through the issue in the group and lacked the resources to do so outside the group.

PREVENTION OF CASUALTIES

In studying the casualty suspects we interviewed many individuals who resembled the casualties in some manner (character structure, goals, type of group, experience in the group, etc) but who did not have a negative experience. What accounted for these different outcomes? Our interviews suggested several *post hoc* explanations which were, for the most part, untestable in the present study.

Many of the subjects interviewed appeared to have taken a more casual stance toward the group than did the casualties. They had neither a pressing need or great expectations for the group. Intellectual curiosity or the three easy academic credits loomed a bit larger; loneliness, depression, or other psychological hang-ups were more rarely mentioned. "Uninvolvement" was often mentioned. They stayed out of the vortex of the group, they "did not take it seriously," the group was "artificial," "not meaningful," "boring," or "plodding." One subject in Synanon stated, "It's unreal, you know, for a group of strangers to meet once a week and scream at one another. How can you really take it seriously?" They detoxified the group by maintaining their objectivity, by forming an alliance with an observing ego which kept before them the fact that the group was an artificial, time-limited aggregation in which deliberate magnification of emotions occurred. Others disengaged themselves physically and dropped out of the group. (Obviously such lack of involvement which reflects a safety or a survival orientation to the group experience also precluded the possibility of positive, constructive gain.)

Others could rely upon their positive self-concept to evaluate with proper perspective a negative group reaction or critical feedback. Their center of gravity remained within themselves, unlike several of the casualties who had low stores of self-esteem and whose sense of worth rocketed up and plummeted down with the appraisal of others. Others used an outside reference group for validation. For example, one subject, an experienced grouper in a type A group, handled attacks upon herself by referring to internalized phantoms of past groups or by actively working it out with members of the commune where she lived. Her commune functioned as a slightly attenuated but perpetual encounter group and emotionally dwarfed the impact of the time-limited group on her. Another well-integrated girl responded very adaptively to the same Synanon attacks which devastated others. She stated that the group pointed out the "dark sides" of herself but she also realized the universality of these aspects. She maintained her ability to objectify: "Yes, they attacked me for being a virgin but I know that they have different cultural backgrounds and different attitudes toward sex. I didn't let it fluster me." The group turned out to be an "eye-opener" for her. She had lead a heavily sheltered life and found the group to be an educational venture which, though smacking of a slumming experience, was a personally meaningful and integrative one.

There were several subjects who, in our view, might well have become casualties were it not for skillful management on the part of the leader. It appeared to us that some subjects started the group in highly vulnerable states, yet benefited considerably from their group experience. Several were not active central members of their groups but seemed to profit both from a sense of belongingness and vicariously from observing others work through problems. Some explicitly expressed gratitude towards their leaders who invited, encouraged, but did not demand participation and who always permitted them to select their own pace. One type B leader who lead a low-risk group, very explicitly asked each member repeatedly to make the choice of what he wanted to work on and how far he wished to proceed in a particular meeting. This is in marked contrast to type A leaders who made that choice for their members and developed a hot-seat, no-escape-hatch format.

One subject early in the group aroused concern in the research staff. He was an encounter group buff, attempted to assume leadership, inappropriately urged the group onto deeper levels of forced intimacy and catharsis, had a grab-bag of group gimmicks for every occasion, and would have been a thorn in the side of any leader. Furthermore, he was a vulnerable individual who joined the group for therapeutic purposes when in the midst of a severe identity crisis and at times veered close to a borderline state. We suspect that without firm leader intervention, he would have soon created an unviable role in the group and evoked a withering degree of group hostility upon himself. The leader very deliberately "kept the lid on." He gently suppressed the subject and guided him into a less vulnerable, albeit less colorful, role in the group. He ended the experience somewhat disappointed and frustrated with his group but none the worse for it.

Another subject assumed a hazardous rule in his group. He declined to participate verbally except for occasional enigmatic comments and from the outset took copious written notes during the meeting—a highly sophisticated method of committing suicide in a California encounter group. The group, as to be expected, focused heavily upon him, but the leader (type B "love" leader) helped to establish tolerant, gentle, nondemanding norms and, even though the subject continued much of this behavior throughout the meetings, the other members were able to accept him as he was without experiencing a sense of failure because they had not broken through his defenses. In the followup interview, the subject expressed a positive attitude toward the group experience.

PREDICTING AND SCREENING OUT CASUALTIES

To what extent does the psychological functioning of the individual and his attitudes and anticipations toward encounter groups predict psychological risk? We have learned that to a considerable extent the type of group a person enters accounts for the amount of risk. The fact that casualties did not occur in some styles of groups and that the population in the various groups was randomized would indicate that the power of prediction of personality variables must be limited in this study. (If, for example, all the groups had been led by leaders with the same style, then the power of prediction of personality factors would be much greater.) The practical implications of screening are, however, so compelling that an attempt was made to determine in this study, *post facto*, what information could be garnered that might help subsequent encounter group leaders predict and screen out subjects likely to have a negative reaction to the group.

A wide variety of tests and questionnaire information was available on all our participants prior to the group experience. From the pregroup data, the following 71 scales or indices were selected to test out whether casualties could be predicted: (1) *Attitudes toward encounter groups* (three scales). (2) *Current status* on such dimensions as intimacy, spontaneity, etc, (seven self-rating scales). (3) *Environmental opportunities*—the amount of opportunities the individual's environment offered to fulfill such needs as intimacy, expressivity, etc (eight scales). (4) The seven current status scales and the eight environmental opportunity scales were also used to measure level of anticipation—the *amount of change the individual anticipated* from his participation in the encounter group. (5) *Interpersonal values*—scales tailored toward the assumed emphases of encounter groups (five scales). (6) *Personal growth orientation*—an open-ended instrument (the life-space questionnaire) was developed for life values and an index was derived from this instrument which assessed the individual's investment in personal growth or change. (7) *Wanted and expressed interpersonal needs* measured by the FIRO-B[8] (four scales). (8) *Self-esteem* measured by the Rosenberg

Self-Esteem Scale.[5] (9) *Self-concept and self-ideal discrepancy* measured by an adaptation of the Kelly Role Repertoire Test.[4] Eight factor-analytically derived self-concept scales and three self-ideal discrepancy scores were developed. (10) *Coping styles*—An instrument was developed which assessed styles of coping with personal dilemmas.[4] Twelve factor-analytically derived scales were used (ie, denial, flight, understanding, take action). (11) Lastly, sex and previous encounter group experience were entered into the pool of predictor variables.

Technical Note

The number of variables hypothesized to be potentially relevant to predicting casualty status were far too numerous to test adequately the predictors' hypothesis. Furthermore, a number of these indices were especially constructed for the research with only minimal test-development and hence the problem of measurement error loomed large for predictive statistics. A series of statistical procedures were designed[9] to reduce measurement error and to make possible an adequate statistical test of the prediction hypothesis. Principal component analyses were computed on those specially constructed instruments which contained multiple scales. Thus, a reduced number of dimensions (the first and second principal component on each instrument) were generated. These new dimensions were then subjected to a linear discriminate analysis which estimated the maximum discrimination on all the variables between the noncasualty and casualty samples. The linear discriminate analysis is a stepwise multivariate analysis which maximizes selection of independent variables for further analysis. In other words, this procedure was used not to test the hypothesis, but rather to develop the most likely independent variables for hypothesis testing. On the basis of these procedures the 71 original separate scores were reduced to 20 dimensions which could be used to test the prediction hypothesis. The statistic chosen for testing the hypothesis was a multivariate analysis of variance.

TABLE 6. *Predictions of Casualty Status*

Variables	Means Noncasualty Nondropout	Casualty	Step Down F	P* (2-Tailed)
1. Previous encounter group experience	1.44	1.47	0.15	0.69
2. Expected danger	26.20	27.30	1.06	0.30
3. Expected superficiality	27.50	29.10	1.37	0.24
4. Acceptance of influence	5.00	4.50	0.83	0.36
5. Desire to control	3.80	2.90	1.50	0.22
6. Self-esteem	3.90	3.50	2.26	0.13
7. Growth orientation	26.50	42.70	4.85	0.02
8. Self-ideal, discrepancy on enthusiasm	5.70	7.60	0.01	0.88
9. Anticipation of change†	0.05	0.00	0.30	0.58
10. Anticipation of opportunity	0.00	0.86	1.84	0.17
11. Positive self-concept	1.36	0.00	3.99	0.04
Coping Styles				
12. Interpersonal perspective	0.00	0.01	0.14	0.70
13. Interpersonal problem-solving	0.35	0.00	5.76	0.01
14. Use of understanding	0.35	0.00	0.70	0.40
15. Taking action	0.00	0.07	0.47	0.49
16. Planned alternatives	0.29	0.00	1.12	0.29
17. Flight-substitutive activity	0.18	0.00	0.63	0.42
18. Escape-leaving situation	0.01	0.11	2.38	0.12
19. Expecting the worst	0.09	0.07	0.17	0.67
20. Denial-not worrying	0.10	0.02	0.02	0.88

*Overall P = 0.086.

†Indices 9 to 20 are based on principal components analyses; means represent transformed scores.

Table 6 shows the means for the noncasualty and casualty samples on these 20 variables as well as giving the step down F value and P levels. The P levels shown are for two-tailed test of the hypothesis, although the anticipation of directionality is clear in many of the dimensions and thus the reader may divide the P levels by 2.

Findings. The multivariate analysis of variance produces an overall probability level of 0.086 which indicates that at a moderate level of confidence indices can be measured prior to an individual's participation in the encounter group that are associated with casualty-noncasualty status. Six of the 20 dimensions were particularly sensitive in discriminating between the casualties and noncasualties. Those who became casualties showed, before beginning the group, significantly lower levels of self-esteem and a lower level of positive self-concept than did those who did not become casualties.

Furthermore the casualties had a higher growth orientation and greater anticipation that the encounter group would provide opportunities for fulfillment of their needs. Perhaps they overinvested in the possibility, perhaps they were more needy individuals who saw in the encounter group the unrealistic possibility of personal salvation. Whatever the origin of the more intense need—or the more "unrealistic" expectation—those individuals who came believing in miracles were more likely to reap pain.

The last area of specific prediction was in the coping-ego-defense scales, which indicate that individuals who are *less* likely to use direct interpersonal modes and *more* likely to use escape modes had a greater probability of becoming casualties.

The entire picture is a consistent one: individuals with generally less favorable mental health with greater growth needs and higher anticipations for their group experience and yet who lacked self-esteem and the interpersonal skills to operate effectively in the group situation were more likely to become casualties.

A history of previous psychotherapy is worth noting, but adds relatively little predictive power. Five (31%) of the 16 casualties had seen a psychotherapist prior to the group as contrasted to 9% of the noncasualty experimental population and 18% of the control population (Table 2). Of these five, four had only brief encounters with a therapist while only one had had on going psychotherapy.

What are the implications of these findings? The instruments we have examined for testing the hypothesis that personality, attitudinal, and anticipatory dimensions are related to development of casualties were in the large not designed for this purpose and, as indicated previously, becoming a casualty was in large part dependent on the particular group the participant found himself in. Nevertheless, our efforts to demonstrate casualty predictability have yielded a model which has considerable psychological consistency. It is reasonable to assume that with closer and more deliberate study some of the individuals who are emotionally traumatized in the encounter groups could be guided away from attending such situations. It is more than likely that some questionnaires which particularly focus on the individual's expectations and anticipations about what it was he would gain from encounter groups would yield the best payoff for screening instruments; the measurement of mental health or its related concepts though complex and inconsistent can serve as a supplemental aid in screening.

COMMENT

Eighteen encounter groups led by leaders with diverse styles were offered as university undergraduate courses. The process and outcome of these groups were intensively researched. We developed several criteria to identify potential casualties of the groups. We defined a casualty as an individual who, as a result of his encounter group experience, suffered considerable and persistent psychological distress. The most effective method of identifying casualties was to ask the group members at the end of the group whether anyone had been harmed by the experience. One of the least effective methods was a rating of negative change by the leaders; indeed many of the leaders were completely unaware that there had been casualties in their groups. This finding has some obvious and significant implications. Group leaders who do not provide themselves with the opportunity for follow-up interviews with their group members simply do not have the necessary information to make a statement about the hazards of their groups. That the members themselves were more accurate in identifying casualties is not surprising. There are a number of studies which attest to the evaluative sensitivity of peers; for example, the Peace Corps candidates were able to predict which of their number would eventually fail in their duties more frequently than were the instructors.[10]

A total of 209 subjects began the encounter groups. There were 16 casualties. This represents a very appreciable casualty rate. Although one aspect of our design—the random assignment of the subjects to one of the 18 groups—may have increased the risk, it was our impression that our casualties rate may, in fact, be a conservative estimate. The overall design of the project, in our opinion, decreased the risk of the groups. The research conditions imposed some restraints on the groups: all groups were observed and tape-recorded and the leaders were cognizant that they were being evaluated. Furthermore, we defined "casualty" in a rigorous manner and, finally, some "high risk" suspects could not be located for study.

A major finding of the study is that the number and severity of casualties and the manner in which the casualties sustained injury are all highly dependent upon the particular type of encounter group. Some leadership styles result in a high-risk group.

Particularly stressful is a leader style (type A) which is characterized by intrusive, aggressive, stimulation, by high charisma, by high challenging and confrontation of each of the members, and by authoritarian control. We shall focus on the A style of leadership since groups led in this manner accounted for far more than their share of the total number of casualties: the five type A leaders accounted for seven (44%) of the 16 casualties. It was our impression, too, that these groups generated more severe casualties and, furthermore, that they bore more responsibility for the casualty. (The casualty seemed truly *caused*, not merely hastened or facilitated, by the leader style, and is thereby preventable by a change in leader style.) The type A leaders were forceful and impatient. If some significant sign of growth or change (crying, testimonial, breakdown, or breakthrough) was not given to them in the group, they increased the pressure on the participants. The "A" leaders appeared to operate on an immediate gratification system. They paid little heed to the concept of "working through" and demanded that their members change and change "now."

Another important characteristic of the type A leaders was their lack of differentiation of the individuals in their groups. It appeared as though these leaders felt that everyone in the group had the same needs and had to accomplish the same thing in the group. There is a curious paradox here. The type A leaders appeared highly unorthodox and innovative; they displayed at the same time the widest and yet the narrowest range of techniques—narrow because of a lack of discernment of the scope of intrapersonal and interpersonal problems. After all, not *everyone* needs to express himself more vigorously and spontaneously, to shuck his societal restrictions, to achieve a greater degree of freedom, to abandon all success-oriented goals. Some individuals may need quite the opposite: they already express themselves with far too much lability; they need more, not fewer controls, they need more, not less of an ego boundary; they need, perhaps, a more structured, more traditionally based hierarchy of values.

One other observation of interest concerning the type A leaders was their religious aura. These charismatic leaders had their own internalized charismatic leader. Synanon is still guided by the hand of Dietrich, its founding father, and many of the Synanon activities have distinct ceremonial, ritualized overtones. The gestalt leaders, too, have a highly revered, idealized leader in the person of the late Fredrick "Fritz" Perls; in fact there is a published gestalt therapy prayer with which some leaders begin their meetings. The fifth type A leader was heavily invested in a Far Eastern religious order, and at the time of this writing he had been persuaded by his religious Elder to abandon his career as a group leader. Perhaps the religious element helps us to understand these leaders' failure to discriminate between individuals since they may tend to imbue the individual with a system of beliefs and values (a single and final common pathway to salvation) rather than to encourage the individual to change according to his own needs and potential. (During the meetings, the type A leaders all revealed, to a greater extent than other leaders, their own personal belief systems.)

Whereas four of the type A groups had a total of seven casualties, one "A" group had no casualties, and although this leader resembled in many ways an "A" leader who had three casualties, he differed from him in a significant fashion. He stated that he realized immediately that there were several restricted, fragile individuals in his group and therefore he deviated from his usual style: "I pulled my punches,

I didn't get into the heavy intrapersonal material I usually focus on, I did more interpersonal work, more classroom work, I gave them a type of tasting session so that they could see what groups could be like . . . I was constantly aware of keeping the lid on my group." The "A" leader whose group had three casualties, on the other hand, commented that it was a stubborn group, full of people "too infantile to take responsibility for themselves and to form an adult contract" with him. "I saw that most of the group didn't want to do anything so what I did was to just go ahead and have a good time for myself."

Occasionally a casualty from attack by the members, not leaders, occurred in groups led by laissez-faire or leaders who modeled little positive, caring behavior. (Laissez-faire leaders paid another type of penalty for their lack of involvement or low stimulus input—large numbers of their groups dropped out because they found the pace slow and plodding.)

Other mechanisms of injury included rejection by the leader or by the other members. That a member may have a truly destructive experience because of rejection is a function of several factors: the norms of the group which mediated the existence and degree of rejection, the consistency of self-image of the subject, the presence of internalized anchor groups, and the presence of other interpersonal resources to which the subject could turn for support.

Other casualties were caused (or perhaps, more accurately, hastened) by "input overload"; they were so challenged and overstimulated that rather than assimilate new perspectives on themselves and their world they were instead sucked into a maelstrom of confusion and uncertainty. The "unfreezing" process that occurs in almost any encounter group may produce this type of casualty. Clearly, we found that these subjects had some preexisting significant disturbance which met the process halfway.

A final mode of injury occurred in a curious manner. The subject observed other members quickly experiencing and expressing high intensity affect. Noting the apparent discrepancy between the others' productions and his own comparatively pallid affect, he judged himself as emotionally deficient and thenceforth identified himself as one of the hollow men.

The low-risk groups were those led by type B leaders and the two tape groups. The subjects in the tape groups had a positive, though not deeply intensive, experience. The Peer Program tapes promoted supportive, low-conflict groups. On the few occasions that negative interaction occurred, it was dealt with by flight: with no leader to help the group understand and resolve conflict, the members generally avoided unpleasant issues. The type B leaders offered considerable positive support for members. They helped create an accepting, trusting climate in the group which permitted members to participate at their own pace.

Although this paper is concerned only with the hazards of encounter groups, we wish to remind the reader that the positive gains from the experience were far-reaching for many subjects. There was, as we describe elsewhere,[11] even more variation amongst the 18 groups in positive outcome than there was in casualty rates.

Although there were pre-group differences apparent between those subjects who went on subsequently to have a destructive experience and those who did not, these differences are not likely to provide us with powerful predictors at the present state of development. Our best means of prediction remains the type of group the subject enters and our best mean for prevention is *self-selection*. If responsible public education can teach prospective encounter group members about what they can, with reasonable accuracy, expect in terms of process, risks, and profit from a certain type of group then, and only then, can they make an informed decision about membership. Individuals who are psychologically vulnerable and who overinvest their hopes in the magic of salvation through encounter groups are particularly vulnerable when they interact with leaders who believe that they can offer deliverance. Such an interaction is a potent synergistic force for destructive outcome.

This study was supported by grants MH-19212-01 from the National Institute of Mental Health and 68-742 from the Ford Foundation and by grants from the Ford Foundation Fund for Innovation in Education, the Mary Reynolds Babcock Foundation, Inc, the Stanford Medical School Student Research Assistantship Grant, the General Research Fund, Division of Biological Sciences, University of Chicago, the Stanford University General Research Support Grant, the Social Science Research Committee, Division of Social Science, University of Chicago, the Clement and Jesse V. Stone Foundation, the Foundation's Fund for Research in Psychiatry, and the Carnegie Foundation.

This report describes one aspect of a larger study in which the principal investigators were Morton Lieberman, Irvin O. Yalom, and Matthew Miles. Peggy Golde and Herbert Wong collaborated in this study. Stephen Miller and E. Kitch Childs contributed to the study of casualties.

REFERENCES

1. *Encounter Groups and Psychiatry*, Task Force Report No. 1. Washington, DC, American Psychiatric Association, 1970.

2. Berzon B, Solomon LN: The self-directed therapeutic group: Three studies. *J Couns Psychol 13*:491-497, 1966.

3. Lieberman M, Yalom I: Dimensions of leader behavior, in Berzon B, Solomon LN (eds): *The Encounter Group: Issues and Applications.* San Francisco, Jossey-Bass, 1971.

4. Lieberman M, Yalom I, Miles M, et al: The group experience: A comparison of ten encounter technologies, in Blank L, Gottsegen G, Gottsegen M (eds): *Encounter Confrontation in Self and Interpersonal Awareness.* New York, Macmillan Co Publishers, 1971.

5. Rosenberg M: *Society and the Adolescent Self-Image.* Princeton, NJ, Princeton University Press, 1965.

6. Asch SE: Interpersonal influence: Effects of group pressure upon the modification and distortions of judgments, in Maccoby EE, Newcomb TM, Hartley EL (eds): *Readings in Social Psychology.* New York, Holt Rinehart & Winston Inc, 1958, pp 174-183.

7. Sherif M: Group influences upon the formation of norms and attitudes, in Maccoby TE, Newcomb TM, Hartley EL (eds): *Readings in Social Psychology.* New York, Holt Rinehart & Winston Inc, 1958, pp 219-232.

8. Schutz W: FIRO: *A Three Dimensional Theory of Interpersonal Behavior.* New York, Rinehart & Co Inc, 1958

9. Childs KE: *Prediction of Encounter Group Outcome as a Function of Selected Personality Variables*, thesis. Committee on Human Development, University of Chicago, 1971.

10. Boulger J, Coleman J: *Research Findings With Peer Ratings*, research note No. 8. Washington, DC, Division of Research, Peace Corps.

11. Lieberman M, Yalom I, Miles M: The impact of encounter groups on participants. *J Appl Behav Sci,* to be published.

26. Case Report: Avoidance Conditioning Therapy of an Infant with Chronic Ruminative Vomiting[1]

PETER J. LANG & BARBARA G. MELAMED

This paper reports the treatment of a 9-mo.-old male infant whose life was seriously endangered by persistent vomiting and chronic rumination. An aversive conditioning paradigm, employing electric shock, significantly reduced the frequency of this maladaptive response pattern in a few brief treatment sessions. Electromyographic records were used in assessing response characteristics of the emesis, and in determining the shock contingencies used in therapy. Cessation of vomiting and rumination was accompanied by weight gains, increased activity level, and general responsiveness to people.

A variety of techniques have been used in the treatment of persistent vomiting in infants and children. In general these therapies are tailored to the known or hypothesized causes of the disorder. Thus, the presence of functional disturbance in the intestinal tract would encourage the use of pharmacologic agents—"tranquilizers," antinauseants, or antiemetics. If gastric, anatomical anomalies can be diagnosed, their surgical removal often proves to be the most effective treatment. Animal studies suggest that surgical manipulation of the central nervous system may also become a vehicle for emesis con-

Peter J. Lang & Barbara G. Melamed, Avoidance conditioning therapy of an infant with chronic ruminative vomiting, *Journal of Abnormal Psychology, 74,* 1969, 1-8. Copyright © 1969 by the American Psychological Association and reproduced by permission.

[1] This study was supported in part by a grant (MH-10993) from the National Institute of Mental Health, United States Public Health Service.

[2] The authors wish to thank David Kass, the physician in immediate charge of the present case, for giving the authors the opportunity to explore this treatment method and for his assistance during its application. The authors are also indebted to Charles Lobeck, Chairman of the Department of Pediatrics of University Hospitals, Madison, Wisconsin, who made facilities available for use, and to the assigned nursing staff without whose help and cooperation the present result could not have been accomplished. The authors also express their appreciation to Norman Greenfield and Richard Sternbach of the Department of Psychiatry, University of Wisconsin, for the loan of a polygraph, and to Karl G. Stoedefalke of Physical Education for providing additional EMG preamplifiers.

trol (Borison, 1959).

When diagnosis excludes obvious, organic antecedents, both the etiology and treatment of the disorder appear less certain. However, clinical workers have described an apparently "psychosomatic" vomiting in children which is generally accompanied by a ruminative rechewing of the vomitus. In reviewing the syndrome, Richmond, Eddy, and Green (1958) adhere to the widely held psychoanalytic hypothesis that it results from a disruption in the mother-infant relationship. They suggest that the condition is brought about by the inability of the mother to fulfill an adult psychosexual role which is reflected in marital inadequacy. She is unable to give up her own dependent needs and is incapable of providing warm, comfortable, and intimate physical care for the infant. This lack of comfort from without causes the infant to seek and recreate such gratification from within. Thus, in attempting to regain satisfaction from the feeding situation, he regurgitates his food and retains it in his mouth. The recommended treatment is the interruption in the mother-infant relationship by hospitalization and the provision of a stimulating, warm environment with a substitute mother figure. This method achieved success in the four cases reviewed. Berlin, McCullough, Lisha, and Szurek (1957) offer a similar psychoanalytic interpretation in reporting a case study of a 4-yr.-old child hospitalized for 8 mo. at Langley-Porter Clinic. Psychotherapy, involving concomitant counseling to improve the relationship between the parents, led to an alleviation of the child's vomiting reaction.

From the point of view espoused by learning theorists, emesis and rumination may be learned habits. In point of fact, vomiting has been clearly demonstrated as a conditioned response in at least three independent studies (Collins & Tatum, 1925; Kleitman & Crisler, 1927; Pavlov, 1927). This prompts the corollary hypothesis that such behavior could be eliminated directly by counterconditioning procedures.

A number of case reports indicate that considerable success may be achieved in modifying alimentary habits in the clinic setting. Both Bachrach, Erwin, and Mohr (1965) and Meyer[3] successfully treated adult anorexic patients by making various social and physical reinforcers contingent on eating behavior or weight gain. Lang (1965) described the therapy of a young adult patient who became nauseous and vomited under social stress. In this case, counterconditioning methods increased the patient's tolerance of formerly aversive social situations, and thus markedly reduced the frequency of nausea and emesis.

The only study reviewed, attempting to apply conditioning methods specifically in the treatment of ruminative vomiting was reported by White and Taylor (1967). Electric shock was applied to two mentally retarded patients (23-yr.-old female, 14-yr.-old male) whenever throat, eye, or coughing gestures signaled rumination. They suggest that the shock served to distract the patient and he engaged in other activities rather than ruminating. Significant improvement occurred after 1 wk. of treatment, and gains were maintained at a 1-mo. follow-up.

The following case report illustrates the efficacy of aversive conditioning in reversing the vomiting and rumination of a 9-mo.-old infant whose life was endangered by this behavior. The case is of general interest because of the extreme youth of the patient, the speed of treatment, and the fact that conditioning procedures were undertaken only after other treatments had been either ruled out by diagnostic procedures, or had been given a reasonable trial without success. These data also have further implications for the understanding of aversive conditioning in clinical practice.

---

[3] Meyer, V. Personal communication, 1964.

HISTORY OF PROBLEM AND FAMILY BACKGROUND

A. T. at the age of 9 mo. was admitted to the University Hospital for failure to retain food and chronic rumination. This infant had undergone three prior hospitalizations for his persistent vomiting after eating and failure to gain weight. Born in an eastern state after an uneventful 39-wk. pregnancy, the patient was bottle fed and gained steadily from a birth weight of 9 lb. 4 oz. to 17 lb. at 6 mo. of age. Vomiting was first noted during the fifth month, and increased in severity to the point where the patient vomited 10-15 min. after each meal. This activity was often associated with vigorous thumbsucking, placing fingers in his mouth, blotchiness of the face, and ruminating behavior. The mother remarked that the start of vomiting may have coincided with her indisposition due to a broken ankle which forced the family to live with maternal grandparents for several weeks. Some friction was reported between the patient's mother and her own adoptive mother concerning care of the child. The patient's father is a part-time college student and the family received financial assistance from the paternal grandfather, a successful dentist. At the time of the most recent hospitalization, the social worker's report suggested that the parents were making a marginal marital adjustment.

Three brief periods of hospitalization which included medical tests (gastrointestinal fluoroscopy, EEG, and neuropsychological testing) failed to find an organic basis for this persistent regurgitation. An exploratory operation was performed and a cyst on the right kidney removed, with no discernible effect on his condition. The patient had no history of head trauma. One previous incident of persistent vomiting in a paternal uncle was noted to be of very short duration. The paternal grandfather and two uncles are reported to suffer ulcers.

Several treatment approaches were applied without success. Dietary changes (Pro-Sobee, skim milk), the administration of antinauseants, and various mechanical maneuvers to improve the feeding situation (different positions, small amounts at each feeding, burping) gave short-lived, if any, relief. As thumb sucking often preceded the response, restraints were tried. However, this did little to reduce the frequency of emesis. An attempt had been made to initiate intensive nursing care "to establish and maintain a one-to-one relationship and to provide the child with warm, friendly, and secure feelings (nurse's chart)." This had to be abandoned because it was not inhibiting the vomiting and some observers felt that it increased the child's anxiety and restlessness.

At the time the present investigators were called in, the infant was in critical condition, down to a weight of 12 lb., and being fed through a nasogastric pump. The attending physician's clinical notes attest that conditioning procedures were applied as a last attempt, "in view of the fact that therapy until now has been unsuccessful and the life of the child is threatened by continuation of this behavior."

THERAPEUTIC PROCEDURE AND RESULTS

The patient was given a private room, continuous nursing care, and assigned a special graduate nurse to assist in the conditioning procedures. The authors closely observed the infant for 2 days during and after normal feeding periods. He reliably regurgitated most of his food intake within 10 min. of each feeding and continued to bring up small amounts throughout the day. Observers on the hospital staff suggested that vomiting was originally induced by thumb pressure at the back of the throat. However, at this stage thumb manipulations were not a necessary part of the vomiting sequence. He did protest, however, if hand restraint was enforced. His frail appearance and general unresponsiveness, made him a pathetic looking child. . . .

In an attempt to obtain a clearer picture of the patterning of his response, electromyograph (EMG) activity at three sites was monitored on a Gilson Polygraph. Responses leading up to and into the vomiting sequence reliably coincided with the nurse's concurrent description of the sequence of behavior. Figure 1 illustrates the typical response pattern. The uppermost channel of information represents muscle potentials recorded just under the chin, and shows the sucking behavior which usually preceded vomiting; the lowest channel is an integrated record taken from the throat muscles of the neck; the center channel which monitors the upper chest region is largely EKG artifact. It can be noted from this segment that the onset of vomiting is clearly accompanied by vigorous throat movements indicated by rhythmic, high-frequency, high-amplitude activity, in contrast with quiescent periods and periods where crying predominated.

The authors were concerned with eliminating the inappropriate vomiting, without causing any fundamental disturbance in the feeding behavior of the child. Fortunately, the child did not vomit during feeding, and the sucking and vomiting could be distinguished readily on the EMG. After 2 days of monitoring, conditioning procedures were initiated. The aversive conditioning paradigm called for brief and repeated shock (ap proximately 1 sec. long with a 1-sec. interpulse interval) as soon as vomiting occurred, continuing until the response was terminated. An effort was made to initiate shock at the first sign of reverse peristalsis, but not during the preceding sucking behavior. The contingency was determined from the nurse's observations of the patient and the concurrent EMG records. In general, the nurse would signal as soon as she thought an emesis was beginning. If EMG confirmed the judgment, shock was delivered. Occasionally, the

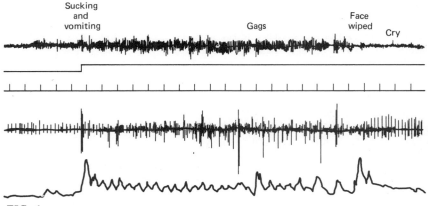

FIG. 1.
Three channels of EMG activity are presented. (The nurse observer's comments are written just above the first channel. The intense muscle activity on this line is associated with sucking behavior, recorded from electrodes on the underside of the chin. The second channel is just below the one pulse per second, timing line, and was taken from electrodes on the upper chest, at the base of the throat. The EKG dominates this channel, with some local muscle activity. Electrodes straddling the esophagus yielded the lowest line, which in this integrated record clearly shows the rhythmic pulsing of the vomiting response.)

FIG. 2

The electrode positions are the same as in Figure 1. (The top line shows the point at which two brief shocks were administered. It may be noted that they follow closely in the first pulse of the vomiting response and that the rhythmic response and that the rhythmic regurgitation observed in Figure 1 never gets underway.)

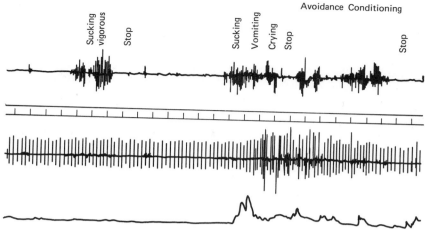

EMG would initiate this sequence with the observational judgment following.[4] Shock was delivered by means of a Harvard Inductorium to electrodes placed on the calf of the patient's leg. A 3,000-cps tone was temporally coincident with each shock presentation.[5] Sessions were chosen following feeding to insure some frequency of response. Each session lasted less than 1 hour.

[4]Particular thanks are due to Mary Kachoyeanos, the nurse who assisted at all the therapy sessions.

[5]Shock level was first determined by applying the electrodes to the Es, who judged it to be quite painful and unpleasant. Intensity was incremented slightly during the first and second sessions on the basis of the patient's response, but was subsequently unchanged. The inductorium does not permit for exact or wholly reliable measures of current level. However, under the conditions of treatment described here, the average current was within a range of from .10 to .30 ma., with a cycle frequency of approximately 50 cps. It should be borne in mind that pulses from an inductorium vary widely in amplitude, and the authors' instrument produced some spikes over 10 ma. Electrodes were first applied to the ball of the foot and then moved to the calf for reasons stated in the text. The accompanying tone was generated by a Hewlett-Packard signal generator and administered by a small oval speaker in a free field. The intensity was loud but not painful (approximately 80-95 db.), and varied considerably because of spontaneous changes in the infant's position. It was employed in order to increase the density of the reinforcer and on the possibility that the therapists might employ it alone, if shock proved to have negative side effects.

After two sessions shock was rarely required. The infant would react to the shock by crying and cessation of vomiting. By the third session only one or two brief presentations of shock were necessary to cause cessation of any vomiting sequence. Figure 2 illustrates the typical sequence of a conditioning trial.

The course of therapy is indicated in Figure 3. Few shocks were administered after the first day of treatment, and both the time spent vomiting and the average length of each vomiting period were abruptly reduced. After only two sessions it seemed that the infant was anticipating the unpleasant consequences of his behavior. He would begin to suck vigorously using his thumb, and then he would remove his thumb and cry loudly.

The data graphed (Figure 3) for the second treatment session represent those reinforcers that the authors are certain were delivered. Early in this session, it became obvious that the infant was not receiving the majority of the administered shocks. The electrodes were at that time attached to the plantar surface of the foot. Observation suggested that the patient had learned to curl his foot, either coincident with emesis or at the first sensation of shock, so as to lift the electrodes off the skin and thus avoid the painful stimulus. At this point, the electrodes were relocated on the calf, and conditioning proceeded nor-

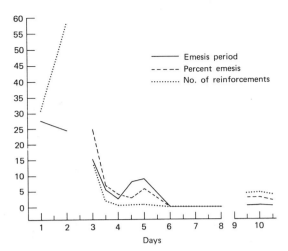

FIG. 3

The abscissa describes successive days (morning and afternoon) on which observation or treatment was accomplished. ("Emesis period" is the length of any continuous period of vomiting. "Percentage of emesis" is the total time spent vomiting divided by the time observed. Sessions varied from 16 min. to 60 min. Treatment began on Day 3 which included two unshocked emesis periods. In Session 10 tone alone was presented on one trial. It is of interest to note that following therapy, nursing staff reported that they could now block the very rare vomiting periods with a sharp handclap.)

mally. If the shock administrations prior to this procedural change are added to those on the graph, Day 3, afternoon figures for emesis period, percentage of emesis, and shock, respectively, are 11 sec., 21.6% and 77.

By the sixth session the infant no longer vomited during the testing procedures. He would usually fall asleep toward the middle of the hour. Figure 4 indicates the sequence of response demonstrating the replacement of vigorous sucking with what the nursing observers described as a "pacifier" use of the thumb.

To vary the conditions under which learning would take place, thereby providing for transfer of effects, the sessions were scheduled at different hours of the day, and while the infant was being held, playing on the floor, as well as lying in bed. Nursing staff reported a progressive decrease in his ruminating and vomiting behavior during the rest of the day and night, which paralleled the reduction observed across therapy sessions.

After three sessions in which there was no occurrence of vomiting, the procedure was discontinued. Two days later there was some spontaneous recovery, which included some vigorous sucking, with a little vomiting and rumination. Three additional sessions were initiated to maintain the reduced frequency of the response (see Figure 3). Except

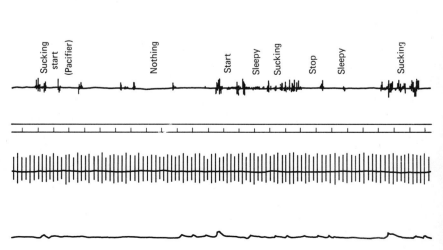

FIG. 4

The above segment is representative of behavior near the end of a conditioning session. (Only mild sucking activity is apparent in the upper EMG channel. The electrode positions are the same as in Figure 1.)

for a brief slackening prior to these trials, there was a steady, monotonic increase in his weight as shown in Figure 5. In general, his activity level increased, he became more interested in his environment, enjoyed playroom experience, and smiled and reached out to be held by the nurse and other visitors.

The mother was reintroduced the day following the last conditioning trial. She took over some of the patient's caretaking needs, including feedings. There was no marked change in his ruminating behavior at this time. The mother responded well and her child reciprocated her attention. He was discharged from the hospital 5 days later, after exhibiting almost no ruminating behavior. . . .

FOLLOW-UP

Correspondence with the mother indicated that there was no further need for treatment. A. T. was eating well and gaining weight regularly. She reported that any thumbsucking or rumination was easily arrested by providing him with other forms of stimulation. He was beginning to seek attention from other people and enjoyed the company of other children. One month following discharge from the hospital, he was seen for a physical check-up. He appeared as a healthy looking 21-lb. child and, aside from a slight anemic condition, was found fully recovered by the attending physician. His local physician reported on a visit 5 mo. later when his weight was 26 lb., 1 oz. "His examinations were negative for any problems. . . .He was eating quite well . . . no vomiting had recurred. He was alert, active and attentive.". . . One year after treatment he continues to thrive. Mother and father are both pleased with his development, and no further treatment is indicated.

DISCUSSION

The rapid recovery of this 9-mo.-old male infant following brief aversive conditioning therapy, argues for the effectiveness of behavioral modification in the treatment of this type of psychosomatic disorder. The vomiting and ruminating were treated as maladaptive behavior patterns, and electric shock was used to inhibit a previously well-established response sequence. Elimination of the response was accompanied by increase in the infant's responsiveness to people, as well as substantial weight gains, and physiological improvement.

Treatment was undertaken without analysis of the disorder's antecedents. Nevertheless, the family history of the infant could be construed as consistent with other cases in the literature. One clinical worker suggested that a feeling of hostility dominated this infant's home. It is true that the parents' wedding was attended by difficulties and the subsequent birth of the patient occurred before the parents were fully prepared for this responsibility. Furthermore, the mother later expressed anxiety about her marriage and complained of the problem of balancing the separate demands of father and child. She also reported her feeling that her own step-mother had not provided a good maternal model. As a consequence she felt inadequate herself and uncertain in the role.

The caseworker's notes are thus rich in "dynam-

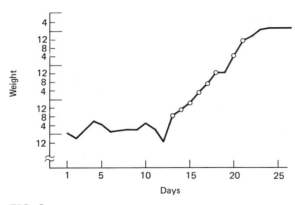

FIG. 5

The infant's body weight as determined from the nursing notes is plotted over time, from well before conditioning therapy was instituted to the day of discharge from the hospital. (Days on which conditioning sessions occurred are marked by circles on the curve. Reinforcers were delivered only on days marked by open circles. The decline in body weight in the few days just prior to therapy was probably occasioned by the discontinuance of the nasogastric pump, in favor of normal feeding procedures. The marked weight gain from Day 13 to 18 is coincident with the first 6 days of therapy. The temporary reduction in weight increase, associated with a resumption of emesis, is apparent at Day 19. The additional conditioning trials appear to have acted immediately to reinstate weight gain.)

ics," and while one is unable to establish the relative accuracy or significance of these statements, it is clear that this case is interpretable within traditional personality theories. Nevertheless, therapies generated by this orientation were not successful in the present case. In deference, it should also be noted that "one-to-one" care was not maintained as long or as consistently as in many cases reported in the literature, and despite evidence of some marital discord, no extensive counseling of the parents was undertaken. However, like many psychiatric treatments, the above are expensive of professional personnel and prolonged in duration. The aversive conditioning procedures used here achieved success in little more than a week, and considering the developing danger to the child's life, speed was of more than usual importance.

No evidence of "symptom substitution" was observed following treatment. On the other hand, positive social behavior increased coincident with the successful conditioning therapy. The infant became more responsive to adults, smiled more frequently, and seemed to be more interested in toys and games than he had been previously. An analogous improvement in social behavior was noticed in the defective adults treated by White and Taylor (1967). Lovaass, Freitag, Gold, and Kassorla (1965) and Lovaas, Schaeffer, and Simmons (1965) have cited similar effects following the avoidance conditioning of tantrum behavior in autistic children. The latter investigators suggest that the Es attained secondary reinforcing value because of their association with shock reduction. This provided the basis for training the children to exhibit affectionate patterns toward adults. In the present case this contingency was very imprecise, and it is not clear that the above mechanism mediated change. What could be called normal infant behavior increased regularly, as the emesis decreased. The social environment appeared simply to replace ruminating as the infant's focus of attention.

Aversive conditioning has been applied widely in adult therapy as well as with autistic children. Eysenck and Rachman (1965) and Feldman (1966) describe its use in treating alchholic and sexual disorders. However, one hesitates to interpret these findings in a straightforward manner. Adult patients may submit to aversive conditioning procedures from a variety of motives, and cognitive factors may blunt the impact or distort the meaning of aversive stimuli. The present case is of particular interest because these procedures were successful in treating an apparently normal child. Furthermore, the absence of language and the limited cognitive development achieved at this age permit one to interpret this change as avoidance conditioning, unmitigated by the above factors.

Finally, it should be noted that the present case represents a productive use of psychophysiologic recording in therapy. Not only did the EMG provide extensive documentation of the response, but concurrent recording was of considerable help in guiding the treatment effort. Specifically, these records confirmed in an objective manner external observations of mouth and throat movements which seemed to precede emesis. Furthermore, they extended these observations, helping the authors to specify those aspects of the response which were unique to the vomiting sequence, thus assuring that shock was never delivered following non-contingent behavior. Finally, observation of the recordings during therapy probably reduced the latency of reinforcement, particularly during the early trials when the validity of external signs seemed less certain, and provided the clearest indicator of the end of the response when shock was promptly terminated. While the importance of this information to the results obtained cannot be unequivocally established, it certainly increased the confidence of the therapists in their method, and, in turn, the speed and precision with which they proceeded. The further exploration of physiological analysis in the therapeutic setting is encouraged.

REFERENCES

Bachrach, A. J., Erwin, W. J., & Mohr, J. P. The control of eating behavior in an anorexic by operant conditioning techniques. In L. P. Ullmann & L. Krasner (Eds.), *Case studies in behavior modification.* New York: Holt, Rinehart & Winston, 1965.

Berlin, I. N., McCullough, G., Lisha, E. S., & Szurek, S. Intractable episodic vomiting in a three-year old child. *Psychiatric Quarterly,* 1957, *31,* 228–249.

Borison, H. L. Effect of ablation of medullary emetic chemoreceptor trigger zone on vomiting response to cerebral intra-ventricular injection of adrenaline, apomorphine and pilocarpine in the cat. *Journal of Physiology,* 1959, *147,* 172–177.

Collins, K. H., & Tatum, A. L. A conditioned salivary reflex established by chronic morphine poisoning. *American Journal of Physiology,* 1925, *74,* 14–15.

Eysenck, H. J., & Rachman, S. *The causes and cures of neurosis.* San Diego, Calif.: Knapp, 1965.

Feldman, M. P. Aversion therapy for sexual deviations: A critical review. *Psychological Bulletin,* 1966, *65,* 65–79.

Kleitman, N., & Crisler, G. A quantitative study of the conditioned salivary reflex. *American Journal of Physiology,* 1927, *79,* 571–614.

Lang, P. J. Behavior therapy with a case of nervous anorexia. In L. P. Ullmann & L. Krasner (Eds.), *Case studies in behavior modification.* New York: Holt, Rinehart & Winston, 1965.

Lovaas, O. I. Freitag, G., Gold, V., & Kassorla, I. Experimental studies in childhood schizophrenia: Analysis of self-destructive behavior. *Journal of Experimental Child Psychology,* 1965, *2,* 67–84.

Lovaas, O. I., Schaeffer, B., & Simmons, J. Building social behavior in autistic children by use of electric shock. *Journal of Experimental Research in*

Personality, 1965, *1,* 99–109.

Pavlov, I. P. *Conditioned reflexes: An investigation of the physiological activity of the cerebral cortex.* Lecture III, Oxford, England; Oxford University Press, 1927.

Richmond, J. B., Eddy, E., & Green, M. Rumination: A psychosomatic syndrome of infancy. *Pediatrics,* 1958, *22,* 49–55.

White, J. D., & Taylor, D. Noxious conditioning as a treatment for rumination. *Mental Retardation,* 1967, *5,* 30–33.

27 *Modification of Social Withdrawal through Symbolic Modeling*[1]

ROBERT D. O'CONNOR

The present experiement was designed to test the efficacy of symbolic modeling as a treatment to enhance social behavior in preschool isolates. Nursery school children who displayed marked social withdrawal were assigned to one of two conditions. One group observed a film depicting increasingly more active social interactions between children with positive consequences ensuing in each scene, while a narrative soundtrack emphasized the appropriate behavior of the models. A control group observed a film that contained no social interaction. Control children displayed no change in withdrawal behavior, whereas those who had the benefit of symbolic modeling increased their level of social interaction to that of non-isolate nursery school children.

Recent years have witnessed increasing applications of principles of learning to psychopathology. Ample evidence has accumulated to indicate that behavioral approaches hold considerable promise for the treatment of diverse psychological conditions (Bandura, 1969; Eysenck, 1964; Krasner and Ullmann, 1967; Wolpe and Lazarus, 1967).

Many of these applications, however, have been concerned with the treatment of highly circumscribed disorders. Only recently have researchers begun to investigate the modifications of interpersonal modes of behavior.

Social interaction, an obviously important factor in personality development, has become the

Robert D. O'Connor, Modification of social withdrawal through symbolic modeling, *Journal of Applied Behavior Analysis, 2,* 1969, 15-22. Copyright © 1969 by the Society for the Experimental Analysis of Behavior, Inc. Reproduced by permission.

[1] This research was supported by Public Health Research Grant M-5162 from the National Institute of Mental Health to Albert Bandura, and by the Louis Haas Research Fund, Stanford University. The author is grateful to Professor Bandura, whose enthusiastic assistance and many suggestions were invaluable during all phases of this project, and to Professor Eleanor E. Maccoby, who provided support and helpful comments during the initial stages of the experiment. Professors Robert R. Sears and Edith Dowley generously assisted in the design and implementation of observational procedures, and Marian O'Connor collaborated on numerous resources which insured the success of the program.

focus of much attention among social-learning theorists, developmentalists, and therapists. There are several reasons for highlighting the role of interpersonal behavior in personality development. First, a child who is grossly deficient in social skills will be seriously handicapped in acquiring many of the complex behavioral repertoires necessary for effective social functioning. Second, children who are unable to relate skillfully to others are likely to experience rejection, harrassment, and generally hostile treatment from peers. Such negative experiences would be expected to reinforce interpersonal avoidance responses, which, in turn, further impede the development of competencies that are socially mediated. Current theories concerning the determinants of personality patterns (Bandura, 1969; Bandura and Walters, 1963; Mischel, 1968; Peterson, 1968) emphasize social variables and underscore the general importance of social interaction.

Several attempts have been made to enhance the social behavior of isolate children (Allen, Hart, Buell, Harris, and Wolfe, 1964; Hart, Reynolds, Baer, Brawley, and Harris, 1968; Hartup, 1964; Patterson and Anderson, 1964) through differential reinforcement. These studies have shown that if peer interaction is reinforced, either socially or otherwise, and isolate play is either punished or ignored, children eventually display a higher level of social behavior. The utilization of a treatment program based solely on reinforcement procedures may encounter difficulties in the development of social responsiveness in extreme isolates. However, while a series of preliminary observations which served as a pilot for the present study found 20% or more of nursery school children exhibiting relatively low levels of social responsiveness, many of whom could be helped by arranging favorable response consequences; a smaller percentage of children either perform no social interaction response or provide only rare opportunities for the application of reinforcement. When such gross deficits exist, the reinforcing agent must either introduce a rather laborious set of "shaping" procedures, which requires waiting for the emission of a reinforceable social response, or resort to more active means for establishing the desired behavior.

Lovaas (1966) showed that relatively complex repertoires can be established to replace gross deficits through a combination of modeling and reinforcement procedures. Of greater interest and relevance to the approach used in the present study is evidence that children can acquire new patterns of behavior on the basis of observation alone (Bandura and Huston, 1961; Bandura and McDonald, 1963; Bandura and Mischel, 1965; Bandura, Ross, and Ross, 1963; Hicks, 1965). Since repertoires can thus be learned on a non-response basis, with no reinforcement to the observer, a modeling program may be particularly effective in the case of gross behavior deficits.

It was noted earlier that in most cases severe withdrawal reflects both deficits in social skills and avoidance of interpersonal situations. An optimal treatment, therefore, should transmit new social competencies and also extinguish social fears. Modeling procedures are also ideally suited for this purpose. A series of studies by Bandura (1968a) demonstrated that various patterns of avoidance behavior can be successfully eliminated through modeling, and that such procedures are readily applicable to therapeutic situations.

By devising a carefully constructed film sequence, the therapist can stage rather complicated situations and events in a dramatic manner that controls the viewer's attention to relevant cues. While the exclusion of extraneous events provides much of this attention control, the enthusiastic and emotionally expressive behavior of models can further enhance attention and vicarious learning in the viewer (Bandura, 1962; Berger and Johansson, 1968). Once the observer's attention has thus been directed toward the filmed events, the therapist may introduce repeated exposure to clearly defined stimuli.

Positive response consequences to the model, such as social praise or material reinforcements for modeled behaviors, which have been shown to increase the performance of similar behavior in observers (Bandura, 1965; Bandura, 1968b), can also incorporated into filmed events. Symbolic modeling processes employing such principles have effectively extinguished severe avoidance behavior in children (Bandura and Menlove, 1968).

The present experiment sought to extend the use of symbolic modeling to the modification of social withdrawal. This approach appears particularly well suited for achieving both of the desired outcomes indicated in the pathology described above, *i.e.,* the transmission of social skills and the extinction of social fears. These two modeling processes, along with the facilitation of interpersonal behaviors which may exist in the observers' repertoire, provided the rationale for the manipulation of social interaction behavior, which in fact comprised the focus of the experimental change assessment.

Children who displayed extreme social withdrawal were shown a sound-film depicting peers engaged in progressively more active social interaction. The viewers were children who not only had very low base-rates of social interaction, according to the dual assessment procedure (below), but whose frequent retreats into corners, closets, and lockers gave observers and teachers a similar impression of active, purposive withdrawal in many instances. The filmed behavior of peers presented to these "isolates" was actively followed by reinforcing outcomes such as peer approval, either verbal or expressional (smiling, nodding, *etc.*); peer acceptance of the model into a game or a conversation, *i.e.,* invitations to join or offering play materials or reaching out to take the model's hand, *etc.*; in most scenes the model behavior resulted in some tangible reinforcement such as a block or other toy, a book to read together with the peers, a dish to wash or dry in a cooperative homemaking activity; and so on. A second group of equally withdrawn children viewed a film that contained no human characters. After exposure to their respective films, the children's social behavior was observed in the nursery school situation. It was predicted that children having the benefits of symbolic modeling would display a significant increase in social interaction with their peers.

METHOD

Selection of Isolates

Head teachers in each of nine nursery school classes were asked to choose from their enrolment lists the five most socially withdrawn children in their class. Each teacher was to rank order these five children "who interact the least with their peers". Of the 365 children enrolled, the 45 nominated in this preliminary selection and 26 children randomly chosen from the remaining non-isolates were then observed in the nursery school setting at randomly selected times throughout the day.

Each child was observed for a total of 32 intervals, each interval consisting of 15 sec, over a period of eight days (with the time of day counterbalanced on consecutive days). During each 15-sec. interval, the children's behavior was scored in terms of five separate response categories; one every 3 sec. These included physical proximity, verbal interaction, "looking at", "interacting with", and the size of the group involved in any interaction sequence. Although the first three response categories, considered social orienting responses, were scored, the measure of social behavior was based entirely on the frequency with which the children interacted with their peers *(i.e.,* category four). The three categories of "orienting" responses and the "size of group" category were included in the observations for intrasample reliability checks and for possible assessment purposes in case the primary "interacts" category had not reflected such notable change in the children's behavior. Obviously, a score in the "interaction" category necessitated "proximity and looking at" responses, and increases in the less critical "verbalizes" and "number in group" categories had to accompany most interactions performed by these former isolates. The major emphasis of the experimental manipulation, therefore, was on the interaction scores, and the changes assessed were in this category alone, although changes in the other behavioral categories were at least as significant as those reported in the response class of interest here. A social interaction was defined as any behavior directed toward another child which involved a reciprocal quality. Neither parallel play nor solitary verbalizations qualified. The two-way nature of a scorable interaction necessitated not only the output of the subject child, but some indication of recognition and attention from the second child in the interaction. Thus, if a subject spoke to or otherwise directed his behavior to another child, but the second child did not respond in any way, at least appearing to be aware of the intended interaction, no score was given for an interaction.

Six trained observers performed the ratings. During a randomly chosen 50% of the sessions, these observers were paired and observed a given child independently but simultaneously. Interscorer reliability on each of these sessions was $r = > 0.92$. (# of agreements/the 32 possible agreements on a given child's interactions), which allowed for matched observer correlations across subjects of $r = 0.90 +$ (product-moment) in all pairs of observers.

Children who scored fewer than five of 32 possible interactions and who had been rated by teachers as isolates were selected as subjects and randomly assigned to either the modeling or the control film conditions. Thus, to qualify for the experiment, children had to meet the dual criteria of having exhibited extreme withdrawal over a long period of time as judged by their teachers, and to have displayed isolate behavior as measured by objective behavioral observations. Of the 20 "isolates" who met these criteria, 13 were included in the experiment; four of the remaining seven were omitted because they were frequently absent from school; and three of the children vigorously refused to leave the nursery room.

The 26 non-isolate children were primarily included to furnish an additional baseline for evaluating any changes produced by the treatment program. These children displayed a mean of 9.1 social interactions, while the means for children assigned to the modeling and control conditions were 1.75 and 1.50 respectively, with the scores in both groups ranging from 0 to 5. The modeling group contained four girls and two boys and the control group, four girls and three boys.

Treatment Conditions

Children in both conditions were brought individually to the experimental room where they were told they could watch a television program. Each child was seated before a large TV console while the experimenter plugged in the set and ostensibly tuned in the picture. The films were shown on a glass lenscreen by means of a rear projector arrangement. As the apparatus was plugged in, the hidden projector and tape recorder were activated simultaneously. An extension speaker directed the sould through the TV set.

The experimenter left the child alone in the room to view the film on the pretext that he had some work to complete and would return before the film had ended. The experimenter then observed the session through a one-way mirror from an adjoining room. All children appeared to be highly attentive to the "TV show" throughout the film. The attention apparently commanded by the television presentation was quite impressive and obviously advantageous to the experimental procedure.

Children in the modeling condition saw a sound-color film lasting approximately 23 min. The film portrayed a sequence of 11 scenes in which children interacted in a nursery school setting. In each of these episodes, a child is shown first observing the interaction of others and then joining in the social activities, with reinforcing consequences ensuing. The other children, for example, offer him play material, talk to him, smile and generally respond in a positive manner to his advances into the activity. The scenes were graduated on a dimension of threat in terms of the vigor of the social activity and the size of the group. The initial scenes involve very calm activities such as sharing a book or toy while two children are seated at a table. In the terminal scenes, as many as six children are shown gleefully tossing play equipment around the room.

Multiple modeling has been shown to be more efficacious than single modeling (Bandura and Menlove, 1968). Also, a second pilot study conducted as a preliminary to the present experiment suggested a powerful effect on social behavior of subjects as a result of multiple, live peer-modeling; the child displaying the social approach behavior was varied from scene to scene in terms of age and sex, including a total of six different models, four girls and two boys, with their ages ranging from 4 to 7 yr.

To accent further the modeling cues and the positive consequences associated with the social behavior of the approaching child, a narrative, sound track was prepared in which a woman's voice, judged by the experimenter to be very soothing, described the actions of the model and the other children in the on-going sequence. The script consisted entirely of descriptions of ongoing social responses and outcomes and was a further attempt to focus the viewers' attention to relevant cues.

The control film depicted 20 min of the acrobatic performances of Marineland dolphins and was accompanied by a musical soundtrack. Since the film contained no human characters, it provided a control for any effects which might have been derived solely from the presentation of a film in the experimental procedure and contact with experimenters. The control group further provided a basis on which to measure any change in the social behavior of isolate subjects which might have occurred as a result of nursery school participation during the course of the project.

Post-Treatment Assessment

Immediately after being shown their respective films, the children were returned to their regular classrooms. They were given 2 min to adapt to the classroom situation, after which they were observed for 32 consecutive intervals, each lasting 15 sec, according to the same observation procedure employed in the pretreatment assessment. The social interaction score was again the number of 15-sec intervals in which the child displayed a direct social interchange (defined according to the "reciprocal quality" criteria mentioned earlier) with one or more children. In order to control for any bias in ratings, observers were kept unaware of condition assignments, and each observed a random combination of treated and control subjects. Aside from the usual "blind assessment" control, this randomizing technique was thought to reduce further any possible observer bias.

RESULTS

Figure 1 represents the mean number of social interaction responses performed by children in the modeling and control conditions during the pretest and immediately after the experimental session.

An analysis of within-group changes showed that the seven control children remained essentially unchanged, whereas the six children who had viewed the modeling film markedly increased their level of social interaction ($t = 2.29; p < 0.03$). The post-test interaction scores of treated subjects were in fact similar to those of non-isolates who had been observed during the pretest period.

A between-groups analysis revealed the change in social interaction to be significantly greater for subjects in the modeling treatment than for controls ($t = 2.53; p = 0.015$). A between-groups comparison of the levels of social interaction achieved at post-test indicated significant differences as evaluated by either the t-test ($t = 2.70$; $p = 0.01$) or the Mann Whitney U-test ($U = 3.0$; $p = <0.004$).

Having measured the powerful effects of the

modeling film in terms of the group comparisons above, data for the individual subjects in the modeling condition were found to indicate consistent positive changes across subjects. All six children in the modeling condition exhibited increased social interaction behavior in the post-film assessment. Children in the control condition performed essentially the same number of interactions before and after viewing the control film, with only slight increases or decreases in the behavior (Figure 2).

DISCUSSION

The present results established symbolic modeling as a highly efficacious procedure for modifying social withdrawal. Children who did not receive the modeling treatment remained socially withdrawn, whereas those who observed a systematic filmed presentation of peer interactions associated with reinforcing consequences displayed a significant increase in social responsiveness.

Follow-up observations could not be made because the nursery school term was completed. However, a second set of teachers' ratings was obtained at the end of the school year. The teachers, who were kept uninformed as to which conditions children had been assigned, again rated the five most withdrawn children from their enrollment lists as they had done in the preliminary selection. Only one of the six subjects who had been in the modeling condition was still rated as an isolate. It is interesting to note that this child, who also improved the least as measured by behavior observation, viewed the modeling film with the sound track 20-sec behind the picture due to a mechanical failure. Four of the seven control subjects were gain judged to be extreme isolates. Although these findings have some suggestive value, they should be accepted with reservations because of the global nature of the ratings and the fact that changes in classroom enrollment may affect their comparability.

Immediate treatment effects achieved by symbolic modeling may produce lasting changes in social interaction without the need of additional procedures, provided that the children's initial social behavior is favorably received by peers. However, the application of systematic reinforcement of appropriate social responses would ensure the maintenance of the induced behavioral changes. Bandura has suggested "the combined use of modeling and reinforcement procedures" as the most efficacious mode of therapy in "eliminating severe behavioral

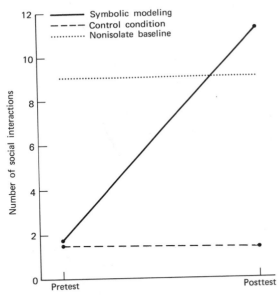

FIG. 1.
Mean number of social interactions displayed by subjects in the modeling and control conditions, before and after the experimental sessions. The dotted line represents the level of interactions manifested by 26 nonisolate children who were observed at the pretest phase of the study.

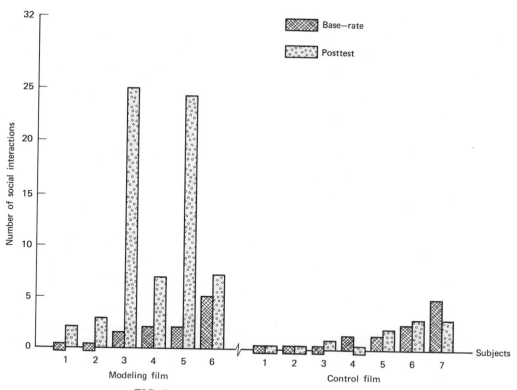

FIG. 2.

Actual number of social interactions displayed by each child in either condition, before, and after exposure to the modeling or control film.

inhibitions" (Bandura, Grusec, and Menlove, 1967). In order to substantiate this hypothesis a study needs to be conducted which extends the design of the present experiment to include durational (follow-up) assessment periods, as well as a comparison of modeling, shaping, and combined treatment procedures. In the present study, social inhibitions were reduced and appropriate social responses were facilitated through symbolic modeling with built-in reinforcement to the model. New responses to familiar social stimuli which were formerly assumed to have elicited avoidance behavior were acquired vicariously within one treatment session.

The subsequent performance of these newly acquired behaviors is seen as primarily resulting from the facilitation and extinction effects which derive from the observation of models performing the target behaviors with no aversive consequences ensuing. This theoretical explanation of the modeling effects achieved is based on the same set of experimental data which guided the construction of the treatment film (an important point in the comparison of differential treatment outcomes). A distinction is drawn between response *acquisition* and response *performance* according to experimental data derived from a recent experiment (Bandura, 1965b) which suggested that novel behaviors may be acquired by observers, even though the models are punished, but that these responses may not be performed readily without the addition of strong incentives beyond those of the situational stimuli in the modeling presentation. The conclusion from this study is theoretically relevant to the present discussion, in that it suggests that a model's reinforcement contingencies may be negative enough to inhibit performance of newly acquired responses, but have little or no effect on their acquisition. Other data, such as the Berger (1962, 1968) studies mentioned earlier and a recent demonstration of arousal reduction in snake phobics through live modeling (Blanchard, 1968), provide support for the additional modeling effects of disinhibition and the facilitation of responses existing in the observer's repertoire, which complete the three-fold theory of modeling effects incorporated into the design of the present film and the theoretical explanation of its effects.

An alternative explanation for the increased social behavior of children who observed the modeling film might be based strictly on the principles of reinforcement theory. Since the data here indicate only changes in the rate of social interaction responses, it might be argued that the simplest behavioral description would identify the filmed presentation as a discriminative stimulus for appropriate matching responses. (Baer and Sherman, 1964; Baer, Peterson, and Sherman, 1967; Peterson, 1968). The approach would be based upon what is often considered the most parsimonious behavioral analysis of observable events, *i.e.*, the performance of measurable behaviors and a description of the stimulus situation in which the matching behaviors, as a "functional response class", occurred. The rationale for such a description might be based upon the observer's prior history of reinforcement for matching models' behavior, or similar conceptions of "imitation", *per se*, with emphasis on the change in reinforcement value of models' behavior, the controlling power of modeled behavior as a discriminative stimulus, *etc.* (Staats, 1963, 1968). Aside from recent suggestions concerning the presumptive nature of these "heavyweight" reinforcement-theory explanations (Glucksberg, 1968); the parsimony deriving from reinforcement approaches, in terms of therapeutic efficiency, has not yet been demonstrated in instances where gross behavior deficits are identified as the changeworthy phenomena. The expense of "shaping time" must be compared to a treatment which may provide for

the acquisition of possibly novel skills according to principles of associative learning (contiguous presentation of modeling stimuli), as well as facilitating the performance of modeled responses and other appropriate behaviors in the observer's repertoire (discriminative stimulus function of non-aversive modeled behavioral outcomes), while reducing negative arousal responses to feared stimuli, all in one treatment session. The explanatory value of reinforcement principles may thus be relevant to performance variables, while an approach that is intended to effect input (learning) variables as well may provide treatment procedures with markedly greater applicability to behavior deficit conditions. The allowance for possible *learning deficits* in treatment strategies designed to modify *behavior deficits, i.e.,* attention to input as well as output deficits, may be much more than a theoretical distinction. The powerful effects of the modeling presentation reported here underscore what appears to be a very practical, therapeutically useful reason to allow for the notion of mediational processes as well as reinforcement principles when these factors may be relevant to the therapeutic strategy.

This brief discussion of two possible explanations of the modeling effects achieved in the present study may serve to direct the reader's attention to further analyses of the modeling process in general. Thoroughly detailed presentations may be found in more appropriate publications (Bandura, 1968c; Bandura, 1969; Mischel, 1968; O'Connor, 1969, Staats, 1968; Ullmann, 1968).

It should be noted in passing that the present experiment achieved significant changes in social behavior among children with relatively severe deficits without developing a therapeutic relationship. Until recently, a fairly intimate client-therapist relationship and the attainment of insight have been considered necessary conditions for personality change. In contrast, the results and discussion above indicate that the social behavior of children can be effectively enhanced by efforts to arrange social stimulus conditions which may ensure the acquisition of requisite competencies, the reduction of inhibiting fears, and the facilitation of appropriate responses. It should also be apparent that attention to learning variables provides for treatment procedures which can optimistically be applied to any program of behavior change. Teachers and other social agents might greatly increase the efficacy of their work with with individual children, as well as in group procedures by employing some of the principles of social learning and symbolic modeling presented here. The use of carefully designed therapeutic films in classroom and experimental situations alike may provide significantly more efficient modification of various behavior deficits and other deviant behaviors.

REFERENCES

Allen, K. E., Hart, B. M., Buell, J. S., Harris, F. R., and Wolf, M. M. Effects of social reinforcement on isolate behavior of a nursery school child. *Child Development,* 1964, *35,* 511-518.

Bandura, A. Influence of models' reinforcement contingencies on the acquisition of imitative responses. *Journal of Personality and Social Psychology,* 1965, *1,* 589-595. (b)

Bandura, A. Modeling approaches to the modification of phobic disorders. *Ciba Foundation symposium: The role of learning in psychotherapy.* London: Churchill, 1968. (a)

Bandura, A. *Principles of behavior modification.* New York: Holt, Rinehart & Winston, 1969, (in press).

Bandura, A. A social learning interpretation of psychological dysfunctions. In P. London and D. Rosehan (Eds.) *Foundations of abnormal psychology.* New York: Holt, Rinehart & Winston, 1968. Pp. 293-344.

Bandura, A. Social learning theory of identificatory processes. In D. A. Goslin (Ed.), *Handbook of socialization theory and research.* Chicago: Rand McNally, 1968. Pp. 213-262 (b)

Bandura, A. Social learning through imitation. In M. R. Jones (Ed.), *Nebraska Symposium of Motivation:* Lincoln: University of Nebraska Press, 1962. Pp. 211-269.

Bandura, A. Vicarious processes: A case of no-trial learning. In L. Berkowitz (Ed.), *Advances in experimental social psychology.* Vol. II. New York: Academic Press, 1965. Pp. 1-55.

Bandura, A., Grusec, J., and Menlove, F. L. Vicarious extinction of avoidance behavior. *Journal of Personality and Social Psychology,* 1967, *5,* 16-23.

Bandura, A. and Huston, Aletha C. Identification as a process of incidental learning. *Journal of Abnormal and Social Psychology,* 1961, *63,* 311-318.

Bandura, A. and McDonald, F. J. Influence of social reinforcement and the behavior of models in shaping children's moral judgments. *Journal of Abnormal and Social Psychology,* 1963, *67,* 274-281.

Bandura, A. and Menlove, F. L. Factors determining vicarious extinction of avoidance behavior through symbolic modeling. *Journal of Personality and Social Psychology,* 1968, *8,* 99-108.

Bandura, A. and Mischel, W. Modification of self-imposed delay of reward through exposure to live and symbolic models. *Journal of Personality and Social Psychology,* 1965, *2,* 698-705.

Bandura, A., Ross, D., and Ross, S. A. Transmission of aggression through imitation of aggressive models. *Journal of Abnormal and Social Psychology,* 1961, *64,* 575-582.

Bandura, A. and Walters, R. *Social learning and personality development.* New York: Holt, Rinehart & Winston, 1963.

Baer, D. M. and Sherman, J. A. Reinforcement control of generalized imitation in young children. *Journal of Experimental Child Psychology,* 1964, *1,* 37-49.

Baer, D. M., Peterson, R. F., and Sherman, J. A. The development of imitation by reinforcing behavioral similarity to a model. *Journal of the Experimental Analysis of Behavior,* 1967, *10,* 405-416.

Berger, S. M. Conditioning through vicarious instigation. *Psychological Review,* 1962, *69,* 450-466.

Berger, S. M. and Johansson, S. L. Effect of model's expressed emotions on an observer's resistance to extinction. *Journal of Personality and Social Psychology,* 1968, *10,* 53-58.

Blanchard, E. B. *Relative contributions of modeling, informational influences, and physical contact in the extinction of phobic behavior.* Unpublished doctoral dissertation. Stanford University, 1968.

Eysenck, H. J. *Experiments in behavior therapy.* New York: Macmillan, 1964.

Glucksberg, S. A self-made straw man. *Contemporary Psychology,* 1968, *13,* 624-625.

Hart, B. M., Reynolds, N. H., Baer, D. M., Brawley, E. R., and Harris, F. R. Effect of contingent and noncontingent social reinforcement on the cooperative play of a preschool child. *Journal of Applied Behavior Analysis,* 1968, *1,* 73-76.

Hartup, W. W. Peers as agents of social reinforcement. *Young Children, 20,* 1965.

Hicks, D. J. Imitation and retention of film-mediated aggressive peer and adult models. *Journal of Personality and Social Psychology,* 1965, *2,* 97-100.

Krasner, L. and Ullmann, L. P. *Research in behavior therapy.* New York: Macmillan, 1964.

Lovaas, I., Berberich, J. P., Perlof, B. F., and Schaeffer, B. Acquisition of imitative speech by schizophrenic children. *Science,* 1966, *151,* 705-707.

Mischel, W. *Personality and assessment.* New York: Wiley & Sons, 1968.

O'Connor, R. D. *Modeling treatment of non-behavior disorders.* Paper presented at 41st annual meeting of the Midwestern Psychological Association, Chicago, March 1969.

Patterson, G. R. and Anderson, D. Peers as social reinforcers. *Child Develop-*

ment, 1964, *35,* 951-960.

Peterson, D. R. *The clinical study of social behavior.* New York: Appleton, Century, Crofts, 1968.

Peterson, R. F. Some experiments on the organization of a class of imitative behaviors. *Journal of Applied Behavior Analysis,* 1968, *3,* 225-235.

Staats, A. W. *Learning, language, and cognition.* New York, Holt, Rinehart & Winston, 1968.

Staats, A. W. and Staats, C. K. *Complex human behavior.* New York, Holt, Rinehart & Winston, 1963.

Ullmann, L. P. Making use of modeling in the therapeutic interview. Paper read at A.A.B.T. meetings, San Francisco, 1968.

Wolpe, J. and Lazarus, A. A. *Behavior therapy techniques.* London: Pergamon Press, 1966.

28. Achievement Place: Experiments in Self-Government with Pre-Delinquents[1]

DEAN L. FIXSEN, ELERY L. PHILLIPS,
& MONTROSE M. WOLF

One of the goals of many treatment programs for pre-delinquent youths is the development of the skills involved in the democratic decision-making process. At Achievement Place, one aspect of the treatment program is a semi-self-government system whereby the seven pre-delinquent youths can democratically establish many of their own rules of behavior, monitor their peers' behavior to detect violations of their rules, and conduct a "trial" to determine a rule violator's guilt or innocence, and to determine the consequences for a youth who violates a rule. Two experiments were carried out to determine the role of some of the procedures in the boys' participation in the self-government system. Experiment I showed that more boys participated in the discussion of consequences for a rule violation when they had complete responsibility for setting the consequence during the trials than when the teaching-parents set the consequence for each rule violation before the trial. An analysis of the rule violations in this experiment indicated that the boys in Achievement Place reported more of the rule violations that resulted in trials than reported by the teaching-parents or school personnel. The boys reported rule violations that occurred in the community and school as well as at Achievement Place, including most of the serious rule violations that came to the attention of the teaching-parents. In Experiment II, the results indicated that more trials were called when the teaching-parents were responsible for calling trials on rule violations reported by the peers than when the boys were responsible for calling trials. When the youths earned points for calling trials the average number of trials per day increased, but more trivial rule violations were reported. These results suggest that aspects

[1] This investigation was supported by Grant MH20030 from the National Institutes of Mental Health (Center for Studies of Crime and Delinquency) and by grant HD03144 from the National Institute of Child Health and Human Development to the Bureau of Child Research and the Department of Human Development, University of Kansas.

of the democratic decision-making process in a small group of pre-delinquents can be studied and variables that affect participation can be identified and evaluated.

Youths and adults who are placed in correctional settings rarely have an opportunity to participate in decisions regarding the formal rules thay have to live by. Instead, administrators, professionsals, and caretakers generally establish rules and policies that are dictated by security precautions and the requirements of a particular approach to treatment (see Johnston, Savitz, and Wolfgang, 1970, pp. 387-392, for a list of typical prison rules). In spite of the formal regulations, many institutional populations develop an informal type of self-government dependent upon group coercion and punishment that often is more severe than that allowed by the formal rules (Fox, 1970; McCorkle and Korn, 1970). The strong influence of the peer group in informal self-government systems has been widely acknowledged by prison and reform school administrators, school officials, probation officers, and parents and has been clearly described by Cohn (1955), Shaw and McKay (1942), and Thrasher (1939). These authors have indicated that much peer group influence is for anti-social behavior.

The attempt has been made in many treatment programs to reduce or eliminate the influence of the peer group in order to carry out the goals of the program. On the other hand, the development of the skills involved in self-government systems has been a primary goal in a few treatment programs. Several authors have described attempts to develop democratic semi-self-governing systems that encourage peer group influence for pro-social behavior. Makarenko (1953) described the development of a self-government system at the Gorky Colony for delinquent youths in Russia. In this program, a governmental system developed over a period of 7 yr that, in its final form, included several detachments of youths, each with an elected commander. The commanders met fre-

quently with Makarenko in a commanders' council to assign specific duties to each detachment and to make decisions that affected the entire colony. According to Makarenko, on most issues considered by the commanders' council he had only one vote and he could be overruled by a majority vote of the commanders. On some issues of special concern, however, Makarenko reported that he would act without the advice of the commanders' council. Nevertheless, the commanders' council had a great deal of authority, even to the extent that the commanders could expel a member of the colony for serious misbehavior.

Another self-government system has been described by Neill (1960) at Summerhill, a residential school for middle to upper-class youths in England. As reported by Neill, the students at Summerhill had complete freedom in determining the rules of the school and providing sanctions for violating the rules. The self-government sessions took the form of a "town meeting" where all interested students would meet, discuss the issues, and vote. Neill reported that he could participate in all phases of the self-government system but his vote counted no more than a student's. Apparently, there were also many rules concerning the law, health, safety, finances, and the reputation of the school that were laregely determined by Neill.

Another attempt to focus peer group influence on pro-social behavior has been in programs for delinquents using *guided group interaction*. Empey (1966) reported that guided group interaction consists of a small group (8 to 12) of youths discussing their current and past problems under the direction of a trained adult leader whose task is to "guide" the discussion toward relevant topics with as little intervention as possible. Each session begins by having each youth recount the problems he had that day. The group then votes to choose which boy's problems to discuss for the remainder of the meeting (about 1 to 2 hr). That boy's problems are then discussed in detail, the group offers possible solutions to the youth, and sometimes consequences are arranged for the boy's misbehavior. At the end of the session the adult leader summarizes what was discussed in the meeting and gives the group feedback on what they covered adequately and on points they may have overlooked. When the youths in a guided group are asked to help solve a boy's problems, the leader and the treatment staff are apparently committed to carrying out whatever solution the group decides (even to the point of having a boy spend the weekend in jail). Other problems, however, are handled by the staff without asking for the advice or consent of the guided group.

An experimental analysis of various administrative systems for pre-delinquent boys at Achievement Place was reported by Phillips, Wolf, and Fixsen (*in press*). In a series of experiments that concerned a specific task Phillips, *et al.*, found that a peer manager system, where the manager was elected by his peers, provided a self-government system that was effective in accomplishing the task and was preferred by the boys. A manager system where the boys bid for the managership was equally effective, but was not as preferred by the boys. Apparently, the opportunity to elect the manager was an important component of this self-government system.

An experimental analysis of a "governmental" system for chronic mental patients who had been hospitalized an average of 18 yr was reported by O'Brien, Azrin, and Henson (1969). In a series of three experiments, O'Brien, *et al.*, found that the number of suggestions made by the patients for changes in the ward treatment procedure was a function of the number of suggestions followed by the staff. When the staff followed 100% of the suggestions, the patients gave more suggestions than when the staff followed only 75%, 25%, or 0% of the patients' suggestions. The patients also made more suggestions when attendance at the meetings was required than when attendance was only invited.

The self-government systems described by Makarenko, Neill, and Empey are interesting because they encompass a broad range of activities, but they are difficult to evaluate because they are described only anecdotally. Phillips, *et al.*, (*in press*) and O'Brien, *et al.*, (1969) provided detailed descriptions of systems that were experimentally analyzed but more limited in scope. The present experiments present an extension of the self-government system developed by Phillips, *et al.*, to other aspects of the treatment program at Achievement Place.

The purpose of the present experiments was to analyze some of the variables that affect the youths' participation in establishing consequences for rule violations (Experiment I) and for calling "trials" for reported rule violations (Experiment II). Also, the descriptive data in Experiment I were analyzed to determine the role of the youths in reporting rule violations.

SETTING

Achievement Place is a residential group home for six to eight court adjudicated delinquent, pre-delinquent, and dependent-neglected boys 12 to 16 yr old. The home is governed by a Board of Directors made up of interested community members. The home is directed by professional teaching-parents who have responsibility for the treatment,

care, and custody of the youths in Achievement Place. The teaching-parents live in the home and are the sole staff of Achievement Place.

The treatment program is based upon a token economy and treatment procedures that were developed during 5 yr of research(Bailey, Wolf, and Phillips, 1970; Bailey, Timbers, Phillips, and

Wolf, 1971; Fixsen, Phillips, and Wolf, 1972; Phillips, 1968; Phillips, Phillips, Fixsen and Wolf, 1971; Phillips, Phillips, Fixsen, and Wolf, *in press;* Phillips, Wolf and Fixsen, 1973; Wolf, Phillips, and Fixsen, 1972). The tokens at Achievement Place take the form of points that are given for appropriate behavior and are taken away for inappropriate behavior. At the end of each day, the boys subtract the number of points they have lost from the number of points they have earned. The resulting point difference is accumulated during the week and the weekly total is used to purchase privileges for the following week. A boy can "live comfortably" by purchasing privileges valued at 15,000 points each week. However, most boys average about 25,000 points each week. By earning the extra points, a boy can permanently return to his natural home.

Achievement Place is a community-based program. As such, the boys who come to Achievement Place continue to attend the same school and have contact with the same teachers and school officials, they retain frequent contact with their parents, they see their friends, and have contact with the general community. Rather than removing a youth from his problems with his teachers, parents, and peer group, a community-based program can keep the youth in contact with all of these problems and seek to work out their solutions. When a boy enters Achievement Place his behavior problems with his teachers, parents, and friends do not automatically go away, of course. So that consequences can be arranged for the problem behavior, the youth's teachers, school officials, and parents are encouraged to report any misbehavior to the teaching-parents. The teaching-parents and the youth's peers at Achievement Place determine these consequences by developing rules of behavior for behavior in the school, the home, and in the community, as well as at Achievement Place.

Development of the Self-Government System

The semi-self-government system at Achievement Place evolved over a period of about 1 yr. The delinquent boys did not have the described self-government skills when they entered the program. The boys first learned to live under a system of rules established by the teaching-parents. Some of the boys then began asking the teaching-parents to make rules to keep the other boys out of their rooms, to stop the other boys from borrowing their clothes and personal belongings without their permission, and to reduce the excessive teasing and bickering that sometimes occurred among the boys. The teaching-parents used these complaints as an opportunity to teach the boys how to make reasonable and fair rules. In the family conference, the teaching-parents asked the boys to make their own rules to govern the behavior they complained about. At first, the boys made very strict rules and established extremely large consequences for anyone who violated the rule in the future. Within a week, someone usually violated the new rule and the teaching-parents gave the rule violator the established consequence. At the next family conference, the rule and the consequence were discussed and the fine was usually reduced to a more appropriate level. After a few weeks, the boys seemed to learn that the rules they made applied equally to all the boys in the home and not just to the boy who was the subject of the original complaint. The boys appeared to learn the cardinal rule of democratic self-government: the "decision makers" as well as the original rule violators have to abide by the same rules. Just because Paulie's behavior was the reason for the rule in the first place did not mean the rule existed just for him; it applied to every one in Achievement Place. In this way, the boys seemed to learn to establish rules that were fair, rules they could "live with", rather than rules that were punitive. Also, they seemed to learn how to continue to modify a rule until it was as satisfactory as possible.

As the boys established more rules they also reported more violations of their rules to the teaching-parents. Occasionally, a boy would also report misbehavior that occurred at school or in the community. The teaching-parents wanted to encourage peer reporting of the more serious misbehaviors and they gave 1000 to 5000 points to a boy who reported such misbehaviors. In addition, they would give a boy a fine of up to 5000 points if he knew of a serious misbehavior but did not report it. As the number of peer reports increased, the teaching-parents gradually withdrew the point rewards and fines and now only occasionally use the point consequences for boys who are new to the program.

As the number of rules and reports of violations of the rules increased, the teaching-parents began discussing the reported rule violations at the family conferences. The teaching-parents would question the accused boy about the circumstances surrounding the reported rule violation, they would discuss the evidence gathered from various sources, and they would discuss the rule violation in terms of how it might affect the relationship between Achievement Place and the Juvenile Court or the Welfare department, how the Board of Directors of Achievement Place might react, how it would affect the reputation of Achievement Place in the community, and what that reputation meant in terms of giving other boys a "second chance". The teaching-parents would also discuss the reasons for assigning a particular consequence for a rule violation. After a few weeks of discussing these aspects of each rule violation, the boys began to participate more in the discussions concerning guilt and consequences. At first, the teaching-parents would give each boy 500 to 2000 points, depending upon how much he participated in each discussion. This would then reduce to about 1000 points for the boy who participated the most. Eventually, the points for participation were eliminated except for occasional points given to a new boy in the program.

In addition to the "trials", the youths were encouraged to criticize any aspect of the program they wanted to change. The youths were required to present reasons why they wanted to change the program and they were asked to present a constructive alternative. In these discussions, the teaching-parents would remind the youths of the goal of the procedure being criticized and would consider any

alternatives that would promote that goal and rectify the problems with the current procedure. If two or more alternatives met both of these criteria, the youths would vote to decide which alternative to put into effect. On some occasions, a youth would complain about some aspect of the program without presenting reasons for the criticism or constructive alternatives. If the youth persisted in his complaints this was sometimes considered a rule violation and a trial was called to decide the consequences for his complaining behavior. Thus, the family conference was a place to discuss serious requests for change and not general complaints that were not justified by a youth.

After the piece-meal development of the components of the self-government system, the teaching-parents began to be more systematic in carrying out each trial until the trial procedure described in the Method section was developed. The boys who were in Achievement Place when the trial system was developed have all graduated and returned to their natural homes and families. However, the trial system continued relatively unchanged. Apparently, with a gradual turnover in the population, the youths who were new to the program quickly learned the rule making, reporting, and participation skills involved in the semi-self-government system at Achievement Place. The instructions by the teaching-parents, consequences for appropriate self-government behavior, and models provided by the other boys were probably important in this regard.

The description of the evolution of the semi-self-government system at Achievement Place is, of course, *post hoc* and ancedotal. However, the self-government system has been replicated in other group homes for adolescent, court adjudicated boys and girls that were based on the Achievement Place model. These self-government systems were developed within three to five months. Apparently, when the necessary self-government skills are objectively defined these skills can be specifically taught in a relatively short period of time.

EXPERIMENT I

Experiment I was conducted to analyze some of the variables that affect the youth's participation in the self-government system and to determine the extent of the youths' participation in the system.

Subjects

Seven delinquent and pre-delinquent boys who resided at Achievement Place participated in the experiment. The boys' ages ranged from 10 to 16 yr with a median age of 15 yr. At the end of the study, which required four months to complete, the boys' median length of residence at Achievement Place was eight months and ranged from three to 40 months.

Procedure

Each day, the teaching-parents recorded any reports of misbehavior or rule violations by a youth from his teachers, school officials, parents, and the youth's peers. The teaching-parents also recorded any rule violations they personally observed. Teachers and parents reported rule violations by telephone to the teaching-parents. Teachers and parents were unaware of the specific rules at Achievement Place but reported misbehavior that in their opinion caused some disruption at school or at home. The peers reported rule violations directly to the teaching-parents by describing the situation surrounding the alleged violation and a youth's behavior in that situation. Many of the rule violations that were reported were not serious and would probably result in point fines of 3000 points or less. In these cases, the teaching-parents simply fined the youth the appropriate number of points. Other reported rule violations, however, were more serious and would probably result in point fines of more than 3000 points. In these cases, the teaching-parents had the option of either fining the youth the appropriate number of points or waiting and letting the youth's peers decide the consequences at the family conference. In either case, in the family conference, the youths in Achievement Place had an opportunity to review the rule violation and establish a new consequence or confirm the consequence given by the teaching-parents.

Family Conference

Each day, at the evening meal, a family conference was held. The family conference provided a time and a place for any complaints or discussions of any aspect of the Achievement Place program (*e.g.*, the rules and reasons for the rules, the consequences provided for certain behaviors). The family conference also provided a time for the "trials" (as the boys came to call them) to occur. The teaching-parents routinely called a trial for any misbehavior that would probably result in a point loss of 3000 points or more and that was reported by teachers, parents, the boys, or the teaching-parents themselves. The trial procedure was as follows:

1. The teaching-parents would identify which boy the trial was about then ask the boy whether he did what he was accused of or not. After the youth stated whether or not he was involved in the rule violation, the teaching-parents asked for further discussion of the incident. These discussions were restricted to information that might bear upon the youth's "guilt" or "innocence".
2. After the discussion was completed, the teaching-parents asked "How many of you agree he didn't do it?" Following each question the boys would raise their hands to indicate their choice. If the vote was not unanimous, the teaching-parents would ask those who voted in the minority to offer their reasons for dissenting, call for further discussion, then ask for another vote. On the second vote, the majority opinion was taken as the opinion of the group.
3. If the majority voted that the boy was "not guilty", the trial ended at that point. If, however, the majority voted that he was "guilty" the teaching-parents asked for a discussion of the consequence that should be applied for this particular rule violation.
4. When the discussion was completed, the teaching-parents summarized the consequence more or

less decided upon in the discussion and called for a vote on "how many agree with this consequence?" Again, the boys raised their hands to indicate their choice. If there were dissenting votes, those voting in the minority were asked to give their reasons, further discussion followed, and a second vote was taken. On the second vote, the majority opinion decided the consequence.

Peer Responsibility

All of the boys, including the accused boy, and the teaching-parents could participate in the discussions of guilt and consequences. However, neither the accused boy nor the teaching-parents could vote on the issues of guilt or consequences. Nevertheless, the teaching-parents did have an important sort of veto power over the group's decision on the consequences. If the boys voted to levy a fine that the teaching-parents considered to be much too low for the rule violation that occurred, the teaching-parents could disagree with the decision and suggest that the boys agree to take responsibility for any similar rule violation that the boy might commit in the future. If the boys chose to accept responsibility it meant that the teaching-parents would set the consequence for any similar rule violation that the accused boy might commit in the future and all the boys, not just the rule violator, would be given the consequence at that time. If the boys chose not to accept this responsibility for their peer's behavior, the teaching-parents would suggest the minimum consequence they would be willing to accept and steps three and four of the trial procedure would be repeated. Thus, the teaching-parents could veto the group's decision on consequences but the veto could be overridden if the boys agreed to take responsibility for any similar rule violation by the same youth in the future and potentially accept the consequences themselves for similar offenses of the youth.

Behavior Definitions

"Agreement" was defined as a youth raising his hand after a vote was called. If more than one vote was taken (when the first vote was not unanimous) the results of the second vote were used for data for the purposes of this study.

"Participation in discussion" was defined as a youth suggesting alternatives, adding information, or making a statement that was directly related to the discussion taking place. In each case, a youth had to do more than agree with what had already been said.

Observation

Each family conference was videotaped. Each evening, the boys would set the video camera in a designated spot, hook up a microphone on each side of the table in the dining room, and test the system to make sure it was working properly. One of the boys would start the video tape recorder when dinner was ready and turn off the system when dinner was finished. An observer later replayed the videotape and recorded the names of the boys who participated one or more times in the discussions of guilt and consequences for each trial and recorded the vote of each boy for each decision of guilt and consequences. Because the number of boys attending each trial varied from four to seven, these observations were converted to the percentage of boys participating in each discussion and the percentage of boys voting in agreement on guilt or consequences.

Inter-observer agreement was measured on four trials during the experiment by having a second observer simultaneously and independently record participation and agreement from the videotapes. The second observer was given the definitions and was asked to record participation and agreement without any special training. The second observer had had considerable experience in recording other behaviors, however. The two observers' records were compared for agreement of recording each boy's name for each trial and the per cent agreement was calculated by dividing the total number of agreements X 100 by the total number of agreements plus disagreements. Inter-observer agreement for participation was 100%, 92%, 100%, and 100% for the four trials. Inter-observer agreement for voting was 100% for all four trials.

Experimental Conditions

Trial-Set Consequences

In this condition, the teaching-parents recorded any reported rule violation that would probably result in at least a 3000-point fine. No consequences for the rule violation were actually delivered before the trial by the teaching-parents, however. At the family conference, the teaching-parents would call a trial on the boy accused of violating the rule and the boy's peers would decide his guilt or innocence and what consequence to deliver, if any.

Pre-Set Consequences

In this condition, the teaching-parents recorded any reported 3000-point (or more) rule violation and delivered a consequence to the boy *at that time* (before the trial). At the family conference, the teaching-parents would call a trial on the boy accused of violating the rule and the boy's peers would decide his guilt or innocence and what consequences to deliver, if any. The only change in the trial procedure in this condition was that the teaching-parents would tell the group how many points they had already fined the boy before asking for a discussion of the consequences. The boys were free to modify any pre-set consequence and the group decision on consequences took precedence over the teaching-parents' pre-set consequence.

Unfair Consequence Probe

The teaching-parents made every attempt to pre-set consequences that were fair and appropriate to the rule violations that occurred. For two trials, however, the teaching-parents set a consequence that was 10 times greater than what they considered to be fair.

Preference Probe

Near the end of this experiment, and after the formal data collection was terminated, the boys were asked on several trials whether they preferred to have the teaching-parents pre-set the consequences for rule violations or to have the consequences decided entirely by trial decisions. The preference measure was taken for nine trials that had Pre-set consequences and for three trials that had Trial-set consequences. The preference question was asked sometimes before a trial began and sometimes after a trial was completed. The boys would vote for the alternative of their choice by raising their hands.

RESULTS

There were 80 trials during the course of this experiment. However, due to mechanical problems, data on participation and agreement were lost for nine trials. The 80 trials occurred over a period of 14 weeks for an average of 5.7 trials per week (range = 1 to 12 per week). The trials averaged about 18 min in duration.

Participation

Figure 1 shows the percentage of boys who participated in each trial decision on consequences. During the first Trial-set consequence condition where the teaching-parents did not pre-set consequences and the peers decided the consequence for rule violations in the trial, there was a median of 80% of the boys participating in each trial. When the teaching-parents began delivering consequences before each trial in the Pre-set consequence condition, the percentage of participation dropped to a median of 40%. When the Trial-set consequence condition was reinstated, the percentage of boys participating in the trial decision increased to a median of 83% and immediately decreased to a median of 0% when the teaching-parents once again began pre-setting consequences. Table 1 shows the per cent of trials each boy participated in during each condition (number of trials participated in/

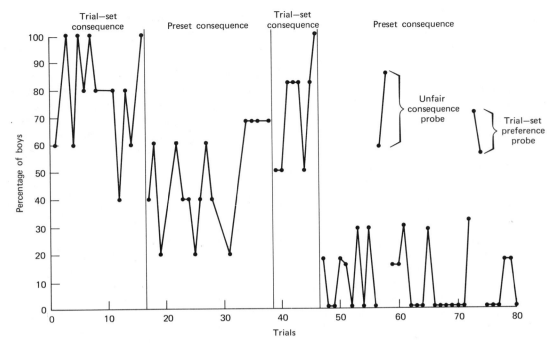

FIG. 1.

The percentage of boys participating in discussion of consequences at each trial under a condition where the boys alone decided the rule violator's consequence during the trial (trial-set) and a condition where the teaching-parents delivered a consequence to a rule violator at the time hte violation was reported and the boys either confirmed or changed the preset consequence during the trial (pre-set). There were two "unfair consequence" trials in the second preset consequence condition in which the teaching-parents preset a point fine that was 10 times greater than what they considered to be fair. There were also two "trial-set consequence preference probe" trials in which the trial-set consequence conditions were used and a measure of the boys' preference was taken.

TABLE 1. *The Percent of Trials Each Subject Participated in During Each Condition of Experiment 1*

	Subjects						
Conditions	1	2	3	4	5	6	7
Trial-set consequences I	83	33	91	75	92	25	..*
Pre-set consequences I	53	40	53	53	53	0	13
Trial-set consequences II	63	75	100	75	75	12	50
Pre-set consequences II	13	7	17	19	3	4	0

*Subject 7 entered the program at the start of the first pre-set consequence condition.

ACHIEVEMENT PLACE: EXPERIMENT

number of trials attended). Table 1 shows that the percentages in Figure 1 were due to similar changes in all the boys. Only Subject 2 did not show a decrease in participation when the first pre-set consequence condition was instituted, although his participation did decrease under the final condition.

The Unfair consequence probe (indicated by the two arrows in Figure 1) occurred during the second Pre-set consequence condition. As shown in Figure 1, the percentage of participation increased sharply when the teaching-parents pre-set a consequence that was judged by them to be inappropriate to the rule violation that occurred.

The percentage of boys who participated in each trial decision regarding guilt (data not shown) did not vary systematically with changes in the experimental conditions. This was primarily due to the fact that the boys admitted their guilt 74 times out of a total of 80 trials. There were only three guilty and one innocent verdicts by trial decision and in two trials there was no decision, due to conflicting evidence. Thus, the participation in decisions of guilt or innocence was uniformly low (median of 0%) across all conditions.

Agreement

There was 100% agreement on all but two trial decisions of guilt. The two exceptions were two trials where guilt or innocence was not decided due to conflicting evidence and no vote was taken.

There was 100% agreement on all but one trial decision regarding consequences, where agreement was 83%. For the two trials that were Unfair consequence probe trials, none of the boys (0%) agreed with the first unfair consequence and only one boy of seven (14%) agreed with the second unfair consequence. However, after the boys discussed a more appropriate consequence and voted on it, there was unanimous agreement on both trial decisions. On the first unfair consequence trial, the youths reduced the unfair consequence of a 100,000-point fine to a warning of a 20,000-point fine the next time the youth violated the same rule. On the second unfair consequence trial, the youths reduced the 50,000-

point fine set by the teaching-parents to a 4000-point fine.

The teaching-parents disagreed with the peers' trial decision on consequences only three times out of the 80 trials. On these occasions, the teaching-parents asked the peers to accept responsibility for similar rule violations committed by the youth in the future. On one occasion, the peers agreed to accept this responsibility and agreed that they would all accept a 100,000-point fine if the same youth committed a similar violation while he was at Achievement Place. On the other two occasions, the peers agreed not to accept this responsibility and voted to set a higher fine for the rule violation, a fine that was considered more appropriate by the teaching-parents.

Preference

On 12 occasions the boys were asked whether they preferred the Trial-set consequence condition or the Pre-set consequence conditions. The boys' preference after four Pre-set consequence trials was unanimously in favor of pre-set consequences. Their preference before five Pre-set consequence trials was unanimously in favor of pre-set consequences on four trials and in favor of trial-set consequences on one trial. The boys' preference before and after all three Trial-set consequence trials was in favor of trial-set consequences.

Descriptive Trial Data

In the Pre-set consequence condition, there was an opportunity to compare the consequences pre-set by the teaching-parents with the consequences agreed upon by the boys. These data are shown in Table 2. Table 2 shows that out of 53 trials, the boys agreed with the teaching-parents on 62% of the trials, increased the consequences on 6% of the trials, and decreased the consequences on 32% of the trials. Table 2 also shows that the boys left the pre-set consequence the same most often for rule violations that were reported by school officials (83%) and least often for rule violations reported by the teaching-parents (31%).

TABLE 2. *Changes in the Teaching-Parents' Pre-Set Consequences by the Peer's Trial Decisions*

Rule Violations Reported by		Change in Pre-Set Consequences by Trial Decision		
		Increase	Same	Decrease
Peers	No.	2	12	5
	%	11%	63%	26%
School officials	No.	—	15	3
	%		83%	17%
Teaching-parents	No.	1	4	8
	%	7%	31%	62%
Parents	No.	—	2	1
	%		67%	33%
Totals	No.	3	33	17
	%	6%	62%	32%

Table 3 shows the types of consequences delivered by the boys' trial decisions. The boys simply fined their peer a number of points on 46 of the 80 trials (57%). On 22 (27%) of the trials, however, they employed a consequence that did not involve points. These non-point consequences included having a boy take a "daily report card" (Bailey, Wolf, and Phillips, 1970) to school each day, take his lunch to school to avoid trouble in the lunch room, calling the teaching-parents at designated times on weekends, warnings of future point consequences, and others. For 12 trials (15%), the boys decided upon a consequence that had both point and non-point components. Table 4 shows the distribution of points levied by the boys in fines for rule violations that were reported by the peers, school personnel, and teaching-

parents. For all 80 trials there was a total of 1,020,750 points lost in 58 fines. The mean fine was 17,600 points and the median was 5000 points.

Table 5 shows the location of each rule violation that was reported by the peers, school personnel, teaching-parents, and parents. The parents reported only those misbehaviors that occurred in the natural

TABLE 3. *The Types of Consequences Delivered by the Peers' Trial Decision*

Types of Consequences	Number	Percent
Points	46	57
Non-points	22	27
Combinations	12	15

TABLE 4. *The Distribution of Point Fines Delivered by Peers' Trial Decisions for Trials Reported by Peers, School Personnel, and Teaching-Parents*

Number of Points Fined	Rule Violation Reported by		
	Peer (n = 24)	School (n = 20)	Teaching-Parents (n = 12)
100,000–200,000	—	15%	8%
50,000– 99,000	8%	—	—
25,000– 49,000	—	20%	8%
10,000– 24,000	17%	10%	—
5000– 9900	38%	25%	25%
3000– 4900	29%	30%	17%
1000– 2900	4%	—	33%
0– 900	4%	—	8%

TABLE 5. *The Location of Rule Violations Reported by the Peers, School Personnel, Teaching-Parents, and Parents*

Reported by		Arch. Place	School	Community	Nat. Home	Totals
Peers	No.	17	7	6	0	38%
	%	57%	23%	20%	0%	
School Personnel	No.	0	27	0	0	34%
	%	0%	100%	0%	0%	
Teaching-Parents	No.	12	1	5	0	22%
	%	67%	5%	28%	0%	
Parents	No.	0	0	0	5	6%
	%	0%	0%	0%	100%	
Totals	No.	29	35	11	5	100%
	%	36%	44%	15%	6%	

home and school personnel reported only those rule violations that occurred on school property. The teaching-parents primarily reported rule violations that occurred at Achievement Place (67%) but also reported a few violations that occurred in the community (28%) and at school (5%). About half of the peers' reports concerned rule violations that occurred at Achievement Place and the other half was evenly divided between violations that occurred at school and in the community. Overall, nearly half (44%) of all rule violations that were reported occurred at school and about one-third (36%) occurred at Achievement Place. More importantly however, Table 5 shows that more than one-third (30/80) of all rule violations were reported by peers.

Table 6 gives the types of rule violations reported by the peers, school personnel, teaching-parents, and parents. The rule violations are ranked in order of seriousness from stealing to not being prompt. Of the first four types of rule violations, the peers reported a majority of the rule violations, in three of the four categories and reported as

TABLE 6. *Types of Rule Violations Reported by Peers, School Personnel, Teaching-Parents, and Parents*

Type of Rule Violation	Peers	School	Teaching-Parents	Parents	TOTALS
Stealing	3 (75%)	1 (25%)	—	—	4 (5%)
Cheating	2 (67%)	1 (33%)	—	—	3 (4%)
Physical agg.	5 (38%)	5 (38%)	2 (15%)	1 (9%)	13 (16%)
Verbal agg.	5 (72%)	1 (14%)	—	1 (14%)	7 (9%)
School rules	5 (20%)	18 (72%)	2 (8%)	—	25 (31%)
Ach. pl. rules	9 (47%)	—	10 (53%)	—	19 (24%)
Promptness	1 (11%)	1 (11%)	4 (45%)	3 (33%)	9 (11%)
TOTALS	30 (38%)	27 (34%)	18 (22%)	5 (6%)	80 (100%)

many as the school personnel in the fourth. Thus, of the 27 rule violations reported for the four most serious violations in Table 6, the peers reported 15 (55%), school personnel reported eight (29%), and the teaching-parents and parents each reported two (8%). The peers also reported rule violations in each of the seven categories.

Four of the peer reported rule violations were self-reports, where a youth reported a rule violation he had committed. Of these four self-reported violations, one was for stealing, two were for physical aggression, and one was for violation of Achievement Place rules.

EXPERIMENT II

Experiment II was conducted to analyze the effects of some variables on the youths' participation in calling "trials" for reported rule violations.

Subjects

Six boys who had been adjudicated by the juvenile court and placed in Achievement Place participated in this experiment. Four of these boys also participated in Experiment I about five months after Experiment II terminated. The boys' ages ranged from 13 to 15 yr with a median of 14 yr. At the end of the study, which required three months to complete, the boys' median length of residence at Achievement Place was five months and ranged from one to 32 months.

Procedures and Results

Under the first condition, the boys were asked to report to the teaching-parents any rule violations committed by their peers. The boys did not earn any points for reporting. If the reported misbehavior would, in the teaching-parents' opinion, merit at least a 3000-point fine, the teaching-parents called a trial on that misbehavior at the next family conference and the peers decided upon a consequence for the violation. As shown in Figure 1, this procedure resulted in an average of 1.4 trials per day over a nine-day period.

The second condition shown in Figure 2 was identical to the first except the boys, and not the

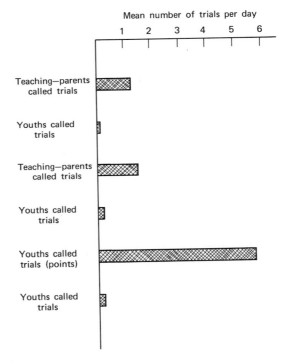

FIG. 2.
The average number of trials per day under conditions where the youths reported rule violations and the teaching-parents had the responsibility of calling a trial (teaching-parents called trials), the youth who reported the rule violation had the responsibility of calling a trial (youths called trials), and the youth who reported the rule violation received points for calling a trial (youths called trials [points]).

teaching-parents, had the responsibility to call for a trial on one of their peers. Under this procedure, when a boy reported a rule violation to the teaching-parents he was asked whether he wanted to call a trial on that violation. If the reporter answered "no", the teaching-parents gave the rule violator what seemed to be an appropriate consequence without going through the trial procedure. If, however, the peer reporter wanted to call a trial, the teaching-parents brought up the rule violation at the next family conference and the boys decided the consequence. As shown in Figure 2, the average number of trials per day under this condition decreased to 0.1 over a seven-day period. These effects were then replicated in the next two conditions. Figure 1 shows that when the teaching-parents again began calling trials, the average number of trials per day increased to 1.6 over an eight-day period and decreased to an average of 0.3 trials per day over eight days when the boys again called the trials.

The fifth condition shown in Figure 2 was identical to the previous condition except that the boys earned 500 points for calling a trial on a rule violation they reported. Under this condition, the average number of trials per day increased markedly to 5.7. This condition was terminated after three days because of the amount of time required to hold five trials each day. In the last condition shown in Figure 2, the boys no longer earned points for calling a trial and the average number of trials each day decreased to 0.3 over three days.

During the conditions where the teaching-parents or the youths called the trials and no points were earned by the youths for calling trials, the average point fine given to the rule violator by his peers in each trial was 2100 points. During the condition in which the boys earned points for calling trials, only one of the 17 trials resulted in a point fine and that fine was only 500 points.

DISCUSSION

The results of these experiments indicate that self-government can be studied experimentally and that variables affecting participation in a governmental system can be identified and evaluated. The results of Experiment I indicated that more youths participated in the governmental system when the teaching-parents did not pre-determine a consequence for a reported rule violation. However, the results of Experiment II showed that the youths called very few trials when they, rather than the teaching-parents, had the responsibility for calling the trials. When the teaching-parents paid points to the youths for calling trials there was a large increase in the number of trials called by the youths, but the rule violations reported were what might be called "technical violations" of rules (e.g., reporting a boy for being 1 min late) that only rarely resulted in a point consequence for the rule violator. Thus, at this time, it appears that the teaching-parents at Achievement Place cannot turn over full responsibility for the self-government system to the youths.

The preference data indicated that in almost every case the youths preferred whatever trial system was being used at the time the preference measure was taken. Since there was no marked preference, the teaching-parents might use either pre-set consequences or trial-set consequences, depending upon the situation. For example, for rule violations that involved rules the boys had established to protect their privacy or belongings or concerning their conduct toward one another, the teaching-parents could use the trial-set consequence procedure to encourage a discussion of individual responsibilities. On the other hand, for violations of rules established by law, for health and safety reasons, or by community agencies such as the schools, the teaching-parents could use the pre-set consequence procedure to establish a consequence appropriate to the seriousness of the rule violation and the youths could review the boy's guilt and the pre-set consequence at the trial. With either procedure, the youths have the opportunity to set a consequence they deem appropriate. The results of the unfair consequence probes indicate that the youths will vote to change a pre-set consequence they consider to be too high.

The semi-self government system that has evolved at Achievement Place consists of at least four important components: developing rules, reporting rule violations, deciding guilt, and assigning consequences. A recent review of 99 rules at Achievement Place indicated that in the boys' opinion they had developed about 50% of the rules and had played a minor role in the development of another 25% of the rules. As shown in Table 5, the boys not only played a major role in establishing the rules, they also reported violations of the rules. According to Table 5, the boys reported 30 of the 80 rule violations that resulted in a trial, more than the number of rule violations reported by school personnel, the teaching-parents, or natural parents Although in 74 of the 80 trials the accused boy admitted his guilt, the boys did have to determine the accused boy's guilt or innocence in six trials. In three cases, the boys decided the accused boy was guilty, one boy was declared innocent, and two trials were undecided due to conflicting evidence. For 58 trials, the boys levied fines that totalled more than one million points. For 22 trials, the boys established non-point consequences that required the boy to avoid the troublesome situation or that required some special behavior of the boy in the situation. The objective results obtained in the present studies appear to confirm the anecdotal descriptions provided by Makarenko, Neill, and Empey that indicate delinquent youths can be taught the skills involved in the democratic decision-making process.

The current treatment program at Achievement Place has evolved during a 5-yr period of intensive research and evaluation. During this period of time, many of the goals of the program have been made objective, a point system involving both point rewards and point fines has been devised and tested for its effectiveness in achieving the goals, and a self-government system has been developed to increase the youths' participation in the treatment program. Although these developments were made primarily by the teaching-parents who direct and operate Achievement Place, they occurred only after much debate and consideration of the issues. Even though the teaching-parents may appear to be "independent operators" because they do not have an immediate superior to supervise their work, they work closely with community agencies and citizens and they must be responsive to various aspects of the community: there is a cross-section of citizens who make up the Board of Directors of Achievement Place, Inc. (a non-profit corporation), the Douglas County Juvenile Court that sends delinquent youths to Achievement Place, the Department of Social Welfare that pays most of the operating costs of the home, the administration of the Lawrence public schools that the youths attend, the youths' parents and relatives, and the opinions and preferences of the youths in the program. And, of course, another important constraint on decisions made by the teaching-parents is effectiveness. Thus, the various aspects of the treatment program must be acceptable to these agencies and citizens and the program must be effective in changing the behavior of the youths or the program would suffer in some way.

When the program began in 1967, one of the first issues that was considered concerned the goals of the program. Should the boys go to public school? Should they be allowed to see their parents? Should they be allowed to go down town? Should the teaching-parents try to teach them appropriate social skills or just keep them out of trouble? There was an extensive list of decisions concerning the goals of the program. Over a period of 2 yr, the teaching-parents and the community agencies and citizens discussed these possible goals and gradually arrived at a consensus. Thus, the goals of the program reflected to a large extent the goals of the community for all its youths, and not just the arbitrary decisions of the teaching-parents.

At the same time the goals were being debated, decisions about the methods to achieve those goals were made. Should a point system be used or should the boys be exposed to a "natural family" situation? Since one early decision was to use a point system in a situation that approximated a "natural family", the remaining questions concerned the kind of point system and how it was to be used. Should there be point fines as well as rewards? How large should the fines be for various misbehaviors? Should the boys be allowed to make up point losses? What should points be given for? After a great deal of discussion and debate it was decided to have a point system that involved both "reward and punishment" and that was flexible enough to allow the boys to make up any points that were lost, so that the youths could still earn all their privileges. This system has proved to be very effective in achieving the goals of the treatment program and has community acceptance because the boys always have the opportunity either to avoid losing points or to make up lost points to obtain all their privileges. The aversiveness of the point system was viewed in terms of the availability of the privileges to the boys rather than in terms of contingent point losses (see Phillips, *et al.*, 1971, for a further discussion of this point).

The fairness of point fines was a more difficult issue to resolve. However, as the goals of the program were made objective and point fines were assigned for failure to meet each goal, these issues became more explicit and decisions were made. Failure to meet some goal behaviors (*e.g.*, truant from school) was seen as more serious than failure to meet other goal behaviors (*e.g.*, not cleaning one's room). Also, some behaviors (*e.g.*, cooperation with parents on the weekend home visit) were more difficult to change than other behaviors (*e.g.*, manners at meals). After considerable experience and discussion, a hierarchy of seriousness and difficulty was established and higher point fines were given for those behaviors that were more serious and difficult to change. Thus, the fairness of the point fines was determined by the community's view of the seriousness of the behavior and by the difficulty the teaching-parents had in modifying the behavior.

Some additional information on the "fairness" of the program was recently obtained. A questionnaire that used the semantic differential technique was administered to the boys. One question asked the boys to rate the teaching-parents on a seven-point scale of fairness where a rating of "extremely unfair" was assigned a score of one and a rating of "extremely fair" was assigned a score of seven. Six of the eight boys gave the teaching-parents a rating of seven, one boy gave them a rating of six, and one boy who had just entered the program gave the teaching-parents a rating of four. Apparently, the boys consider themselves to be fairly treated by the teaching-parents.[2]

When the self-government system began, the decisions about the goals of the program and the point system had been made. The community agencies and representatives gave their complete support to instituting a self-government system that would increase the boys' participation in the treatment program. The one self-government issue that generated discussion was having the boys report the misbehaviors of their peers (some called it "squealing","informing","tattling", being a "stool pigeon", or "ratting"). Was peer reporting an example of "ratting" or of "good citizenship"? Was this a "big brother" or a "natural family" behavior? In these discussions an important distinction was made. "Ratting" and "informing" were seen as reports of misbehavior to an authority or agency that used the information in a way that could not be controlled by the informant. This was seen as "big brother" behavior. However, "reporting" was seen as giving information about a peer's misbehavior to an authority (the teaching-parents) whose function was later (at the family conference) to bring the matter before the accused youth and his peers for *their decisions* concerning his guilt and the consequences of his behavior. Thus, the "reporter" maintained some control over the outcome of his reporting. This was seen as a behavior that occurred in most "natural families".

[2]We would like to thank D. Stanley Eitzen, Department of Sociology, University of Kansas, for composing and administering the questionnaire and for making these data available to us.

Although these issues have been fairly well resolved by the teaching-parents, community agencies, and citizens in the Lawrence community, these same issues will probably arise when similar programs are started in other communities. It is important to note that the objective specification of goals and treatment procedures that are among the strengths of the experimental analysis of behavior also increase its exposure to criticism and feedback from other professionals and the public. It seems important, therefore, for behavior modifiers to develop treatment programs that take into careful consideration the ethical and moral standards of society as well as the opinions and preferences of those who have any input into the program. In this way, we can develop programs that are not only effective but acceptable to potential users as well.

REFERENCES

Bailey, J. S., Wolf, M. M., and Phillips, E. L. Home-based reinforcement and the modification of pre-delinquents' classroom behavior. *Journal of Applied Behavior Analysis,* 1970, *3,* 223-233.

Bailey, J. S., Timbers, G. D., Phillips, E. L., and Wolf, M. M. Modification of articulation errors of pre-delinquents by their peers. *Journal of Applied Behavior Analysis,* 1971, *4,* 47-63.

Cohn, A. *Delinquent boys: The culture of the gang.* Glencoe, Ill.: Free Press, 1955.

Empey, L. T. *The Provo experiment: a brief review.* Youth Studies Center, University of Southern California, 1966.

Fixsen, D. L., Phillips, E. L., and Wolf, M. M. Achievement Place: the reliability of self-reporting and peer-reporting and their effects on behavior. *Journal of Applied Behavior Analysis,* 1972, *5,* 19-30.

Fox, V. Prison disciplinary problems. In N. Johnston, L. Savitz, and M. E. Wolfgang (Eds.), *The sociology of punishment and correction.* New York: John Wiley and Sons, 1970. Pp. 393-400.

Johnston, N., Savitz, L., and Wolfgang, M. E. (Eds.), *The sociology of punishment and correction.* New York: John Wiley and Sons, 1970.

Makarenko, A. S. *The road to life.* Moscow: Foreign Language Publishing House, 1953, Vol. I, II, III.

McCorkle, L. W. and Korn, R. Resocialization within walls. In N. Johnston, L. Savitz, and M. E. Wolfgang (Eds.), *The sociology of punishment and correction.* New York: John Wiley and Sons, 1970. Pp. 409-418.

Neill, A. S. *Summerhill.* New York: Hart Publishing Co., 1960.

O'Brien, F., Azrin, N. H., and Henson, K. Increased communications of chronic mental patients by reinforcement and by response priming. *Journal of Applied Behavior Analysis,* 1969, *2,* 23-29.

Phillips, E. L. Achievement Place: token reinforcement procedures in a home-style rehabilitation setting for "pre-delinquent" boys. *Journal of Applied Behavior Analysis,* 1968, *1,* 213-223.

Phillips, E. L., Phillips, E. A., Fixsen, D. L., and Wolf, M. M. Achievement

Place: modification of the behaviors of pre-delinquent boys within a token economy. *Journal of Applied Behavior Analysis,* 1971, *4,* 45-59.

Phillips, E. L., Phillips, E. A., Fixsen, D. L., and Wolf, M. M. *The teaching-family handbook.* Champaign, Ill.: Research Press, (in press).

Phillips, E. L., Wolf, M. M., and Fixsen, D. L. An experimental analysis of governmental systems at Achievement Place, a group home for pre-delinquent boys. *Journal of Applied Behavior Analysis,* 1973, (in press).

Shaw, C. and McKay, H. *Juvenile delinquency and urban areas.* Chicago, Ill.: University of Chicago Press, 1942.

Thrasher, F. *The gang.* Chicago, Ill.: University of Chicago Press, 1939.

Wolf, M. M., Phillips, E. L., and Fixsen, D. L. The teaching-family: A new model for the treatment of deviant child behavior in the community. In S. W. Bijou and E. L. Ribes. (Eds.), *Behavior modification: issues and extensions,* New York: Academic Press, 1972. Pp. 51-62.